"A wealth of natural beauty resides in the Bay Area's coastal mountains and their rolling foothills—redwood forests, wooded streamsides, oak-studded grasslands, rocky peaks, steep mountainsides, lush meadows, and sunny chaparral slopes."

"The windswept, rocky soil beside the path supports one of San Francisco's last remaining habitats of native plants that harbor the endangered Mission Blue butterfly. In spring, indigenous pink checkerblooms, blue and white lupines, and orange poppies brighten the landscape."

"The prints of many trail users mark the sandy surface—the corrugated tread of athletic shoes, the continuous pattern of bicycle tires, U-shaped prints of equestrians' steeds, and the paw prints of an

"From this vantage point, Spanish soldiers scanned the Golden incoming ships carrying supplies from the Old World. The the waters for unfriendly ships that might threaten this tin at the entrance to San Francisco Bay."

Loma Prieta from Santa Teresa County Park.

THE BAY AREA RIDGE TRAIL

Ridgetop Adventures
Above San Francisco Bay

Jean Rusmore

in cooperation with the
Bay Area Ridge Trail Council

Foreword by George Miller,
United States House of Representatives

WILDERNESS PRESS
BERKELEY, CALIFORNIA

Copyright © 1995, First Edition, Jean Rusmore
© August 2002, Second Edition, Jean Rusmore

Published in cooperation with the Bay Area Ridge Trail Council

Cover design: Jaan Hitt
Book design and production: Scott Perry, Archetype Typography
Map design and production: Ben Pease
Book editor: Jessica Lage
Managing editor: Jannie Dresser

All photos by the author except where otherwise noted.

Cover photo: © 2002 by Jean Rusmore, *Indian Tree OSP*
Back cover photos: © 2002 by Jean Rusmore
Frontispiece photo: *Loma Prieta from Santa Teresa County Park*

Manufactured in the United States of America
Published by Wilderness Press
            1200 5th St.
            Berkeley, CA 94710
            (800) 443-7227
            www.wildernesspress.com
            Contact us for a free catalog.

Library of Congress Card Number 95-35393
ISBN 0-89997-280-2
UPC 7-19609-97280-8

Library of Congress Cataloging-in-Publication Data

Rusmore, Jean.
      The Bay Area Ridge Trail : ridgetop adventures above San Francisco
      Bay / Jean Rusmore ; maps by Ben Pease, Pease Press.
         p.   cm.
      Includes index.
      ISBN 0-89997-280-2
      1. Hiking—California—Bay Area Ridge Trail—Guidebooks.
      2. Cycling—California—Bay Area Ridge Trail—Guidebooks.
      3. Horsemanship—California—Bay Area Ridge Trail—Guidebooks.
      4. Bay Area Ridge Trail (Calif.)—Guidebooks.   I. Title.
      GV199.42.C22B387   1995
      917.94'6—dc20   95-35393

TABLE OF CONTENTS

Introduction 3

Bay Area Setting
The Bay Area's Heritage of Outdoor Enjoyment
A Land Conservation Ethic
Development of Parks and Open Spaces
The Role of Private, Nonprofit Groups

The Bay Area Ridge Trail 11

The Beginnings
Bay Area Ridge Trail Accomplishments
The Next Step—Closing the Gaps
Other Regional Trails in the Bay Area
Other Long Trails

About this Guidebook 19

A Proposal Takes Shape
How to Use This Guidebook
Sharing the Trails
Some Hazards for Trail Users
What to Wear and Take Along
Where to Stay

SAN FRANCISCO

THE NORTH BAY

THE EAST BAY

THE SOUTH BAY & PENINSULA

To my husband Ted

Ferns and shade-loving shrubs flourish in Huckleberry Preserve.

ACKNOWLEDGEMENTS

Since the Bay Area Ridge Trail concept was first proposed, many people have contributed their efforts and enthusiasms into completing 230 miles of the trail. Leading this achievement have been Bay Area Ridge Trail Council's Board of Directors—Brian O'Neill, its longest serving chairman, Marcia McNally, Doug Kerseg, and presently, Bill Long. To these dedicated people and the many board members who have given their energies and talents to guide the Ridge Trail along its successful way, I offer my thanks. I also extend to them my appreciation for approving the idea for the first edition of this book and for endorsing this second edition.

For the splendid support and considerable skills of the Bay Area Ridge Trail Council staff I am most grateful: to Marti Leicester, first executive director; Barbara Rice, who served during its rapidly growing years; interim executive director Mary Burns; Bob Power, who as interim executive director generously piloted the organization through a transitional period and its move to the Presidio; and to Holly Van Houten, its current executive director. It has been a pleasure to know and work with all of them. To the very helpful field coordinators, Dee Swanhuyser and Bob Power, and to the capable and friendly office staff, I offer many thanks.

The directors, superintendents, and planners of the parks, open space agencies, and water districts through whose lands the Bay Area Ridge Trail trips travel were most cooperative. I extend my appreciation for their specialized knowledge, for their maps and background materials, and for their helpful comments on the trip descriptions. To the rangers, many of whom hiked the trails with me, and to all the field staff who shared their special knowledge of the trails and the natural, historic, and cultural features of their parks, watersheds, and preserves, I offer my thanks. Their love of the lands in their care was truly inspiring.

I salute and thank Larry Orman, Mark Evanoff, and Judy Kanofsky, whose pioneering work at Greenbelt Alliance stimulated Bay Area leaders to reactivate William Penn Mott's dream of a ridgetop trail around San Francisco Bay.

It's been a pleasure to work with the able members of the San Mateo County Committee of the Bay Area Ridge Trail Council. I thank them and all the nine Bay Area County Committees for their volunteer leadership in exploring, planning, and promoting the Bay Area Ridge Trail and for their long-term efforts to complete the Ridge Trail around the Bay Area.

Many friends hiked the trails with me: Doris Lindfors, a special friend and hiking companion, who generously contributed her firsthand knowledge of Bay Area trails and cheerfully hiked almost every mile of the Bay Area Ridge Trail route with me. My monthly hiking friends, the Walkie-Talkies, heartened me with their pleasure in exploring most of the South Bay and the peninsula segments of the Bay Area Ridge Trail. Elna Cunningham and J'Anny and Ed Nelson also joined me on several North Bay trips. To these and all who shared the Bay Area Ridge Trail trips, I extend my appreciation for their company and their delight in the beautiful country we traveled through.

To Ron Brown for his comprehensive mileage data, to Ben Pease for his careful maps, to Paula Tuerk for photography assistance, and to volunteer Rollye Wiskerson for his trailbuilding expertise, my sincere thanks.

To my friend and longtime co-author Frances Spangle, I extend my appreciation for contributing her original, copyrighted text to four Marin County trips and the Wunderlich to Huddart county parks trip.

During the process of producing this guidebook, the staff of Wilderness Press efficiently managed a significant part—my thanks to Mike Jones, publisher; Jannie Dresser, managing editor; Jessica Lage, editor; and Jaan Hitt, cover designer. To Wilderness Press founding publisher Tom Winnett, now retired, I owe my thanks and appreciation for his unfailing interest in producing excellent outdoor guidebooks.

Jean Rusmore
Portola Valley, California
May 2002

FOREWORD

I am honored to once again write the foreword for the *Bay Area Ridge Trail: Ridgetop Adventures Above San Francisco Bay.* This spectacular 425-mile recreational trail connects parks, people, and communities in the nine Bay Area counties. The preservation of our natural heritage is perhaps the most important legacy for our children's children and the most urgent task facing the Bay Area's rapidly growing population. I want to congratulate the Bay Area Ridge Trail Council for its extraordinary leadership and commitment to the project in the thirteen years of its existence. The council partners with more than 200 community groups and land management agencies, a growing number of corporate supporters, and thousands of trail enthusiasts of all ages and interests—no other urban trail in the United States has reached this level of complexity.

The Bay Area Ridge Trail is an outstanding example of volunteerism. The special mix of people—private citizens, parks and trails professionals, and nonprofit and corporate leaders—involved in planning, promoting, and developing the Ridge Trail provides an example of people working together toward a common vision. It is only with efforts of this magnitude that completion of the 425-mile trail will be realized. Without the leadership and talent of the hundreds of individuals throughout the Bay Area, the trail would not be where it is today, with over 230 miles dedicated. We are indeed fortunate to have such dedicated volunteers, and I want to offer my personal thanks for their tremendous efforts to forever preserve the unique and world-renowned natural beauty of the Bay Area. I pledge to continue to work with you to meet the goal of completing the Ridge Trail in ten years.

A special thanks to those state legislators, especially the Bay Area delegation, who have taken a leadership role in supporting funding for the Ridge Trail, including Senator John Burton, Senator Wesley Chesbro, Senator Byron Sher, Senator Don Perata, Senator Liz Figueroa, Senator Jackie Speier, Assemblywoman Pat Wiggins and Assemblyman Fred Keeley.

Congressman George Miller
7th District, California
May 2002

15 YEARS OF SUCCESS DUE TO VOLUNTEERISM AND CIVIC COMMITMENT

Just 15 short years ago, a visionary leader, William Penn Mott, inspired a small band of citizens and park managers to begin a journey to protect and connect the region by way of a continuous ridgeline trail. As the organization that formed to promote the idea prepares to celebrate its 15th Anniversary, there are a long string of successes to look back on with pride. Supporters have grown from about 50 to a 5,000-member-strong organization with a staff, dozens of agency and private landowner partners, and hundreds of volunteers all working together to complete the Bay Area Ridge Trail.

These are the folks who scouted potential routes; put up with blisters, poison oak, and sore muscles to build sections of the trail; talked with their political representatives to spread the idea; led group outings; tirelessly attended local planning committee meetings; hosted events; raised funds; and took friends and family out to enjoy the emerging trail. Because of their collective passion, dedication, and commitment, we have been able to complete 230 miles of trail so far.

What motivated them? The chance to leave a legacy, protect something special, or have a place to go with their children and their children's children to enjoy the outdoors. Some were captivated with the notion of hiking or riding all around the San Francisco Bay on a trail. Still others were motivated by the sheer challenge of creating a trail of this magnitude.

And that challenge continues. Although the 230 completed miles of trail represent significant progress, much more remains to be done. Each day, the Ridge Trail Council—its staff, board, partners, and volunteers—is working towards making this guidebook out of date, having set a goal for ourselves to get another 70 miles of trail opened to the public by 2005.

Until then, we are proud to present, in partnership with Wilderness Press, this 2nd edition of *The Bay Area Ridge Trail: Ridgetop Adventures Above San Francisco Bay*. We are especially indebted to Jean Rusmore, whose contributions as a council volunteer have made this book possible. Since 1989, Jean has hiked, researched and written about each and every leg of the completed Bay Area Ridge Trail.

As you hike, ride, and read about the wonders of the Bay Area Ridge Trail, consider how you might take up the challenge to help complete the trail—if you haven't already. To learn more, to volunteer, or to contribute to the Ridge

Trail, contact the Bay Area Ridge Trail Council at 1007 General Kennedy Avenue, Suite #3, San Francisco, CA 94129, (415) 561-2595 or on the web at www.ridgetrail.org.

Brian O'Neill
Chairman Emeritus, Board of Directors, Bay Area Ridge Trail Council
Superintendent, Golden Gate National Recreation Area
May 2002

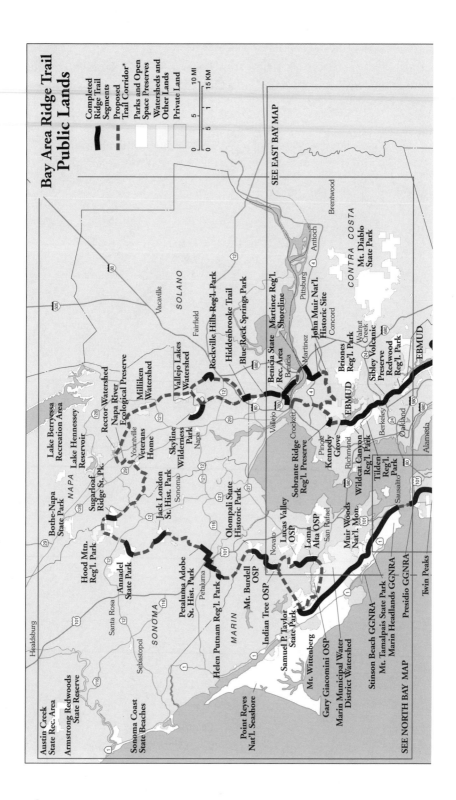

Bay Area Ridge Trail
Public Lands

Completed
Ridge Trail
Segments

Proposed
Trail Corridor*

Parks and Open
Space Preserves

Watersheds and
Other Lands

Private Land

0   5   10 MI
0 5   15 KM

SEE EAST BAY MAP

Austin Creek
State Rec. Area

Armstrong Redwoods
State Reserve

Sonoma Coast
State Beaches

Point Reyes
Nat'l. Seashore

Healdsburg

Santa Rosa

Sebastopol

SONOMA

Hood Mtn.
Reg'l. Park

Annadel
State Park

Jack London
St. Hist. Park

Sonoma

Petaluma Adobe
St. Hist. Park

Petaluma

Helen Putnam Reg'l. Park

MARIN

Mt. Burdell OSP

Indian Tree OSP

Samuel P. Taylor
State Park

Mt. Wittenberg

Gary Giacomini OSP

Marin Municipal Water
District Watershed

Stinson Beach GGNRA

Mt. Tamalpais State Park

Marin Headlands GGNRA

Presidio GGNRA

Twin Peaks

SEE NORTH BAY MAP

Bothe-Napa
State Park

Sugarloaf
Ridge St. Pk.

NAPA

Lake Berryessa
Recreation Area

Lake Hennessey
Reservoir

Rector Watershed

Napa River
Ecological Preserve

Milliken
Watershed

Yountville
Veterans
Home

Skyline
Wilderness
Park

Napa

Olompali State
Historic Park

Lucas Valley
OSP

Loma
Alta OSP

San Rafael

Muir Woods
Nat'l. Mon.

Sausalito

Novato

Vallejo Lakes
Watershed

SOLANO

Vacaville

Fairfield

Rockville Hills Reg'l. Park

Hiddenbrooke Trail

Blue Rock Springs Park

Benicia State
Rec. Area

Benicia

Vallejo

Sobrante Ridge
Reg'l. Preserve

Pinole

Kennedy
Grove

Richmond

Wildcat Canyon
Reg'l. Park

Tilden
Reg'l.
Park

Berkeley

Oakland

Alameda

Martinez Reg'l.
Shoreline

Martinez

John Muir Nat'l.
Historic Site

Concord

Briones
Reg'l. Park

Walnut
Creek

Sibley Volcanic
Preserve

Redwood
Reg'l. Park

EBMUD

EBMUD

Pittsburg

Antioch

CONTRA COSTA

Mt. Diablo
State Park

Brentwood

Crockett

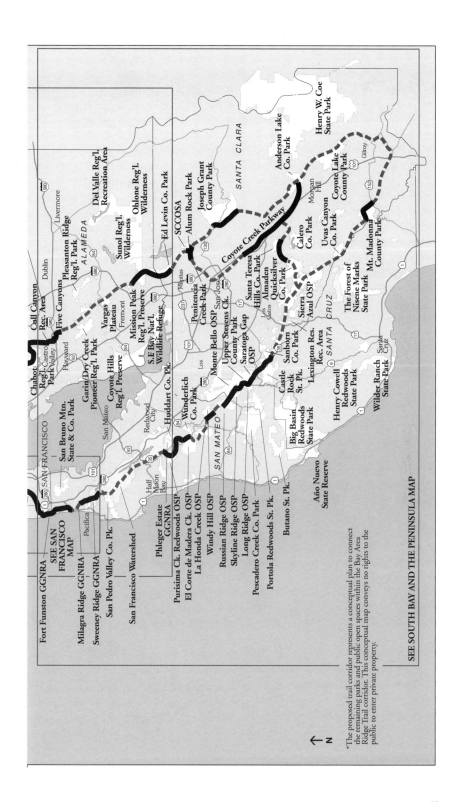

N

*The proposed trail corridor represents a conceptual plan to connect the remaining parks and public open spaces within the Bay Area Ridge Trail corridor. This conceptual map conveys no rights to the public to enter private property.

SEE SOUTH BAY AND THE PENINSULA MAP

Fort Funston GGNRA

SEE SAN FRANCISCO MAP

Milagra Ridge GGNRA

Sweeney Ridge GGNRA

San Pedro Valley Co. Pk.

San Francisco Watershed

Purisima Ck. Redwoods OSP

El Corte de Madera Ck. OSP

La Honda Creek OSP

Windy Hill OSP

Russian Ridge OSP

Skyline Ridge OSP

Long Ridge OSP

Pescadero Creek Co. Park

Portola Redwoods St. Pk.

Butano St. Pk.

Año Nuevo State Reserve

SAN FRANCISCO

Pacifica

San Bruno Mtn. State & Co. Park

Garin/Dry Creek Pioneer Reg'l. Park

Coyote Hills Reg'l. Preserve

Phleger Estate GGNRA

Huddart Co. Pk.

Wunderlich Co. Park

Half Moon Bay

San Mateo

Redwood City

SAN MATEO

Castro Valley

Hayward

Dublin

Livermore

ALAMEDA

Pleasanton Ridge Reg'l. Park

Del Valle Reg'l. Recreation Area

Sunol Reg'l. Wilderness

Vargas Plateau

Mission Peak Reg'l. Preserve

Fremont

S.F Bay Nat'l. Wildlife Refuge

Milpitas

Penitencia Creek Park

San Jose

Los Gatos

Monte Bello OSP

Upper Stevens Ck. County Park

Saratoga Gap OSP

Sanborn Co. Park

Lexington Res. Rec. Area

Castle Rock St. Pk.

Big Basin Redwoods State Park

Henry Cowell Redwoods State Park

Wilder Ranch State Park

Santa Cruz

SANTA CRUZ

The Forest of Nisene Marks State Park

Sierra Azul OSP

Almaden Quicksilver Co. Park

Santa Teresa Hills Co. Park

Calero Co. Park

Uvas Canyon Co. Park

Coyote Lake County Park

Mt. Madonna County Park

Gilroy

Morgan Hill

SANTA CLARA

Ohlone Reg'l. Wilderness

Ed Levin Co. Park

SCCOSA

Alum Rock Park

Joseph Grant County Park

Anderson Lake Co. Park

Henry W. Coe State Park

Coyote Creek Parkway

Call Canyon Rec. Area

Chabot Reg'l. Park

Five Canyons

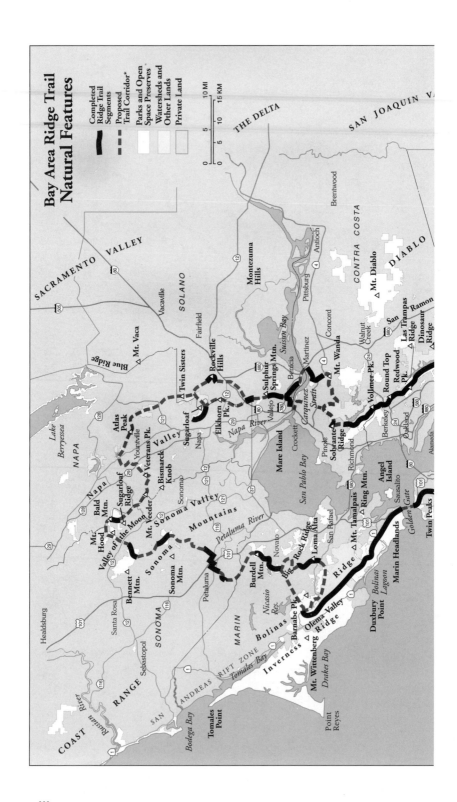

Bay Area Ridge Trail
Natural Features

Completed
Ridge Trail
Segments

Proposed
Trail Corridor*

Parks and Open
Space Preserves

Watersheds and
Other Lands

Private Land

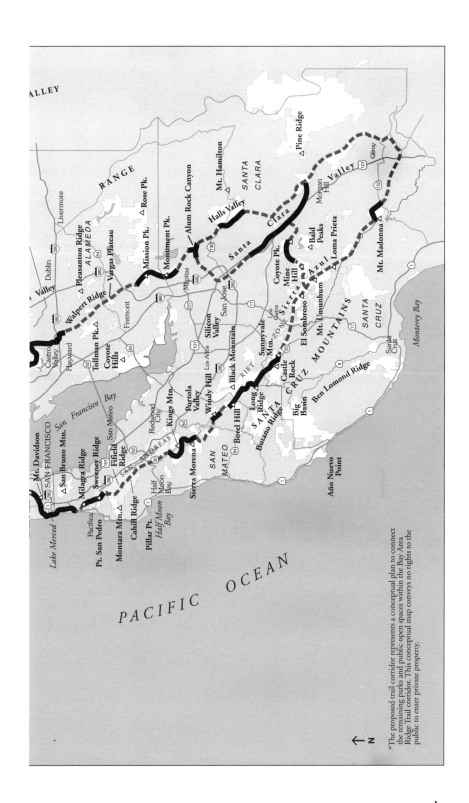

Map Legend

=== Freeway
=== Road
——— Minor Road

Bay Area Ridge Trail (shown by use)

Multi-Use Trail (horses, bikes, and hikers)
Equestrian & Hiking Trail
Bicycle & Hiking Trail
Hiking Only Trail
Designated Connector Trails
Other Trail (use not specified)

Bay Area Ridge Trail
San Francisco Bay Trail
EBRPD Regional Trails

Parks along Bay Area Ridge Trail
Watersheds and Adjacent Parks
Private Property

P Parking
LP Limited Parking
EP Equestrian Parking
T Transit Stop
(R) Restroom
π Picnic Area
▲ Campground
i Park Office/ Visitor Center
■ Structures
• Point of Interest
ı Gate

1250'△ Peak (elevation in feet)
Stream
Lake/ Pond/ Bay/ Ocean
Marsh

THE BAY AREA RIDGE TRAIL

Ridgetop Adventures
Above San Francisco Bay

View towards Butano Ridge.

INTRODUCTION

Bay Area Setting

The San Francisco Bay Area, with its remarkable juxtaposition of bay, mountains, and sea, is one of the world's premier natural settings. The jewel of this region is San Francisco Bay, one of the largest bays in the United States and a unifying feature for the nine counties that ring its shores. Two arms of the Coast Range cradle the bay as they run northwest-southeast along the length of the region. The hills and valleys of the North and South Bay counties loosely connect the inner and outer Coast Ranges.

A wealth of natural beauty resides in the Bay Area's coastal mountains and their rolling foothills—redwood forests, wooded streamsides, oak-studded grasslands, rocky peaks, steep mountainsides, lush meadows, and sunny chaparral slopes. During the last seventy years, public agencies as well as private land trusts have set aside tracts of land in the mountains and foothills that are now parks, open space preserves, and watersheds. Extensive public open space now occupies the land between the Coast Ranges—on shady creek banks, in hillside forests, and in greenspaces within residential areas. In several Bay Area counties this land now forms a continuous open space corridor—a Bay Area Greenbelt.

These public open spaces are peaceful backdrops to a bustling urban area—places for adventure, discovery, recreation, and relaxation. Here is "room to breathe," habitat for diverse plant and animal species, and areas for forests to thrive and cleanse our air. Here too, is the route of the multi-use Bay Area Ridge Trail. When complete, 425 miles of trail will link more than 75 public parks and open spaces on the ridgeline surrounding San Francisco Bay.

These public open space lands in the Bay Area lie close to the homes of nearly seven million residents, most of whom live in the valleys of the Coast Range and on the sloping plains that border the bay. From almost any place in the Bay Area, the ridgelands, accented by taller peaks, are visible to Bay Area residents. For them, the sun rises and sets over these mountains, literally and figuratively. Bay Area natives, especially, are fiercely proud and protective of their mountains.

The Bay Area's Heritage of Outdoor Enjoyment

The physical grandeur of this setting and its moderate climate, influenced by the bay and the Pacific Ocean, make the Bay Area ideal for outdoor recreation. You can hike, run, bicycle, or ride horseback somewhere in the Bay Area on almost any day of the year.

Hikers on the Sonoma Mountain Trail in Jack London State Park.

The area's earliest inhabitants—the Ohlone, Yurock, Pomo, and other Native American tribes—indicated that this was a gentle land. The first explorers marveled at its beauty, its great redwood forests, and its Mediterranean climate. After the Gold Rush, a wave of settlers arrived to farm and work in its salubrious weather. The first California Geological Survey team report, written by William H. Brewer under the direction of Josiah D. Whitney in the early 1860s, found delight in the variety of terrain and glowingly praised its marvelous scenery. Brewer's book *Up and Down California* describes some Bay Area scenery that is today preserved as parklands in the great Bay Area greenbelt.

As the Spanish built missions and settlements in California, the Spanish government gave large land grants to some colonists as rewards for their service. On vast domains known as "ranchos," these "rancheros" kept thousands of cattle, which they managed with well-trained horses. The rancheros displayed their fine horses and their equestrian skills at rodeos and games that became important social events. The Spaniards established a tradition of skilled horsemanship and a love for riding that the Mexican rancheros later carried on.

Anglo cattle ranchers blazed trails as they herded their stock and allowed friends—and a relatively small public interested in walking and riding—to cross their lands on these trails; some are in public use today. These ranchers also carried on a tradition of fine horsemanship and riding for pleasure.

European immigrants who grew up in the mountains of Germany, Austria, and Switzerland recognized the natural beauty of the Bay Area and took pleasure in walking with friends on weekends. They could wander freely through orchards, along farm roads, through friendly neighbors' meadows, and along hillside animal paths. Mt. Tamalpais was a favorite destination after passenger ferry service from San Francisco reached Marin County in the 1920s.

Eventually many hiking and horseback riding groups sprang up to offer trips in the Bay Area countryside on trails made by the rancheros, cattlemen, early settlers, and weekend explorers. Today, trail enthusiasts can find outings geared for a great variety of skills and interest levels. Trained volunteers for the Bay Area Ridge Trail Council lead trips to many scenic, historic, and cultural sites along the ridges surrounding the bay. Local Sierra Club chapters, as well as sports groups and commercial outfitters, offer outings to many Bay Area destinations.

A Land Conservation Ethic

In 1892, John Muir and others devoted to the outdoors and its natural wonders founded the San Francisco-based Sierra Club. The club grew out of a land conservation ethic that was dedicated to preserving areas of natural beauty and unique wilderness for posterity. It promoted the establishment of many western national parks, including Yosemite. The Sierra Club continues its conservation mission today at local, national, and international levels.

Local chapters of the Sierra Club sprang up to lobby for the acquisition of public open space and to support its use. In the Bay

Wheat stalks dry in an orchard at John Muir National Historic Site.

Area, a large membership includes hikers, backpackers, mountain climbers, kayakers, bicyclists, advocates for all types of trail use, and people involved in saving land for parks.

Since nine Bay Area counties border San Francisco Bay, all have an impetus for cooperation and collaboration. Recent studies, such as Bay Vision 2020, promote regional unity and planning, and preservation of the area's natural resources. Governmental organizations—the Association of Bay Area Governments, the Metropolitan Transportation Agency, the Regional Air Quality Control Board, the Bay Conservation and Development Commission (BCDC), and the California State Coastal Conservancy—seek unity by organizing and managing regional affairs.

Nonprofit grassroots organizations address current needs or glaring deficiencies in government long-range regional planning and land-use problems. The Bay Conservation and Development Commission, for example, brought about by a vigorous grassroots Save the Bay campaign, now regulates use and care of the bay and monitors its shores. The non-profit Planning and Conservation League, based in Sacramento, works to promote good legislation for parks, transportation, and land use.

Recognizing that the Bay Area needed a defining greenbelt of open space for its cities, far-sighted citizens and committed activists joined the late Dorothy Erskine to form a group dedicated to achieving this ideal. First known as People for Open Space, then Greenbelt Congress, and now Greenbelt Alliance, this organization mobilized a regional fight to establish a ring of parks, preserves, open space, farms, and ranches around the Bay Area. As the crusaders grew in numbers, so did the greenbelt around the bay.

Development of Parks and Open Spaces

As the Bay Area population grew, especially in the years following World War II, outdoor lovers began to appreciate the importance of obtaining recreation lands for all to enjoy. More and more people gravitated to the outlying hills and valleys to walk or ride horseback freely.

Even before World War II, East Bay citizens began to realize the need for parks adjacent to their growing cities. Inspired and dedicated Alameda and Contra Costa county citizens, aided by civic leaders, launched the East Bay Regional Park District (EBRPD) in 1934 by an overwhelming vote. The EBRPD's first acquisition, Tilden Regional Park, marked the beginning of its present-day 93,000-acre greenbelt of parks, historic units, and recreation complexes.

Other cities and counties eventually followed suit, setting aside small and large areas for parks and open space. Most of these parklands lie on the ridges, mountainsides, and foothills of the Coast

Ranges. However, with the recognition that San Francisco Bay was diminishing in size and purity, agencies around the bay began establishing shoreline parks to increase stewardship and appreciation of the bay. A notable example is the Don Edwards San Francisco Bay National Wildlife Refuge, a federal unit under the Fish and Wildlife Service of the Department of the Interior. The refuge seeks to preserve the plant and animal life of the wetlands, to help cleanse bay waters (an unknown or unheeded need until recently), and to educate the public about these goals. The California Coastal Commission, set up by a statewide ballot initiative that was later resoundingly renewed by public vote, has a mandate to protect the entire state's coastal viewshed and to preserve public access to the shoreline.

As the appreciation of our need for breathing space and stretching room grew, other new agencies also took up the cause. Successful examples include the Marin County Open Space District and the Midpeninsula Regional Open Space District in Santa Clara and San Mateo counties. Recently, Sonoma County organized an Agricultural Preservation and Open Space District, and Santa Clara County passed a ballot measure to set up an open space authority. Cities and counties have passed several bond measures and initiatives to promote good land use, limit urban sprawl, provide recreational opportunities, and preserve agriculture at city edges. Napa County has adopted land-use regulations designed to protect its world-famous vineyards.

Today, as a result of these many efforts, hundreds of thousands of protected acres in the foothills and mountainsides surround the urbanized bayside, and more acreage edges the bay's shores. In coastal counties—particularly Marin, San Francisco, and San Mateo—thousands of acres are permanently protected by the National Park Service. Local Coastal Plans in Sonoma, Marin, San Francisco, and San Mateo counties afford a measure of protection as well. There is at least one unit of the California State Park System in each Bay Area county and most Bay Area counties have a county park system; Marin, Sonoma, Alameda, Contra Costa, Santa Clara, and San Mateo counties are blessed with an additional regional park agency.

Many Bay Area parks were established on closed military bases. The military declared Forts Baker, Barry, Cronkite, and Funston, and Milagra and Sweeney ridges surplus bases in post-WWII downsizing. In 1994, the San Francisco Presidio became a national park under the jurisdiction of the Golden Gate National Recreation Area. A provision of federal law that required these bases to be offered to public entities before the commercial market led to many of the parks that grace our ridgetops and baylands.

Watersheds, too, preserve open space in Marin, Alameda, Contra Costa, Santa Clara, and San Mateo counties. In order to assure a steady water supply to San Francisco's growing population, a group of individuals formed the Spring Valley Water Company in the mid-1880s; the San Francisco Water Department later grew out of this company. Eventually the SFWD began to pipe water from the Sierra Nevada to service the needs of its customers—now more than a million—in San Francisco, the East Bay, and on the peninsula.

Other jurisdictions began to develop stable water supplies and to store water in reservoirs. Most of these storage areas are in the foothills surrounding the bay plain. For many years these reservoirs were off-limits to the public. However, with the development of modern purification techniques, some agencies began to open their gates to quiet, passive recreation, such as nature walks and hiking. Today, most water agencies allow some public access, although the SFWD restricts access to groups.

The Role of Private, Nonprofit Groups

Private, nonprofit organizations, such as Trust for Public Land, Peninsula Open Space Trust (POST), and Sempervirens Fund, have worked for many years to preserve and protect open space lands for eventual public use. Through gifts, purchases, and easements these organizations can make choice lands available to public agencies. A recent outstanding example is POST's 4262-acre purchase of choice coastal land at Rancho Corral de Tierra in San Mateo County, adjacent to existing federal, state and county parks, and to San Francisco Watershed lands. Cooperation among agencies, citizens, large donors, and the federal government brought about this remarkable acquisition. A connector trail through this land will someday reach the Bay Area Ridge Trail on the crest of the Santa Cruz Mountains.

View of the bay from the Anniversary Trail
at Windy Hill Open Space Preserve.

THE BAY AREA RIDGE TRAIL

A combination of unique characteristics primed the Bay Area for the establishment of the Bay Area Ridge Trail: a glorious physical setting; a long history of outdoor recreation; a growing greenbelt; a conservation ethic; and a population of avid outdoor enthusiasts, conservationists, and educated and willing volunteers. Designed as a multi-use ridgeline route, this proposed 425-mile trail will connect public parklands and watersheds of the Bay Area greenbelt that circles San Francisco Bay. It will eventually link over 75 parks and public lands and provide magnificent views, visits to important historic sites, glimpses of the area's cultural heritage, and firsthand experience in the Bay Area's diverse ecosystems.

On a network of paths that traverses a broad corridor along the ridgelands, the Bay Area Ridge Trail provides recreational opportunities for hikers, bicyclists, and equestrians. Some segments of the trail are accessible to wheelchair users. At least one segment of the Ridge Trail lies less than a half-hour's drive or bus ride from any Bay Area community. The scenic trail links communities along the ridgeline and will connect to bayside population centers and the San Francisco Bay Trail via feeder trails through existing city, county, regional, and federal parks.

The Beginnings

When William Penn Mott, Jr. was General Manager of the East Bay Regional Park District in the 1960s, he proposed a trail around the entire ridge of the Bay Area. His vision also included a trail around the bay, close to the water, and connector trails to the Sierra Nevada.

In the late 1980s, when he returned from his position as director of the National Park Service, he lent his strong support and encouragement to achieving his vision of a ridgeline trail around the bay.

THE BAY AREA RIDGE TRAIL

In 1986, during the review of the Land Use Element of the San Francisco General Plan, language was inserted that promoted public access to the watershed lands of the City and County of San Francisco. People for Open Space (POS), the predecessors of Greenbelt Alliance, began an effort to acquaint the city with the public-access policies of the region's other water departments. POS brought together the managers of water departments, county, regional, state, and federal parks departments, trail activists, and leaders of environmental organizations at a meeting in 1987, intending to demonstrate to San Francisco that other Bay Area watersheds' less restrictive public access policies did not harm water quality. As an important outgrowth of that meeting, these groups recognized that watershed lands, parks, and preserves that surround the bay could be linked with a regional trail.

A coalition of activists, spurred by the energy and commitment of William Penn Mott, Jr. (then Director of the National Park Service), set up the Bay Area Trails Council in September 1987, followed by the Bay Area Ridge Trail Council in late 1987. Brian O'Neill, Superintendent of the Golden Gate National Recreation Area (GGNRA), was the first chairman. The Bay Area Ridge Trail Council was established as a project of POS/Greenbelt Alliance, which provided office space and administrative support in the early years. The National Park Service provided first-year funding, and GGNRA contributed staffing. The outpouring of support for the Bay Area Ridge Trail led the informal council to incorporate in 1992 as a private, nonprofit organization. Today, the council has a membership of 5000, two regional field coordinators, and a growing corps of dedicated, grassroots volunteers.

The Bay Area Ridge Trail Council's Mission

The Bay Area Ridge Trail Council, a coalition of volunteers and agencies, plans, promotes, builds, acquires, and maintains the 425-mile Bay Area Ridge Trail, a multi-use trail that, when complete, will connect over 75 parks and open spaces on the ridgeline surrounding the San Francisco Bay. Recognizing the growing recreational needs of the Bay Area's diverse populations, along with the desire of individuals to connect with their communities and the outdoor environment, the council creates links between parks, people, and communities. The council also fulfills and accomplishes the pioneering vision of William Penn Mott, Jr.

Cutting the ribbon at a dedication for the Ridge Trail through Jack London State Park.

Bay Area Ridge Trail Accomplishments

As of May 2002, 230 miles of the Ridge Trail have been completed and are dedicated, signed, and in use. An additional 10.5 miles of trail are under construction and will be dedicated by the end of 2002. The total Ridge Trail mileage is calculated along the main route on a single alignment and does not include alternate routes, connector trails to the main route, or side trips.

There is at least one Ridge Trail segment in each of the Bay Area counties. Most of the trail traverses public parklands around the Bay Area. However, the 4.5-mile trail in Skyline Wilderness Park is on land leased from the State of California and operated as a park by a private group that offers its use to the public for a nominal fee.

This treasury of public lands unites the nine Bay Area counties that touch San Francisco Bay. The Bay Area Ridge Trail is a composite necklace of trails, made up of diverse jewels, for a variety of users, from hikers, equestrians, and bicyclists, to all who appreciate the beauty of this land. The public spaces it threads offer magnificent views of our Bay Area, places to sit, contemplate and relax, places to restore the spirit, places to test endurance and build stamina. Along these paths, an observant user can see many of the area's

13

animal species, countless birds, and hundreds of different wildflowers in season. The parks through which the Bay Area Ridge Trail runs offer a wide variety of experiences depending on each trail's exposure to sun, rain, and wind. The presence of animal and plant life will vary according to such exposure, past usage, and present management. You will enjoy a unique experience on each segment of the Ridge Trail.

The Next Step—Closing the Gaps

Since 1987, the Bay Area Ridge Trail Council has been particularly successful in completing Ridge Trail segments on public lands. Approximately 66% of the total miles to be completed are in existing public parks and open spaces along the route. Another 23% of the miles are proposed for publicly owned watersheds and relatively short, undeveloped segments on public road rights-of-way or sidewalks.

The additional miles of the Bay Area Ridge Trail that remain to be completed may be proposed for private lands. The Bay Area Ridge Trail Council actively reaches out to private landowners, works to build sound public policies that support the Ridge Trail, and assists community partners in fund-raising and trail maintenance efforts—critical components in the completion of the remaining Ridge Trail miles.

Closing these gaps in the Bay Area Ridge Trail presents an immediate and immense challenge that will take years to fulfill. However, the council's long-range strategic target is to complete 400 miles of the Ridge Trail by 2010. Success in this effort relies on the council's leadership and the on-going involvement and commitment of its members, volunteers, and public agency partners.

Volunteers play a key role in the programs and projects of the council. From an active corps who serve on the Board of Directors, to those who build trails, plan and carry out Ridge Trail events, and others who raise needed funds, the volunteers are the heart of the Bay Area Ridge Trail Council. Two outstanding volunteers, Dinesh Desai and Bob Cowell, hiked the entire Ridge Trail route in the summer of 1999. Newspaper, magazine and TV coverage of this event raised public awareness and financial support of the trail. Several hiking and bicycling groups challenged themselves to hike or ride a large number of Ridge Trail segments over an extended period. A Santa Clara County group hiked 18 segments in a one-year period.

Dinesh Desai and Bob Cowell hiked the entire
Ridge Trail route in summer 1999.

Young people too, can contribute to the Ridge Trail mission. The High Adventure Team of the Santa Clara County Council of the Boy Scouts of America created a patch for youths who hike or bike one segment in any of the four Bay Area sections of the Ridge Trail. Completing a trip in each of the four sections earns the participant all four patches for the full 4 × 4-inch Bay Area Ridge Trail "map." It is open to Brownies and Cub Scouts, Girl and Boy Scouts, and other youth and school groups. Trail maintenance or construction of the trail under supervision of the public land agency is an alternate way to earn a patch. (A pamphlet is available through the Boy Scout office at 408-280-5088 or South Bay Scout Shop at 408-279-2086.)

Other Regional Trails In the Bay Area

After World War II, Californian's enthusiasm for a round-the-state, border-to-border loop trail surged, and easements were secured and rights of way developed for the California Riding and Hiking Trail. However, due to rapid building activity along the route and to lack of legal rights to the trails, most trail segments fell into disrepair and were subsequently closed. Today, the Bay Area Ridge Trail follows some segments of this early trail in Contra Costa and San Mateo counties. (See *Carquinez Strait Regional Shoreline to John Muir Historic Site* in the East Bay section and *Wunderlich County Park to Huddart County Park* in the South Bay and Peninsula section).

The Anza Trail, a National Historic Trail, follows Captain Juan Bautista de Anza's attempt to find a land route from Mexico to San Francisco. In the Bay Area, the Anza Trail runs through Santa Clara, San Mateo, and San Francisco counties. The statewide Coastal Trail hugs the shoreline through San Mateo, San Francisco, Marin, and Sonoma counties. In Marin, San Francisco, and San Mateo counties, the Ridge Trail and Coastal Trail share the same alignment. The San Francisco Bay Trail proposes to circle the shoreline of the entire bay, following a plan originally developed and funded by legislation introduced by Senator Bill Lockyer. The Association of Bay Area Governments, the Metropolitan Transportation Commission, and the nonprofit San Francisco Bay Trail Project are now implementing plans for the Bay Trail, and as of 2002, more than 200 miles are completed.

The Skyline-to-the-Sea Trail connects Castle Rock State Park, on the crest of the Santa Cruz Mountains, with Big Basin State Park, on the Pacific Coast at the mouth of Waddell Creek. Since the inception of this 26-mile trail in 1969, hundreds of volunteers have built and maintained it during California Trail Days, with support and sponsorship from Sempervirens Fund, the State of California Department of Parks and Recreation, and presently, the California Trails and Greenways Foundation. The Skyline-to-the-Sea Trail also serves as a connector from the coast to the Bay Area Ridge Trail at Saratoga Gap in Santa Clara County.

Three Bay Area trails have been granted national trail status: The Anza Trail is a National Historic Trail; the Skyline Trail, which traverses six regional parks on the ridges above East Bay cities, and the Creek Trail, which follows Penitencia Creek in Alum Rock Park, are designated National Recreation Trails. The Bay Area Ridge Trail follows the Skyline and Creek trails and parts of the Anza Trail.

The Bay Area Ridge Trail Council seeks to connect neighboring communities by linking the Ridge Trail to other regional trails and to local trail networks. The connecting trails offer many local residents the opportunity to reach the long regional trails without ever starting a car. These links bind the communities together, like the spokes of a bicycle wheel.

Other Long Trails

Long-distance trails connecting several sites, cities, and/or regions are a challenge to distance hikers and a source of volunteer action and pride in the areas they traverse. The oldest of these trails in the United States is the Appalachian Trail, which stretches from Mt. Katahdin in Maine to Springer Mountain in Georgia. Other well-known trails include the Long Trail in New England, the John Muir Trail in California's Sierra Nevada, and the Pacific Crest and Coastal trails from Mexico to Canada. Around Lake Tahoe, the Tahoe Rim Trail traverses ridgetop lands, and in Southern California, the Santa Ana River Trail offers paved paths on both sides of the river leading to Huntington Beach. Other communities and regions are taking up the long trail idea.

The State of California's Recreational Trails Committee coordinates California's statewide effort to build trails that link communities and promote stewardship of and appreciation for the wealth of public land at our doorsteps. Along with the California Trails and Greenways Foundation, it conducts an annual conference for trail advocates and sponsors the annual spring California Trail Days, to help build and maintain trails throughout the state.

The Bay Area Ridge Trail
Ridgetop Adventures Above San Francisco Bay

Jean Rusmore
in cooperation with the
Bay Area Ridge Trail Council

Official Guide
to the
Bay Area
Ridge Trail

Front cover of this book's first edition.

ABOUT THIS GUIDEBOOK

A Proposal Takes Shape

In late 1989, author Jean Rusmore and Tioga Press publisher Karen Nilsson submitted a proposal to the Bay Area Ridge Trail Council to produce a small guide for each completed Ridge Trail segment. Eventually, these guides were to be assembled in a book. The council accepted the proposal and agreed to make the maps and print the guides. Frances Spangle, who co-authored other guidebooks with Jean Rusmore, wrote the first four Marin County trips and one in San Mateo County. The Bay Area Ridge Trail Council eventually produced 18 guides, printed in two colors on a folded 11″ × 17″ sheet, and offered for a small fee. After Karen Nilsson's untimely death, Thomas Winnett, publisher of Wilderness Press, a premier national guidebook press, graciously took over the project. The first edition of this book, dedicated to Karen, is the outgrowth of that proposal. This second edition of the Bay Area Ridge Trail incorporates and updates the early guides and the previous edition.

How to Use This Guidebook

This book includes all the completed segments of the Bay Area Ridge Trail, as of press time, in 45 trips, totaling 230 miles. The trail descriptions here are arranged in clockwise order around San Francisco Bay, beginning in San Francisco, followed by Marin County, Sonoma County, then Napa County, and so on around the bay. Hence, the Marin County descriptions are written to start at the south end and finish at the north end of each segment. As the route heads across the interior valleys of the North Bay, trail descriptions begin at the west end and finish at the east end. The East Bay descriptions start in the north and end in the south, and across the Santa Clara Valley the trips go from east to west. Heading up the peninsula and into San Francisco, the route is described from south to north.

The trips are listed in four main sections: San Francisco, the North Bay, the East Bay, and the South Bay and the peninsula. Each trip lists length; access for different groups; regulations and facilities specific to each park, preserve, or open space; and trip highlights and information about the trail surface and elevation gain/loss. Trips also include a map, directions to the trailhead, and a detailed description of the trail.

Maps

At the beginning of each section, you'll find a map of the Ridge Trail route through the region that section covers; the Ridge Trail segments are shown as black, bold lines. A separate map for each trip marks the Ridge Trail segment as well as other trails, park trailheads, and major landmarks. Different thicknesses and dash patterns indicate at-a-glance the trails and their user-groups: a thick dashed line indicates a multi-use route; medium dashed lines show hiking and equestrian segments; medium dash-dot lines show hiking and bicycling segments; dots indicate hiking-only trail segments. Designated connector trails are similarly coded, but colored gray. Wheelchair-accessible trails are marked by the standard wheelchair symbol. Each map displays a legend of the dash symbols for easy reference.

The combination of user-group symbols on the map, the accessibility information at the beginning of each trip, and the material in the text clarify the Ridge Trail route and appropriate users within each park or preserve. Additional information on the maps includes trailhead parking areas, major roads, and nearby landmarks, which when combined with the text, will direct you to the park.

The maps are generally based on the 7.5-minute series of United States Geological Survey topographic maps, which are available from some sporting-goods stores and from the USGS at 345 Middlefield Road, Menlo Park, CA 94025. The Map Center, located at 2440 Bancroft Way, Berkeley, CA 94704 and at 63 Washington Street, Santa Clara, CA 95050, stocks all the 7.5-minute and 1:250,000 USGS topographic maps for the State of California.

Some additional trails in each park are shown on the maps, but user groups are not distinguished. For complete information, consult a guidebook or request a park map from the managing agency. There are maps at some trailheads, but they may not be available when you visit. For other trails in the South Bay and on the peninsula, excellent guides are *Peninsula Trails* and *South Bay Trails*, co-authored by Jean Rusmore, Betsy Crowder and Frances Spangle and published by Wilderness Press, Berkeley, CA. *North Bay Trails* and *East Bay Trails* by David Weintraub, also published by Wilderness Press, are useful sources for major parklands in the region that the Bay Area Ridge Trail traverses. Additional references and selected readings are in Appendix 6.

Sections

For each trip, **Getting There** gives directions to the trailhead from the nearest major road for each end of the trip. In a few instances, the trailhead differs for each class of user. Bus lines are given for trailheads that are serviced by public transportation. See Appendix 2 for a list of transportation agencies, their addresses, phone numbers, and websites.

Regulations lists the hours of operation for each park or preserve, dog and bicycle rules, and fees. Rules regarding dogs range from parks that do not allow dogs on any trail to those that only require them to be under voice control. In general, dogs must be on a six-foot leash. Some trails pass through the jurisdictions of more than one agency, each with different dog regulations.

Many parks charge an entrance fee, although some only require it on weekends, and group fees may be lower. There is usually a fee for amenities such as camping, horse rental, and swimming. Fees change every few years, so the exact charge is not given in this book. Call the agency that manages the park or special facility or check its website for current fees.

Bicycle rules vary depending on the managing agency. Some allow bicyclists on fire or service roads; a few allow them on narrow trails. Bicyclists should note the Ridge Trail routes in this guide and observe the map information and icons on trailhead signs.

A complete list of agency addresses, phone numbers, and websites is in Appendix 2. The Bay Area Ridge Trail website also supplies this information.

On the Trail describes the route, gives directions for trail junctions, tells you what you may see along the way, mentions animal and plant life, and sketches some geologic, historic, and cultural features that add to the interest of the trip. Since the author took these trips at different times of the year, and since the appearance of flowers, shrubs, and trees, and the presence of animal life vary season-

Even a llama came to the dedication in Jack London State Park.

ally, some aspects of the trail's surroundings may differ from what you see.

Sharing the Trails

Hikers, equestrians, and bicyclists share many segments of the Bay Area Ridge Trail. Wherever possible, the Ridge Trail tries to accommodate all users on a single route. If this is not possible, the Bay Area Ridge Trail policy states "...due to policy or regulation restrictions, environmental concerns, safety or physical terrain, the Bay Area Ridge Trail Council works cooperatively to secure an additional route that offers an equivalent trail experience."

Variations in speed, height, and power of each type of user require that there be some trail etiquette rules. Some general rules are:

- Observe trail use signs.
- Be responsible, safe, and considerate.
- Stay on the trail.
- Respect private property.
- Minimize your impact.
- Protect plants and wildlife.

Some rules are generally accepted for yielding to other users:

- Hikers and bicyclists yield to equestrians; stop and remain quiet while an equestrian is passing.
- Bicyclists yield to hikers; dismount and allow the hiker to pass.

A number of agencies have adopted additional rules for bicyclists: Maximum speed is 15 miles per hour; slow to 5 miles per hour when passing or when sight distance is limited. Helmets are a standard requirement of most agencies. Some agencies use radar systems to increase awareness of park speed limits and to help bicyclists know their speed.

Some Hazards for Trail Users

Poison oak is ubiquitous in the Bay Area. It takes different forms, usually as a trailside shrub, but mature plants climb trees and occasionally become small trees themselves. It has three-lobed leaves that are shiny green in spring and turn beautiful shades of red and orange in the fall, and it is extremely harmful to those allergic to it. Just to touch its leaves, berries, or leafless twigs can cause an itchy, blistery rash that takes several weeks to heal. Learn to recognize it and avoid it carefully.

Rattlesnakes are indigenous to the Bay Area, but far less widespread than poison oak. They have triangular-shaped heads, diamond markings on their backs, and rattles or segmented sections on their tails. They will try to avoid contact with humans. However, it is well to look down on warm spring days when a rattlesnake may be sunning itself on the trail. Look where you put your hands when climbing on rocks.

Lyme disease is a potentially serious disease caused by the bite of the western black-legged tick. In their active months, between December and June, these tiny ticks can brush off trailside grasses and bushes onto your clothes. Wear light-colored clothing so you can see the ticks, keep your arms and legs covered, and tuck your pant legs into your socks.

Mountain lions are shy, native residents of wild lands in the Bay Area. Sightings of these creatures have become more frequent in recent years due to increased human use of their habitat. A mountain lion is about the size of a small German Shepherd with a furry tail as long as its body. Trail users should stand facing any mountain lion they encounter and make loud noises while waving their arms; do not run away.

Feral pigs have spread over many acres of wild lands since they were introduced in the 19th century as hunting animals. While generally not dangerous to humans, they can be fierce when cornered.

What to Wear and Take Along

Some basic rules for all trail users are to carry plenty of water and some food and snacks, have the appropriate equipment for your mode of travel, take an extra sweater and a windbreaker, wear a hat, and carry sunscreen. A small packet of Band-Aids can be useful. All these items can easily fit in a light day pack. Although many people prefer a small waist pack because it is lighter, this equipment may not have room for an extra sweater or windbreaker.

Specialized equipment for trail users is readily available, but not required. Many hikers prefer to wear boots; others find that sturdy shoes with good tread and adequate support are appropriate for most Bay Area trails. Some bicyclists prefer special mountain-biking shoes and many equestrians like to wear a protective helmet.

Where to Stay

Many Bay Area Ridge Trail travelers will hike or ride one or two segments of the trail on day trips from their Bay Area homes. For those who want to take a longer trip, a weekend or more, there are many miles of continuous Ridge Trail through Marin, Contra Costa, Alameda, Santa Clara, and San Mateo counties. A Ridge Trail trip through the city of San Francisco would fill two hiking days.

Hostels, primitive camps, and public park campgrounds, located within 2 to 6 miles of the trail, are generally the least expensive places to stay overnight. See *Camping and Hostels On and Near the Bay Area Ridge Trail* map, Appendix 4, and Appendix 2 for contact information.

Charming bed and breakfast inns, comfortable motels, and some luxurious hotels in towns and tourist areas near the trailheads are listed in local telephone books or with travel agencies. As the public discovers the outstanding scenic and recreation qualities of the Bay Area Ridge Trail, local and national outing companies will undoubtedly offer hiking and riding trips on the Ridge Trail including transportation to the trailheads and overnight accommodations.

On the following pages are 45 Ridgetop Adventures above San Francisco Bay. To help you choose the right trip for the weather, your abilities and interests, see Appendix 3—*A Bay Area Ridge Trail Sampler—Trips for Many Reasons.*

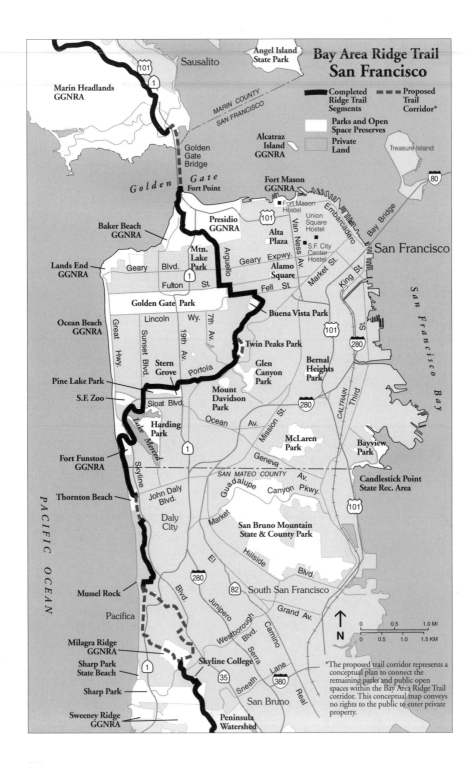

Bay Area Ridge Trail
San Francisco

Completed Ridge Trail Segments
Proposed Trail Corridor*

Parks and Open Space Preserves
Private Land

Angel Island State Park

Sausalito

Marin Headlands GGNRA

101 1

MARIN COUNTY
SAN FRANCISCO

Golden Gate Bridge

Golden Gate

Fort Point

Alcatraz Island GGNRA

Treasure Island

80

Fort Mason GGNRA

Fort Mason Hostel

Presidio GGNRA

Baker Beach GGNRA

101

Union Square Hostel

Embarcadero

Alta Plaza

Van Ness Av.

S.F. City Center Hostel

San Francisco

Mtn. Lake Park

Arguello

Geary Expwy.

Alamo Square

Lands End GGNRA

Geary Blvd. Park

1

Fulton St.

Market St.

King St.

Fell St.

San Francisco Bay

Golden Gate Park

Lincoln Wy.

7th Av.

Buena Vista Park

101 280

Ocean Beach GGNRA

Great Hwy.

Sunset Blvd.

19th Av.

Twin Peaks Park

Bernal Heights Park

Pine Lake Park

Stern Grove

Portola

Glen Canyon Park

S.F. Zoo

Sloat Blvd.

Mount Davidson Park

280

Third

CALTRAIN

Ocean Av.

Mission St.

McLaren Park

Bayview Park

Harding Park

Fort Funston GGNRA

Lake Merced

1

Geneva Av.

Candlestick Point State Rec. Area

Skyline

SAN MATEO COUNTY

Thornton Beach

John Daly Blvd.

Guadalupe

Canyon Pkwy.

101

Daly City

Market

San Bruno Mountain State & County Park

Hillside Blvd.

280

El Camino

Mussel Rock

Blvd.

82 South San Francisco

Pacifica

Junipero Serra Blvd.

Grand Av.

0   0.5   1.0 MI
0   0.5 1.0   1.5 KM

N

Milagra Ridge GGNRA

Westborough Blvd.

Camino

Sharp Park State Beach

Skyline College

380

*The proposed trail corridor represents a conceptual plan to connect the remaining parks and public open spaces within the Bay Area Ridge Trail corridor. This conceptual map conveys no rights to the public to enter private property.

Sharp Park

1 35

Sneath Lane

Real

Sweeney Ridge GGNRA

San Bruno

Peninsula Watershed

SAN FRANCISCO

Fog streams through the Golden Gate, but the Ridge Trail
route through San Francisco remains in sun.

1   Fort Funston to Stern Grove
From Hang-Glider Viewing Deck to the Trocadero

2   Stern Grove to the Presidio
From Wawona Street at 21st Avenue to Arguello Gate

3   San Francisco Presidio
From Arguello Gate to the Golden Gate

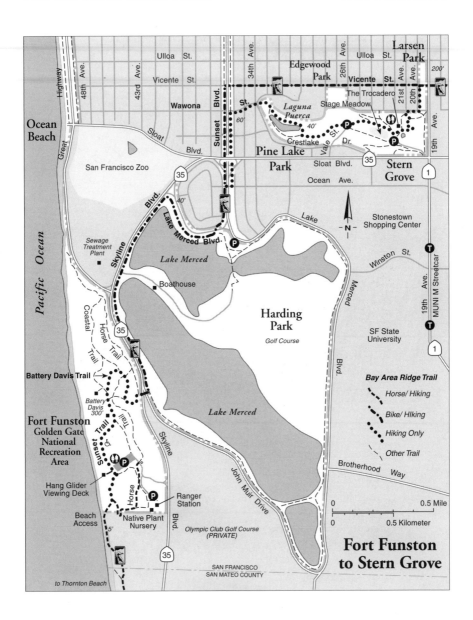

FORT FUNSTON TO STERN GROVE
From Hang-Glider Viewing Deck to the Trocadero

Length: 3.2 miles

Accessibility: Hikers, bicyclists, wheelchair users

Regulations: Fort Funston—Sunrise to sunset. Dogs on
                     6-foot leash.
                     Pine Lake Park and Stern Grove—7 a.m. to
                     10 p.m. Dogs on leash on park trails and city
                     streets.

Facilities: Water, restrooms, and phone at Fort Funston;
                     water, restrooms, and phones at Stern Grove.

WATCH HANG GLIDERS SOAR on ocean breezes at the launching site in Fort Funston and take in sweeping vistas from a former military observation point. Begin this diverse San Francisco stroll at a defunct military site, now part of Golden Gate National Recreation Area, on foggy, bluff-top dunes. You'll pass two freshwater lakes, dip into sunny and protected glens, and cross residential neighborhoods on mostly paved trails on your way to historic Stern Grove. A steep 115-foot climb in the last 0.1 mile gives you a sense of accomplishment.

Getting There

By Car

South trailhead, Fort Funston: Going south on Skyline Blvd. (Hwy. 35) towards Lake Merced, go 0.1 mile past John Muir Dr. and turn right (west) into Fort Funston. At fork in road, bear right and continue to extensive parking area. Sunset Trail entrance on **north**

side of parking area near hang-glider viewing deck on bluff above beach.

Going north on Skyline Blvd. (Hwy. 35), make a U-turn at John Muir Dr. and go south on Skyline Blvd. 0.1 mile, turn right (west) into Fort Funston, and follow directions above.

When leaving Fort Funston, autos and bicycles must turn right. To go north, continue south on Skyline Blvd. to John Daly Blvd. and make a U-turn.

North trailhead, Stern Grove (between Sloat Blvd. and Wawona St., just west of 19th Ave.): Traveling north on 19th Ave., no left turns are allowed. Therefore, pass Stern Grove and turn right on Ulloa St. Turn right on the next street, 18th Ave., and then right again on Vicente St. Cross 19th Ave., turn left on 20th Ave., and go one block to Wawona St., where there is on-street parking. To park in the grove, go left (east) on Wawona St. and then turn right on 19th Ave. Continue to corner of Sloat Blvd. and 19th Ave. and then turn right to parking at Stern Grove.

Traveling south on 19th Ave., turn right into Stern Grove parking area from corner of Sloat Blvd. and 19th Ave. Additional parking: turn right on Wawona St. from 19th Ave. for on-street parking. Or turn right on Sloat Blvd. from 19th Ave. and right again on Vale Ave. to park in Pine Lake Park.

 By Bus

SF MUNI line 18 daily to Skyline Blvd. at John Muir Dr. Lines 23 and 28 daily to Stern Grove.

On the Trail

As you leave Skyline Boulevard for Fort Funston, consider how "beating swords into ploughshares" benefits the Bay Area and its Ridge Trail. This former military site, as well as several others used in World Wars I and II for coastal defense, is now open for public enjoyment as part of the vast Golden Gate National Recreation Area. Today Fort Funston's paved parking area covers the site of former Nike silos, and the elevated hang-glider viewing deck and the adjacent hang-glider launching site encompass an earlier military observation point.

Be sure to walk out to the viewing deck for sweeping vistas of the Pacific Ocean from Point San Pedro in the south to Point Reyes in the north. On a clear day, the view extends 25 miles offshore to the Farallon Islands. You may see an aerial display by hang-gliders soaring on the ocean breezes.

To start the trip from the parking area, **hikers** and **wheelchair users** take the wide, paved Sunset Trail north along the bluffs. At a junction after about 200 yards, go left on the Sunset Trail to continue on the Ridge Trail route. Soon the trail veers east and passes through the concrete arch of Battery Davis, the site of a World War II gun emplacement.

Wheelchair users turn right (south) at a junction on the other side of the battery tunnel and return to the trailhead on a paved trail that rejoins the first segment of the Sunset Trail. From this junction they then return to the parking area.

Hikers continue east, cross an equestrian trail, and after 100 yards take a footpath to the top of a sandy hill. From here, you descend on a flexible ladder made of wooden cross-bars secured on each side to heavy ropes. The ropes are attached to sturdy posts at the top and bottom of the sand dune. When wet, the wooden cross-bars can be slippery. At the foot of the dunes, you make a short jog north to the Skyline Boulevard/John Muir Drive intersection. Cross with the signal and go left (north) on the paved path beside fenced Lake Merced.

To access the Bay Area Ridge Trail from the hang-glider viewing deck, **bicyclists** must take the paved road in Fort Funston to Skyline Boulevard (Highway 35) and go right (south) to John Daly Boulevard. Make a U-turn and ride north on Skyline Boulevard to John Muir Drive. Across John Muir Drive, join the paved path around Lake Merced.

Hikers, **bicyclists**, runners, and strollers share the path around Lake Merced. This now-freshwater lake occupies an ancient valley that was flooded at the end of the last ice-age. As the sea coast rose, dunes built up, thus isolating this lake and Pine Lake in Stern Grove. Gradually, springs and groundwater changed the new lakes into a freshwater environment.

As you round the northwest corner of Lake Merced, you may hear the roar of a lion or the piercing scream of a peacock emanating from the forested west side of the street, which bounds one side of the San Francisco Zoo. The Bay Area Ridge Trail route now turns southeast following the path between Lake Merced and the boulevard of the same name. After passing parcourse stations set in a broad lakeside band, you cross Lake Merced Boulevard to the west

Sunset Trail at Fort Funston with Golden Gate
and Marin Headlands in the distance.

side of Sunset Boulevard. This wide avenue, laid out in the tradition
of the grand boulevards of Paris and Washington, D.C., has landscaped borders and a park-like center strip, and runs from Lake
Merced to Golden Gate Park.

 Bicyclists cross Ocean Avenue at Sunset Boulevard and follow
the west-side path to Vicente Street. Here you cross Sunset Boulevard and travel east on Vicente Street to 20th Avenue, the end of this
Ridge Trail trip for bicycles. Follow the next segment of the Ridge
Trail another 7 miles to the Presidio for a longer ride.

At Ocean Avenue, **hikers** cross Sunset Boulevard and take the
graveled path on its east side. Follow this path for four blocks, then
turn right (east) on Wawona Street, continuing for three blocks to
Pine Lake Park at Crestlake Drive and 34th Avenue.

Now you leave city streets to enter a steep-sided, tree-lined
canyon. The paved path, often strewn with fragrant eucalyptus and
cypress seedpods, descends rather steeply to marshy Laguna Puerca,
then levels off on a dirt footpath hugging the north edge of the lake.
(Although early Spanish settlers used this term—translated from
the Spanish as "Sow Lake"—no pigs are in sight today. However, you
will still see the pine trees that give this park its name.) Blackberry

bushes and tall reeds crowd the path, which soon emerges at the first of four narrow meadows filling the rest of the canyon.

Take the asphalt path that heads east up the meadow to a parking area. Beside two large eucalyptus trees at the north edge of the lot, you will find a trail, constructed by volunteers, which joins paths above Stern Grove's West Meadow and Stage Meadow. The paths are edged with handsome, low stone walls which also serve as additional seats for the crowds that come on summer Sundays to enjoy the free concerts held here. The long-standing tradition of fine public performances was started by Mrs. Sigmund Stern in 1931, when she gave the grove to San Francisco in honor of her husband.

Beyond Stage Meadow on the north hillside sits the charming Trocadero Inn, built in 1892 as a public hotel by George M. Greene, who owned the land for 40 years. The Trocadero Inn, with its deer park, restaurant, dancing pavilion, rowing lake and trout farm, flourished until the Prohibition Amendment to the Constitution took effect in 1920. Refurbished in 1986, the Trocadero appears today much as it did at the turn of the century.

You'll find picnic tables beside a small lily pond in a dense redwood grove near the yellow-painted Trocadero. When the day is warm, this is a shady place for a backpack lunch after your hike. If your shuttle car is parked in Stern Grove or at Pine Lake, you have a short walk to reach it. If your shuttle car is parked on Wawona Street, climb the steep hillside on a zigzag asphalt path just east of the Trocadero to its end at 21st Avenue and Wawona Street. If you would like to continue on the Bay Area Ridge Trail, see the next segment, *Stern Grove to the Presidio*, for descriptions of attractive parks to visit along the route.

For those returning to Fort Funston, another 3.2 miles of views from a new perspective await. Sunsets over the ocean are particularly dramatic from the hang-glider viewing deck.

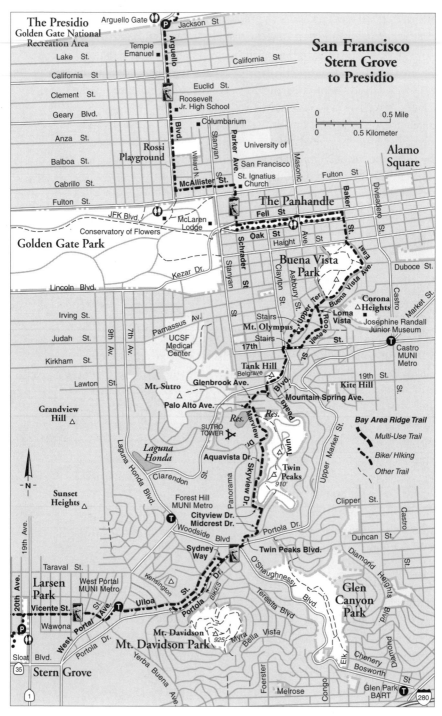

The Presidio
Golden Gate National
Recreation Area

Arguello Gate

Jackson St

San Francisco
**Stern Grove
to Presidio**

Lake St.

Temple
Emanuel

California St

California St

Euclid St.

Clement St.

Roosevelt
Jr. High School

0   0.5 Mile

Geary Blvd.

Columbarium

0   0.5 Kilometer

Anza St.

Rossi
Playground

University of

Alamo
Square

Balboa St.

San Francisco

Cabrillo St.

McAllister St.

St. Ignatius
Church

Fulton St.

Fulton St.

JFK Blvd.

McLaren
Lodge

The Panhandle

Fell St

Conservatory of Flowers

Oak St

Baker St.

Divisadero St.

Golden Gate Park

Haight

Duboce St.

Kezar Dr.

Buena Vista
Park

Lincoln Blvd.

Clayton St.

Corona
Heights

Irving St.

Parnassus Av.

Stairs

Loma
Vista

Josephine Randall
Junior Museum

Judah St.

UCSF
Medical
Center

Mt. Olympus

Stairs

Castro
MUNI
Metro

Kirkham St.

17th

St.

Lawton St.

Tank Hill

Belgrave

19th St.

Mt. Sutro

Glenbrook Ave.

Kite Hill

Grandview
Hill

Palo Alto Ave.

Mountain Spring Ave.

Bay Area Ridge Trail

Res.

Res.

Multi-Use Trail

SUTRO
TOWER

Twin
Peaks

Bike/ Hiking

Laguna
Honda

Aquavista Dr.

Twin
Peaks
910'

Other Trail

Sunset
Heights

Clarendon

Clipper St.

Forest Hill
MUNI Metro

Cityview Dr.
Midcrest Dr.

Portola Dr.

Duncan St.

Castro St.

Woodside Blvd.

Sydney
Way

Twin Peaks Blvd.

Taraval St.

West Portal
MUNI Metro

**Larsen
Park**

Vicente St.

Ulloa

O'Shaughnessy Blvd.

**Glen
Canyon
Park**

Wawona

Mt. Davidson

925'

Bella Vista

Sloat Blvd.

35

Stern Grove

Mt. Davidson Park

Yerba Buena Ave.

Myra

Chenery

Bosworth St.

1

Foerster

Melrose

Congo

Glen Park
BART

280

STERN GROVE
TO THE PRESIDIO
From Wawona Street at 21st Avenue to Arguello Gate

Length: 7 miles

Accessibility: Hikers, bicyclists

Regulations: Dogs on leash

Facilities: Water, restrooms, and phone at Stern Grove.

S AN FRANCISCO'S SPECTACULAR bay and ocean views reward you on gradual climbs along city streets and park paths. Visit unique and lively neighborhoods, parks, and playgrounds. You'll gain significant elevation on detours to the city's high peaks—a steep stairway to Mt. Olympus and a 685-foot ascent to Twin Peaks, plus three other climbs to viewpoints. Be prepared for San Francisco's notorious foggy and breezy weather.

Getting There

By Car

North trailhead, Stern Grove (between Sloat Blvd. and Wawona St., just west of 19th Ave.): Traveling north on 19th Ave., no left turns are allowed. Therefore, pass Stern Grove and turn right on Ulloa St. Turn right on the next street, 18th Ave., and then right again on Vicente St. Cross 19th Ave., turn left on 20th Ave., and go one block to Wawona St., where there is on-street parking. To park in the grove, go left (east) on Wawona St. and then turn right on 19th Ave. Continue to corner of Sloat Blvd. and 19th Ave. and then turn right to parking at Stern Grove.

Traveling south on 19th Ave., turn right into Stern Grove parking area from corner of Sloat Blvd. and 19th Ave. Additional parking: turn right on Wawona St. from 19th Ave. for on-street parking. Or turn right on Sloat Blvd. from 19th Ave. and right again on Vale Ave. to park in Pine Lake Park.

North trailhead, San Francisco Presidio, Arguello Gate: Take Arguello Blvd. to the Presidio. Limited parking on west side of Arguello Blvd. 100 yards inside Presidio or at Inspiration Point less than 0.1 mile farther north on Arguello Blvd. MUNI buses recommended.

 By Bus

MUNI lines 23 and 28 serve Stern Grove. MUNI lines 1, 2, 4, 33 and 38 stop on Arguello Blvd. several blocks south of the Presidio.

San Francisco's Past

This trip begins at Stern Grove in San Francisco's Sunset District in the area of the former San Miguel Rancho. The rancho was originally granted to José Noé in 1839 and passed to Adolph Sutro. Sutro was the entrepreneur of the former Sutro Baths, now part of the Golden Gate National Recreation Area, as well as a philanthropist and former mayor of San Francisco. Rancho San Miguel was mostly composed of shifting sand dunes beyond city limits at the time and remained undeveloped for nearly forty years—used only for horse racing and some farming and cattle grazing.

When the Twin Peaks Tunnel opened in 1918, and rapid transportation by trolley to downtown became possible, an era of residential building away from the city center began. It culminated in San Francisco's feverish expansion in post-World War II years. Row upon row of houses of varied façades and trims filled the former sand dunes. The wooded glen now known as Stern Grove escaped development because it was occupied by the George M. Greene family from 1847 until 1931, when Mrs. Sigmund Stern gave it to the City of San Francisco.

On the Trail

 Hikers and **bicyclists** start this trip where the paved trail emerges from Stern Grove at 21st Avenue and Wawona Street. Following the Bay Area Ridge Trail signs, you go east one block on Wawona Street, turn left on 20th Avenue and skirt the Larsen Park greensward. At the turn of the century, Carl Larsen had a chicken ranch here, which supplied eggs for his Tivoli restaurant downtown. Today, a swimming pool, tennis courts, and children's play equipment serve neighborhood families.

From the corner of Vicente Street and 20th Avenue, proceed east, cross 19th Avenue and continue uphill on Vicente. St. Cecelia's is the first of several churches you'll see on this trip, its façade graced by handsome bronze doors.

Soon eucalyptus-covered Mt. Davidson in Mt. Davidson Park and its 103-foot concrete cross looms on your right; the soaring, spare, rusty-orange frame of Sutro Tower rises on your left. These will be landmarks for the first half of your trip. Mt. Davidson, the

On the route from Stern Grove to the Presidio.

city's highest peak at 927 feet, commemorates surveyor George Davidson for exposing a false ownership claim to vast acreage in the southwest quarter of the city.

You leave Vicente Street's flowery front gardens and curve left (northeast) onto West Portal Avenue. Here is a one-block opportunity to stop at a neighborhood restaurant or buy a deli lunch for a picnic later in Buena Vista Park. Turn right, uphill, on Ulloa Street, just before the streetcar line disappears into its tunnel. As you progress along Ulloa Street, look for a steep cliff on your left with wavy lines of red chert. This rock is composed of layers of silica and clay, uplifted from the ocean floor and deposited on the edge of California by movement of the earth's tectonic plates.

Continue to the heights of Rockridge Terrace, crowned by the colorful mosaic bell tower of St. Brendan's Church. At the intersection of Ulloa and Laguna Honda streets, you'll have a sweeping view across the Bay to the Marin Headlands and Mt. Tamalpais.

Now you descend gradually and curve right (east) onto Sydney Way, before turning left (northeast) on Portola Drive. Across Portola Drive there are more neighborhood shops and restaurants. In a few blocks you bear left onto Twin Peaks Boulevard. Pause at the Portola Drive/Twin Peaks Boulevard junction and glance southeast across tree-filled Glen Canyon Park to see Mt. Diablo rising above the East Bay Hills across the bay.

Hiker Side Trip to Twin Peaks Summit

To get the kite-flyer's view from Twin Peaks, **hikers** turn right onto a foot trail at the junction of Marview and Farview ways. You'll pass a reservoir the city set aside for fighting fires, remembering the conflagration after the 1906 earthquake. **Bicyclists** can lock their bikes to the chain-link fence surrounding the reservoir and make the trek to the summit. From the foot trail, you emerge beside Twin Peaks Boulevard and walk south to the summit path that is flanked by boulders of weathered red chert. The windswept, rocky soil beside the path supports one of San Francisco's last remaining habitats of native plants that harbor the endangered Mission Blue butterfly. In spring, indigenous pink checkerblooms, blue and white lupines, and orange poppies brighten the landscape.

You have a 360-degree view from your vantage point at 910 feet above sea level: the Pacific Ocean, the Golden Gate, and the Coast Range mountains that encircle San Francisco Bay. Other segments of the Bay Area Ridge Trail lie along the ridges of these mountains: Mt. Tamalpais and Sonoma Mountain to the north; Vollmer, Mission and Monument peaks to the east; and Mt. Madonna and Kings Mountain to the south. Spread out before you is the magical city of San Francisco. With a good map you can identify its famous hills, its historic buildings, its new skyscrapers, its bracelets of bridges across the bay, and its many parks.

When you've had your fill of vistas near and far (on very clear days you can see north to Mt. St. Helena), retrace your steps.

Onward and upward, make a quick left turn on Panoramic Drive and in 50 yards a sharp right onto Midcrest Way. After turning left on Cityview Way, make a right turn (north) on Skyview Way. The street names attest to the remarkable vistas this Bay Area Ridge Trail route offers. In a quick succession of right turns on Aquavista and Marview ways, you skirt the steep sides of Twin Peaks. On windy days you may see people flying kites from the top.

If you don't make the trek to Twin Peaks' summit, go past San Francisco's Central Radio Station to the lee of Christmas Tree Point for a more intimate view east, north, and south of city neighborhoods, hilltop parks, and landmark public structures, such as the bronze-domed City Hall.

Bear northwest on Marview Way. At the intersection with Palo Alto Avenue, a path to the left through the trees circumnavigates yet another reservoir.

You pass houses with intricate brickwork facing, charming garden gates, and handsome redwood siding and jog right (northeast) on Glenbrook Avenue for a quick, steady descent. Bear right on Mountain Spring Avenue and then arc sharply left (north) on Twin Peaks Boulevard. In the late 1860s, the popular roadhouse, Mountain Spring House, was situated near here on Corbett Road, a predecessor of present-day Twin Peaks Boulevard. Corbett Road continued past the Trocadero Inn, still standing in Stern Grove, to the now-defunct San Miguel Ocean House and its nearby race track at the beach.

Watch for the Bay Area Ridge Trail signs and stay on Twin Peaks Boulevard as it turns right (east), past a former water tank site, Tank Hill Open Space, pausing to note its exposed, convoluted, layered chert and greenstone rocks. Sighting northwest from here, beyond the Golden Gate you see the Point Bonita Lighthouse, and on a clear day, farther still to the tip of Point Reyes. Twin Peaks Boulevard becomes Clayton Street, where another reservoir sits encased in a solid steel tank.

Hikers and bicyclists diverge here and rejoin at Buena Vista Park.

Hikers turn right (east) on 17th Street, walk a few yards on its north side, and then mount a steep stairway to Upper Terrace. Head left (northeast) at the top, continuing to Mt. Olympus Park, a tiny, circular green space in the geographical center of the city, which surrounds a raised pedestal.

You then descend the stairway on the circle's north side to the lower leg of Upper Terrace, and pass well-kept gardens and attractive homes, following a fairly level route to Buena Vista Park. If the day is sunny, you can see the ocean sparkling at the end of intersecting side streets, named for surveyors and developers of this area. At the entrance to Buena Vista Park your view northwest points to the forested Presidio, where you are headed.

Hiker Side Trip to Buena Vista Park

Hikers can take a short side trip into Buena Vista Park, a 36-acre hilltop preserved in 1894 for its trees and views. Take the wide, paved path from the end of Upper Terrace and follow it to a grassy summit knoll with lacy, tree-framed views—a fine lunch stop. It's said that the ornate marble gutters edging the path that circles the knoll are recycled tombstones from relocated cemeteries. Rejoin the signed Bay Area Ridge Trail route on Buena Vista Avenue East by retracing your steps or by taking one of many paths descending the park's east side.

 Bicyclists turn right (east) as well on 17th Street and go left (northeast) on Roosevelt Way, which then becomes Loma Vista. Turn right (northeast) on Upper Terrace before rejoining hikers at Buena Vista Park.

 Along Buena Vista Avenue East, **hikers** and **bicyclists** pass refurbished Victorian mansions, lovingly known as Painted Ladies, and a former hospital converted to residences. Continue downhill on this avenue to cross Haight Street. On the other side of Haight Street, Buena Vista Avenue East becomes Baker Street; follow Baker Street for two blocks north to the Panhandle, a long, tree-canopied, grassy strip that leads to Golden Gate Park.

 Hikers bear left (west) on a park path in the Panhandle that parallels Oak Street.

 Bicyclists continue one block on Baker Street, then turn left on the Panhandle's Fell Street path. Rambling under some of the city's oldest trees, these paths replace a boulevard that once cut through the middle of the park, a space now filled with basketball courts, hopscotch games, and children's play equipment.

Just before Golden Gate Park, **hikers** and **bicyclists** turn right (north) onto Shrader Street and pass St. Mary's Hospital. Shrader Street ends at Fulton Street; the Ridge Trail route makes a slight jog right on Fulton Street and continues north on Parker Street.

You go one block on Parker Street past twin-towered St. Ignatius Church on the University of San Francisco campus to McAllister Street, where you turn left (west). Admire the tight row of venerable, tiny, stick-style homes, each trimmed in different, but harmonious, dark colors.

Turn right onto Stanyan Street; jog north slightly, and cross Stanyan to pick up McAllister again. At the corner of Willard North and McAllister, note two small houses on the right, vestiges of pre-1906 San Francisco, tucked in among taller homes and apartments. Growing next to a white picket fence surrounding the corner house is a patriarch among buckeye trees with gnarled, twisted limbs.

The last leg of this trip brings more San Franciscana to those who travel it slowly. Turn right (north) onto Arguello Boulevard from McAllister Street. In a few blocks, you'll come to a playground donated by former mayor Angelo J. Rossi. Mount the concrete steps graced by circular flower-filled planters to see the playing fields, tennis courts, and swimming pool. To continue your trip, descend the second set of steps 50 yards to the north.

In the last mile of your trip along this busy boulevard, look on its west side for Roosevelt Middle School, an imposing, brick-faced public school, designed by the distinguished architect Timothy Pflueger.

Two houses of worship stand on opposite corners of the intersection of Lake Street and Arguello Boulevard. The brown-shingled St. John's Presbyterian Church, dating from 1905, contains stained-glass windows from two churches of the late 1800s. The monumental, neo-Byzantine style Temple Emanu-El, has a fine courtyard and stained-glass windows designed by Mark Adams. (It's possible to enter these churches at posted times to see their windows and to sample the architectural and cultural variety of this City of Saint Francis.)

After climbing a little in the last two blocks, you reach the Arguello Gate of the Presidio of San Francisco. The Spaniards established the Presidio here in 1776 to guard their colony at the edge of the Pacific.

On the next segment of the Bay Area Ridge Trail, hikers and bicyclists leave from Arguello Gate to explore the Presidio's northwest-trending ridges, between the military station and the mission settlement. The trip ends at the Golden Gate Bridge. (See *San Francisco Presidio—From Arguello Gate to Lincoln Boulevard.*)

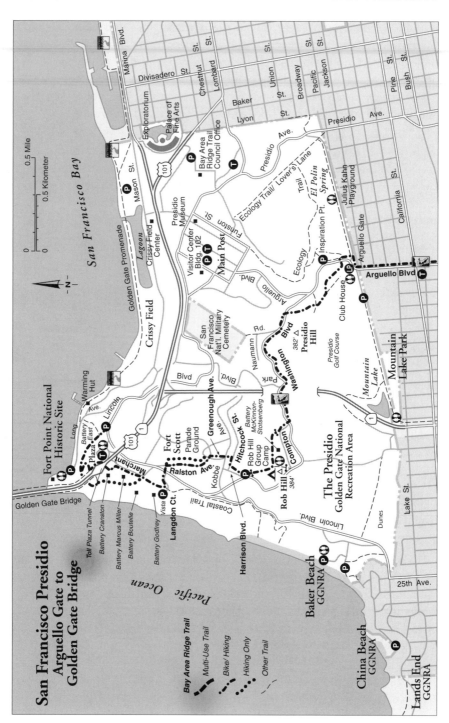

San Francisco Presidio
Arguello Gate to
Golden Gate Bridge

Bay Area Ridge Trail
— Multi-Use Trail
— Bike/ Hiking
••• Hiking Only
-- Other Trail

SAN FRANCISCO PRESIDIO
From Arguello Gate to the Golden Gate

Length: 2.5 miles

Accessibility: Hikers, bicyclists, wheelchair users

Regulations: Presidio Trails—Daylight hours. Dogs on leash. No horses.

Facilities: Water, restrooms, and phone at clubhouse and at Rob Hill Campground and Picnic Area; water, restrooms, and phone at Golden Gate Bridge Plaza.

E XPLORE THE CHARM, seclusion, natural wonders, and historic and cultural variety of the Presidio. Stunning views await you on this short trip through forests and grasslands and along coastal bluffs, from the Presidio's south-central entrance to its northwest tip. You'll travel sidewalks along the Fort Scott segment and gently sloping dirt paths with between 2 and 10 percent elevation change. In summer, coastal fog often lingers until afternoon.

Getting There

By Car

South trailhead, Arguello Gate: Take Arguello Blvd. to the Presidio. Limited parking on west side of Arguello Blvd., 100 yards inside Presidio adjacent to golf course, or at Inspiration Point less than 0.1 mile farther north on Arguello Blvd. Cross Arguello Blvd. in a crosswalk from the southern Presidio Golf Course parking lot to join the trail there.

North trailhead, Golden Gate Bridge Toll Plaza: Going south on Hwy. 1, turn right immediately after toll booth, turn right again, and turn right yet again; then go under bridge approach, and into toll plaza and metered parking area.

Going north on Hwy. 1, turn right into parking plaza immediately before toll booths.

To continue to Lincoln Boulevard free parking area east of toll plaza, leave plaza on road going downhill (south), and turn left (east) on Lincoln Boulevard. Unpaved parking area is on your left. Look for BATTERY EAST sign.

Alternate North parking, Langdon Court: From Lincoln Blvd. just west of Fort Winfield Scott, turn west on Langdon Court to an unpaved parking area near Battery Godfrey beside the Coastal Trail.

 By Bus

South trailhead, Arguello Gate: MUNI lines 1, 2, 4 and 38 stop on Arguello Blvd. several blocks south of Presidio.

North trailhead, Golden Gate Bridge Toll Plaza: Any Golden Gate Transit bus southbound to San Francisco from Marin and Sonoma counties will stop at plaza on request. MUNI lines 28 and 29 daily to the toll plaza; line 76 on Sundays and holidays.

On the Trail

As you enter the Presidio through the Arguello Gate, take note of the gate's flanking stone columns. A prominent stars-and-stripes emblem proclaims the founding of the Presidio in 1776, and the insignia of the Infantry, Cavalry, and Artillery decorate the columns. In the more than 200 years since the founding of the Presidio, these gates have been closed only once—at the beginning of World War II.

 Beyond the gate, **hikers** and **bicyclists** veer right, cross West Pacific Street, and bear right on the paved trail. In less than 50 yards the trail swings left and proceeds north beside Arguello Boulevard. After 100 yards, cross the street at the crosswalk that leads to the Presidio Golf Course clubhouse. The signed entrance to the Bay Area Ridge Trail is just north of the clubhouse driveway and leads uphill into the forest. (If you have parked at Inspiration Point, go south on Arguello to this crosswalk.)

Side Trip to Inspiration Point

Before or after your trip, visit Inspiration Point, less than 0.1 mile north from Arguello Gate on Arguello Boulevard. From this vantage point, Spanish soldiers scanned the Golden Gate for incoming ships carrying supplies from the Old World. They scouted the waters for unfriendly ships—British, French, and Russian—that might threaten this tiny toe-hold at the entrance to San Francisco Bay; in its early days, the Presidio was Spain's northernmost outpost.

Steps lead downhill from Inspiration Point to a new, unpaved trail that joins the Ecology Trail as it meanders around the southern quarter of the Presidio. A large area of serpentinite, California's state rock, is exposed along this trail. Placards tell about plant species that thrive on soils composed of this rock, bringing luxurious spring-wildflower displays to California's grasslands.

On the hillside north of Inspiration Point, you can also glimpse a remnant of the native serpentine grassland that once stretched across San Francisco. The National Park Service is rehabilitating this area to protect small colonies of two endangered species—the Presidio clarkia and the Marin dwarf flax. If you would like to learn more about the native flora here, you can join a wildflower walk led by a park naturalist. Inquire at the Visitor Center, Building 102, at the Main Post Parade Ground. After this short side trip from Inspiration Point, wend your way back to the parking area and cross Arguello Boulevard to the Bay Area Ridge Trail route.

You thread through mature forests of Monterey pine and cypress and a scattering of redwoods. In 1883, Major W. A. Jones had trees planted on three ridgetops and around the parade ground. He intended to beautify the windswept sand dunes and the coastal scrub landscape, as well as to provide much-needed wind protection and to camouflage the military fort.

Today, angled sunlight glancing through these trees creates an ethereal, peaceful effect as you traverse this trail. Major Jones would be amazed to see the height and proliferation of the forest. The ridgetop trees planted for windshields grew so well that they spread into the valleys, where abundant moisture encouraged vigorous growth. Today's forest is composed of tall, spindly trees, so closely spaced that most of their branches are clustered at the top reaching for sunlight. The National Park Service is selectively removing some nearly dead trees to afford better bay views and to introduce sunshine into grasslands, valleys, and riparian corridors.

As you continue up a gentle rise, you see the fence that surrounds the post reservoir in a eucalyptus grove uphill on your left.

Through the trees on your right you can glimpse San Francisco's famous skyline.

You descend gradually to Washington Boulevard and cross it. Turn left and stay on the roadside trail for a short distance to Naumann Road, where a spur trail skirts the back side of former Army officers' housing and leads to the San Francisco National Military Cemetery.

Side Trip to San Francisco National Military Cemetery

On a short side trip, follow Naumann Road along a unique urban wildlife habitat. The huge blackberry bramble is perfect cover for quail and rabbits; in early morning or at dusk, you may see quail at the bramble's edge or even on the road. At most any time of day, you can hear the quail's distinctive call, "Be careful, be careful." Halfway around curving Naumann Road, look into the eucalyptus forest on your right for a trail surfaced with decomposed granite that leads downhill to a corner of the San Francisco National Military Cemetery. Built in the 1850s, this was the Presidio's first post cemetery; in 1884, it was converted to a National Military Cemetery. Robert Todd Lincoln, son of Abe, is buried here. General Funston, who commanded the rebuilding of the Presidio after the 1906 quake and for whom the southernmost coastal fort of the GGNRA is named, also rests here.

Among the many famous people also interred here are the relatively unknown Native American scout "2 Bits" and Pauline Cushman Fryer, a Union spy in the Civil War. Phillip and Sala Burton, heroes today for preserving the Marin Headlands and the San Francisco beaches and bay fronts in the GGNRA, are also buried here. Here too, lie the remains of 400 "Buffalo Soldiers," outstanding African-American soldiers, many of them Medal-of-Honor winners. You can walk through a wide opening in the cemetery wall to find these historic grave markers.

From a vantage point at the corner of the cemetery wall, you can look beyond the cemetery's white markers, arranged in symmetrical rows on a gentle slope, to the opposite side of the Golden Gate. There, you'll see the World War II bunkers of Fort Barry and the Coast Guard installations at East Fort Baker, more recent military installations.

From Washington Boulevard at Naumann Road, cross the street and follow the sidewalk past a row of former military housing units. Beyond the houses, the Ridge Trail route follows a graveled path along a grassy strip outside the golf course fence. Shortly the trail passes beside three stately Monterey cypress trees at the corner of the Park Boulevard intersection. Here a unique sign gently

The National Military Cemetery in the Presidio overlooks San Francisco Bay.

reminds visitors that wildlife still inhabits these forests: QUAIL IN AREA—DRIVE CAREFULLY.

After 0.3 mile, you cross Washington Boulevard and take Compton Road under a high canopy of mature Monterey cypress. Go about 100 yards on this minor road (no path) bordered by blackberry brambles, native grasses, and clumps of native iris that bloom in purple springtime splendor. Then turn right, uphill, onto a wide path covered with soft duff. On your left is a raised area topped by yellow bush lupines—the former Battery McKinnon-Stotsenberg, dating from 1892. Then on your right is a sunken concrete structure, the fenced-off, 1938 Central Magazine. Though in disuse, the mossy complex is still surveyed by a raised wooden guard tower.

The trail veers right and passes the Rob Hill Picnic Area, the highest point in the Presidio and a good picnic spot on a warm day. Here the Juan Bautista de Anza Trail joins your route. A nearby signpost bears its symbol, and that of another long-distance trail, the American Discovery Trail, together with the Ridge Trail emblem.

Passing between lichen-covered posts, you continue on a quiet stretch of trail under a tall forest canopy. At Hitchcock Street, go

47

right (east) on this little-used road, and in about 150 yards, watch for a low, cream-colored building on your left. Just beyond it, turn left (north) on a short path lined with pavers and cross Kobbe Street. Pass a low brick building (#1339) and then follow Greenough Street going due north. Behind a brick wall lies the spacious garden of a 1915 officer's residence, whose Georgian style façade contrasts with the mossy, presently unused, wooden barracks on your left.

Shortly you reach Ralston Avenue, where the hiker and bicyclist routes briefly diverge.

Bicyclists go left on the marked Ridge Trail route.

Hikers go a few feet farther to walk through the arched entrance to Fort Winfield Scott and veer left (west) on the broad Fort Scott promenade in front of the buildings. (This promenade is suitable for **wheelchair** use.)

Named for a commanding general of the U.S. Army during the Mexican-American War, Fort Winfield Scott became the headquarters for the coastal defenses of San Francisco in 1912. The Post Parade Ground, an elongated, open greensward, is partially surrounded by former Army buildings.

When the fort was built, this extensive open space commanded an uninterrupted view of the Marin Headlands, the Golden Gate, and Richardson Bay. Now trees block some of the near view, but you can still see these landmarks and the Golden Gate Bridge's dramatic, rust-colored towers, which clearly define the entrance to the bay. Even on foggy days, the towers' tops might be visible, swept clear of fog by fresh ocean winds.

As you walk along around the parade ground on a clear day, look out at the blue bay waters filled with sailboats heeling in the wind, windsurfers skimming across the waves, and great ships, mostly ocean-going freighters, cruising to or from distant ports. Alcatraz Island sits in a swirl of swift bay currents, first a fortress, then a federal prison. Alcatraz is now a National Park and part of the GGNRA. You can reach it by ferry from San Francisco.

To the east lie Coit Tower, the Transamerica Pyramid, other downtown skyscrapers, and the Bay Bridge leading to the populous East Bay cities. The Campanile's tall shaft rises on the UC Berkeley campus, and forested public parklands crown the surrounding hills. Topping the distant view are two East Bay landmarks—triangular-shaped Mt. Diablo and half-spherical Round Top, both within public parklands.

Continuing north along the west side of the Fort Scott Parade Ground, you pass buildings constructed in Mission Revival style, popular in the early 20th century. The square, two-story building on the far northern side is the former Fort Scott stockade, now devoid of inmates.

When **hikers** arrive at a passageway between Buildings 1207 and 1208, they swing left and proceed to Lincoln Boulevard.

Bicyclists join **hikers** and both cross this busy street and continue on Langdon Court. Go through a parking lot and then pass Building 1648, the former Nike Missile Building. Pick up the Coastal Trail here, on your right. Continue north along this trail past coastal defense batteries built from 1891 to 1900; plaques tell the story of these coastal defenses, the earliest of which had a one-mile range. Later, Nike missiles had a 75-mile range.

Just seaward from the missile building is Battery Godfrey. On its landward side you see a ramp used to transport ammunition stored below ground to guns behind low walls on upper concrete platforms. Its rifles were mounted on disappearing carriages and retracted below the battery's walls after firing so the soldiers could safely load the guns.

Just beyond the next battery, Battery Boutelle, you reach an opening with a fabulous view of Land's End, the Point Bonita Lighthouse, and the Marin Headlands. The Golden Gate's high cliffs are indented by small, crescent-shaped beaches. In good weather, these picturesque cliffs and rugged shores seem quite benign. But when it's foggy, the many-voiced warning horns, now computer-driven, announce the imminent danger of rocky points, small islets, and treacherous tides to ship traffic navigating the hazardous waters at the entrance to San Francisco Bay. On a clear day, you'll see west to the Farallons—small, rocky islands 25 miles offshore.

After Battery Boutelle, **bicyclists** go straight onto Marchant Street for 1 block. Turn left just before the freeway entrance, then turn right and go through the narrow tunnel beneath the Golden Gate Bridge Toll Plaza.

Hikers continue to the next battery, Marcus Miller. It retains a small, square, concrete lookout, known as a base-end station, which in conjunction with another such station, could triangulate the position of its targets or the site of its shell landing.

To continue toward the Golden Gate Bridge, bear left onto the Coastal Trail, a narrow, cliff-top path. You'll hear the crashing surf and screeching seagulls and get a slight approximation of a ship's view as it enters the Golden Gate. After traversing the wild and scenic bluffs west of Battery Marcus Miller and Battery Cranston, the Coastal Trail dips under the bridge and reaches a paved trail. Go uphill (south) to the Golden Gate Bridge Plaza, where tourists and locals alike flock on clear days to enjoy the world-class views of the Golden Gate, the bridge, San Francisco, the bay, and the enclosing hills.

If the weather is too windy and foggy to appreciate the bluffs, you can take the bicycle route on the east side of Battery Marcus Miller. Follow it through the bridge-maintenance yard, cross to the sidewalk under the bridge's south portal, and emerge at the Golden Gate Bridge Plaza.

To reach the Lincoln Boulevard parking area on the east side of the bridge plaza, return to the Coastal Trail and follow it east through a short tunnel built of brick, part of the original Battery East (1876). Beyond the tunnel, you can climb to an observation deck to look down at the top of the fortifications, the bay, and Fort Point. As you continue east on the Coastal Trail, look for a path that

---

Side Trip to Fort Point

Before you cross the bridge to Marin County, take a short, 0.4-mile walk from the toll plaza to Fort Point. Return to the Coastal Trail from the Toll Plaza and descend north toward the bay at the Golden Gate Bridge. Fort Point stands directly beneath the bridge, reminding us of over 200 years of Golden Gate defenses. The Spaniards first established Castillo de San Joaquin here at White Cliff Point, with a small bastion of 13 guns. It fell into disrepair during the Spanish and Mexican periods, and was claimed by Army Lt. John C. Fremont in 1846.

In the late 1850s, the United States Army planned to build three forts to defend the bay and the Golden Gate from attack. A fortification of about 109 cannon batteries and two mortars was established on Alcatraz Island; a fort planned for Lime Point in Marin, directly across the Golden Gate, was never completed. Fort Point, this massive three-story brick fortress, was first occupied in 1861 and used intermittently through World War II. Now a National Historic Site, it is open for guided day tours and special evening programs by the National Park Service.

---

bears right (south) to the alternate parking area on Lincoln Boulevard, where you could have a shuttle car waiting. From this parking area, you drive along Lincoln Boulevard southeast under Highway

101, pass the National Military Cemetery, and reach the Main Post Parade Ground and Visitor Information Center.

This trip only samples the remarkable story of the Presidio at San Francisco—from establishment of the first Spanish military outpost in 1776 through Spanish and Mexican settlements, the Gold Rush, and the early California statehood period to its present National Park status. Although the military presence is diminished, its influence will stay on with an outstanding military museum, the 19th and 20th century coastal defenses, and the intact, historic Civil War building, Fort Point. Many interesting tours led by experienced volunteers and National Park Service staff offer more detailed information about this historic site. Inquire at the Visitor Information Center, Building 102, a former enlisted men's barracks, situated in the row of historic brick buildings on Montgomery Street facing the Main Post Parade Ground.

The next leg of the Bay Area Ridge Trail begins across the Golden Gate Bridge in Marin County. Five completed segments of the Bay Area Ridge Trail lead 35 miles north without interruption through the Marin Headlands, along the flanks of Mt. Tamalpais, and then down Bolinas Ridge to Samuel P. Taylor State Park. (See *Marin Headlands—Golden Gate National Recreation Area*.)

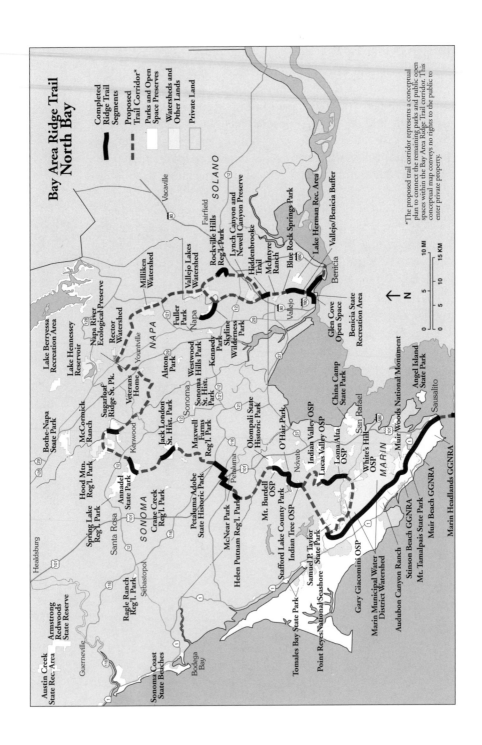

Bay Area Ridge Trail
North Bay

Completed Ridge Trail Segments

Proposed Trail Corridor*

Parks and Open Space Preserves

Watersheds and Other Lands

Private Land

*The proposed trail corridor represents a conceptual plan to connect the remaining parks and public open spaces within the Bay Area Ridge Trail corridor. This conceptual map conveys no rights to the public to enter private property.

N

0   5   10 MI
0   5   10   15 KM

SOLANO

NAPA

SONOMA

MARIN

Austin Creek State Rec. Area
Armstrong Redwoods State Reserve
Sonoma Coast State Beaches
Guerneville
Bodega Bay
Sebastopol
Santa Rosa
Healdsburg
Ragle Ranch Reg'l. Park
Spring Lake Reg'l. Park
Hood Mtn. Reg'l. Park
Annadel State Park
Crane Creek Reg'l. Park
Bothe-Napa State Park
McCormick Ranch
Lake Hennessey Reservoir
Lake Berryessa Recreation Area
Napa River Ecological Preserve
Rector Watershed
Sugarloaf Ridge St. Pk.
Veterans Home
Kenwood
Sonoma
Milliken Watershed
Vacaville
Vallejo Lakes Watershed
Fuller Park
Napa
Rockville Hills Reg'l. Park
Fairfield
Hiddenbrooke Trail
McIntyre Ranch
Lynch Canyon and Newell Canyon Preserve
Blue Rock Springs Park
Lake Herman Rec. Area
Vallejo/Benicia Buffer
Benicia
Vallejo
Glen Cove Open Space
Benicia State Recreation Area
Alston Park
Yountville
Westwood Hills Park
Sonoma St. Hist. Park
Kennedy Park
Skyline Wilderness Park
Jack London St. Hist. Park
Maxwell Farms Reg'l. Park
Petaluma Adobe State Historic Park
Petaluma
Olompali State Historic Park
O'Hair Park
Novato
Indian Valley OSP
Lucas Valley OSP
Loma Alta OSP
White's Hill OSP
China Camp State Park
San Rafael
Muir Woods National Monument
Angel Island State Park
Sausalito
McNear Park
Helen Putnam Reg'l. Park
Mt. Burdell OSP
Stafford Lake County Park
Indian Tree OSP
Samuel P. Taylor State Park
Gary Giacomini OSP
Marin Municipal Water District Watershed
Audubon Canyon Ranch
Stinson Beach GGNRA
Mt. Tamalpais State Park
Muir Beach GGNRA
Marin Headlands GGNRA
Tomales Bay State Park
Point Reyes National Seashore

THE NORTH BAY

Blue oaks cast welcome shade for hikers and bicyclists.

10 Indian Tree Open Space Preserve to O'Hair Park
    From Vineyard Road to Indian Tree and through Verissimo Hills
    and Little Mountain Preserves to O'Hair Park

11 Mt. Burdell Open Space Preserve
    From O'Hair Park and San Andreas Fire Road
    to Olompali State Historic Park

12 Helen Putnam Regional Park and McNear Park
    to Petaluma Adobe State Historic Park
    From Helen Putnam Park to Oxford Street and
    from 11th and G Streets to Casa Grande/Adobe Roads

13 Jack London State Park
    From Sonoma Mountain Trail to Hayfields/Cowan
    Meadows Trails Junction

14 Annadel State Park
    From Spring Lake Park to Annadel Park East Gate
    at Lawndale Road

15 Sugarloaf Ridge State Park
    From Visitor Center to Bald Mountain Summit

16 Skyline Wilderness Park
    From Park Entrance to South Boundary

17 Rockville Hills Community Park
    From North Entrance to Green Valley Road

18 Hiddenbrooke Trail
    From McGary Road to Trail's Southern Terminus

19 Vallejo-Benicia Buffer
    From Blue Rock Springs Park to Rose Drive

20 Benicia-Vallejo Waterfront
    From Benicia State Recreation Area East to Benicia
    Point at F Street and West to Carquinez Bridge

(Above) Pink checkerbloom dots grassy slopes in spring.
(Below) California poppies.

55

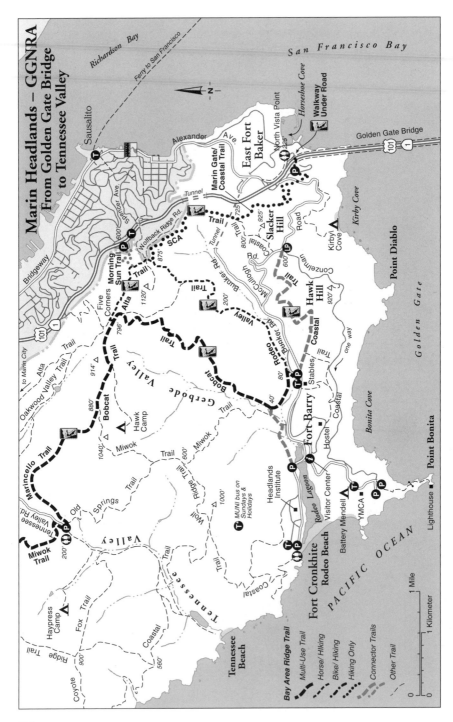

Marin Headlands – GGNRA
From Golden Gate Bridge
to Tennessee Valley

San Francisco Bay

Richardson Bay

Ferry to San Francisco

Sausalito

Walkway Under Road

Golden Gate Bridge

Horseshoe Cove

North Vista Point
225'

Alexander Ave.

East Fort Baker

Kirby Cove

Point Diablo

Bridgeway

Spencer Ave.

600'

Morning Sun Trail

Tunnel

725'

Marin Gate/Coastal Trail

925'

Coastal Trail

Slacker Hill
800'

Conzelman Road

Kirby Cove

Wolfback Ridge Rd.

875'

SCA Trail

600'

Tunnel

McCullough Rd.

Hawk Hill
920'

Golden Gate

Five Corners

Alta Trail

1120'

Bunker Rd.

200'

Valley Trail

Rodeo Trail

Coastal Trail

Hawk Hill

one way

Bonita Cove

to Marin City

Oakwood Valley Trail

796'

914'

Alta Trail

Bobcat Trail

880'

Gerbode Valley

Bobcat Trail

80'

40'

Fort Barry

Stables

Coastal Trail

Point Bonita

Marincello Trail

Hawk Camp

1040'

Miwok Trail

Miwok Trail

600'

1000'

Rodeo Lagoon

Visitor Center

Headlands Institute

MUNI bus on Sundays & Holidays

Hostel

Battery Mendell

YMCA

Lighthouse

Point Bonita

Tennessee Valley Rd.

200'

Miwok Trail

Old Springs Trail

Wolf Ridge Trail

Fort Cronkhite

Rodeo Beach

PACIFIC OCEAN

Haypress Camp

Fox Trail

Tennessee Valley

Coastal Trail

Tennessee Beach

Ridge Trail

Coyote

900'

560'

Bay Area Ridge Trail
Multi-Use Trail
Horse/Hiking
Bike/Hiking
Hiking Only
Connector Trails
Other Trail

1 Mile

1 Kilometer

MARIN HEADLANDS— GOLDEN GATE NATIONAL RECREATION AREA
From Golden Gate Bridge to Tennessee Valley

Length: 4.6 miles

Accessibility: Hikers, equestrians, bicyclists

Regulations: No dogs on Bay Area Ridge Trail (on leash on some other Marin Headlands trails).

Facilities: Water, restrooms, and phone at Marin Headlands visitor center; restrooms and phone at Tennessee Valley.

A DRAMATIC TRIP from the landmark Golden Gate Bridge into the hills of the Marin Headlands—climb through open grassland and coastal chaparral to the ridge above Sausalito and descend into the wide ravine of Tennessee Valley. You'll have spectacular views of San Francisco Bay, the Marin Headlands, and the Pacific Ocean. On narrow paths and wide service roads, you'll climb and descend 600 feet; come prepared for wind and fog.

Getting There

By Car

South trailhead, Golden Gate Bridge northwest parking (hiker trailhead): Going north on Hwy. 101, take Alexander Ave. exit and turn left to go under highway. Go right on Conzelman Rd. and make an immediate left turn onto the road to parking lot. Ample parking.

Going south on Hwy. 101, take the Sausalito exit, go left at stop sign, go right on Conzelman Rd., and then immediately turn left onto the road to parking lot.

Bunker Road trailhead (bicyclist/equestrian trailhead): Going north on Hwy. 101, take the Alexander Ave. exit and turn right toward Sausalito. Take the first left turn (west) into the Fort Baker-Fort Barry tunnel. Signals regulate one-way auto traffic through the tunnel. Bicycle traffic in both directions; watch for flashing yellow light. Follow Bunker Rd. about 1.25 miles beyond tunnel to trailhead on your right. Parking for horse trailers and all trail users.

Traveling south on Hwy. 101, take the Sausalito exit, turn right at the stop sign and go under the highway toward Sausalito. Turn left at the second stop sign; entrance to tunnel is on your left. See directions above.

Additional parking for all trail users at Miwok Trailhead at east end of Rodeo Lagoon near Headlands Institute.

Limited parking for all trail users at Conzelman/McCullough roads junction with access to Coastal Trail.

North trailhead, Tennessee Valley: From Hwy. 101 near Mill Valley take Stinson Beach/Mt. Tamalpais exit and go west on Hwy. 1 (Shoreline Hwy.) for about 0.4 mile. Turn left (south) on Tennessee Valley Rd. and continue to parking lot at end of road.

By Bus

Golden Gate Transit buses 20, 60, 70, and 80 stop at Spencer Ave. on Hwy. 101 daily for access to the Morning Sun Connector Trail. MUNI bus 76 to Marin Headlands on Sundays only.

On the Trail

Hikers, equestrians, and **bicyclists** take different trails to reach the Bay Area Ridge Trail route, and then they travel the same route from a junction often called Five Corners. Each user's route to this junction is described separately below, beginning with hikers, then equestrians, then bicyclists. Trails in Marin County have a long history, and some trails retain their historic names. This narrative and the maps use the long-established names, although some of these do not appear on trail signs. However, the Ridge Trail route is clearly marked on signposts with the blue, white, and red logo.

Hikers start at the trailhead parking near the northwest portal of the Golden Gate Bridge. From the northwest corner of the parking lot, cross the road and pick up the Bay Area Ridge Trail, also the Coastal Trail, which starts in a Monterey cypress forest and climbs 0.2 mile to Conzelman Road. Cross Conzelman Road to railroad-tie steps that begin a 600-foot climb up the open hillside. You zigzag along this narrow trail through coastal scrub that seems nondescript, but as the signs warn, it is habitat for the endangered Mission Blue butterfly.

Pause partway up the hill to look back at Lime Point. Juan Ayala, the first European to enter San Francisco Bay, called Lime Point a "white island rock" and anchored his ship, the *San Carlos,* nearby. The rock was later named for its covering of bird lime. Beyond the point lie the waters of the Golden Gate. The Golden Gate Bridge, completed in 1933, spans the narrow entrance to the bay that Ayala navigated more than two centuries ago, in 1775.

The trail climbs steeply northwest above Highway 101; traffic sounds fade and the view northeast widens to include Richardson Bay and the Belvedere Peninsula. At your feet, a bright variety of yellow daisies, blue lupines, pearly everlastings, and brilliant red Indian paintbrush grow amid bracken fern and the ubiquitous poison oak.

A small footbridge crosses seeping springs where moisture-loving yellow mimulus thrive. Turn around here to enjoy magnificent views of San Francisco's skyline, Alcatraz and Angel islands, and the East Bay Hills beyond. Below you to the northeast, you can see the red-tiled roofs of East Fort Baker's historic buildings in Horseshoe Cove. This old fort, part of the Golden Gate National Recreation Area, is home to the Bay Area Discovery Museum, which offers imaginative activities for young people. Beyond Horseshoe Cove, you can see the bay, enlivened by the sight of yachts heeling over in the brisk winds coming through the gate.

At the ridgecrest, you come to a trail junction; to stay on the Ridge Trail route, go right (northwest) on the 0.8-mile SCA Trail, named for and built by the Student Conservation Association. The Coastal Trail goes left over Slacker Hill, then descends west to Rodeo Lagoon. If the day is clear, the views around the compass from this ridge are dramatic; you'll have your first views west to the Pacific Ocean and northwest over the GGNRA's 12,000-acre Marin Headlands.

Continue northwest on the SCA Trail. After climbing up a slope where rattlesnake grass and oats blow in the wind, you come to a sign that states, HIKERS, PRIVATE PROPERTY, TURN WEST HERE. The single track Ridge Trail heads west here at the head of Rodeo Valley; it follows the contour of the hillside below a row of houses. From this trail you can look 600 feet down into Rodeo Valley and see the

59

From Rancho Sausalito to Golden Gate National Recreation Area

The open hills before you—from the Marin Headlands to Stinson Beach—were once part of the vast Rancho Sausalito. In 1822, an enterprising Englishman, William Richardson, left his ship in San Francisco; two years later he married the daughter of the Mexican Commandante of the Presidio. In 1841, the Mexican governor of California granted him the 20,000-acre Rancho Sausalito. Failing ventures forced Richardson into debt and he had to sell his land to Samuel Throckmorton in 1860.

The land was subdivided, and many ranches were bought for use as dairies by Portuguese immigrants from the Azores. Hay to feed the dairy cows did not thrive along this foggy coast, however, and by the mid-1890s the Portuguese had abandoned their dairies.

The U.S. Army also occupied land in the headlands. The Army bought the tract that now serves the north end of the Golden Gate Bridge in 1855, and in 1873, it began installing fortifications there, the last of which was a Nike missile site, dismantled in 1974.

Today, most of the original Rancho Sausalito is part of the Golden Gate National Recreation Area. The grizzlies and elk that vaqueros and early settlers hunted are long-gone, but bobcat, deer, fox, and an occasional mountain lion still range over these hills.

---

west entrance of the tunnel beneath the ridge you have just walked along.

The narrow trail climbs gently along a grassy slope, accented by jagged outcrops of white rock and flowery in spring. You pass through a small eucalyptus grove and continue for half a mile before climbing to the ridgetop high above Sausalito. On the ridge, you meet the Rodeo Valley Trail, the Bay Area Ridge Trail equestrian route, which has climbed northeast from the Bunker Road trailhead.

 Equestrians begin at the Rodeo Valley trailhead off Bunker Road at the junction of the Coastal and Rodeo Valley trails in the Marin Headlands. Cross the wooden bridge, signed RIDGE TRAIL, over willow-bordered Rodeo Creek and head north along the lower slope of the hill between Rodeo and Gerbode valleys. In spring, the field above the creek is bright with yellow mustard and the air is filled with the calls of red-wing blackbirds.

Head east on the Rodeo Valley Trail for about a mile, along the edge of the valley, past rock outcrops. The trail winds towards the

Hikers cross Wolf Ridge en route to Tennessee Valley.

ridgetop for another mile, over steep pitches and gentle grades. At the ridgetop, it meets the north end of the SCA Trail, where equestrians join hikers to continue to Five Corners.

Now **hikers** and **equestrians** continue past a private road on the right and go left around a white, metal fire-protection gate onto the Alta Trail. Then you round the east side of a wooded, antenna-crowned hill, where you pass the 0.5-mile Morning Sun Trail, a 300-

61

foot connector trail of railroad-tie steps from the Highway 101 Spencer Avenue exit in Sausalito. At this trailhead, you'll find parking, a telephone, and Golden Gate Transit bus connections.

Hikers and equestrians on the Bay Area Ridge Trail continue northwest from the Morning Sun Trail intersection along an oak-shaded hillside. Occasional views of the bay and patches of apricot-colored sticky monkeyflowers grace the trail. Look west to the Clyde Wahrhaftig Memorial Bench dedicated in 1998 to honor the memory of this renowned geologist who contributed greatly to the understanding of Marin Headlands' geology.

In about half a mile, you reach the convergence of five trails, known as "Five Corners" to Marin Headlands regulars, although no sign identifies it as such. Watch carefully for this junction—on foggy days it may be hard to see. Jog left (west) about 30 feet to meet the Bobcat Trail and turn right (northwest) on it. This is where bicyclists coming up from Gerbode Valley meet hikers and equestrians.

Bicyclists begin at the same trailhead as equestrians on Bunker Road (you can also park at the Miwok trailhead at the east end of Rodeo Lagoon near the Headlands Institute). Cross the wooden bridge signed RIDGE TRAIL and turn left (west) on the Rodeo Valley Trail (multi-use going west only). Turn right (northeast) at the Bobcat Trail junction and begin your 2-mile trip up Gerbode Valley. Look for blue bush lupines blooming by the trailside in spring. Ahead is the site of the former Sam Silva dairy, one of the many Portuguese dairies along this coast in the mid-1800s. All that remains today are the groves of eucalyptus and Monterey cypress and a few persistent fruit trees and rose bushes. You can make out the cistern that supplied water to the site, high on the hill above.

Past the dairy, the trail begins its climb up a hillside and you look out over the floor of the valley. In the 1960s, developers planned the city of Marincello in this valley. Martha Gerbode and other staunch conservationists succeeded in preventing the development plans by buying the land and turning it over to The Nature Conservancy; the headlands then became part of the Golden Gate National Recreation Area. The Bobcat Trail winds up the valley to the ridge and Five Corners junction.

From Five Corners, **all trail users** follow the Bobcat Trail due west up a slight incline to a spectacular view: Mt. Tamalpais to the northwest, Richardson Bay to the east, and the Pacific Ocean to the west. At the top of the incline you pass a little meadow fenced for "Resource Protection" against footsteps, hoof prints, and wheel tracks; buttercups, poppies, brodiaea, scarlet Indian paintbrush, and native grasses flourish.

After a small dip and rise, you pass the trail that goes southwest half a mile downhill to primitive Hawk Camp. Pause here to look back for a last glimpse of San Francisco's skyline and the tip of the Golden Gate Bridge tower. Hawks soar above, watching for field mice and voles in open grasslands and for wary rabbits hurrying across the road to the cover of chaparral. Bear right to continue past the camp on the rocky, rutted, Bobcat Trail.

In less than a quarter of a mile you reach the Marincello/Bobcat trails junction, where you veer right again on the wide, 1.7-mile Marincello Trail, the Bay Area Ridge Trail route to Tennessee Valley. (The Bobcat Trail veers left, uphill.) You follow the road laid out in the 1960s to the proposed Marincello development. Modest stands of Monterey pines, cypresses, and a few eucalyptus planted by the would-be developers of this city now crown the steep road banks. Clumps of willows and tall woodwardia ferns watered by seeping springs dot the roadside.

The hillside falls off steeply to the east into Oakwood Valley, beyond which lie Richardson Bay and Belvedere. The trail makes a wide curve west as you near the trailhead in Tennessee Valley, and the Miwok stables and corrals, part of an old dairy ranch, come in view.

At the Tennessee Valley trailhead you will find pleasant picnic tables under a grove of pines. The next segment of the Ridge Trail route continues north from here on the Miwok Trail to Shoreline Highway and Mount Tamalpais State Park beyond. (See *Golden Gate National Recreation Area, Marin Headlands—Tennessee Valley to Shoreline Highway.*)

For an easy 4-mile side trip from Tennessee Valley, follow a trail that leads 2 miles to the coast at Tennessee Cove.

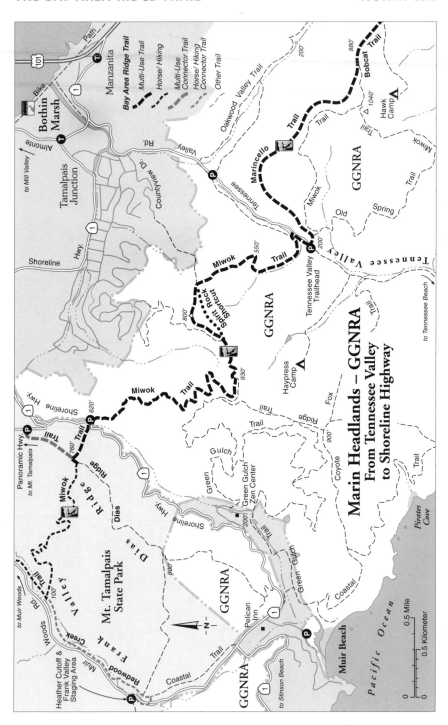

Marin Headlands – GGNRA
From Tennessee Valley
to Shoreline Highway

MARIN HEADLANDS— GOLDEN GATE NATIONAL RECREATION AREA
From Tennessee Valley to Shoreline Highway

Length:	3.8 miles
Accessibility:	Hikers, equestrians, bicyclists
Regulations:	Dogs on leash on Bay Area Ridge Trail. Not allowed on other trails.
Facilities:	Restrooms and phone at Tennessee Valley.

T HE TRAILHEAD IN TENNESSEE VALLEY lies at a low divide between Coyote and Wolf ridges, from which creeks flow east to Richardson Bay and west to the ocean. The Bay Area Ridge Trail route climbs northwest along the Miwok Trail, a narrow and sometimes steep trail that ascends 800 feet towards Coyote Ridge; you'll have sweeping views of San Francisco Bay, see bountiful spring wildflowers, and catch cool ocean breezes. Fog and wind will often accompany you over these coastal hillsides. You reach Highway 1 on a gentle descent along a wide service road.

A network of trails extends south into Gerbode and Rodeo valleys and north to Muir Beach and Green Gulch. These trails are popular and very busy on weekends. One trail leads 2 miles west to Tennessee Cove, well-known for its powerful surf. It was here in 1853 that the three-masted sidewheel steamship *Tennessee*, on a voyage from Panama, ran aground in a fog. All aboard were saved.

Getting There

By Car

South trailhead, Tennessee Valley: From Hwy. 101 near Mill Valley take Stinson Beach/Mt.Tamalpais exit and go west on Hwy. 1

(Shoreline Hwy.) for about 0.4 mile. Turn left (south) on Tennessee Valley Rd. and continue to parking lot at end of road.

North trailhead, Shoreline Hwy: From Hwy. 101 in Mill Valley take Stinson Beach/Mt. Tamalpais exit and go 2.7 miles west on Hwy. 1 (Shoreline Hwy.). Continue 0.4 mile beyond Panoramic Hwy. turnoff north to roadside parking. Room for four cars on north side of highway and six cars on south side. Do not block fire road gate.

On the Trail

To begin this trip to Shoreline Highway, **hikers, equestrians,** and **bicyclists** find the Bay Area Ridge Trail/Miwok Trail sign on the north side of the parking area at the east end of Tennessee Valley Road. Cross a bridge over a small creek, and follow its course upstream through a grove of native scrub oaks and non-native eucalyptus, commonly imported and planted as windbreaks for dairy ranches along the coast.

Biker on the Miwok Trail.

After 0.25 mile, the Ridge Trail/ Miwok Trail begins to climb out of the canyon on switchbacks. Across the stream, you see a scattering of oaks and madrones on the grassy hillside and apricot-colored blossoms of sticky monkeyflower grow along the trail. In spring, open grasslands are bright with flowers—pink mallow, blue brodiaea, golden poppy, and blue ground iris.

You climb several flights of innovative hard rubber water bars—alternatives to railroad ties designed to prevent erosion and to allow both bicyclists and equestrians to maneuver—the trail rises quickly toward the ridge ahead. Look west to see the Pacific Ocean through a notch in the hills at the end of Tennessee Valley. Soon you see east across Richardson Bay to Belvedere and Angel Island, and beyond to the East Bay. Such vistas are surely what were envisioned for the Bay Area Ridge Trail.

Amid chaparral and rock outcrops, pink mallow, silver-leafed lupine, and blue-eyed grass bloom in open grassy patches. Silver-leafed lupine is an important host plant for the endangered Mission Blue butterfly; in order to protect the plants, the park service re-routed the trail on this steep grade.

Above your trail to the north, you see a grove of tall eucalyptus crowning the hill ahead. The Miwok Trail circles east of the grove. As you approach the grove, a narrow path marked for **hikers** only turns left (west) on a shortcut to Coyote Ridge ahead. Detour along this steep, grassy hillside in spring to see an extravagant display of wildflowers.

The Bay Area Ridge Trail route continues north on the Miwok Trail, then west, beside a sheltered, shady forest where wood ferns carpet the ground. As you round the hilltop, you'll see the Miwok Trail extending north from Coyote Ridge. Near the ridgetop, you meet the Coyote Ridge Trail. You turn right on the Miwok Trail and wind in and out of deep canyons and cross chaparral-covered hills as you drop steeply into Tamalpais Valley. The Coyote Ridge Trail continues southwest to meet the Green Gulch and Fox trails and then meets the Coastal Trail.

The Miwok Trail/Bay Area Ridge Trail continues into Tamalpais Valley, with views of houses nestled on the hills. As you near the highway, you pass through woods of eucalyptus and oak, where ferns line the trail, and toyon and elderberry flourish.

Just before the highway, a short section of trail buttressed with railroad ties and flanked by posts directs you to a point where hikers, equestrians, and bicyclists have enough sight distance to safely cross Shoreline Highway. To the west you can see Muir Beach and the Pacific Ocean. Across the road, the Bay Area Ridge Trail route continues on the Miwok Trail over Dias Ridge, through Mount Tamalpais State Park.

Find the trail in a small parking area on the far side of the highway. (See *Mount Tamalpais State Park—From Shoreline Highway to Pantoll.*)

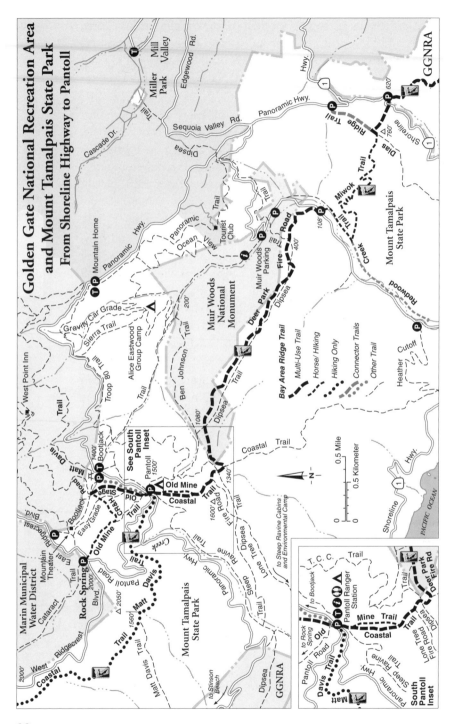

Golden Gate National Recreation Area and Mount Tamalpais State Park
From Shoreline Highway to Pantoll

Bay Area Ridge Trail

Multi-Use Trail

Horse/Hiking

Hiking Only

Connector Trails

Other Trail

0.5 Mile

0.5 Kilometer

—N—

Miller Park

Mill Valley

Edgewood Rd.

Hwy.

620

GGNRA

Ridge Trail

Shoreline

Dias

760

Panoramic Hwy.

Sequoia Valley Rd.

Cascade Dr.

Dipsea

Trail

Trail

Miwok

Trail

Mount Tamalpais State Park

Creek

Redwood

108

400

Mountain Home

Panoramic Hwy.

Panoramic

Ocean

View

Tourist Club

Muir Woods Parking

Fire Road

Deer Park

Dipsea

Multi-Use Trail

Horse/Hiking

Gravity Car Grade

Sierra Trail

Alice Eastwood Group Camp

Ben Johnson Trail

200'

Trail

1080'

Dipsea

Trail

West Point Inn

Trail

Troop 80

Muir Woods National Monument

Heather Cutoff

Coastal Trail

Matt Davis

Bootjack

1400'

See South Pantoll Inset

Pantoll 1500'

Old Mine

Coastal Trail

1340'

1600' Fire Road

Marin Municipal Water District

Mountain Theater

Bootjack

Easy Grade

Old Mine Trail

Stage Rd.

Creek

Dipsea Trail

Ravine Trail

Lone Tree

Ridgecrest Blvd.

Pantoll Road

Davis

Matt

2000'

Rock Spring

2050'

Cataract Trail

West Ridgecrest Blvd.

2000'

Coastal Trail

Matt Davis Trail

1560'

Mount Tamalpais State Park

Panoramic Hwy.

Steep Ravine Trail

to Stinson Beach

Dipsea Trail

GGNRA

to Steep Ravine Cabins and Environmental Camp

Shoreline Hwy.

1

PACIFIC OCEAN

South Pantoll Inset

T.C.C. Trail

Deer Park Fire Rd

Pantoll Ranger Station

Mine Trail

Coastal

Old

Lone Tree Fire Road

Dipsea Trail

to Bootjack

to Rock Spring

Pantoll Road

Davis Trail

Matt

Steep Ravine Trail

Panoramic Hwy.

GGNRA

MOUNT TAMALPAIS STATE PARK
From Shoreline Highway to Pantoll Ranger Station

Length: 5.4 miles

Accessibility: Hikers, equestrians, bicyclists

Regulations: Open 7 a.m. to sunset (approximately). No dogs. Bicycles limited to fire roads.

Facilities: Water, restrooms, and phone at Pantoll Ranger Station.

WATCH RAPTORS SOAR above open grassy slopes, take in views of the Pacific, follow a moist creekbed, and cross shaded oak woodlands and Douglas-fir forests; this trek through Mount Tamalpais State Park crosses the northwest corner of Muir Woods. You begin with a 500-foot elevation loss on the gentle, 2.1-mile Miwok Trail and then gain 1400 feet on a steady climb to Pantoll Ranger Station.

Getting There

By Car

South trailhead, Shoreline Hwy: From Hwy. 101 in Mill Valley, take Stinson Beach/Mt. Tamalpais exit and go 2.7 miles west on Hwy. 1 (Shoreline Hwy.). Continue 0.4 mile beyond Panoramic Hwy. turnoff north to roadside parking. Room for four cars on north side of highway and six cars on south side. Do not block fire road gate.

Alternate trailhead on Panoramic Hwy: Follow directions above, but turn north on Panoramic Hwy, continuing north around the first sharp bend to roadside parking. Pass through gate on west side of road to well-signed Dias Ridge Fire Trail and continue south 0.33 mile to the Miwok Trail.

Equestrians: A staging area off Frank Valley Rd. provides access to the Redwood Creek Trail and the Deer Park Fire Road.

Bicyclists: Deer Park Fire Road access off Frank Valley Rd. and Muir Woods Rd.

North trailhead, Pantoll Ranger Station: From Hwy. 101 in Mill Valley follow directions above, but turn north on Panoramic Hwy. and continue approximately 6 miles northwest to parking at ranger station. Parking fee. Additional parking at Bootjack Picnic Area, 0.2 mile before Pantoll, if Pantoll is full (group parking fee).

By Bus

Golden Gate Transit bus 63 to Pantoll weekends and holidays.

On the Trail

This Bay Area Ridge Trail trip runs from the Golden Gate National Recreation Area through the southeast corner of 6,000-acre Mount Tamalpais State Park. **Hikers, equestrians,** and **bicyclists** begin on the Miwok Trail from Shoreline Highway and climb switchbacks on a gentle grade. In spring, purple iris and lavender bush lupine enliven the greasewood-covered hillside. At the ridgetop, you turn left (southwest) on the Dias Ridge Fire Road.

On clear days, you'll have far-reaching views from broad, grassy Dias Ridge: west to San Francisco; east to Richardson Bay,

---

The Sleeping Lady

The 2571-foot East Peak of Mt. Tamalpais towers over the Bay Area; it has been upthrust by fault movement over millions of years. The mountain was revered by Coast Miwoks, who settled by its streams and along its coast and bay waters more than 7000 years ago. New arrivals to this area were drawn to its peaks and slopes, and by the late 1800s, thousands of hikers thronged its trails on weekends. In 1896, the Mt. Tamalpais Railroad was extended to the summit. The Tamalpais Conservation Club, formed in the early 1900s, and other hiking clubs helped construct and maintain trails. In 1928, Mount Tamalpais State Park was created.

Belvedere, Angel Island, and across to the East Bay. Mt. Tamalpais rises before you to the north.

The Miwok Trail branches right (northwest) after 0.15 mile on the Dias Ridge Trail.

Bicyclists continue west on the Dias Ridge Trail to Highway 1, where you go north 0.25 mile and then turn right (north) on Frank Valley and Muir Woods roads and join hikers and equestrians on the Deer Park Fire Road.

Hikers and **equestrians** turn on the Miwok Trail and descend into Frank Valley. The trail loses 500 feet on a comfortable grade; switchbacks pass through grassy clearings and oak groves, with views into the valley and of the ridge you will follow on Deer Park Fire Road. A meadow-side bench halfway down the trail offers a good place to pause.

You follow a tributary to Redwood Creek and arrive at a junction with the Redwood Creek Trail. A handsomely turned signpost notes that the Miwok Trail was built by the Youth Conservation Corps in 1981. The Miwok Trail ends here and you go upstream on the Redwood Creek Trail.

Redwood Creek begins high in the canyons above Muir Woods and flows into the ocean at Muir Beach. In fall and winter, you may see fish swimming in the creek (no fishing). The trail follows the creek as it bends around a jumble of rocks where giant bay laurels spread a wide canopy. A pool reflects the sky and overhanging branches of alders, making this an inviting place to stop for a snack before the long climb to Pantoll. Continuing upstream, you cross a footbridge and then head north to Muir Woods Road.

The main entrance to Muir Woods National Monument is 0.75 mile up the road. However, you pick up the gated, signed Deer Park Fire Road directly across the road. Here, **bicyclists** join **hikers** and **equestrians** on this broad, unpaved fire road, which swings up through scanty chaparral into oak woodland. For 2.8 miles you climb steadily up the ridge to the Pantoll Ranger Station, a gain of 1,400 feet.

In about half a mile, the fire trail crosses the Dipsea Trail, the route of the 7-mile foot race from Mill Valley to Stinson Beach, held every June since 1905. The Dipsea Trail affords an alternate route for hikers; it more or less parallels the fire trail, crossing it several times as they climb to the ridge. In another half a mile, the fire trail emerges on a stretch of meadow from which you can see the domes of a military installation on Mt. Tamalpais' west peak.

In spring, these grassy hillsides are bright with flowers. Red-tailed hawks and turkey vultures with wingspreads of nearly six feet often circle above the meadows, scanning them for hapless field mice or carrion. You may not see any black-tailed deer, but you can be sure they are nearby from their tracks along the trail.

The trail enters the forest again, where the shade is welcome on sunny days. Tall redwoods remind you that you are on the edge of Muir Woods National Monument, which you pass through farther up the trail, in a Douglas-fir forest. The trail steepens, veering left to emerge onto broad grasslands below Pantoll.

To the west, you have a view of the Pacific Ocean, or as is often the case, the fog bank covering it. South and east are the bay and San Francisco's skyline.

You join the Coastal Fire Road and head due north, passing the Dipsea Trail as it veers west on its way to Stinson Beach. Shortly you pass the Lone Tree Fire Road and continue north for about 0.7 mile to the Pantoll Ranger Station.

Hikers and **equestrians** can follow the Old Mine Trail to Pantoll through a Douglas-fir forest; the trail begins just beyond the Lone Tree Trail junction and runs adjacent to the Coastal Fire Road.

Bicyclists stay on the Coastal Fire Road to Pantoll.

From Pantoll, **hikers** can continue north on the Matt Davis Trail, which begins the next segment of the Bay Area Ridge Trail. The trailhead is just across Panoramic Highway from Pantoll. **Bicyclists** do not have a designated Ridge Trail route north from Pantoll to the Bolinas-Fairfax Road; **equestrians** take the Old Stage Road to begin the next trip. (See *Mount Tamalpais State Park and Golden Gate National Recreation Area—From Pantoll to Bolinas-Fairfax Road.*)

If you are not continuing north, you could arrange to meet friends at the Pantoll Ranger Station and have lunch at nearby Rock Spring or Bootjack picnic areas. Or make advance reservations to stay at the campground at Pantoll.

MOUNT TAMALPAIS STATE PARK AND GOLDEN GATE NATIONAL RECREATION AREA
From Pantoll Ranger Station to Bolinas-Fairfax Road

Length: 6.4 miles

Accessibility: Hikers, equestrians, bicyclists

Regulations: Pantoll Rd. and Ridgecrest Blvd.—Open 7 a.m. to sunset (approximately); may be closed in times of high fire danger or hazardous road conditions. Parking fee at Pantoll Ranger Station.
Mount Tamalpais State Park—Open 7 a.m. to sunset (approximately). No dogs. Bicycles on fire roads only.
GGNRA and MMWD—Dogs on leash.

Facilities: Water, restrooms, and phone at Pantoll Ranger Station; water and restrooms at Rock Spring; water and restrooms at nearby Mountain Theatre.

HIGH ON THE SLOPES of Mt. Tam and along Bolinas Ridge, this route takes full advantage of the mountain's challenging trails, breathtaking views, forested glades, and flowery slopes. Coastal fog often obscures vistas in the morning and late afternoon. Choose a clear winter or spring day to appreciate views up and down the coast and the wildflowers that bloom along the trail. Hikers gain and loose several hundred feet in elevation.

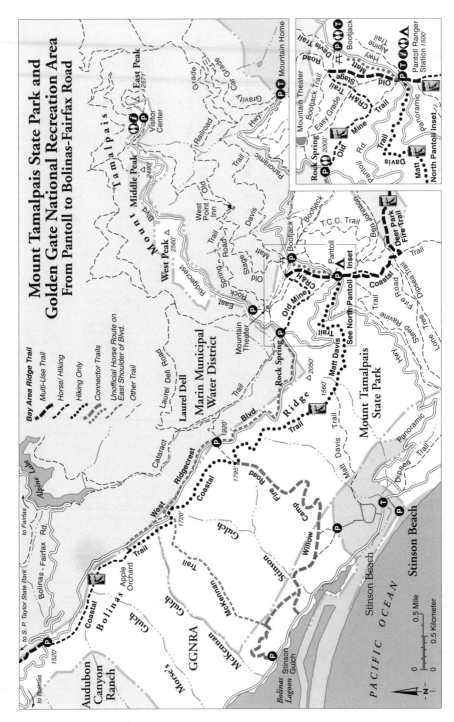

Mount Tamalpais State Park and Golden Gate National Recreation Area From Pantoll to Bolinas-Fairfax Road

Bay Area Ridge Trail
Multi-Use Trail
Horse/Hiking
Hiking Only
Connector Trails
Unofficial Horse Route on East Shoulder of Blvd.
Other Trail

Getting There

By Car

South trailhead, Mount Tamalpais Pantoll Ranger Station: From Hwy. 101 in Mill Valley, take Stinson Beach/Mt. Tamalpais exit and go 2.7 miles west on Hwy. 1 (Shoreline Hwy.). Turn north on Panoramic Hwy. and continue approximately 6 miles northwest to parking at ranger station. Parking fee. Additional parking at Bootjack Picnic Area, 0.2 mile before Pantoll, if Pantoll is full (group parking fee).

North trailhead, Bolinas-Fairfax Rd.: From Pantoll Ranger Station in Mt. Tamalpais State Park, take Pantoll Rd. 1.3 miles to Ridgecrest Blvd. and Rock Spring. Turn left onto East Ridgecrest Blvd. and continue northwest to Bolinas-Fairfax Rd. junction. Park on south side of road and cross road to trail entrance. Or, take Bolinas-Fairfax Rd. west from Fairfax or east from Hwy. 1 to its junction with Ridgecrest Blvd; parking on south side of Ridgecrest Blvd. Road subject to closure.

By Bus

Golden Gate Transit bus 63 to Pantoll, weekends and holidays only; continues to Stinson Beach.

On the Trail

Hikers, equestrians, and bicyclists start this trip at Pantoll on different routes. Each route is described separately below.

Hikers begin on the Matt Davis Trail, at the stone steps across Panoramic Highway from the Pantoll parking lot. This well-kept old trail crosses the mountain and descends to Stinson Beach. A hiker's favorite, it is named for the "dean of Mt. Tamalpais trail builders" and has been built and rebuilt over the years.

The trail curves to the left around a serpentine rock outcrop and for the next half a mile, contours through a forest of oaks and firs. Soon it enters a small ravine where a stream splashes over moss-covered rocks, and giant ferns stand 6 feet tall. Around the next bend, a grassy spot above the trail is blue with hound's tongue blossoms in March. Douglas irises bloom by the trail's edge in April.

As the trail rounds a south-facing slope, it emerges from the woods to cross a steep, grassy hillside and climb over a saddle. From this vantage point, you see Bolinas Lagoon ahead (west) in the distance and, looking back (southeast), the San Francisco skyline. The trail winds in and out of a tree-filled gully, and—again on grassy slopes—reaches the junction with the Coastal Trail. You head north here and the Matt Davis Trail continues down (left) to Stinson Beach.

Now a narrow path, the Coastal Trail (Bob Cook Memorial) turns upward to round a steep slope. From these heights you look down on the town of Stinson Beach, and on a still day you can hear the roar of the surf. As the trail enters a forested ravine, the sounds of surf fade in the presence of a splashing creek. From the far side of the ravine, you see the long curve of Stinson Beach, the Bolinas Lagoon, and the white line of waves breaking on Duxbury Reef beyond.

The trail continues across steep hillsides punctuated by great serpentine outcrops. Spreading bay trees, their roots buttressed by these rocks, cling to the hillside in gullies. Deer tracks crisscross open slopes above dark, forested ravines. At the forest's edge far below, grazing does and their fawns raise their heads as they sense intruders.

In the sky, vultures with wingspans of six feet circle on strong updrafts that rise from the steep slopes. On fine days, bright-winged hang gliders share the skies, born aloft by the same updrafts. From launch sites near Ridgecrest Boulevard, they slowly wheel their way down to land on Stinson Beach.

By March, buttercups and California poppies begin to appear in the grass, soon followed by a colorful array of spring wildflowers.

The Coastal Trail continues in and out of folds across the ever-steeper hillside, climbing toward a spur of Bolinas Ridge. Here you meet the Willow Camp Fire Road, which descends to Stinson Beach from Ridgecrest Boulevard; you continue on the Coastal Trail, across a small saddle, and enter a ravine. On the other side of the ravine, a stone bench beside the trail overlooks the sea. It honors Bob Cook, the Eagle Scout who conceived this trail and persisted in its completion by volunteers.

Around another open slope, the trail enters woods of bay trees where a lively creek rushes down Stinson Gulch. Across a bridge, ferns, mossy rocks, and a grove of moisture-seeking maples grow in damp contrast to the exposed hillsides.

From the creek, the trail climbs up the hillside to Ridgecrest Boulevard, and you walk on the roadside around a bend for about

500 feet to the McKennan Gulch Trail gate. You have your first views of the Marin hills and mountain peaks to the northeast. On clear days, you can see Mt. St. Helena in the distance.

The Coastal Trail resumes beyond the McKennan Gulch Trail gate and drops down into a tight gully. Railroad-tie steps lead to a rivulet where a Bay Area Ridge Trail sign marks the route. At this point you leave Mount Tamalpais State Park and enter GGNRA lands for the last 2 miles of the trip.

You are above the woods of McKennan Gulch and below a small knoll. After crossing a little flat dotted with great boulders, where a fence keeps out feral pigs, the trail follows close to Ridgecrest Boulevard. Below you, an apple orchard in a green, spring-fed meadow marks the site of a mountain cabin. Here the unsigned equestrian trail from the east side of Ridgecrest Boulevard joins the Coastal Trail on the Bay Area Ridge Trail route.

Equestrians leave Pantoll Ranger Station, cautiously cross Panoramic Highway, and take the paved Old Stage Road past three left-branching hiking trails. You continue to the junction of the historic California Riding and Hiking Trail, marked by a water trough, and follow this shaded trail up steep slopes. From the open grasslands above, you have spectacular panoramic views of San Francisco, the ocean, and the multiple peaks of Mt. Tamalpais. After negotiating railroad-tie steps, you join the Old Mine Trail for a short stretch, and then cross Ridgecrest Boulevard to Rock Spring parking lot.

There is no signed equestrian trail for the next 3 miles, northwest from Rock Spring to "Apple Orchard." Therefore, from the Rock Spring parking lot, riders head northwest on the California Riding and Hiking Trail, which follows the east shoulder of Ridgecrest Boulevard. You pass the Laurel Dell Fire Road (roadside parking available) and continue to the McKennan Gulch Trail gate (west side of Ridgecrest Boulevard) to join hikers on the Coastal Trail along Bolinas Ridge. Although an authorized equestrian route does not exist on the east side of Ridgecrest Boulevard, the Bay Area Ridge Trail Council will continue to pursue viable alternatives. For current information regarding both the bicycle and equestrian alignments, please contact the Bay Area Ridge Trail Council.

Ahead, a tall fir forest extends over the ridgetop. The Bay Area Ridge Trail, accessible at this point to **hikers** and **equestrians**, bears west under the trees to cross a broad chaparral-covered hillside. You then descend switchbacks through scrub oaks and cross a seasonally dry stream bed before climbing steeply into a mixed woodland.

The trail levels off and 0.25 mile farther, enters a ridgetop redwood forest. Trees in this forest, some as much as 50 feet in circumference, were heavily logged in the 1850s to build Gold Rush San Francisco. Today, a grove of stately second-growth redwoods shades the summit of Bolinas-Fairfax Road at the end of Ridgecrest Boulevard.

Bicyclists use Pantoll Road north from Pantoll Ranger Station to Rock Spring, then bear left on Ridgecrest Boulevard.

At the junction of Bolinas-Fairfax Road and Ridgecrest Boulevard, the next leg of the Bay Area Ridge Trail begins on the Bolinas Ridge Trail, open to hikers, equestrians, and bicyclists. (See *Golden Gate National Recreation Area and Samuel P. Taylor State Park*.)

View across the headlands to Mt. Tamalpais.

GOLDEN GATE NATIONAL RECREATION AREA AND SAMUEL P. TAYLOR STATE PARK
From Bolinas-Fairfax Road to State Park Entrance

Length: 12.8 miles to Samuel P. Taylor State Park; 12.2 miles to parking at Platform Bridge at Tocaloma; 11.1 miles to alternate trailhead at Olema Hill on Sir Francis Drake Boulevard.

Accessibility: Hikers, equestrians, bicyclists

Regulations: Bolinas Ridge Trail and Cross Marin Trail— Daylight hours. Subject to closure in times of high fire danger. Dogs on leash on Bolinas Ridge Trail. Leave gates to cattle-grazing lands as you find them. When in doubt, close gate. Pantoll Rd. and Ridgecrest Blvd.—Open 7 a.m. to sunset; may be closed in times of high fire danger or hazardous road conditions.

Facilities: Water and restrooms at Samuel P. Taylor State Park.

FROM THE HEIGHTS OF BOLINAS RIDGE you'll have magnificent views of the sparkling ocean, tree-covered ridges, deep canyons, oak-dotted hills, and distant peaks. You'll also glimpse Marin County history as you pass trails named for early landholders and tread the paths of Mexican ranchers, Anglo settlers, rugged loggers, and prosperous dairymen.

A wide, unpaved road descends northwest along the crest of Bolinas Ridge, gradually losing 1300 feet in over 12 miles. You'll travel through damp forests on soft and springy leaf duff; wind through tall chaparral on bare, rocky sandstone; and cross open, cattle-grazed grasslands. Weather and temperature vary as well:

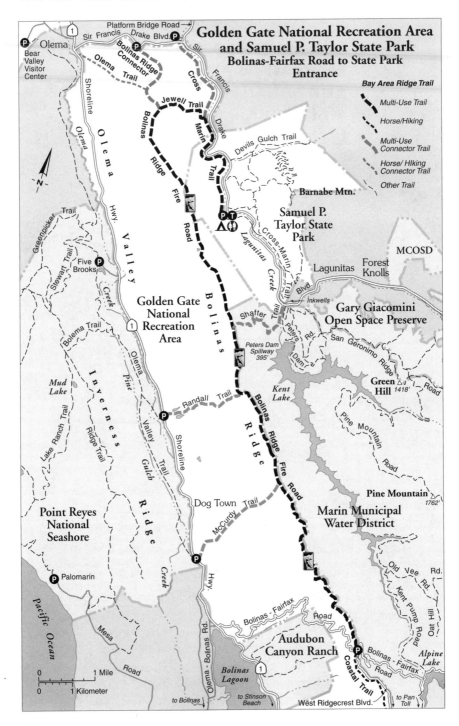

Golden Gate National Recreation Area and Samuel P. Taylor State Park
Bolinas-Fairfax Road to State Park Entrance

Bay Area Ridge Trail

Multi-Use Trail

Horse/Hiking

Multi-Use Connector Trail

Horse/ Hiking Connector Trail

Other Trail

Platform Bridge Road

Sir Francis Drake Blvd.

Olema

Bear Valley Visitor Center

Bolinas Ridge Connector

Olema Trail

Shoreline

Cross

Marin Trail

Sir Francis Drake

Jewell Trail

Bolinas

Ridge

Fire

Road

Devils Gulch Trail

Barnabe Mtn.

Samuel P. Taylor State Park

MCOSD

Olema Valley

Greenpicker Trail

Stewart Trail

Five Brooks

Creek

Laguinitas Creek

Cross-Marin Trail

Lagunitas

Forest Knolls

Blvd.

Golden Gate National Recreation Area

Inkwells

Shafter Trail

Peters Rd.

San Geronimo Ridge

Gary Giacomini Open Space Preserve

Bolema Trail

Olema

Pine

Valley

Gulch

Trail

Inverness

Mud Lake

Lake Ranch Trail

Ridge Trail

Shoreline

Trail

Ridge

Peters Dam Spillway 395'

Dam

Kent Lake

Bolinas

Ridge

Green Hill 1418'

Pine Mountain

Road

Randall Trail

Point Reyes National Seashore

Dog Town Trail

McCurdy

Creek

Pine Mountain 1762'

Marin Municipal Water District

Palomarin

Hwy.

Ridge

Fire

Road

Old Vee Rd.

Kent Pump Road

Oat Hill Rd.

Mesa

Road

Olema - Bolinas Rd.

Bolinas - Fairfax

Road

Audubon Canyon Ranch

Bolinas - Fairfax Road

Alpine Lake

Pacific Ocean

Bolinas Lagoon

Coastal Trail

0   1 Mile

0   1 Kilometer

to Bolinas

to Stinson Beach

West Ridgecrest Blvd.

to Pan Toll

long, exposed stretches of trail can be windy or hot, and summer fog often covers the open ridge. The Cross Marin Trail is paved from Platform Bridge south through Samuel P. Taylor State Park, mostly in shade.

The San Andreas Fault runs through Olema Valley, just west of the trail; it made history in 1906 when it gave San Francisco and Marin County a violent shake. In the sheltering arm of Point Reyes, to the northwest, Drake's Bay is named for Sir Francis Drake, who is said to have anchored there in 1579.

Getting There

By Car

South trailhead, Bolinas-Fairfax Rd./Ridgecrest Blvd. junction: From Pantoll Ranger Station in Mount Tamalpais State Park, take Pantoll Road 1.3 miles to Ridgecrest Blvd. and Rock Spring. Turn left onto Ridgecrest Blvd. and continue northwest to Bolinas-Fairfax Rd. junction. Park on south side of road and cross road to trail entrance. Or, take Bolinas-Fairfax Rd. west from Fairfax or east from Hwy. 1 to junction of Ridgecrest Blvd.; parking on south side of road. Road subject to closure.

North trailhead, Jewell Trail: Take Sir Francis Drake Blvd. to Samuel P. Taylor State Park. Park at main entrance and go northwest 2.1 miles on Cross Marin Trail to junction with Jewell Trail. No off-road parking and no bridge across creek at Jewell Trail.

Limited additional parking at Tocaloma at Sir Francis Drake Blvd./Platform Bridge Rd. junction, 3.5 miles north of main park entrance (park along the road on Sir Francis Drake or off-road behind the bridge, accessible from Platform Rd.). Go south 1.5 miles on Cross Marin Trail to Jewell Trail junction.

Equestrian trailhead: Devils Gulch trailhead along Sir Francis Drake Blvd. Park on roadside.

Alternate north trailhead, north terminus of Bolinas Ridge Trail at Olema Hill: On Sir Francis Drake Blvd. go 4.1 miles northwest of Samuel P. Taylor State Park or 0.6 mile west of Tocaloma (Sir Frances Drake Blvd./Platform Bridge Rd. junction) to parking area on south side of road.

Rock outcroppings on a hillside along Bolinas Ridge,
looking south through Lagunitas Creek Valley.

By Bus

Golden Gate Transit bus 65 to Samuel P. Taylor State Park
weekends and holidays.

On the Trail

To start your trip at the Bolinas-Fairfax Road summit, **hikers**,
equestrians, and **bicyclists** walk or ride into the cool, dark Douglas-fir and redwood forest. As you wind along the wide service road,
you'll notice a low, wire-mesh fence on your left, designed to exclude feral pigs from Audubon Canyon Ranch, west of the ridge.
Feral pigs were once imported for sport hunting, but have prolifer-
ated, and are now a menace to wild plants and animals; humans
should avoid them.

Before long, you emerge from the conifer forest to pass into
chaparral and coastal scrub, where dense vegetation makes a low,
prickly border on both sides of the trail. From occasional openings
in the chaparral you can see to the coast and even hear breakers crashing on Duxbury Reef. Look south behind you to see Mt.
Tamalpais, Marin County's most prominent landmark.

After 3.4 miles, you pass the McCurdy Trail, where it begins
a 1.7-mile descent west. It reaches Highway 1 at Woodville (also

Redwood Logging on Bolinas Ridge

Like much of this area, this part of the ridge and surrounding slopes were once clothed with a majestic redwood forest. The demand for lumber during the Gold Rush obliterated the forest within a few years. Oxen dragged cut logs down to Bolinas Bay, which was deep enough for ships at that time, before erosion-born silt filled it. The devastation of the redwoods was so great that even some loggers expressed dismay. Today, some second-growth trees have attained splendid heights, and salal, Oregon grape, and huckleberry form a shiny undergrowth.

known as Dogtown), which once boasted a number of flourishing lumber mills during the logging period. You stay on the Ridge Trail and continue through a luxuriant second-growth forest. In 2 miles, you reach the Randall Trail, which also descends 1.7 miles to Highway 1 in Olema Valley. The widowed Sarah Seaver Randall, a pioneer in the valley, had a ranch here where she operated a successful dairy and raised a large family. Her home, awaiting historic designation, still stands nearby.

Along the ridge beyond the Randall Trail, the forest thins and pastures edge the trail. Turkey vultures wheel through the skies, and a cacophony of bird song comes from the trees. The cows that graze here may remind you of pictures of Mexican ranchers who raised cattle for their hides and hunted the once-numerous elk. When the Anglos arrived, their dairy herds grazed in these fields and supplied milk to dairies that became famous for their products. The cows you see today are mostly beef cattle.

You pass the Shafter Trail, named for the Shafter brothers, astute lawyers from Vermont who became rich landowners in Marin county. James Macmillan Shafter's house, "The Oaks," still stands on private property near the Bear Valley Trail in Point Reyes National Seashore; it now functions as a retreat center for the Vedanta Society. According to legend, one of the Shafter cows fell into a large fissure created by the 1906 earthquake.

Although the Shafter Trail (open to hikers, equestrians, and bicyclists) descends east to the Shafter Bridge over Lagunitas Creek on Sir Francis Drake Boulevard, this trail is not recommended as a route to Samuel P. Taylor State Park. No bridge crosses Lagunitas Creek to the Cross Marin Trail, and fording the creek can be hazardous at high water. In addition, lack of adequate shoulders on Sir Frances Drake Boulevard makes walking or riding on it unsafe.

Beyond the Shafter Trail junction, the Bay Area Ridge Trail route along the Bolinas Ridge Trail is completely out in the open; it drops into little ravines and then climbs up rounded knolls to take in views west to wooded Inverness Ridge and north to Tomales Bay. On clear days, the blue waters of Tomales Bay shimmer in the sunshine, carrying your eye to the bay's outlet on the coast. The San Andreas Fault continues north through this long finger of water into the Pacific Ocean.

Beside a spring-fed pond you come upon evidence of past habitation—a depression for house foundations and five eucalyptus trees planted in a tight row. The Longley family occupied a house here until 1888, where Thomas Longley reportedly operated a roadhouse. The house was later moved several miles downhill and eventually destroyed. Today the eucalyptus trees, called "The Five Sisters," can be seen from Tomales Bay. Nothing else remains to tell the settler's tale, but cows still come to drink from the pond.

You continue through this pastoral scene for 4 miles beyond the Shafter Trail turnoff. Open grasslands extend up to the forested ridgeline and down to the barns nestled in Olema Valley. The Bolinas Ridge Trail curves east around cattle chutes and corrals and you reach a junction with the Jewell Trail. From here, the Bay Area Ridge Trail route follows the Jewell Trail 0.9 mile to the Cross Marin Trail; the Bolinas Ridge Trail goes 1.3 miles north to Sir Francis Drake Boulevard.

You descend east on the Jewell Trail, following the ridgecrest through steep grasslands punctuated by white, lichen-covered outcrops. Clumps of wind-sculpted oaks frame dramatic views of Barnabe Mountain in the east and Pine Mountain farther south. In spring, many-hued wildflowers brighten this spare landscape. Rounding a curve at the former Omar Jewell ranch homesite, you pass another line of eucalyptus and a few fruit trees.

Now you drop down rapidly to a gate at the Cross Marin Trail on the edge of Lagunitas Creek. Samuel P. Taylor's mill on this stream, formerly called Papermill Creek, once produced paper bags and newsprint for San Francisco. The Bay Area Ridge Trail route continues on the Jewell/Cross Marin trails to 2700-acre Samuel P. Taylor State Park. It follows Lagunitas Creek on the historic North Pacific Coast Railroad (later the North Shore and then the Northwestern Pacific Railroad) right-of-way. The railroad, bankrolled by the Shafter brothers and other financiers in the 1870s, extended from Sausalito to Samuel P. Taylor's mill and continued on to logging camps in Cazadero.

To reach park headquarters, go right (south) for 2.1 miles on the Cross Marin Trail. However, if you parked at Platform Bridge or have a shuttle car waiting there, go left (northwest) 1.5 miles on the Cross Marin Trail.

Equestrians heading to Devils Gulch Camp and trails east can follow the Cross Marin Trail south to the old horse corral and ford Lagunitas Creek, then cross Sir Francis Drake Boulevard to the camp's entrance road.

The next leg of the Bay Area Ridge Trail starts west of Novato in Loma Alta Open Space Preserve. The exact alignment of a Ridge Trail route between Samuel P. Taylor State Park and Loma Alta has not been determined, but preliminary plans include using the proposed Inkwells Bridge across Lagunitas Creek and a route through Giacomini and White's Hill open space preserves. Until then, see *Loma Alta to Lucas Valley Open Space Preserve.*

Platform bridge at Tocaloma.

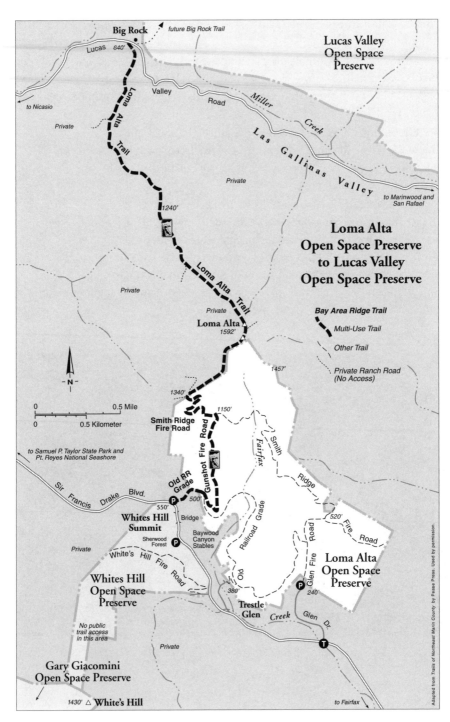

Big Rock
640'
future Big Rock Trail

Lucas Valley
Open Space
Preserve

Lucas

Loma Alta Trail

Valley

Road

Miller

Creek

Las Gallinas Valley

to Nicasio

Private

Private

1240'

to Marinwood and
San Rafael

Loma Alta Trail

**Loma Alta
Open Space Preserve
to Lucas Valley
Open Space Preserve**

Private

Private

Loma Alta
1592'

Bay Area Ridge Trail

Multi-Use Trail

Other Trail

1457'

Private Ranch Road
(No Access)

1340'

-N-

1150'

0   0.5 Mile

0   0.5 Kilometer

Smith Ridge
Fire Road

Gunshot Fire Road

Smith
Fairfax

Ridge

to Samuel P. Taylor State Park and
Pt. Reyes National Seashore

Sir Francis Drake Blvd.

Old RR
Grade

550'

500'

Railroad Grade

520'

Glen Fire Road

Fire Road

**Whites Hill
Summit**

Bridge

P

Sherwood
Forest

P

Baywood
Canyon
Stables

Old

Private

White's Hill Fire Road

**Whites Hill
Open Space
Preserve**

**Loma Alta
Open Space
Preserve**

380'

240'

P

Glen Fire Road

No public
trail access
in this area

**Trestle
Glen**

Creek

Glen

Glen Dr.

Private

T

**Gary Giacomini
Open Space Preserve**

1430' △ **White's Hill**

to Fairfax

Adapted from Trails of Northeast Marin County by Pease Press. Used by permission.

LOMA ALTA OPEN SPACE PRESERVE TO LUCAS VALLEY OPEN SPACE PRESERVE
From Sir Francis Drake Blvd. to Lucas Valley Road

Length: 3.7 miles

Accessibility: Hikers, equestrians, bicyclists

Regulations: Open dawn to dusk. Dogs on leash on Lucasfilm lands; voice control on MCOSD fire road. See MCOSD bike rules.

Facilities: No water, restrooms, or telephone.

CROSS OPEN GRASSLANDS on old ranch roads with around-the-compass views. This steep trip climbs the hill that separates San Geronimo and Lucas valleys (1092'/1052' elevation gain/loss) on a wide, rocky, and exposed trail. It is best taken on cool mornings in summer or bright sunny days in winter.

Getting There

By Car

South trailhead: From Hwy. 101 take San Anselmo exit (4th Street), cross over freeway, after 2 miles bear right on Sir Francis Drake Blvd. and continue 4 miles to parking on east side of road. Note: After completion of Whites Hill bridge over Sir Francis Drake, trail entrance will be under east side of bridge.

North trailhead: From Hwy. 101 take the Lucas Valley Rd. exit and go west on Lucas Valley Rd. After about 6 miles, you reach the summit and the landmark Big Rock. Roadside parking.

On the Trail

Hikers, equestrians, and **bicyclists** begin on the wide ranch road laid out on a segment of the old narrow-gauge North Pacific Coast Railroad bed. After a short descent through a small glen (one of two shaded stretches on the trip), you reach a wooden gate with the familiar MCOSD logo. Continue to the left beyond the gate, where another trail branches right (downhill). You soon make a sharp turn north to mount open grasslands with wide views on your 1.62-mile ascent to Loma Alta.

To the south, Mt. Tamalpais looms over the entire North Bay, while San Pedro Mountain and its long, lower line of hills stretches east to the edge of the bay. At your feet grow orange poppies, blue-eyed grass, and other spring wildflowers. By summer, most flowers have disappeared, but clumps of native bunchgrasses, nibbled by wildlife, still line the road. Ever higher you climb, and after turning due north, your views expand to include the San Rafael/Richmond Bay Bridge and all of San Francisco and San Pablo bays.

At about 800 feet, you enter a shaded corridor where a cluster of oak trees flourishes, nourished by a spring on the hill to your left. It is a pleasant place to pause for water and map reading. A little rivulet, fed by runoff from the spring and by winter rains, splashes its way south through the narrow ravine below the trail to join Fairfax Creek.

Beyond the tree canopy, the vegetation on this south-facing ridge reverts to sun-loving plants—sage, sticky monkeyflower, and ubiquitous poison oak. Perky stalks of pearly everlasting topped by creamy-white flower tufts stand tall above the grasses. The trail continues unwaveringly straight up this ridge, aptly matching its name, Gunshot Fire Road. Off to the left (northwest), you may notice a huge rock outcrop, its surface weathered to a dull gray. Although unnamed, it is probably twice the width and taller than Big Rock, which marks the end of this trail. These and other outcrops in this area are known as "knockers," probably composed of Franciscan mélange.

After a short, almost-level stretch, you climb another steep pitch to reach a junction. Turn left (west) here, on the Smith Ridge Fire Road (now 0.78 mile from the trailhead); a right turn here would take you about 4 miles southeast to the preserve boundary. Pause at this junction to take in splendid views south—of Angel Island, the Bay Bridge and the San Francisco skyline.

The trail now heads due west on a gentler route. Scattered clumps of young bay trees grow along the edges, and wildflowers flourish in the roadside drainage ditches. When the sun warms the air, you may detect the turpentine scent of yellow tarweed; Indians ground the seeds of this sticky-leafed plant into edible dry cakes. The blue-gray rocks underfoot appear to contain serpentine, the California state rock.

Fine views of sometimes fog-shrouded Bolinas Ridge and Pine Mountain open up before you, and on clear days, you'll see all the high peaks of West Marin, from Mt. Tamalpais in the south to Black Mountain in the north. Much of this land is public open space, including Whites Hill, Gary Giacomini, and Roys Redwoods open space preserves, in the nearer view. What a treasure trove to enjoy and support!

Now you climb steadily, winding up the ridge. A few small and mostly unused trails branch right (east), but you stay on the wide Ridge Trail. After less than a mile on the Smith Fire Road, you enter the Lucasfilm Ltd. property on an easement trail. This easement, graciously offered to MCOSD users, crosses George Lucas' Loma Alta and McGuire ranches and includes just the trail itself. Watch carefully to stay on the trail; you will pass several junctions with trails that are not open to the public.

From the entrance into the Lucasfilm property, a working cattle ranch, turn right (east) and ascend beside the fenced property line. Tight clusters of redwood and bay trees fill the canyon below you, where moisture assures their growth. In late spring, the sun glances off the shiny surfaces of dry oatgrass. The wide, steep Ridge Trail route soon reaches a junction, where you veer left towards the summit of Loma Alta—only 0.42 mile further; the right-branching trail enters public property.

Continue upward on a brief but steep climb. At the broad, rounded summit (1592'), the trail levels off a bit and you look down on the other side of the mountain. Savor the views over lunch or a snack: grassy ridges indented by tree-filled canyons, distant mountains traversed by other Ridge Trail routes, and valleys cut by rushing streams. Big Rock Ridge lies to the north—a long flank of mountain above Lucas Valley with two communication towers on its 1895' summit. A route over this ridge is planned for the next phase of the Bay Area Ridge Trail through Marin County.

The rocky road meanders down the east and north-facing hills of the Lucasfilm ranches; your descent is gentle and undulating at

Big Rock marks the end of this Ridge Trail segment.

first, but steepens farther along. You can see houses nestled in Lucas Valley and the Luiz Fire Road zigzagging up Big Rock Ridge through the Lucas Valley Open Space Preserve.

Huge rocks are scattered among the grasslands; some shelter emerging oaks from sun and wind damage. After passing a farm road on the left and going under a single-strand powerline, you see two corrals—one built of shiny new wire, the next a venerable, well-used wooden structure. An unnamed ridge rises to your left, creased by canyons filled with oak and bay trees.

As you descend close to the fence line on your right, you look into a wooded canyon (private property) and a hill beyond scarred by a vertical barren patch. The trail makes a wide swing left (west) and winds down the north side of an open hillside. Your view now takes in grassy Shroyer Ridge straight ahead, topped by a patchy forest of redwoods that extends into its indented south side.

At 2.65 miles, you pass a ranch road heading left, downhill, and you see a semicircular fenced area in a quiet glen of the former McGuire Ranch. Here, in the protection of the enclosing hills, the air is filled with birdsong and the soft hush of wind in the trees. Losing elevation at every step (foot or hoof) or turn of the bicycle wheel, look left at a spring above the road. It is probably responsible for the muddy trail and lush growth on the right hillside—bay trees, bracken ferns, and of course, poison oak. A nasty thistle, known as knapweed, thrives along this road, its tangled web of small branches armed with sharp barbs and light purple flowers.

The east-facing ridge above you is topped by windblown trees, pruned high by cattle. The steep slope is strewn with serpentine boulders and rocky rubble. As you drop farther downhill, fractured, almost dusty serpentine rock extends out onto the trail.

Around the next curve you can see east down Lucas Valley to the bay, with Mt. Diablo looming beyond. You lose a few hundred more feet in elevation, pass another wooden corral, and reach Lucas Valley Road. Big Rock lies on the other side, marking the end of this 3.7-mile Ridge Trail segment. Future plans for the Ridge Trail include a tunnel under Lucas Valley Road to a limited parking area for trail-users.

In the meantime, the next completed leg of the Bay Area Ridge Trail begins in Indian Tree Open Space Preserve, six or seven miles as the crow flies, but about 14 miles longer via West Marin roads to the trailhead on Vineyard Road in Novato. (See *Indian Tree Open Space Preserve to O'Hair Park.*)

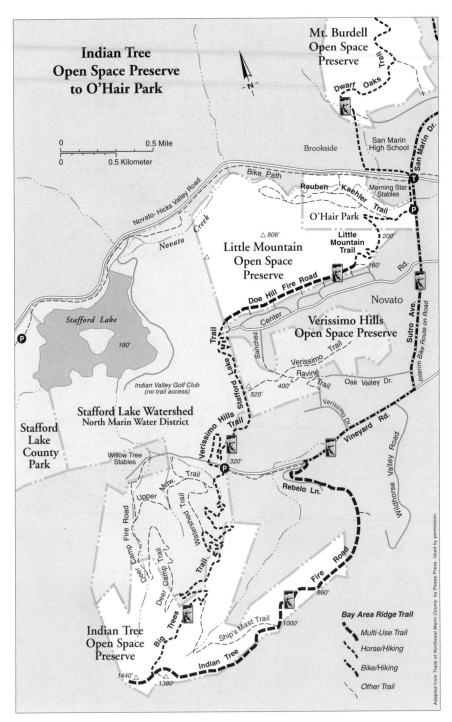

**Indian Tree
Open Space Preserve
to O'Hair Park**

Mt. Burdell
Open Space
Preserve

Dwarf Oaks

San Marin High School

Brookside

Novato-Hicks Valley Road

Bike Path

Reuben   Kaehler   Morning Star
Trail   Stables

O'Hair Park

0   0.5 Mile

0   0.5 Kilometer

Novato Creek

△ 806'

Little
Mountain Trail

200'

**Little Mountain
Open Space
Preserve**

160'

Doe Hill Fire Road

Novato

Stafford Lake

190'

Center

Sanchez

Trail

Little Mountain Trail

**Verissimo Hills
Open Space Preserve**

Sutro Ave.

Interim Bike Route on Road

Rd.

Indian Valley Golf Club
(no trail access)

Verissimo   Trail

Ravine   Trail

Oak Valley Dr.

△ 400'

△ 525'

Stafford Lake Watershed
North Marin Water District

Verissimo Hills Trail

Stafford Lake Trail

Verissimo Dr.

Vineyard Rd.

**Stafford
Lake
County
Park**

Willow Tree
Stables

320'

Rebelo Ln.

Wildhorse Valley Road

Upper   Mdw.   Trail

Watershed Trail

Deer Camp Fire Road

Deer Camp Trail

Trail

Big Trees

Fire   Road

860'

Bay Area Ridge Trail

1000'

Ship's Mast Trail

Indian Tree

1440' △

△ 1380'

**Indian Tree
Open Space
Preserve**

— Multi-Use Trail

··· Horse/Hiking

▪▪ Bike/Hiking

- - Other Trail

Adapted from Trails of Northeast Marin County by Pease Press. Used by permission.

INDIAN TREE OPEN SPACE PRESERVE TO O'HAIR PARK
From Vineyard Road to Indian Tree and through Verissimo Hills and Little Mountain Preserves to O'Hair Park

Length: 9 miles (includes 6 miles round trip to Indian Tree and 3 miles to O'Hair Park)

Accessibility: Hikers, equestrians, bicyclists

Regulations: No bikes on Indian Tree, Verissimo Hills, Stafford Lake, or Little Mountain OSP trails.

Facilities: None

EXPLORE INDIAN TREE'S redwood and Douglas-fir forests on a shady and well-graded out-and-back trip (elevation gain/loss 720'/720'). Then head north over grassy hillsides above Stafford Lake, around Little Mountain, and through forest to O'Hair Park. The Little Mountain Trail starts on fire protection road; otherwise, narrow, well-graded, and shaded trails cross these preserves, with minor elevation change.

Getting There

By Car

Northern trailhead: From Hwy. 101 in Novato, turn west on San Marin Dr. Cross Novato Blvd. onto Sutro Ave. and go over the Novato Creek bridge to roadside parking at O'Hair Park.

Southern trailhead: Follow directions above but continue south on Sutro Ave. past O'Hair Park to Vineyard Rd. Turn right (west). Follow Vineyard Rd. for a little over a mile and park on the south side of the street, immediately after last house, in unpaved area.

By Bicycle

Follow directions above on Novato city streets marked INTERIM BICYCLE ROUTE to Vineyard Rd., go about three quarters of a mile, turn left (south) on Rebelo Lane, and then turn uphill on MCOSD Indian Tree Fire Road.

Each trailhead is marked with a Ridge Trail logo as well as the distinctive Marin County Open Space District sign.

On the Trail

Indian Tree Open Space Preserve

As of now, there is no trailhead at the south end of Indian Tree Open Space Preserve, so this segment of the Ridge Trail first visits Indian Tree on a 6-mile out-and-back trip, before continuing northwest through Verissimo Hills and Little Mountain open space preserves.

Hikers and **equestrians** descend gently from the trailhead on Vineyard Road along a fenced trail into a small meadow, lusciously green in springtime and sprinkled with shiny yellow buttercups. Shortly you pass a green gate and turn left. You ascend switchbacks through oaks and sparse redwoods. The open understory allows a riot of springtime wildflowers to flourish—magenta shooting stars, white and light pink milkmaids, deep red Indian warriors, and later, blue hounds tongue.

In a small clearing, notice a huge rock slab seemingly teetering on a narrow point. Moisture-loving bay laurel trees are scattered among the oaks, Douglas-firs, and redwoods. You'll recognize the bay tree by its aromatic leaves, similar to those of the Greek bay tree, but somewhat stronger. (Some people call them "spaghetti" leaves.) After about 0.75 mile you reach a clearing that offers splendid views east to the bay and north to the bare, 1440-foot peak of Mt. Burdell (the destination of the next Ridge Trail segment).

The trail makes a wide swing west and continues uphill, passing a trail that goes right, into the Stafford Lake Watershed. Where the forest is dense, especially on north- and east-facing slopes, moss grows on older oak-tree trunks and shade-loving plants thrive—maidenhair and printer's ferns, chocolate-colored mission bells, creamy-white globe lilies and white coral bells.

Indian Tree Trail.

On a narrow ridge between two canyons, you stroll under a canopy of tall redwoods, Douglas-firs, and a few tall madrones that stretch for sunlight. Fine-leafed huckleberry bushes fill the understory; deer and birds favor their small, blue-black berries. Soon you pass the Deer Camp Trail and curve left along a split-rail fence to continue on the Big Trees Trail. After about 0.25 mile, you emerge from the forest into chaparral on the edge of a deep canyon. A pause here will reward you with views east to the Novato baylands, the former Hamilton Air Base, and Mt. Diablo in the distance. The Indian Tree Fire Road, the bicycle route to the Indian Tree Preserve Summit, snakes up the opposite ridge. On a chilly day this southwest-facing stretch feels good; on a hot day, you will hurry by.

Back in the cool forest, you soon arrive at a junction with the Shipmast Trail, which was probably named for the very tall, perfectly-straight redwoods growing here. You continue straight on the Big Trees Trail, while the Shipmast Trail contours around the head of the deep canyon you looked into from the chaparral area; it eventually connects to the Indian Tree Fire Road.

You climb steadily on the last leg of the Big Trees Trail, then level off a bit and emerge in a wide meadow. Join a dirt road that runs through the meadow and follow this road through a gentle swale. Veer right uphill on a narrow footpath that leads to a lush meadow bursting with spring wildflowers of every hue—cream colored iris, purple lupine, and yellow buttercups. Ahead are the big trees—a solitary clump of immense redwoods. From the footpath between them, take a few steps left (just a few!) to stand at the edge of an abrupt drop-off above the deep canyon you saw from the trail. Now the whole North Bay spreads before you.

When you have savored the flowers, trees, and views, return on the dirt road through the meadow and bear right on the footpath into the forest to start your downhill trip. Return to Vineyard Road and turn left (west).

 Bicyclists are not allowed on the Big Trees Trail, so you begin the out-and-back Indian Tree segment by following Vineyard Road to Rebelo Lane and picking up the Indian Tree Fire Road there. Take the fire road to the top of the preserve. Return the same way and go right on Vineyard Road to Sutro Avenue. Turn left and continue to O'Hair Park.

Verrissimo Hills and Little Mountain Preserves to O'Hair Park

Hikers and **equestrians** go west on unpaved Vineyard Road for less than 0.25 mile to the Verissimo Hills Trail entrance. The trail begins on the north side of the road at a stile and green MCOSD gate. Go through the gate, making sure to close it behind you (and the cows).

Start up the trail in a tight canyon and soon cross a little bridge. The intermittent creek nourishes an immense bay tree with an almost-hollow trunk. Making a switchback to the right, you begin a serious ascent of the east side of this canyon. At an overlook with a bench, you can see the densely forested hillside you just traversed in the Indian Tree Preserve.

You ascend several switchbacks under the intermittent shade of live oaks and bays. On a quiet spring morning the author heard only birdsong and the rustle of leaves in a gentle breeze. After reaching the top of the first hill the trail follows the contour of the shady north-facing hillside and then turns sharply north. A sign on a gate in an open expanse announces that you are now on the Stafford Lake Trail. The narrow trail undulates up and down small hills, just below the eastern ridgeline boundary of the Stafford Lake Watershed. Small openings through the trees allow quick views of Stafford Lake, with its little island and the dairy farms surrounding it. As hawks and turkey vultures quietly ride the winds above you, the distant sound of lawn-mowing tractors reminds you that the intense green meadows below are the Indian Valley Golf Course.

Soon you leave the hilltop and descend a north-facing hillside through a deciduous-oak forest. When the young, yellow-green leaves unfurl in spring against the dark brown limbs, these trees are uniquely beautiful. After a cold snap in fall, their leaves turn a rich tawny, golden-brown. Rounding several switchbacks you reach the end of this trail in a damp meadow in the Verissimo Hills Open Space Preserve. Cross the meadow and go through the stile in the fence that surrounds a cluster of homes at the end of Center Street. Bear right on the Doe Hill Fire Road in the Little Mountain Open Space Preserve.

Signs ask **all users** to avoid the trail after heavy rains. You skirt the base of Little Mountain on this wide trail; the south-facing exposure can be hot in summer. Tree-filled canyons indent the grassy hillside, collecting rain and spring water. You cross several streams on sturdy wooden bridges built over small dams made of rock-filled gabions. Stands of live oaks beside the trail provide shade for you and refuge for the many birds you may see or hear, especially in early morning or late afternoon.

Bicyclists are allowed on the short, wide Doe Hill Fire Road, accessible from Center Road, but must turn around after about a mile, when the wide trail ends.

Hikers and **equestrians** veer left on the narrower Little Mountain Trail at the base of a steep creek canyon. In May, early-blooming blue brodiaea wave above drying grasses, and clusters of orange poppies cover the sloping hillside. You enter a cool woods of bay and oak trees and after a couple of zigzags, descend gradually along the east side of Little Mountain. Crossing little streams that tumble down the mountainside, this well-graded trail takes you through dense woods of tall, rather spindly trees reaching high for light. After a long traverse beside a handsome split-rail fence, the trail turns to the right and descends quickly to a junction. If you make a sharp left turn on the Reuben Kaehler Trail, you will reach the roadside path along Novato Boulevard. Signs on both sides of this road advise motorists that equestrians and hikers may cross here. However, if you go straight past a private pasture and horse stall, you come to O'Hair Park beside Novato Creek on Sutro Avenue and the end of this trip.

If you are going on to Mt. Burdell, the next leg of the Bay Area Ridge Trail, the hiker/equestrian entrance is across Novato Boulevard just west of San Marin High School. The multi-use entrance is on San Andreas Drive, less than a mile north of O'Hair Park. (See *Mt. Burdell Open Space Preserve.*)

From O'Hair Park, **hikers** go north on the Sutro Way sidewalk, cross Novato Boulevard, and turn left on the sidewalk in front of San Marin High School. Turn right just beyond the west end of the high school property and go through the gate to the Brookside Trail in Mt. Burdell Open Space Preserve.

Equestrians use the unsurfaced edge of Sutro Way sidewalks, cross Novato Boulevard, and turn left on the sidewalk in front of San Marin High School to the Brookside Trail gate in Mt. Burdell OSP.

Bicyclists continue on San Marin Drive to San Andreas Drive, turn left, and go to the preserve gate on San Andreas Fire Road in Mt. Burdell Open Space Preserve.

MT. BURDELL OPEN SPACE PRESERVE
From O'Hair Park and San Andreas Fire Road to Olompali State Historic Park (West Entrance)

Length: 7.1 miles (includes 1.9 miles from O'Hair to San Andreas Fire Rd. and 5.2 miles round trip to Mt. Burdell)

Accessibility: Hikers, equestrians, bicyclists

Regulations: Dogs on leash; not allowed on Dwarf Oak Trail.

Facilities: None

C LIMB THROUGH GRASSLANDS dotted with ancient oaks to spectacular vistas of North Bay ridges from the 1558-foot peak of Mt. Burdell. The largest of Marin County Open Space District's holdings, these nearly 1600 acres of oak savanna and grasslands are interspersed with dense woodlands. Hikers and equestrians can begin from O'Hair Park and cross a Sensitive Wildlife Area on a shaded trail. Bicyclists join them at San Andreas Fire Road and all users follow wide fire roads to the peak; the trails are steep and rocky, with little shade. Summers are hot here, so be sure to get an early start and come prepared.

Getting There

By Car

O'Hair Park trailhead: From Hwy. 101 in Novato, turn west on San Marin Dr. Cross Novato Blvd. onto Sutro Ave. and go over the Novato Creek bridge to roadside parking at O'Hair Park.

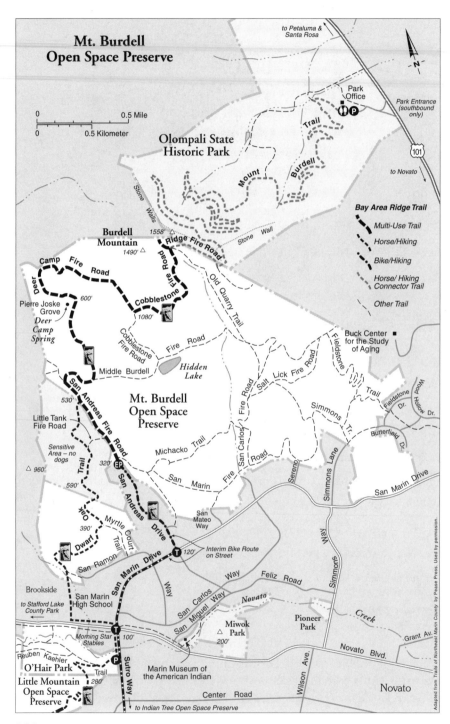

Mt. Burdell
Open Space Preserve

to Petaluma &
Santa Rosa

N

Park
Office

Park Entrance
(southbound
only)

0   0.5 Mile

0   0.5 Kilometer

Olompali State
Historic Park

101

to Novato

Trail

Mount

Burdell

Bay Area Ridge Trail

Multi-Use Trail

Horse/Hiking

Bike/Hiking

Horse/ Hiking
Connector Trail

Other Trail

Stone   Walls

Stone   Wall

Burdell
Mountain

1558'

1490'

Ridge Fire Road

Camp   Fire   Road

Deer

Cobblestone Fire Road

Old Quarry Trail

600'

Cobblestone
Fire Road

1080'

Pierre Joske
Grove
Deer
Camp
Spring

Buck Center
for the Study
of Aging

Fieldstone

Fire   Road

Hidden
Lake

Middle Burdell

Salt Lick Fire Road

Trail

Fieldstone

Hollow Dr.

Dr.

San Andreas Fire Road

530'

San Carlos

Fire   Road

Simmons Tr.

Butterfield Dr.

Little Tank
Fire Road

Sensitive
Area – no
dogs

960'

320'

EP

Trail

Michacko   Trail

San   Marin   Fire   Road

590'

Simmons Lane

Sereno

San Marin Drive

San   Andreas   Drive

Oak

390'

Myrtle Court

Trail

Dwarf

San Mateo
Way

Interim Bike Route
on Street

120'

San Ramon

Way

San Marin Drive

T

Feliz Road

Way

Simmons

Way

Brookside

to Stafford Lake
County Park

San Marin
High School

San Carlos

San Miguel Way

Novato

Creek

Pioneer
Park

Miwok
Park

200'

Grant Av.

100'

T

Novato Blvd.

Morning Star
Stables

Reuben Kaehler

Trail

O'Hair Park

P

Sutro Way

Marin Museum of
the American Indian

Wilson Ave.

Novato

Little Mountain
Open Space
Preserve

280'

Center   Road

to Indian Tree Open Space Preserve

Adapted from Trails of Northeast Marin County by Pease Press. Used by permission.

San Andreas Fire Rd. trailhead: From Hwy. 101 in Novato, turn west on San Marin Dr. At San Andreas Drive, turn right and continue about a half mile to preserve entrance, marked by green gate and MCOSD sign. Park on street. Do not block driveways.

By Bicycle

From Hwy. 101 in Novato **bicyclists** take San Marin Drive south to San Andreas Drive, turn right (northwest) and go to parking at the preserve gate on San Andreas Fire Rd. in Mt. Burdell Open Space Preserve.

On the Trail

From O'Hair Park to San Andreas Fire Road

Hikers and **equestrians** can begin this trip across Novato Boulevard from the last leg of the Indian Tree to O'Hair Park segment. From roadside parking on Sutro Avenue, go north to Novato Boulevard. Cross it and turn left (west) on the sidewalk in front of San Marin High School. Continue to the gated trail into Mt. Burdell OSP. The short, shady 0.6-mile trail dedicated in October 2001 traverses an easement between the school fence and the enclosed gardens of the Brookside subdivision. Cross the rust-colored steel bridge over a tributary of Novato Creek and soon enter Mt. Burdell's 6-acre southwest meadow. In spring, this meadow glows with bright orange California poppies and yellow suncups; by summer, golden oat grass covers the sloping fields. Red-tailed hawks soar overhead and rusty-breasted bluebirds dart after insects on the wing.

Just past a sturdy vehicle bridge at the end of San Ramon Drive, you head northwest on the Dwarf Oak Trail and climb grassy slopes. On this Ridge Trail segment, dedicated in 1990, you head east and traverse the hillside above a neighboring subdivision. Deciduous oaks crowd the banks of a tiny stream that courses through a fold in the hillside. Shortly, you enter an evergreen oak and bay forest, punctuated in fall by the golden leaves of a few Kellogg oaks. Little streams tumble over rocks in shady canyons in the Sensitive Wildlife Area; white milkmaids and blue hounds tongue brighten the trailside. You leave the forest momentarily and reach a mossy rock garden and a mound with seemingly stunted oak trees growing from cracks in the rock—probably the trees that give their name to the Dwarf Oak Trail.

When you leave the rock garden, you cross a grassy slope where several streamlets trickle down the hillside in spring. Head due north across a meadow filled with bright yellow buttercups in spring. Shortly, you come to the gate at San Andreas Fire Road and the beginning of the multi-use trip up Mt. Burdell.

Mt. Burdell's Early Residents

The Coast Miwoks lived in this area since 1300, subsisting on shellfish from the marshes and acorns and wild game from the oak-studded hills to the west. The Miwoks' last chief, Camilo Ynitia, received a Spanish land grant in 1834 and named the village and surrounding lands Rancho Olompali. Ynita later sold part of the rancho to James Black, who passed some of the land to his daughter as a wedding present.

Mary Black married Galen Burdell, the first San Francisco dentist and the man for whom the mountain was named. The Burdells built a fine house on the east side of the mountain and developed orchards and gardens on the site of the large Miwok village, Olompali.

From San Andreas Fire Road to Olompali State Historic Park

The multi-use Ridge Trail route begins on the San Andreas Fire Road, a wide park patrol road that heads north from the San Andreas gate. The trail hugs the wooded east side of the Sensitive Wildlife Area and ascends gradually through a canyon to reach the preserve's central valley.

Northwest across this valley, your gaze stretches to surrounding 1200-foot hills, fringed with dark tree silhouettes. To the east, Mt. Burdell rises 1558 feet; to the west is the low hill of the wildlife area. In the near foreground, a cattle pen beyond the preserve boundary sets a pastoral tone for the trip. If you are in this valley at sunset, you may be rewarded with a spectacular view of the northwest mountains outlined against a glowing, red-orange sky.

You veer east from the valley on the Middle Burdell Fire Road, through sloping grasslands to a grove of ancient, deciduous white oaks. One old giant's diameter measures close to five feet. In winter the gnarled, widespread limbs of these trees present striking, gaunt silhouettes against the greening fields. In their summer dress these oaks cast welcome shade for human visitors and seasonal bovine residents. (Huge fallen limbs serve as convenient resting places.) The Ridge Trail's Mt. Burdell segment was dedicated in this handsome grove in October 1990.

Just across from this majestic grove, the marked Ridge Trail route goes left on the Deer Camp Fire Road. You head due north through the grasslands, and then climb to a broad, wooded plateau. Here, shady Deer Camp, a 25-acre picnic and camping site fenced against cattle intrusion, invites you to pause for a snack or lunch. Organized groups can get permission for overnight camping; they must carry their own water, and no fires are allowed. You'll find a portable toilet, hitch racks and a circle of log benches situated under some fine Kellogg (black) oaks, large live oaks and many bay trees.

Buckeye along Deer Camp Fire Road.

Resuming your upward way, follow a long, steep curve around an isolated clump of buckeye trees on your right. The buckeyes' bare limbs shine silvery in winter, but burst with new growth as early as February to herald spring. By May, the spikes of white flowers tinged with pink fill the air with a sweet fragrance. In dry years, the buckeye trees' leaves shrivel and drop in early summer to compensate for lack of water.

103

As you ascend steadily for the next half a mile, look for the preserve's biggest elderberry tree standing alone beside a curve in the trail: leafless in winter, covered with branchlets of fine leaves and clusters of cream-colored flowers in summer, and heavy with blue-gray, edible berries in fall.

Shortly after the trail levels off beside a luxurious woods, you reach the Cobblestone Trail junction, where you turn left for the summit. As you start your climb, the relay tower near the west shoulder of Mt. Burdell appears above the forested ridgetop. But your destination is still 400 vertical feet and about 1 mile away. This trail takes its name from the basalt rock that was quarried here to pave San Francisco streets in the 1860s and '70s. Basalt, a dark igneous stone, is readily split, chipped and made into cobbles. From pits on the west side of Mt. Burdell, Chinese laborers dug out and chipped rectangular stone blocks (about 6 inches wide, 15 inches long and 4 inches thick). The workers loaded the cobbles onto wooden sleds and slid them down the steep mountainside. Scars of the sleds' descent are still visible from this trail.

Continue uphill on the rocky trail, past lush clumps of California bay trees growing among boulders on north-facing slopes. It's said that the Olompali Miwok Indians used these boulders as hunting blinds, or perhaps set game traps near them.

As you approach the summit of Mt. Burdell, on the left you see a private road to the relay tower, a telephone company repeater station. On the right, the Old Quarry Trail, for hikers and equestrians only, drops 800 feet in elevation down the steep canyon between Mt. Burdell and the ridge you just conquered.

With the summit just a few feet beyond the preserve boundary, you bear right onto the paved Burdell Mountain Ridge Road leading to the rock quarries. The main quarry is on your left, well-worth a short walk to see the exposed, layered rock walls of the pits where cobbles were removed. Although small trees and shrubs have gained toeholds in the crevices and masked some of the walls, the size of the pit helps you empathize with the Chinese laborers who excavated it by hand. Just beyond the main pit are smaller diggings, even more overgrown.

An overlook on the other side of the road offers a hawk's eye view of the preserve and the distant, high ridges that almost circle northern Marin County. If the day is bright, you can make out Hicks Mountain to the northwest, Mt. Tamalpais to the south and the shoulder of Mt. Burdell curving around to the west; when fog lies in the valleys, the ridgetops seem like islands floating in a misty sea.

After enjoying the vistas and the red-tailed hawks and turkey vultures that may circle aloft, return past the quarries to a trail on your right. It leads to a very old rock wall, hand-built by Chinese laborers, that marks the boundary of Olompali State Historic Park. Step into a high meadow on the other side of the wall to see the Petaluma River flowing through flat marshlands toward San Francisco Bay. Or take the 5-mile Mt. Burdell Trail to Olompali State Historic Park, which descends through white oak and madrone woodlands to the site of the largest Miwok village in Marin County and the Burdell home and gardens.

To return to your trailhead, retrace your steps downhill on the Cobblestone Fire Road to the Deer Camp Fire Road junction. For different views, a bit steeper route and a rainy-winter surprise, veer left on the Cobblestone Fire Road. The road curves south to enter a beautiful, mature oak and bay woods. Soft duff under the great tree branches erupts with mushrooms in spring and nurtures ferns year-round; in early spring, white milkmaids and blue hound's tongue greet the observant eye.

Follow the trail southwest along a high, open, west-facing shoulder and a sparse, steep mountainside on your left. At the Middle Burdell Fire Road junction lies a great meadow nestled in a high valley, surprisingly inundated in wet winters by storm waters washed from the surrounding slopes. The fenced, flooded meadow is known as Hidden Lake, said to have been deep enough for swimming 40 years ago. Today, when dry, it provides seasonal cattle-grazing.

Bear right on the Middle Burdell Fire Road and go around the meadow/lake under a lush forest canopy to the crest of a west-facing, steep hillside. You descend rapidly, curving northwest, through grasslands ablaze with brilliantly colored wildflowers in spring.

Soon you reach the Deer Camp Fire Road junction in the grove of handsome white oaks. Continue 0.25 mile downhill on the Middle Burdell Fire Road to the preserve's central valley.

The next segment of the Bay Area Ridge Trail begins in Petaluma's Helen Putnam Regional Park. (See *Helen Putnam Regional Park to Petaluma Adobe State Historic Park.*)

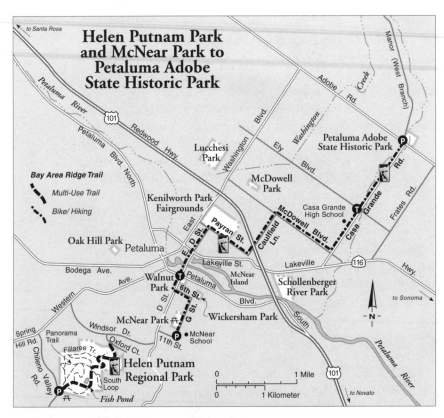

Helen Putnam Park and McNear Park to Petaluma Adobe State Historic Park

New leaves emerging on oak trees.

HELEN PUTNAM REGIONAL PARK AND McNEAR PARK TO PETALUMA ADOBE STATE HISTORIC PARK

From Helen Putnam Park to Oxford Street and from 11th & G Streets to Casa Grande/Adobe Roads

Length: 5.9 miles (includes 1.2 miles through Helen Putnam Park and 4.7 miles from McNear Park to Petaluma Adobe)

Accessibility: Hikers, bicyclists

Regulations: Helen Putnam Regional, McNear, and Walnut parks—Open daylight hours. Petaluma Adobe State Historic Park— Open 8 a.m. to 5 p.m. Entrance fee.

Facilities: Water and restrooms at Helen Putnam and McNear parks; water and restrooms at Petaluma Adobe.

THIS PLEASANT STROLL through a regional park and Petaluma's historic neighborhoods is rich in history. You'll pass restored Victorian houses around McNear and Walnut parks and cross the Petaluma River on a historic drawbridge to arrive at General Vallejo's adobe ranch. The relatively level sidewalks and bike lanes are shaded until you reach city limits along Casa Grande Road, where trees are few; you'll follow the paved road shoulder to reach Petaluma Adobe State Park, where a large eucalyptus grove awaits.

Getting There

By Car

West trailhead, Helen Putnam Regional Park: From Hwy. 101 take East Washington Blvd. exit. Continue on East Washington and cross the Petaluma River. Turn left on Petaluma Blvd. and right on Western Ave. Go 2 miles and turn left (south) on Chileno Valley Rd. Continue another mile to parking area.

McNear Park: From Hwy. 101 take East Washington Blvd. exit, go west on it to Payran St. and turn left (south), then turn right (west) on East D St. Turn left (south) on 6th St. and right (west) on G St. to parking along this street or on 11th and F streets.

East trailhead, Eucalyptus Grove, at Adobe Rd./Casa Grande Ave. intersection: From Hwy. 101 take East Washington Blvd. exit and go east on it to Adobe Rd. Turn right (south) and proceed to off-road parking at edge of a large eucalyptus forest on west side of road.

By Bus

Golden Gate Transit bus 80 to 4th and C streets daily.

On the Trail

In late fall 1995, the Bay Area Ridge Trail Council dedicated a trail in Helen Putnam Regional Park and the route from McNear Park to Petaluma Adobe State Park as an official segment of the Bay Area Ridge Trail.

The paved 1.2-mile trail through Helen Putnam Regional Park begins the southwest corner of the park near the playground and picnic area. It passes a cattail-lined fish pond and the creek that feeds it. The trail then heads northeast and rises 480 feet to the top of a pretty knoll that offers views of the surrounding hills and the town of Petaluma. The trail ends at Oxford Court but it is hoped that someday the short gap between Helen Putnam and McNear parks will be closed.

The next Bay Area Ridge Trail route begins at McNear Park on the corner of 11th and G streets. A small grove of redwoods shades the picnic tables, benches, and horseshoe pits on lush green lawns. Nearby are tennis courts and brightly colored slides, swings, and climbing apparatus for young children, with plenty of benches from which parents can supervise the juvenile scene.

Petaluma's "First Citizen"

Longtime Petaluma residents may remember McNear Park's benefactor, George P. McNear, who was born here in 1857. He gave the land for the park, as well as a handsome sum to maintain it. He also gave land for McNear School, just east of the park, and for a local golf course. George McNear was prominent in many civic affairs and played an important part in the poultry industry here, which earned Petaluma the name "Egg Basket of the World." In 1937, when McNear was an active 80 years old, a historian declared him "the first citizen of Petaluma."

Hikers and **bicyclists** leave the park, heading east along G Street. Opposite sides of the street offer sun or shade—take your pick depending on the day's weather. Turn left (north) on 6th Street and admire several large and handsome Victorian houses. Mature trees in well-kept gardens surrounded by picket fences cast shade over the sidewalk, welcome in summer.

At East D Street you go right (east) and pass more Victorians and the historic city post office. At the East D Street/South Petaluma Boulevard intersection, a few black walnut trees in Walnut Park remain to give credence to the park's name. In yet another of this city's many parks, you will find green lawns, benches, and picnic tables. From each of the park's four corners, a broad walkway leads to the charming, round bandstand in its center.

Side Trip to McNear Building

An optional two-block detour to the historic McNear Building heads north along South Petaluma Boulevard from the east side of Walnut Park. Petaluma's downtown has 99 buildings recorded in the National Register of Historic Paces. The McNear Building's graceful iron front is typical of the sheet- or cast-iron façades popular here in the 1880s and 1890s; they were prefabricated in San Francisco and shipped here by boat along the Petaluma River.

The Petaluma River was an important commerce route for other goods as well, beginning with the Gold Rush, when it was used to ship supplies for 49ers. Until 1950, grain and farm products were transported downriver to San Pablo Bay and San Francisco.

Continue along East D Street to the Petaluma River, just three blocks beyond Walnut Park. You cross the river on the historic D **109**

Street drawbridge, one of the oldest drawbridges still in use in California; its steel roadbed lifts for water craft too tall to pass under it. Vacationing boaters from San Francisco Bay often use the mooring and landing facility upstream of the bridge. As you cross the river, look downstream to McNear Island, zoned for eventual park use by the town's General Plan.

In the next half a mile, you go through a mixed commercial and residential neighborhood on East D Street. At the Sonoma-Marin Fairgrounds and Kenilworth Park on Payran Street, turn right (south) and continue for 0.5 mile to a shopping center on the corner of Caulfield Lane. Turn left (east) on Caulfield Lane, where you will find sidewalks on the north side of the street and bike lanes on both sides. New subdivisions fill the land on either side of the street, and tall fences and flowering plum trees line the sidewalks. Make a right turn (south) on McDowell Boulevard to find ranch style housing, wide bike lanes, and only a little shade.

At Casa Grande Road you turn left, continuing east past even newer subdivisions and the playing fields and sprawling buildings of Casa Grande High School. A planted median strip and new trees along the sidewalks continue until Ely Boulevard. You are now about a mile from La Casa Grande, General Mariano Vallejo's partially restored adobe ranch headquarters and the end point of this segment. Since crossing the Petaluma River, you have traveled over what was once part of Vallejo's vast land holdings. The Sonoma Mountains to the northeast, the land east to Sonoma Creek, and thousands of acres from the shores of San Pablo Bay north to Glen Ellen were part of Vallejo's huge Rancho Petaluma. Vallejo grazed Mexican longhorn cattle on his extensive acreage, raised sheep and goats, and grew a variety of crops to supply the ranch's needs. Today, some of the land along Casa Grande Road remains in agricultural use.

Your route rises toward the foothills, where California oaks, sycamores, and bay laurel trees fill gentle folds in the hillsides. You reach the state-owned eucalyptus grove, on your left at the southwest corner of Adobe and Casa Grande roads, the end of this Bay Area Ridge Trail trip. You may have left a shuttle car here at off-road parking on Adobe Road. If you are returning to McNear Park, you might enjoy a visit to Petaluma's riverside shops and restaurants on 2nd Street, just two blocks north of the Ridge Trail route on D Street.

Across busy Adobe Road is Vallejo's adobe ranch headquarters, where you can visit some of its rooms and learn the story of food and meat production in the days of the Mexican ranchos. Several picnic tables under mature trees, a running stream, and a monument to Vallejo enhance the grounds outside the adobe. Although your Petaluma trip ends here, you will traverse other lands in Vallejo's holdings as you circumnavigate the Bay Area on its ridgelines. (See Ridge Trail trips *Vallejo-Benicia Buffer* and *Benicia-Vallejo Waterfront.*)

The next leg of the Bay Area Ridge Trail starts in Jack London State Park near Glen Ellen on the other side of the Sonoma Mountains. As yet, the route to this park has not been designated. (See *Jack London State Historic Park.*)

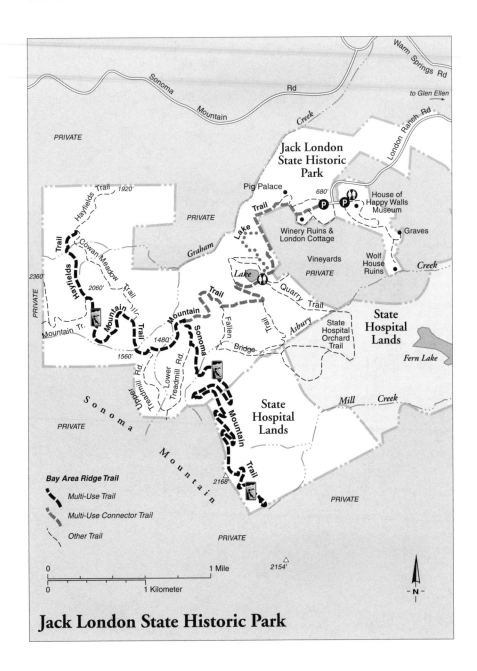

Jack London State Historic Park

JACK LONDON STATE HISTORIC PARK
From Sonoma Mountain Trail to Hayfields/Cowan Meadows Trails Junction

Length:	11.7 miles round trip (includes 4.4 miles round trip on connector trail, 4 miles round trip on Sonoma Mountain Trail, and 3.3 miles round trip to Hayfields/Cowan Meadows junction; additional 0.8 mile round trip to park's northeast boundary)
Accessibility:	Hikers, equestrians, bicyclists
Regulations:	Open 8 a.m. to dusk
Facilities:	Water, restrooms, and phone

JOIN A NEW LEG of the main Ridge Trail route—the Sonoma Mountain Trail—from a connector trail through redwood and oak forests. After an out-and-back trip on this new trail, follow the Ridge Trail along lively streams, through dense forests, and across scattered grasslands on the eastern flank of Sonoma Mountain. You'll travel wide park service roads and new, well-designed, narrow trails to reach lofty heights: a gain of 608 feet in elevation on the Sonoma Mountain Trail and 1220 feet on the Hayfields Trail, where you'll have grand views of the Valley of the Moon.

Getting There

From Hwy. 101 in Sonoma County, take Hwy. 12 to Glen Ellen, turn southwest on Arnold Drive. Turn left (west) on London Ranch Road to park entrance on left. Turn right to the western parking area.

On the Trail

Since there is no trailhead at the southern extension of the main Bay Area Ridge Trail, the first 2 miles of this trip follow connector trails (the Lake and Mountain trails) to meet the Ridge Trail route, the new Sonoma Mountain Trail, due to open in 2002. (Call park headquarters for particulars or check the Ridge Trail website. For the first year after its dedication, this segment will have seasonal closures while the trail compacts.)

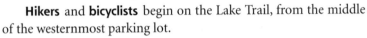

Hikers and **bicyclists** begin on the Lake Trail, from the middle of the westernmost parking lot.

Equestrians take the trail from the parking area's north corner and follow short paths through the trees to join the Lake Trail. Bear right on this park service road.

The multi-use Lake Trail skirts the north and west sides of a beautiful private vineyard, the vines of which add lovely shades of red and tawny gold to the fall scene. Once the prized vineyard of Jack London, who laid it out on stepped terraces, it still produces wine today. After 0.4 mile on the road, **hikers** can cut right onto a narrow trail through redwood and fir woods and then rejoin **bicyclists** and **equestrians** at the reed-rimmed lake, created by London for swimming, fishing, and poolside partying. Today, the lake's curving stone dam offers park visitors a sunny place to rest on their trek up the mountain.

Beyond the lake you turn right (due west) to join the Mountain Trail, which in 0.15 mile swings south through a cool, dark forest of redwoods and Douglas-firs. In openings where large redwoods were cut long ago, tanoaks, madrones, and big-leaf maples now fill the void. After climbing steadily for 0.2 mile, you reach a junction with the Fallen Bridge Trail, which goes left toward Asbury Creek. Mays Clearing lies before you, a wide meadow with fine views south over the valley and east to the mountains that rise above it. In fall, look for the clear red berries that hang from long tendrils of the native honeysuckle vine; in winter, white snowberries attract deer and birds, but are poisonous to humans.

Follow the Bay Area Ridge Trail sign that points the way right and uphill on the Mountain Trail. You climb through Woodcutters Meadow, where fallen tree limbs are strewn among scattered, moss-covered rocks, and clumps of California fescue and ferns wave in the breeze. As you pass the Upper Fallen Bridge Trail on the left, the trail swerves right to make a hairpin turn north, then south through

Swaths of blue lupine on the Sonoma Mountain Trail.

lovely Pine Tree Meadows. Filled with many native flowers in spring, especially purple iris, pink checkerbloom, and shiny yellow buttercups, this meadow is a delight to behold.

South Along the Sonoma Mountain Trail

Continue on the Mountain Trail as it swings right and climbs again through woods to reach the Sonoma Mountain Trail. Turn left to begin the out-and-back trip to the park's southern boundary. The trail heads generally south through a forest of Oregon white oak, California bay, and big-leaf maple, zigzagging on wide sweeps. Here and there, young Douglas-firs spring up in openings created by fallen trees. You cross the deep trough of Asbury Creek, lined by ferns and large-leafed, creamy-blossomed aralia.

Beyond the creek, small, lacy-leafed hazelnut trees and California buckeyes grow under a high canopy of magnificent deciduous Oregon white oaks. In spring, large candles of buckeye blossoms, white to light pink, fill the air with their fragrance. Numerous specimens of hound's tongue, a tall, blue-blossomed cousin of forget-me-not (in the Borage family) grow along the trail. You may also see mission bells nodding their bell-shaped heads—deep purple and greenish spotted—a special springtime treat.

115

Low walls demarcate this carefully designed trail, constructed from rocks and downed tree logs that trail builders removed to smooth the trail surface. From a few clearings, you can see Fern Lake and the red-roofed buildings of the developmental center in the valley below. A ring of mountains encloses the valley, and almost due north, Mt. St. Helena rises to 4344 feet. From another opening you can look back northwest to 2463-foot Sonoma Mountain, topped by its radio transmitter tower.

The trail sweeps widely to the west and then east; you then head due south through the forest and into the Sonoma Developmental Center property. A sign announces the trail's name and its builders—crews of volunteers and California Conservation Corps members under the able direction of park ranger, Toni McRorie. Now on the second leg of the Sonoma Mountain Trail, at about 2000 feet, you follow several small switchbacks in and out of the forest. In spring, flowers bloom in small sunny meadows—deep blue lupines, purple-tufted brodiaea, and tiny pink linanthus. Bring your wildflower book to identify the glorious specimens. From a wide clearing, you can see the Napa River to the east, where it flows through the marshlands to San Pablo Bay. Mt. Diablo rises beyond, easily visible on a clear day.

Just after crossing the indistinct track of an old road on your left, you come to the south boundary of the developmental center. Beyond is private property—DO NOT ENTER! Loop to the right on a short trail and retrace your route to the junction with the Mountain Trail, which you left some 2 miles back.

North to Hayfields/Cowan Meadows Trails Junction

At the Sonoma Mountain/Mountain trails junction, turn left from the Sonoma Mountain Trail or continue straight on the Mountain Trail if you skipped the Sonoma Mountain Trail round trip. Shortly you cross South Graham Creek; in winter and spring it may overflow onto the road, but you can usually rock-hop across. In the rainy season, rushing water cascades over rocks in a moist, fern-clad canyon upstream. Bear right at the junction with Upper Treadmill Road, continuing on the Mountain Trail for 0.1 mile to Middle Graham Creek. After crossing the creek, you come to a rest area with a picnic table. Ferns grace the trail banks beneath large redwoods, and hazelnut leaves glow golden against the dark redwood trunks in fall.

Just 0.2 mile beyond the rest area, and after a third Graham Creek crossing, you reach the Mountain/Cowan Meadows trails junction. Your multi-use Ridge Trail route stays on the Mountain Trail, swinging left and gaining more than 400 feet in elevation in 0.65 mile. You pass another vista point with views south to a tree-topped knoll and west toward the Sonoma Mountain summit. Bear right at the next junction, on the Hayfields Trail. After 0.2 mile, you begin to descend rapidly for another 0.2 mile, north toward the marshy confluence of three arms of North Graham Creek and the upper junction with the Cowan Meadows Trail. The Ridge Trail ends here, as of this writing, but you can continue 0.4 mile northeast under the powerlines to the park boundary at about 1920 feet.

Your return descent is speedier than your ascent, and you soon reach the historic buildings of the former Jack London ranch.

Jack London's Beauty Ranch

No trip to this park is complete without a visit to Beauty Ranch, Jack London's cherished estate. By 1876, London had already achieved international fame for his adventure stories *Call of the Wild* and *The Sea Wolf*. Jack and his wife moved to Sonoma Valley to escape busy city life and began work on Beauty Ranch. Over the remaining years of his life, he embarked on continual projects to improve the land and repair or construct buildings.

The 0.5-mile Beauty Ranch Trail leads to the ranch buildings, the winery and distillery, and the House of Happy Walls, built by Charmian London after Jack's death. Charmian lived at the ranch until her death at the age of 84, after which the House of Happy Walls became a museum with artifacts of the London legend; today it is also the park visitor center. Jack London's gravesite is 0.45 mile by trail from the House of Happy Walls. Follow the park road just 0.15 mile beyond to the handsome rock walls of Wolf House, all that remains of the London's dream house. In 1959 the state acquired some 40 acres of the original ranch; today, Jack London State Park has expanded to over 800 acres.

In the future, proposed trails will connect this Bay Area Ridge Trail segment to segments in Petaluma to the south, and Annadel and Sugarloaf Ridge state parks to the north. For now, the next segment begins 7 miles north in Annadel State Park. (See *Annadel State Park*.)

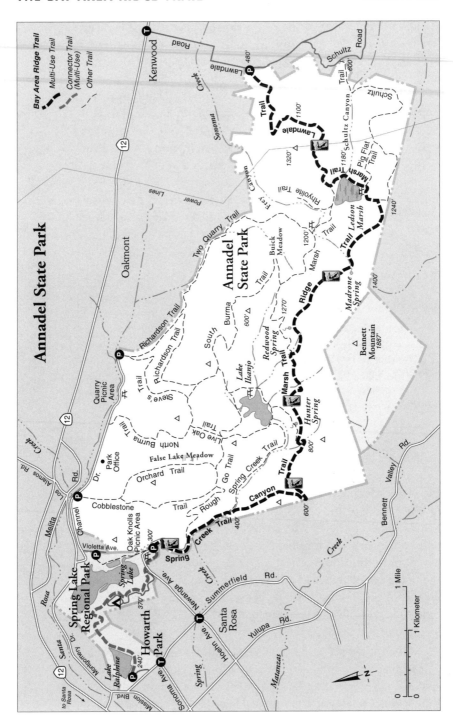

Annadel State Park

ANNADEL STATE PARK
From Spring Lake Park to Annadel Park East Gate at Lawndale Road

Length: 9 miles

Accessibility: Hikers, equestrians, bicyclists (Trails not suitable for road bicycles or inexperienced riders.)

Regulations: Spring Lake Park—Open 8 a.m. to sunset. Entrance fee.
Annadel State Park—Open sunrise to sunset. No dogs on trails. Bicyclists must observe state park rules.

Facilities: Water, restrooms, and phone at Oak Knolls Picnic Area in Spring Lake Park; water and restrooms at Channel Dr. parking lot and restrooms at Lake Ilsanjo and at Marsh/Two Quarry trails intersection in Annadel State Park.

G RADUALLY CLIMB OVER GRASSY HILLSIDES and through oak woodlands and conifer forests on the west side of Bennett Mountain along wide, rocky service roads. You gain 1100 feet and then lose 1000 feet as you descend past spring-fed meadows on a new, well-graded trail to Annadel's east side. West- and south-facing slopes can be hot in summer; north- and east-facing slopes are forested.

Getting There

West trailhead, Spring Lake Park: From Hwy. 101 in Santa Rosa, take Hwy. 12 east. At Farmers Lane (marked Hwy. 12), continue straight onto Hoen Ave. and pass Summerfield Rd. Turn onto first street on left (Newanga Dr.), and follow Newanga Dr. as it veers right after one block. Continue to Spring Lake Park entrance and go right to parking at Oak Knolls Picnic Area.

East trailhead, Lawndale Rd.: From Hwy. 101 in Santa Rosa, take Hwy. 12 east about 9 miles, then turn right (south) on Lawndale Rd. and continue about 1.5 miles to small parking area on right side of road.

On the Trail

Two local parks are connected by trail to Annadel State Park—Howarth City Park and Spring Lake County Park. This trip begins in Spring Lake Park at the Oak Knolls Picnic Area and follows a graveled road due south on the levee beside Spring Creek. In summer the creek is dry, but in winter water flows from the northwest side of Bennett Mountain through Annadel State Park to the flood-control basin of Spring Lake. The levee trail, much favored by local bicyclists, hikers, and equestrians, runs along the base of a west-facing hillside, just outside Annadel State Park's boundary.

After half a mile, the trail crosses the creek and then continues another 0.3 mile to the Annadel State Park boundary. You cross a concrete weir for Spring Creek flood control and go straight ahead to enter an oak-and-buckeye woodland on the Canyon Trail in Annadel State Park's 5000 wilderness acres. The stone foundations on your right are all that remain of a cabin built by one Dr. Summerfield, a former owner of this land. Annadel State Park was once part of Rancho Los Guilicos, granted in 1839 to a Scottish sea captain, John Wilson. Wilson was married to Ramona Carrillo de Pacheco. Since he was away at sea most of the time, his nearly 19,000 acres remained relatively untouched.

You continue on the wide, rocky Canyon Trail and emerge from the shady forest into a gentle valley. Ahead you see the low, rounded ridge of Taylor Mountain with the large homes of a nearby subdivision in the foreground. After you make a hairpin turn to the left, your uphill way begins in earnest. From the open hillside you look north to Spring Lake and beyond to Rincon Valley. On clear days, Mt. St. Helena's long shoulder and its taller, prominent left hump, is visible in the distant north. Looking south from this trail at 1000 feet, you see Bennett Mountain's 1887-foot summit just outside the

Land of the Bitakomtara

Native American tribes were the first inhabitants of the land this Bay Area Ridge Trail segment traverses. The Bitakomtara, a southern group of Pomos, occupied approximately 200 square miles in the Santa Rosa area, from Laguna de Santa Rosa east to Sonoma Creek, and south from Mark West Creek nearly to Cotati. Probably about 20 tribelets lived in the area, and each spoke a slightly different dialect.

The Bitakomtara lived well on this land, harvesting acorns from several species of oaks, fishing the creeks, and hunting or trapping game, especially deer, squirrels, and rabbits. Many years have passed, but little has changed this lands' meadows and woods since then. You will find a near wilderness here, especially on remote sections of the Bay Area Ridge Trail route. Oak trees stud the hillsides and their acorns litter the trails, springs feed bubbling creeks, and the bulbs, berries, seeds, and grains that Native Americans harvested grow in meadows and forests.

park. If you come here in late March or early April, you may find the rare white fritillary blooming in moist grasslands.

After 1.8 miles on the Canyon Trail, you reach a junction with the Marsh Trail. Make a sharp right turn and continue climbing on the re-designed, narrower Marsh Trail. You'll see splendid examples of northern oak woodlands made up of Oregon white oaks, black oaks, buckeyes, and occasional manzanitas along this trail. Beautiful, lush stands of California fescue, a native gray-green bunchgrass with tall, graceful stalks and feathery flower heads, fill the spaces between rounded, moss-covered boulders on the forest floor. The Pomo people collected fescue seeds for food.

In the shade of redwoods and Douglas-firs, with soft duff underfoot, you cross the headwaters of Spring Creek. Here, where ferns drape the road banks and redwoods tower overhead, a quiet serenity seems to prevail. You proceed through the forest, and after 1.3 miles on the Marsh Trail, reach a junction with the newly re-aligned Ridge Trail. Make a sharp right turn onto the 2.7-mile Ridge Trail, formerly Upper Steve's Trail, and head south on a gentle grade. A high forest canopy arches over skeletons of huge manzanitas, and in moist places, spring blossoms of scarlet columbine stand one-to-three feet tall.

You enter a woods of oak and buckeye and curve around the head of an intermittent stream, traveling due east. As you cross rivulets and streams on this trail, notice that the drainages are **121** covered with large flat-topped rocks which replace former culverts. Known as armored drains, these wide, gently scooped-out aprons are easier to maintain and are more pleasant to cross in all seasons.

You emerge from the woods and skirt a sloping meadow southwest of Ledson Marsh; the meadow grasses are golden in summer and vivid green in winter and spring. You see the results of a controlled burn conducted here in 1994: oaks and manzanita survived the fire well, manzanita and toyon have root-sprouted, and spring wildflowers and bunchgrasses fill the meadow after winter rains.

Oregon white and California black oaks dot your route through the grasslands. Some of these trees are over 200 years old; although they continue to set seed, an overabundance of rodents—mice, voles, and squirrels—that eat the acorns are preventing the oaks from regenerating. Hawks, owls, and coyotes are the rodents' natural predators. You cross a historic rock wall that marks the boundary of early landowners. These rocks, and those strewn about the hillsides, are mostly basalt, an igneous rock of the Pliocene Age Sonoma Volcanics formation that is found throughout the Sonoma and Mayacmas Mountains.

From your vantage point at 1198 feet, look northeast across the meadows and Ledson Marsh to 2730-foot Hood Mountain, named in honor of William Hood, who owned Rancho Los Guilicos for almost 30 years. Just east of Hood Mountain lies 2729-foot Bald Mountain (on the Bay Area Ridge Trail route through Sugarloaf Ridge State Park). Lower Red Mountain, immediately west of Sugarloaf Ridge State Park on private property, is easily recognized by its unusual color.

The Ridge Trail ends and you turn left (north) on the Marsh Trail toward Ledson Marsh. In 0.2 mile you reach a picnic table under a huge, double-trunked oak and flanked by three large manzanitas. This shady spot offers fine views of the reed-rimmed marsh and your route across the meadow above it. In fall, the reeds' gold and brown tones present a subdued contrast to the dark green woods.

When you feel refreshed, rejoin the Marsh Trail and pass the Pig Flat Trail junction. Continue 0.3 mile around the east side of the marsh and cross a bridge over the outlet stream; a low dam contains winter run-off from the surrounding hillsides. When summer's heat prevails, the marsh dries up. Continue through a veritable coyote-bush forest (*baccharis*), accented by a few struggling live and blue oaks, to another junction on the north side of the marsh. Then

Oregon white oaks shade the Marsh Trail.

swing right onto the Lawndale Trail, here a rocky road, to begin your descent to the park's east entrance.

In the next 0.3 mile, look for piles of dark basalt rock, remains of late 19th century cobblestone quarrying. European immigrants chipped and shaped basalt rocks into paving stones and sent them by barge and train to San Francisco. Cobblestone quarrying was a thriving industry until modern auto users preferred smoother rides.

On the final leg of this Ridge Trail trip, watch for a left turn onto the new, 2.1-mile section of the Lawndale Trail. This well-designed trail was built by state park ranger, Toni McRorie and volunteers. It ambles through a redwood-and-fir forest, following a gentle downhill slope. A study of fire ecology has left black scars on some redwoods, although the trees are still alive. Upon leaving the wooded area, you traverse a south-facing hillside in a grassy canyon and go through a gate at the Lawndale Road parking area.

After your trip, stop in at the park office to see an exhibit of quarrying done by the Pomo people, who shaped obsidian into arrowheads, knives, scrapers, and spearheads. Since these artifacts are significant clues to the Native American culture, visitors are asked to leave them intact.

The next leg of the Bay Area Ridge Trail begins in Sugarloaf Ridge State Park, about 6 miles northeast of this parking area. (See *Sugarloaf Ridge State Park*.)

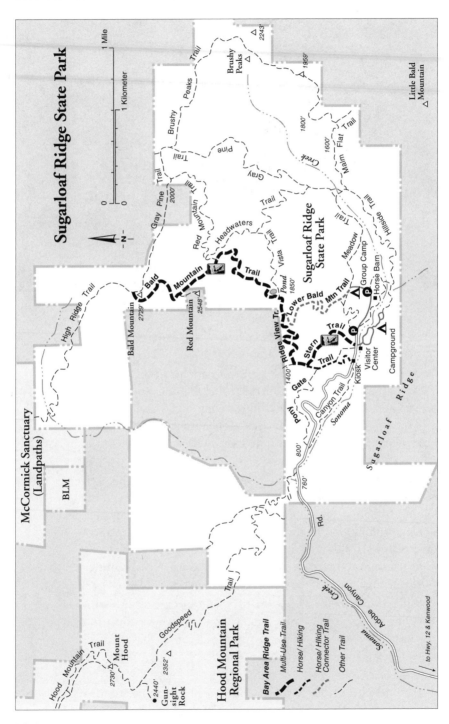

Sugarloaf Ridge State Park

1 Mile

1 Kilometer

△ 2243'

Brushy Peaks

△ 1959'

Little Bald △ Mountain

Brushy Peaks Trail

1800'

Pine Trail

1600'

Gray Pine Trail

2000'

Gray Creek

Malm Flat Trail

Red Mountain Trail

Headwaters

Trail

Sugarloaf Ridge State Park

Hillside Trail

Bald Mountain Trail

Pond Vista Trail

1850'

Meadow Trail

High Ridge Trail

△ Bald Mountain 2729'

Red Mountain △ 2548'

Lower Bald Mtn Trail

Group Camp

P Horse Barn

Ridge View Tr.

1400'

Stern Trail

P

Visitor Center

△ Campground

McCormick Sanctuary (Landpaths)

Gate

Pony Trail

Canyon Trail

Kiosk

Sonoma

BLM

800'

Sugarloaf Ridge

760'

Rd.

Sonoma Creek

Adobe Canyon

to Hwy. 12 & Kenwood →

Hood Mountain Trail

Goodspeed Trail

Mount Hood

2730' △

△ 2352'

• 2440' Gun-sight Rock

Hood Mountain Regional Park

Trail

Bay Area Ridge Trail

Multi-Use Trail

Horse/ Hiking

Horse/ Hiking Connector Trail

Other Trail

SUGARLOAF RIDGE STATE PARK
From Visitor Center to Bald Mountain Summit

Length:	5.4 miles round trip; 6.7 miles using hikers' alternate return
Accessibility:	Hikers, equestrians, bicyclists
Regulations:	No dogs on trails. Entrance fee.
Facilities:	Water and restrooms. Phone at visitor center.

A CHALLENGING 1550-FOOT CLIMB from an enclosed, remote valley to the top of Bald Mountain, where you'll take in far-flung views of Northern California. Cross oak woodlands and chaparral slopes and detour to a seasonal vernal pool on wide service roads with a short paved segment. These trails are hot in summer.

Getting There

From Hwy. 12 east of Santa Rosa or northwest of Kenwood, turn north on Adobe Canyon Rd., and continue to end. Parking area is on left after park entrance kiosk and visitor center. Horse trailers park just past barn 0.5 mile beyond kiosk.

On the Trail

Equestrians ride from the barn to the group campsite parking area to join the Lower Bald Mountain Trail. Go west, uphill, and meet the hiker and bicyclist route at the Bald Mountain Trail.

Hikers and **bicyclists** start this trip on the Stern Trail, just across the entrance road from the visitor center. The wide Stern Trail heads uphill (northwest) through grasslands and past scattered clumps of scrub oak. When you meet the Bald Mountain Trail, look west over the Sonoma Creek canyon to ridge after ridge of coastal mountains that stretch to the sea. When early morning fog lies in the interior valleys, the ridgetops peek out, giving the effect of islands rising from misty inland seas. Conical-shaped Hood Mountain rises to the northwest—at 2750 feet, it is the highest point in neighboring Hood Mountain Regional Park. Due south beyond the park's boundary is the rugged linear ridge from which Sugarloaf Ridge State Park takes its name. The bare rock columns on its north face are remnants of nearby Mt. St. Helena's volcanic activity some seven million years ago.

Turn right on the Bald Mountain Trail, a paved road built for service vehicle access to the microwave station on Red Mountain. Go around a metal gate across the road and begin your ascent in earnest. The road cuts reveal large veins of bluish-green serpentine, California's state rock and an indicator of fault zones. The St. John's Mountain Fault crosses this mountain.

High road banks and modest oak-fir-madrone woodlands offer much-needed shade on summer mornings. In spring, clumps of iris brighten the road with lavender or cream blossoms. Apricot-colored sticky monkeyflowers, purple asters, and the tawny, two-foot flower stalks of native bunchgrass last into summer.

In less than half a mile, you reach the junction with the Lower Bald Mountain Trail, where equestrians join the main Ridge Trail route. On clear days, you can see south to Mt. Tamalpais in Marin County. Below you are the park's meadows, barns and visitor center.

Hikers, equestrians, and **bicyclists** continue steadily uphill on the Bald Mountain Trail. You pass the Vista Trail, on which a short detour takes you to a lovely vernal pool. When winter rains fill this seasonal wetland, a unique community of plants blooms; as the water recedes, they die in concentric rings. Enjoy the pool from the trail and respect its fragile environment.

Return to the Bald Mountain Trail, where the vegetation alternates between woodland and chaparral, depending on soil and exposure. Chaparral covers the slopes on south-facing stretches of the trail. Farther uphill, oaks and madrones fill little ravines, often accompanied by bay trees. The oaks and madrones on these hillsides are old-growth trees, unlike the hardwood forest in the valley below, which was stripped by a settler in the 1880s. He burned the wood to make charcoal and sold it to heat homes and run steam engines in nearby communities.

Sugarloaf Ridge History

There is evidence of Native American habitation here since about 5000 B.C. The most recent peoples were the Wappos, whose village was called Wilikos. Their firm resistance to the intruding Spaniards earned them the name *Wappo*, a derivative of the Spanish word for brave or handsome, *guapo*. However, weakened by cholera and smallpox, their numbers diminished and they were eventually relocated to a Pomo reservation. The last full-blooded Wappo died in 1909.

The Spaniards ran cattle on these hills before the arrival of the first settlers in 1867. Farming was not successful here, and in 1920 the State of California purchased these lands for a reservoir, which never materialized. Later, Sonoma State Hospital built a swimming pool and cookhouse for a summer camp program. Finally, in 1964 this land became part of the California State Park System.

Turn back as you climb to look over this steep, rugged terrain. There is little agricultural activity in these mountains, except for a large vineyard just outside the southern boundary of the park and a few large ranches to the west. Instead, many acres of this land are public open space, including this 2700-acre park—Sugarloaf Ridge State Park—and Hood Mountain Regional Park, just west of here.

Continue upward on the paved road, around bends that head into small ravines. At about 2200 feet, you pass the Red Mountain Trail and begin to see black oaks and big-leaf maple trees on the east-facing slopes that drain into Sonoma Creek's headwaters. Across a steep ravine to the northeast, you see the grass and brush-covered slopes of the park's northern ridge, along which the Gray Pine Trail extends to meet the Brushy Peaks Trail.

You leave the paved road where it turns sharply left to ascend private Red Mountain. Your route, still the Bald Mountain Trail, goes right and then immediately left. You descend a very steep dirt road and then traverse open, sloping grasslands dotted with bright wildflowers in spring and glowing, rosy-red buckwheat in fall.

A short half a mile from the turnoff you round the north side of Bald Mountain's summit and reach the junction with the High Ridge and Gray Pine trails. The former heads downhill, a tempting direction after the last upward pitch; but you take the Gray Pine Trail right for about 100 yards and then go right again to reach the rounded, bare summit. An exhilarating 360-degree sweep around the compass greets you. Two vista displays identify (clockwise from San Francisco): the towers of the Golden Gate Bridge, Mt.

127

View from Bald Mountain.

Tamalpais, the Sonoma hills, Mt. St. Helena, long Blue Ridge between Napa County and the Central Valley, Mt. Diablo, and then San Francisco. Even Snow Mountain to the north and the Sierra Nevada to the east are visible on a clear winter day. With Northern California at your feet, this is a pleasant place for a picnic. For a view north to Mt. St. Helena, find a protected shelf just below the summit.

Since the Bay Area Ridge Trail route between this park and the next completed segment in Napa County (see *Skyline Wilderness Park*) is not determined, you must return to the trailhead in Sugarloaf Ridge State Park—the downhill trip is faster.

Hikers can combine the Gray Pine and Meadow trails for an interesting and extended return trip.

SKYLINE
WILDERNESS PARK
From Park Entrance to
South Boundary

Length: 8.8 miles round trip

Accessibility: Hikers, equestrians, bicyclists

Regulations: Open 9 a.m. to 1 hour before sunset, Monday
to Thursday; 8 a.m. to 1 hour before sunset,
Friday, Saturday, and Sunday. Closed on
Christmas day. Entrance fee. No dogs.

Facilities: Water and restrooms at picnic area near park
entrance.

A FTER A STEEP CLIMB in the first mile, this trail ambles
through oak forests and high grasslands to views of North
Bay marshes and mountains, and then follows a perennial stream to
the eastern edge of the park. The narrow, rocky trail can be hot in
summer and is best suited for hardy hikers and careful equestrians
and bicyclists.

Getting There

From Hwy. 29 south of Napa, turn east on Imola Ave. Look for
the park entrance on the right (south) about 1 mile beyond Napa
State Hospital.

On the Trail

Skyline Wilderness Park was established in 1980 when 900 acres
of Napa State Hospital grounds were declared surplus by the State
of California. A dedicated local group formed the nonprofit Skyline
Park Citizens Association to preserve the beautiful Marie Creek
Canyon and its surrounding watershed. The association leases the

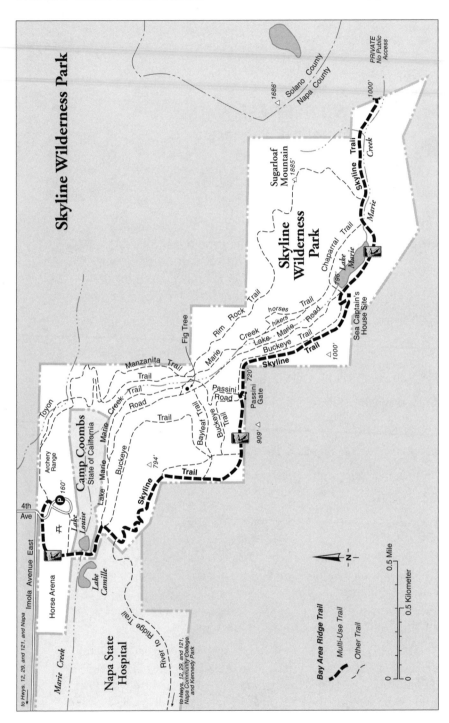

Skyline Wilderness Park

Skyline Wilderness Park

Sugarloaf Mountain
△ 1885'

Solano County
Napa County

△ 1686'

PRIVATE
No Public
Access

1000'

Skyline Trail

Marie Creek

Chaparral Trail

Lake Marie

Sea Captain's
House Site

Rim Rock Trail

Fig Tree

Marie Creek Trail

horses Trail
hikers

Lake Marie Road

Buckeye Trail

Skyline Trail

△ 1000'

Manzanita Trail

Trail

Creek Trail

Road

Trail

Passini Road

Passini Gate

720'

Bayleaf Trail

Buckeye Trail

909' △

Toyon

Archery Range

Camp Coombs
State of California

Buckeye Lake Marie Creek

Skyline Trail

△ 794'

Skyline Trail

Lake Louise

160'

4th Ave

Napa State
Hospital

Horse Arena

Lake Camille

Marie Creek

River to Ridge Trail

to Hwys. 12, 29, and 121, and Napa

Imola Avenue East

to Hwys. 12, 29, and 121,
Napa Community College
and Kennedy Park

N

Bay Area Ridge Trail

Multi-Use Trail

Other Trail

0.5 Mile

0.5 Kilometer

0

0

land from the state and county and manages these foothill forests and grasslands for public enjoyment. Many trails crisscross the park, including one to Sugarloaf Mountain, the park's highest point at 1685 feet. The Skyline Trail, the designated Bay Area Ridge Trail route, reaches the southeastern park boundary near the Solano County line and is the park's longest trail. Plan for an 8+-mile round trip, take plenty of water, and start early, especially on warm days.

Hikers, **equestrians**, and **bicyclists** begin this trip on the graveled Lake Marie Road that leaves from the picnic area near the park entrance. Cross the fenced causeway between Lake Louise and Lake Camille, two ponds that are still part of the State Hospital grounds. You follow the road as it bends left (east), and about 600 feet beyond the Buckeye Trail, you turn right (southwest) onto the Skyline Trail.

The Skyline Trail zigzags up a steep hill studded with volcanic rock outcrops. At each bend west, the trail comes close to a low wall built of these rocks in early ranching days. In spring, bright orange, yellow, and blue native wildflowers accent the green grasslands; in summer, golden oats contrast with the dark lichen-covered rocks.

After an elevation gain of almost 600 feet in less than a mile, the trail straightens and levels off a bit as it enters an oak-and-buckeye woods. You head south now, with lovely views of the Napa marshlands at the edge of San Francisco Bay and majestic Mt. Tamalpais beyond. The open jaw of an immense rock quarry gnaws close to the park boundary, a less attractive view.

Past the left-branching Bayleaf Trail (you stay right on the Skyline Trail past all junctions on the outward-bound trip), you reach a high grassy meadow, where you'll see the light-pink blooms of bitterroot (Montana state flower) in spring. Although bitterroot implies an unpleasant taste, California Indians considered it a delicacy when peeled and cooked.

The trail veers east through chaparral shrubs and ubiquitous poison oak and traces the contour of the hillside. It then heads downhill and crosses a spur of Lake Marie Road which enters a private holding outside the park. You start climbing to the high grasslands at the western edge of the park. On clear days, you can see chaparral-covered Mt. George due north and Mt. Tamalpais in the southwest. Hawks and scrub jays, woodpeckers and towhees are just a few of the many birds that the quiet hiker can observe in this wilderness park. You may also see the prints of many animals— deer, raccoons, bobcats, and even feral pigs in the path's soft dirt.

Just over 2 miles from the trailhead, you traverse a steep hillside above the deep cleft of perennial Marie Creek that lies between you and 1630-foot Sugarloaf Mountain. Ferns festoon the trailside in this dense forest. Then, in a small clearing, you come upon the skeleton of a house—a tall chimney and stonework foundations. Although known as the Sea Captain's House, local historians say that it was originally built for the gatekeeper who tended the dam at Lake Marie, just a few hundred feet below. When the state decided it no longer needed the gatekeeper, it took down his house.

The Chaparral Trail branches left to the lake, but you continue on the Skyline Trail, along an old, rocky roadbed through a mature oak-and-fir forest. You then descend to cross the creek upstream from the lake. On the north side of Marie Creek, look for some boulders to perch on while eating your knapsack lunch. This beautiful, remote wilderness truly befits the park's name.

Continue on the Skyline Trail for the next 1.1 miles. (Note another left turnoff (northwest) for the Chaparral Trail, an alternate return route.) You follow meandering Marie Creek, and skirt a sloping meadow to cross a tributary creek. On a gentle forest path, you soon reach the end of the trail at a locked gate.

Retrace your steps along the route you just followed or return to the trailhead by any of several other trails. The Chaparral and Marie Creek trails (hikers only) and Lake Marie Road (multi-use) return through the valley.

The proposed "River to Ridge Trail" will soon connect the Skyline Trail to other Bay Area Ridge Trail segments in Solano County. For now, the next segment of the Bay Area Ridge Trail begins in the hills west of Fairfield. (See *Rockville Hills Community Park.*)

ROCKVILLE HILLS COMMUNITY PARK
From North Entrance to Green Valley Road

Length: 7 miles round trip

Accessibility: Hikers, bicyclists

Regulations: Open 8 a.m. to dusk. Bicyclists must wear helmets, stay on trails, and yield to hikers. Horses not allowed in park.

Facilities: None

C LIMB GENTLY THROUGH THESE VOLCANIC ROCK HILLS to a remote, grassy valley with a great stand of blue oaks. On your descent, you'll have views of Mt. Diablo, Elkhorn Peak, and the Twin Sisters. Most trees in the park are deciduous, so on a winter day these trails can be comfortably sunny, yet in summer, the predominant blue-oak forest offers welcome shade. This trip begins on a paved road, then travels wide, unpaved service roads to a paved trail through a private subdivision.

Getting There

North trailhead: From I-80 take Suisun Valley exit and go north on Suisun Valley Rd. Pass Solano Community College and turn left on Rockville Rd. Rockville Hills parking area is on left after 0.8 miles. The main Bay Area Ridge Trail route begins from the north trailhead, 0.6 miles farther on Rockville Rd., at a gated entrance on the south side of the road; off-road parking on either side.

South trailhead: There is no parking at the end of the trail on Green Valley Rd.

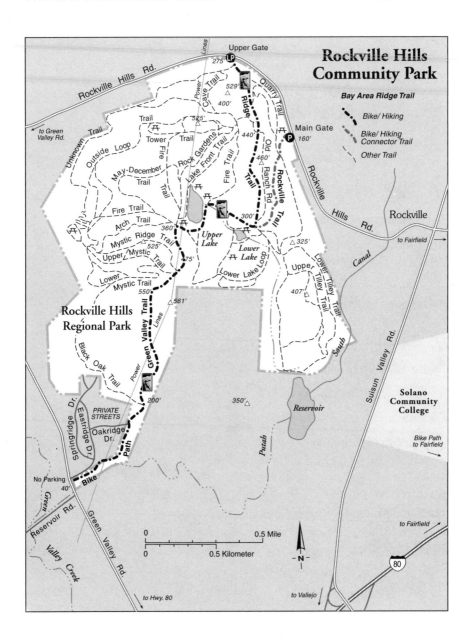

Rockville Hills
Community Park

Bay Area Ridge Trail

Bike/ Hiking

Bike/ Hiking
Connector Trail

Other Trail

The Creation of a Park

Rockville Hills Community Park was once part of a large cattle ranch owned by the Masons, a local ranching family. In the 1970s, the City of Fairfield bought these rocky, wooded highlands to build a golf course. The city laid out golf-cart paths on the hills and in the interior valleys and improved existing stock ponds for irrigation, but Fairfield citizens defeated a bond issue to fund further development of the golf-course, and the land became a city park instead. The Solano County Farmlands and Open Space Foundation took over the management of the 600-acre park in 1991, and installed picnic tables on shady knolls and beside level lakeside lookouts.

The Crossroads Settlement of Rockville

The settlement of Rockville once lay on the old stage route between Benicia and Sacramento. In the early 1850s, it was nothing more than a group of summer encampments where settlers attended prayer meetings. Locals sought a more permanent prayer house and contributed money and volunteer labor to build a church, on land given by an early pioneer family. The stone walls, quarried in the Rockville Hills, withstood the 1906 earthquake, but fell into disrepair in the 1920s; in 1940, the church was restored as a pioneer monument. Today it stands just north of the Suisun Valley and Rockville Hills crossroads in the Rockville Public Cemetery, shaded by ancient oaks.

On the Trail

If you parked at the Rockville Hills Community Park fenced parking area, you begin this trip on a 0.5-mile connector trail that ascends to meet the main Bay Area Ridge Trail route about a mile from its start. To follow this Ridge Trail segment in full, park at the north trailhead on Rockville Road.

Three trails begin from the north entrance. The main Bay Area Ridge Trail route follows the wide, paved road on the left, which ascends through trailside cover of red-berried toyon, shiny-leafed, mahogany-trunked manzanita, and shrubby coyote bush. Live oaks cling to steep hillsides above and below the trail, offering shade on warm days. In late spring, blue Douglas iris and light-orange sticky monkeyflower fill the banks with color.

You climb around a northeast-facing hillside and pass a couple of left-branching trails to the main parking area, potential alternate connectors to this route. You stay on the paved trail and soon have views south across the farmlands to Suisun Bay and its fleet of unused, decommissioned Navy vessels moored there—the mothball fleet. The low Potrero Hills lie northeast of the Suisun Bay marshes, partially surrounded by Rush Ranch, a 2000-acre estuarine nature preserve of the Solano County Farmlands and Open Space Foundation. In addition to protecting and restoring marshland and riparian habitats, this foundation strives to conserve agricultural lands and preserve key open space lands between Solano County's established communities.

You pass a right-branching trail and continue on the paved road beneath sizable deciduous white oaks; their great branches arch over the trail to provide filtered shade. At the crest of the hill, look west to see a high, rocky ridge topped by tall towers supporting ribbons of electric transmission lines. The park's central valley lies between this ridge and your trail.

As you descend past some very large specimens of manzanita, you look down at the lakes nestled among stands of mature blue oaks. David Douglas, a botanist in the early days of western-states plant collecting, first identified these blue oaks, a species unique in that it can withstand the high summer temperatures and scant rainfall of these Inner Coast Range foothills. When blue oaks begin to leaf out in late spring, their thick, slightly lobed leaves take on the blue-gray color their name indicates.

About 1 mile from the trailhead, you meet the connector trail to the main parking area that joins your trail from the left. A picnic site in a knoll-top grove of blue oaks offers vistas over the surrounding plain. The Bay Area Ridge Trail route swings right (west) from the junction and heads into grasslands on an unpaved trail. You pass close to Lower Lake and continue toward Upper Lake, your way brightened by masses of spring wildflowers, including low-growing daisy-like goldfields, bright yellow Johnny-jump-ups, and tall blue brodiaea.

At the top of Upper Lake's low dam, you may find tame, year-round resident ducks and geese, which swim and waddle toward any hapless visitor who spreads out lunch at lakeside tables. Migratory water birds, winter visitors only, are less sociable. Birds of the surrounding blue-oak woodland—acorn woodpeckers, flickers, and western bluebirds—are even less interested in visitors, but their bright plumage will reward you with quick displays of color.

From the dam you can look across the lake to the rocky cliffs that form the backbone of the park. This rock formation, known as Sonoma Volcanics, is made up of undifferentiated volcanic and sedimentary rocks, ash, basalt and andesite, dating from the late

Miocene and Pliocene epochs, some two to ten million years ago. Rockville Hills Park marks the southern limit of a 40-mile-long band of Sonoma Volcanics.

Bear left at Upper Lake to follow the trail along the east side of the lake; pass one left-branching trail and veer right around the south end of the lake. At a second trail intersection, you turn left to follow the Ridge Trail route toward the Green Valley trailhead.

Side Trip to "Magic Valley"

For a short, delightful side trip into "Magic Valley," continue straight ahead at the Green Valley trailhead sign. Immense live oaks co-exist with valley and blue oaks at the base of these north-facing slopes. You continue past a left-branching trail and veer south to reach a picnic table on a knoll overlooking Green Valley. The trail then turns east to rejoin the Ridge Trail, about 1 mile from the beginning of the "Magic Valley" side trip.

After a short, steep ascent, the trail reaches the ridgetop and levels off in a saddle. It then drops down to the Green Valley gate, which marks the entrance to a one-hundred-acre donation from the adjoining subdivision developer. Go through the gate to a narrow trail on a thickly wooded, steep slope. Shiny-faced buttercups on tall stems herald spring here, and poppies last into summer.

You emerge on a high, treeless plateau, where you look due south to the 3849-foot summit of Mt. Diablo, rising prominently above the surrounding plain. Overhead, hawks circle lazily, searching the grasslands for their prey of mice, voles, and gophers. With luck, you may spot a pair of black-shouldered kites, frequent visitors to this area, identifiable by their long white tails and sharply pointed wings.

The trail veers right and then shortly bends left (south), across the plateau. If you continue straight (west) at this bend, you reach the edge of the plateau. From here, you have an uninterrupted view of Green Valley's lush fields; the mountains that serve as a natural boundary between Napa and Solano counties rise in the background. Twin-topped, 1330-foot Elkhorn Peak, fringed with a thatch of trees, stands due west. Visually follow this line of mountains north along undulating, tree-cloaked slopes, to the Twin Sisters in Solano County, each over 2000 feet high.

Return to the main trail and continue across the plateau into a grove of ancient evergreen oaks, their branches sculpted by the prevailing northwest winds and their trunks 4-6 feet in diameter. Following the path through these widely spaced, venerable trees is like walking down a *grande allée* of some fabled estate of yesteryear. A pause here will give you time to bask in their shady grandeur and enjoy spring wildflowers or the bluish-white flowers of the soap plant on summer evenings.

Beyond the ridgetop, the wide trail descends a steep, east-facing hillside dotted with California buckeye trees. Their gnarled, white bark stands out against dry winter grasses, and their long, erect spikes of dense, pinkish-white blossoms scent the air in spring. From this hillside you see across a small valley to the park's eastern wooded ridge.

A short descent on a south-facing hillside takes you under transmission lines to a wide, fenced corridor that leads to a gate to a private housing development. Continue half a mile on this urban trail to Green Valley Road; signs remind you to stay on the paved path and not to stray onto private streets or lawns in this private community.

Since there is no designated southern staging area and no parking on Green Valley Road, retrace your steps through Rockville Hills Park or opt for an alternate route on the many other trails. In the late afternoon, red-wing blackbirds calling from the reeds in Lower Lake and swallows snatching insects in mid-air will provide aerial entertainment.

The next segment of the Bay Area Ridge Trail begins at Hiddenbrooke in Vallejo. (See *Hiddenbrooke Trail.*)

HIDDENBROOKE TRAIL
From McGary Road to
Trail's Southern Terminus

Length: 5 miles round trip

Accessibility: Hikers, equestrians, bicyclists

Regulations: Open 6 a.m. to dusk. No dogs.

Facilities: None

THESE ROLLING GRASSLANDS offer expansive views of San Francisco and San Pablo bays and the mountains that encircle them, from Mt. Tamalpais to Mt. Diablo. You'll gain 550 feet on short, steep climbs along this broad, exposed trail. Take this trip on cool summer mornings or late afternoons; some spots are muddy after heavy rains.

Getting There

From I-80 northeast of Vallejo and west of Fairfield, take American Canyon Rd. exit east onto Hiddenbrooke Parkway. Immediately turn right (south) onto McGary Rd. and park along the road. Follow the paved sidewalk with landscaped border along Hiddenbrooke Parkway for 0.5 mile to trailhead on right. A signpost **bears** Bay Area Ridge Trail insignia.

On the Trail

Your trip begins on an unpaved trail that runs between the tree-lined, landscaped border of the Hiddenbrooke Parkway and the fenced property line. As you climb upward beside graceful, gray-green olive trees, look right over the adjoining grasslands and ahead to the first hill and fine views.

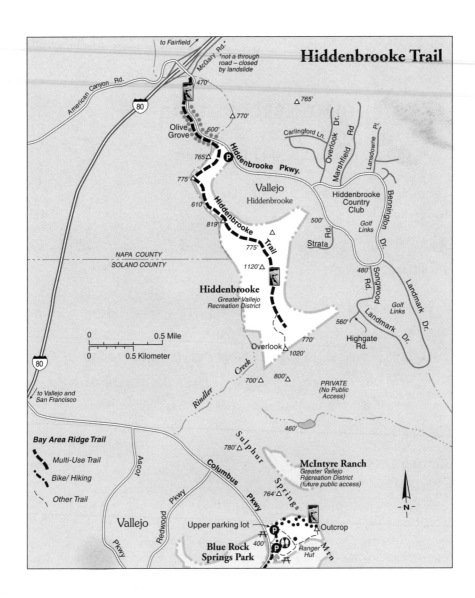

Hiddenbrooke Trail

Bay Area Ridge Trail

- Multi-Use Trail
- Bike/ Hiking
- Other Trail

At the top of the first rise, veer to the right, away from the parkway, and round the south side of the hill. Across a wide canyon ahead, you glimpse a distinctive clump of wind-sculpted trees that top an otherwise bald hill. The trail climbs a steep hill along the property-line fence to reach your first viewpoint. On a clear day, you can see west across the community of American Canyon to the Napa River, as it flows south past the former Mare Island Naval Shipyard. Slightly northwest of the island, the Napa-Sonoma Marshes Wildlife Area, fed by several arms of the Napa River, extends to the shores of San Pablo Bay. Across the water are the low hills of Napa County and the taller peaks of the North Bay.

Hiddenbrooke Trail.

The trail turns left and descends along the fence line, then climbs again to a zigzag cattle gate, just wide enough for hikers and for bikes held vertically. (Equestrians use the patrol gate, and please close it behind you.) Look due north to locate the distinctive double points of Twin Sisters rising above the surrounding plain.

You drop into a small valley where clumps of oak and bay trees hug a rocky ridge 10 feet above the trail. Veined with red-brown ore, the rocks recall the mining days of this region, when mercury was extracted for processing the gold found in the Sierra foothills. The mines are now closed and sealed, but one gave its name—St. Johns Mine Hill—to a nearby knoll on private property.

141

You round a shoulder of the trip's central hill and ascend its south side, past a cow path on the left. Then turn left sharply onto the wide trail beneath the brow of the central hill. Continue to a gap in the hills, where you can see south to Suisun Bay and Mt. Diablo beyond it. To the north lie the expansive green fairways and greens of the Hiddenbrooke Golf Course and the homes along the meandering roads of Hiddenbrooke Estates. In early spring, you may see bright yellow tufts of a ground-hugging plant, commonly known as hog fennel.

Soon you reach a junction marked END RIDGE TRAIL SEGMENT. A short path leads to 360-degree views of the Bay Area from the trip's highest point at 1020 feet. Follow this path to the preserve boundary; after a winter storm has cleared the air, you will see east to the snowy Sierra peaks and west to the Golden Gate, spanned by the famous bridge. You can identify the prominent mountaintops around the bay and trace the circular Bay Area Ridge Trail on or near them; begin just north of the bridge with Mt. Tamalpais, then to Mt. Burdell, Sonoma Mountain, Mt. Diablo, Mission and Monument peaks, Mt. Madonna, Loma Prieta, Mt. Umunhum, Black Mountain, Kings Mountain and back to the bridge. You can also look south to a broad valley where a proposed route of the Ridge Trail would head toward the McIntyre Ranch and the existing Blue Rock Springs and Vallejo-Benicia Buffer Trail.

Descend from the rocky high point of this trip and retrace your steps to the parking area, noting unique aspects of the immediate terrain and of the Bay Area beyond.

The next segment of the Ridge Trail begins in Blue Rock Springs Park. (See *Vallejo-Benicia Buffer.*)

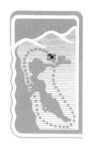

VALLEJO-BENICIA BUFFER
From Blue Rock Springs Park to Rose Drive

Length: 5.9 miles (includes 1-mile round trip on northeast extension, 1.9 miles on sidewalks and bike lanes, and 3 miles on Buffer Trail)

Accessibility: Hikers, equestrians, bicyclists

Regulations: Blue Rock Springs Park—Open 8 a.m. to dusk. No dogs. Parking fee.
Buffer Trail and Rollye Wiskerson Connector Trail—Open dawn to dusk.

Facilities: Water, restrooms, and phone at Blue Rock Springs Park.

TAKE THIS VARIED TRIP along the ridgeline greenbelt between Vallejo and Benicia. Begin on a short round trip to a rocky ridge and return to the rolling green lawns and shady picnic areas of Blue Rock Springs Park to follow a paved path or bike lane to the Buffer Trail. Meander through the open space easement, up and down hilly grasslands, towards Benicia State Recreation Area. Little shade protects you from the hot summer sun on this unpaved trail; the ridge may be windy or foggy. Elevation gain/loss 300 feet/540 feet.

Getting There

North trailhead, Blue Rock Springs Park: From I-80, take Columbus Pkwy. east for 2.5 miles; turn left (east) into park. Ample parking. Use upper lot for northeast hillside leg.

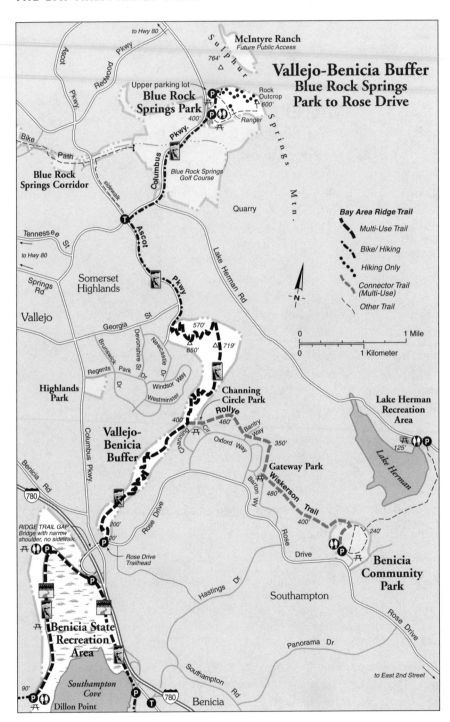

Vallejo-Benicia Buffer
Blue Rock Springs
Park to Rose Drive

McIntyre Ranch
Future Public Access

to Hwy 80

Redwood Pkwy

Ascot Pkwy

Bike Path

Upper parking lot
Blue Rock Springs Park
400'

Rock Outcrop 600'

Ranger

Columbus Pkwy

Blue Rock Springs Golf Course

Blue Rock Springs Corridor

sidewalk

Quarry

Tennessee St

to Hwy 80

Springs Rd

Vallejo

Somerset Highlands

Ascot Pkwy

Georgia St

570'

650'

719'

Bay Area Ridge Trail

Multi-Use Trail

Bike/ Hiking

Hiking Only

Connector Trail (Multi-Use)

Other Trail

N

0   1 Mile
0   1 Kilometer

Brunswick Park Dr

Regents Dr

Devonshire St

Newcastle Way

Windsor Way

Westminster

Highlands Park

Channing Circle Park

Rollye

400'

460'

Bantry Way

Oxford Way

350'

Vallejo-Benicia Buffer

Channing Cir

Gateway Park

Barton Wy

Wiskerson Trail

480'

400'

Rose Drive

Lake Herman Recreation Area

125'

Lake Herman

240'

Benicia Community Park

Columbus Pkwy

Benicia Rd

780

RIDGE TRAIL GAP
Bridge with narrow shoulder, no sidewalk.

200'

20'

Rose Drive

Rose Drive Trailhead

Southampton

Hastings Dr

Benicia State Recreation Area

90'

Southampton Cove

Dillon Point

780

Southampton Rd

Benicia

Panorama Dr

Rose Drive

to East 2nd Street

South trailhead, Rose Dr.: From I-780 east (Vallejo-Benicia Fwy.), take Benicia State Park Rd. exit, bear right, and circle around to cross over the freeway. Continue to Columbus Pkwy. and cross it onto Rose Dr. Park in first block on west side of street only. Trail entrance on north side of day-care center.

From I-780 west (Vallejo-Benicia Fwy.), take Columbus Pkwy. exit, and turn right (northeast) on Rose Dr. Find parking and trail entrance as above.

General Mariano Vallejo

As you begin your trip over the lands north of Carquinez Strait, consider that they were once part of a vast, 11-square-league land grant encompassing most of present-day Vallejo, Benicia, and Cordelia, approximately 99 square miles. Known as Rancho Soscol, the grant was awarded in 1844 by Governor Micheltorena to General Mariano Vallejo for his military service and generous loans to the Mexican government.

In 1847 the present-day Carquinez Strait town of Benicia was named Francesca, after General Vallejo's wife. When the older settlement of Yerba Buena was renamed San Francisco, Francesca changed its name to Benicia, another of Señora Vallejo's names.

Although today's thriving City of Vallejo was named for the general, he never resided there. Instead, he lived comfortably and well in Sonoma, protected by his own army of Mexican soldiers. Nevertheless, General Vallejo worked hard to make Vallejo the second California state capital, and contributed land and a building to house the state legislature.

On January 5, 1852 the legislature met in the new Vallejo capitol building, but their stay was short. By January 12 of that year, the dissatisfied legislature moved to Sacramento, returning to Vallejo only for a brief stay in 1853 due to floods in Sacramento. However, the legislature did compliment Vallejo for his generosity by naming today's city after him, even though Vallejo himself had suggested "Eureka."

Vallejo and subsequent landowners ran cattle over these hills and shipped hides through the Carquinez Strait to San Francisco and on to world ports. Today, the cattle are gone and houses cover the hillsides, except for a 500-foot-wide easement between the cities of Vallejo and Benicia. This ridgeline greenbelt is called a buffer, although it serves as open space joining the two cities bearing the Vallejo family names.

On the Trail

This trip over General Vallejo's former lands begins in Blue Rock Springs Park, once the site of an elegant home and lavish gardens built by General Frisbie, son-in-law of General Vallejo. It later became a popular picnic place and is now managed by the Greater Vallejo Recreation District; its green lawns, spring-fed pond, picnic tables and big trees attract visitors year-round.

Northeast Extension

A short Bay Area Ridge Trail segment now extends the Vallejo-Benicia Buffer half a mile north toward the Hiddenbrooke Trail. The planned Ridge Trail route will eventually connect the Hiddenbrooke Trail to Blue Rock Springs Park via McIntyre Ranch. In the meantime, this short but interesting round trip offers an opportunity to climb to the rocky ramparts in the northeast corner of the park.

The trail begins on the park's north side; to reach it, park in the upper parking area or follow the sidewalk north from the lower lot. Continue on the sidewalk or a paved park path past the green lawns to a grassy hillside. Just beyond three young pine trees on your right, climb the wooden steps outlined by native rocks. The trail soon bears right around the developed park's perimeter.

Pass through a zigzag cattle gate on your left after 0.1 mile to begin your uphill route. Seven switchbacks (dangerously ignored by downhill speeders) climb to the summit of a rocky ridge. Along the way, two sturdy benches built and installed by Gregory Basham, an Eagle Scout of Vallejo Troop 12, offer the opportunity to pause and enjoy the North Bay ambience; you have fine views of the bay and surrounding hills, the golf course, and the Vallejo-Benicia Buffer route. Uphill from these benches, a wall of huge rocks with crenellations is reminiscent of ancient fortresses; on your left, these ragged outcrops top another hill. These hills and those you passed on the Columbus Parkway are part of the Sulphur Springs Mountain chain.

You reach the summit after about a third of a mile; turn around to survey your climb and then continue on the trail through an opening in the high rock wall ahead of you. Despite the harsh terrain, a few rangy live oaks, some hardy toyon bushes, and a buckeye tree grow in clefts between the rocks. Wend your way carefully to the other side, where small boulders scattered among trees offer perches from which you can survey the wide views southeast. You can see and hear the trucks and bulldozers in a rock quarry nearby. To the left is a canyon between the hills, a possible future Ridge Trail route northward. After you have enjoyed the views, retrace your steps to the parking area.

South to the Buffer Trail

To continue on the Ridge Trail route toward the Vallejo-Benicia Buffer, find the path just south of the park entrance road. Follow it to a paved sidewalk or the bike lane along the east side of Columbus Parkway, bordered by the municipal golf course. You pass Lake Herman Road and reach Ascot Parkway, where you turn left at the signaled crossing. Young trees and clipped green lawns dot the well-landscaped banks along Ascot Parkway.

Buffer Trail

After less than a mile on the parkway, you pass Georgia Street and look for a landscaped entry in front of a weathered-gray fence on the east side of the street. Turn left to begin the Buffer Trail, signed as the Bay Area Ridge Trail route. Manzanita, toyon, coffeeberry, and springtime blue lupine, all native California plants installed by volunteers, fill the space beside the trail for the first 50 feet.

The single-track trail zigzags to the 640-foot summit of the first of this trip's many hilltops. Before you lies the long sweep of the greenway's undulating terrain that stretches almost to the shores of Southampton Bay on Carquinez Strait. The homes that edge both sides of the Buffer highlight the importance of activists' persistent efforts to convince the Vallejo and Benicia councils to create this linear open space, which now serves as a trail and a wildlife corridor.

Beyond the first hilltop, the trail heads north into a swale. Then after a long traverse and switchback, it reaches the highest point on the trip. You have views of impressive bodies of water from this vantage place: due east is Lake Herman, the local water supply; beyond, the Navy's mothball fleet floats on the quiet waters of Suisun Bay; below you to the south, one-third of California's water surges through Carquinez Strait, drained from the Sierra Nevada into the San Joaquin and Sacramento rivers. Beyond the strait, San Francisco Bay spreads out over a vast expanse of tidelands, marshes, sloughs, and open waters. On a clear day you can see the towers of the Golden Gate Bridge under which these waters flow to the Pacific.

For the next half a mile, you follow a wide track south over the hilltops. A Ridge Trail sign directs you right (west), on a narrower trail, built by a team of volunteers. Continue downhill on a gentle grade along the west-facing hillside. When you reach a concrete-sided drainage ditch with a V-cross section, again head south, paralleling the ditch.

In spring, these rolling grasslands are ablaze with orange poppies and blue lupines. As the season progresses, yellow-flowered mule ears on strong, erect stems add their color to the hillsides. Heavenly blue brodiaea and lemon-yellow mariposa lilies are special floral treats that peek through the grasses in early June. The roasted bulbs of these plants were favorite foods of Native Americans.

The Rollye Wiskerson Connector Trail joins your route from the east; built and named for the Solano County master trail-builder, this trail runs along the north edge of a residential neighborhood and connects three community parks to the Buffer Trail.

Past the junction, your trail is again a wide track that undulates up and down along the fence line. Veer right (south) on a single-track trail to avoid a very steep hill. Follow the contour of the hillside and round a couple of switchbacks. You then dip into a little valley and trend left, into the Benicia side of the easement, where pretty gardens and colorful children's play equipment hug the fence line.

On three more switchbacks, you climb to the crest of another hilltop; from there you have good views of Southampton Bay and the Benicia State Recreation Area, which this trail will someday reach. If the day is clear, you'll see, and sometimes hear, ships on the fast-flowing waters of Carquinez Strait. The trail zigzags along the fence line, with moderate undulations over the last hilltops, and finally descends steeply to the trail's end at Rose Drive in Benicia.

There is a short gap between Rose Drive and the beginning of the next segment of the Bay Area Ridge Trail along the Benicia Waterfront. (See *Benicia-Vallejo Waterfront*.) If you are returning to Blue Rock Springs Park, allow plenty of time for the uphill trip, especially on hot summer days.

BENICIA-VALLEJO WATERFRONT
From Benicia State Recreation Area East to Benicia Point at F Street and West to Carquinez Bridge

Length: 3.5 miles east on Benicia Waterfront Trail
3.5 miles west on Vallejo Waterfront Trail
to Carquinez Bridge

Accessibility: Hikers, equestrians, bicyclists, wheelchairs

Regulations: Benicia State Recreation Area—Open 6 a.m. to ½ hour after sunset. Entrance fee. No dogs. State fishing license required for those 16 years and older. No bicycles on unpaved trails.
City of Benicia Waterfront Trail and City of Vallejo Trail—Open daylight hours. No bicycles on unpaved trails.

Facilities: Water and restrooms at Benicia State Recreation Area; water, restrooms, and phone at City of Benicia 9th Street Park.

TAKE A TRIP THROUGH Mexican and early California history: two routes follow the Carquinez Strait waterfront through the thriving towns of Benicia and Vallejo. Enjoy brisk breezes and occasional fog as you watch the San Joaquin and Sacramento rivers funnel into San Francisco Bay. This route travels mostly level trails, including sidewalks, paved and unpaved trails, and paths.

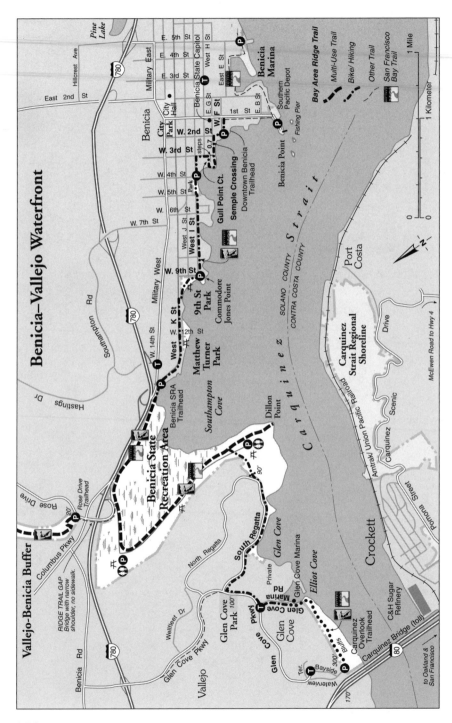

Getting There

Benicia State Recreation Area: From I-80 take I-780 (Vallejo-Benicia Fwy.) to exit marked Benicia State Recreation Area. Follow the road as it curves right, then jog to the left (south) and turn right into recreation area.

On the Trail

East to Historic Benicia

All trail users head southeast on the paved trail from the recreation area that skirts the marshlands around Southampton Bay. Among the shorebirds and waterfowl that feed in the marshes, you may see the 30-inch-tall, stately white egret. You will certainly see many runners, strollers, and bicyclists on this trail.

Across Southampton Bay to the south, Dillon Point juts into the strait, named for a rancher who, in 1855, bought the 400 acres that now lie within the state recreation area. Patrick Dillon's homesite is marked by towering eucalyptus, and a few of the fruit trees from the orchards he planted remain, but his vineyard, quarry, and brickyard are gone.

Equestrians and **wheelchair users** end this segment at the east boundary of the State Recreation Area.

At K Street, **hikers** and **bicyclists** continue on the Waterfront Trail on the sidewalk. Near West 14th Street, you reach the first of many historical sites. A sign tells of the famous 1889 boxing match between James J. Corbett and "Battling Joe" Choynski. The first rounds were fought in Fairfax, and the fight was continued a week later on a barge in Southampton Bay.

Turn right (south) on West 12th Street to the Matthew Turner Shipyards Park, where you'll have your first close-up view of the Carquinez Strait. Around 1900, 169 ships were launched here; today you'll find benches, picnic tables and pretty gardens, and another historical marker. Across the strait, Port Costa was once an important depot for transporting grain by barge, ship, and rail. The Southern Pacific Railroad still runs transcontinental freight and Amtrak operates a fleet of passenger trains on waterfront tracks.

Now return to K Street, where a bluff-top path runs diagonally across the 9th Street Park to Jones Point. Commodore Thomas Jones was founder of the U.S. Naval Academy and Commander of the Pacific Fleet in the 1840s. Southampton Bay is named for one of his supply ships. Jones feared war with Mexico and advocated a port here in Benicia's deep offshore waters. Modern-day sailors launch their craft beside Jones Point to ply these same waters.

Follow I Street beyond the park, past houses with charming gardens. In the 1860s, two tanneries near here processed hides from vast inland cattle ranches. Each hide was marked with the ranch's unique registered brand. Further on, barriers exclude motor vehicles from I Street, but Ridge Trail signs assure bicyclists and pedestrians that they can pass. At 4th Street, you'll find picnic tables and children's play equipment that overlooks a small crescent-shaped bay.

Turn right (south) on West 3rd Street and go two blocks to Gull Point Court.

Hikers can descend to Semple Crossing, one street below, on a stairway near a handsome, restored Victorian house.

Bicyclists follow Gull Point Court to Semple Crossing.

From Semple Crossing, **hikers** and **bicyclists** continue on an unpaved path to F Street, where, as of this writing, the Benicia Waterfront Trail ends.

Fischer-Hanlon House.

Touring Historic Benicia

The centerpiece of Benicia's attractions stands at West 1st and G streets—an imposing, red brick building with white, two-story columns: our state's third capitol. Although the legislature convened here only in 1853, the building is now faithfully restored and open as a state historic park. The Fischer-Hanlon house is next door, a fine example of Victorian architecture. Until recently, it was occupied by the original owner's descendants; it is now open for tours.

You are in the heart of Benicia's old town, where saloons, hotels, and the 1847 Von Pfister adobe (to be restored) bring to life the years before and after the Gold Rush. If you continue down West 1st Street to Benicia Point, you'll see where 400-foot-long barges once ferried trains across to Port Costa. Cars were also ferried across the strait until the Benicia-Martinez Bridge was built. In just a few minutes walk, you'll reach the 1850s military buildings—the Benicia Arsenal with its landmark clock tower, the Camel Barn Museum, and the Commandant's House.

Today Benicia bustles with activity that matches its lively past—huge ships unload Japanese cars at the port, and slick condominiums, shopping malls, and subdivisions cover the hillsides and crowd its shores. However, open space trails along the waterfront and through the Vallejo-Benicia Buffer join these cities and former capitals of California that bear General Mariano Vallejo's family names. (See *Vallejo-Benicia Buffer* for more about the Vallejo family.)

West to the Carquinez Bridge

To take the waterfront trail west, **all trail users** again begin at the entrance to Benicia State Recreation Area. Follow the paved park road (hikers and equestrians on the shoulder) as it skirts the marshes and western shore of Southampton Bay on its way to Dillon Point, about 1.5 miles from the entrance gate.

Turn right on a path, marked by a Bay Area Ridge Trail sign, just past the first picnic area along this road. The path crosses the low hill that runs north-south through the park, where some of Patrick Dillon's fruit trees survive. Look due west from the crest of the hill for a view of the Carquinez Bridge and your route along the town of Vallejo's bluffs, high above the strait.

Equestrians and **wheelchair users** end their trip at the South Regatta Drive Gate.

To continue, **hikers** and **bicyclists** take the short footpath that descends to a gate to South Regatta Drive. (Don't veer off into the long swale on your left.) Turn left and follow sidewalks through several new subdivisions to Glen Cove Parkway. For the first half a mile, you have an unobstructed view out to the strait and its maritime traffic; then you see west through the trees to Glen Cove, where the City of Vallejo is planning a shoreline park. In the future, the Ridge Trail will go through this park.

Continue on South Regatta Drive to Glen Cove Parkway—0.9 mile from the Benicia State Recreation Area gate—and turn left. Pass Vallejo's Glen Cove Park, with attractive plantings and brightly painted children's play apparatus. After just 0.2 mile on Glen Cove Parkway, turn left again on Glen Cove Marina Road, and go 0.1 mile downhill to a cul-de-sac and the entrance to the Glen Cove Marina.

The Victorian yacht club once served as the residence for personnel at the Carquinez Lighthouse and Life Saving Station, and was formerly situated just west of the Carquinez Bridge at the mouth of the Napa River. After the lighthouse was automated in 1955, the building was sold and barged to its present site at Elliot Cove in 1957. The three-story building, painted white with gray trim, now presides over the yacht basin.

Bicyclists end their trip here.

The Ridge Trail route for **hikers** continues from the west shore of the yacht basin, where a crushed granite path heads up a broad easement (check with the Greater Vallejo Recreation District about repairs to and routes around a recent slide here). From the bluffs above the strait, you look down on tankers and freighters from ports around the world, barges, naval vessels, and pleasure craft. On a foggy day, the horns of ships and the bells of buoys reverberate eerily from the strait's watery canyon. High above the strait, the Carquinez Bridge carries its noisy load of land-based traffic.

Connecting trails from tiny parks in the adjoining subdivision intersect with this segment of the Bay Area Ridge Trail. The trail ends at a dramatic vista above the bridge, just above the park on Waterview Place. The swiftly moving strait joins San Pablo Bay, with Mt. Tamalpais and the Coast Ranges as a backdrop. West of the Carquinez Bridge, there are two historic maritime facilities—the Mare Island Naval Shipyard and the California Maritime Academy.

On your return, you'll see the port communities of Vallejo, Benicia, and Martinez, with Mt. Diablo in the distance. This waterfront trail, the route of the Bay Trail, crosses the river to Martinez on a bridge that is being retrofitted for bicycle and pedestrian traffic. (See *Martinez City Streets to Carquinez Strait Regional Shoreline*.)

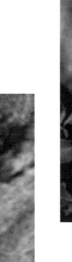

(Top) Hound's Tongue; (middle) *Gilia* on serpentine; (bottom) Mariposa lilies.

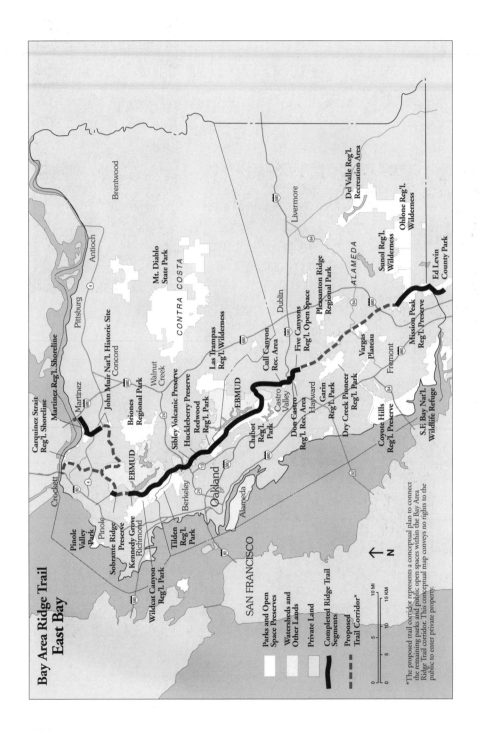

Bay Area Ridge Trail
East Bay

SAN FRANCISCO

Carquinez Strait Reg'l. Shoreline
Martinez Reg'l. Shoreline
Pinole Valley Park
Sobrante Ridge Preserve
Kennedy Grove
Richmond
Pinole
Crockett
Wildcat Canyon Reg'l. Park
Tilden Reg'l. Park
Berkeley
Alameda
Oakland

Martinez
John Muir Nat'l. Historic Site
Concord
Briones Regional Park
EBMUD
Walnut Creek
Sibley Volcanic Preserve
Huckleberry Preserve
Redwood Reg'l. Park
Chabot Reg'l. Park
EBMUD

Pittsburg
Antioch
Brentwood

Mt. Diablo State Park
CONTRA COSTA
Las Trampas Reg'l. Wilderness
Castro Valley
Don Castro Reg'l. Rec. Area
Hayward
Garin Reg'l. Park
Dry Creek Pioneer Reg'l. Park
Coyote Hills Reg'l. Preserve
S.F. Bay Nat'l. Wildlife Refuge

Cull Canyon Rec. Area
Five Canyons Reg'l. Open Space
Pleasanton Ridge Regional Park
Dublin
Livermore

Del Valle Reg'l. Recreation Area
Ohlone Reg'l. Wilderness
Sunol Reg'l. Wilderness
ALAMEDA
Vargas Plateau
Mission Peak Reg'l. Preserve
Fremont
Ed Levin County Park

N

- Parks and Open Space Preserves
- Watersheds and Other Lands
- Private Land
- Completed Ridge Trail Segments
- Proposed Trail Corridor*

0   5   10 MI
0   5   10   15 KM

*The proposed trail corridor represents a conceptual plan to connect the remaining parks and public open spaces within the Bay Area Ridge Trail corridor. This conceptual map conveys no rights to the public to enter private property.

THE EAST BAY

Uplifted rocks with embedded fossilized shells surmount Dinosaur Ridge.

Clumps of blue-eyed grass bloom on trailsides in spring.

MARTINEZ CITY STREETS TO CARQUINEZ STRAIT REGIONAL SHORELINE
From Benicia Bridge to Martinez Regional Shoreline and East Staging Area

Length: 2 miles

Accessibility: Hikers, bicyclists

Regulations: City of Martinez—Helmets required for bicyclists under age 18.
Martinez Regional Shoreline—Open 5 a.m. to 10 p.m., unless otherwise posted.

Facilities: Water and restrooms at Martinez Regional Shoreline.

TAKE A WALK OR BIKE RIDE along the Carquinez Strait shoreline and discover the area's rich history, from early Spanish explorers and rancheros to Gold Rush forty-niners; and from sea captains of grain ships and oil tankers to the founders and public leaders of Contra Costa County's capital city. This route follows sidewalks and bike lanes with only 100 feet in elevation gain.

Getting There

East trailhead: From I-680 south of Benicia Bridge, take Marina Vista exit. Follow it to on-street metered parking; or to park in Martinez Regional Shoreline, continue to Ferry St., turn right, and cross railroad tracks. Turn right on Joe DiMaggio St. and then left on N. Court St. to several parking areas.

West trailhead: From I-80 or I-680 in Contra Costa County, take Hwy. 4 (John Muir Pkwy.) to Martinez. Take Alhambra Ave. exit and go 1.75 miles north through Martinez, turn left on Escobar, right on Talbart, and then veer left on Carquinez Scenic Dr. Just after cemeteries, turn left into East Staging Area.

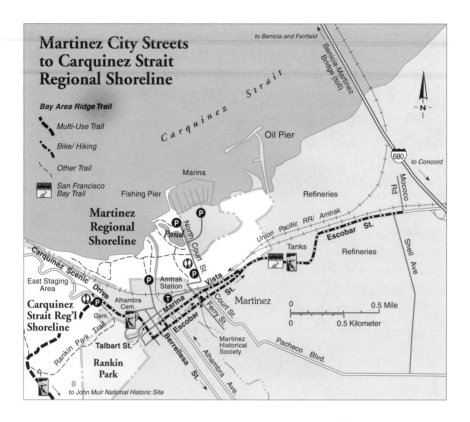

Martinez City Streets to Carquinez Strait Regional Shoreline

MARTINEZ CITY TO CARQUINEZ STRAIT REGIONAL SHORELINE

From I-680 south of Benicia Bridge, take Marina Vista west, turn left on Berrellesa, and right immediately on Escobar. Turn right on Talbart, veer left on Carquinez Scenic Dr. and then turn left into East Staging Area.

On the Trail

The Ridge Trail route starts at Mococco Road, about a quarter of a mile west of the Benicia Bridge, but since there is no parking at Mococco Road, you must start your trip by going east from Marina Vista Avenue or from Martinez Regional Shoreline. (Bicyclists should use Escobar Street going east to Mococco.)

Bicyclists start your westward trip at Mococco Road on the Marina Vista bike lanes.

Hikers begin at Shell Avenue, 0.1 mile west, on the paved sidewalk along Marina Vista's south side. **Hikers** and **bicyclists** travel near railroad tank cars on sidings and loaded freight trains passing refineries and oil storage tanks. Huge pipes snake along the hillside,

Enjoy views of the Carquinez Strait from Martinez Shoreline and fishing pier.

then form shiny, high bridges over the thoroughfare to reach storage tanks and railroad tank cars. Sounds of switching engines and sights of parked tanker cars on sidings plus oil refinery odors offer a different ambience from rural parkland trips.

161

Tall Italian cypresses soon camouflage the refinery and dense plantings partially shield the view of the railroad tracks. About half a mile beyond Shell Avenue your route swings south, away from the tracks, and hugs the hillside below the refineries. It curves northwest and passes below hillside homes with porches that overlook the strait.

At Miller Street, tall eucalyptus mask the railroad view; after Huntington Drive, Marina Vista splits at a "Y" and becomes a one-way street going west. Hikers can safely cross to the north side of Marina Vista at Miller Street or continue west on Escobar Street. After the split, a landscaped island lies between Marina Vista and Escobar streets. On a hillside to your left, a sturdy blue Victorian house and summer cottages of several vintages have broad views of the strait and the Benicia hills beyond.

Soon you reach the busiest section of town, where county and city government buildings—courthouses, office buildings, finance and postal departments—fill several square blocks. When the

---

Historic Martinez

The Martinez Museum is housed in the Moore house, a historic building on the corner of Escobar and Ferry streets. You can view artifacts from the town's long history and pick up a brochure for a walking tour of historic buildings in Martinez. Learn about Don Ignazio Martinez, who received 17,000 acres in this valley for his military services to the Mexican government. His daughter, who inherited some of this acreage, married San Francisco businessman, William Smith. Smith first surveyed and laid out 20 of the land-grant acres for the original city of Martinez.

Martinez was the first city in present-day Contra Costa County. With the onset of the Gold Rush, it grew into a busy port and became the county seat in 1851. Ocean-going vessels carried grain grown in the Central Valley from Martinez docks to international ports. The completion of the transcontinental railroad through Martinez in 1876 brought the "iron horse" into Martinez. Shell oil established its refineries and pipelines here in 1915. The city continues to be an important shipping center and governmental center.

Today, this Bay Area Ridge Trail segment follows the shoreline route used by explorers and early settlers. The route was dedicated as a joint Ridge Trail and Bay Trail segment on November 7, 1998.

---

author walked this trail, a farmers market and a "whatchamacallit" rummage sale occupied Ferry Street between Ward and Marina

Vista, and government employees strolled the streets on lunch break, giving a festive feel to the heart of the city. The historic Moore house, on the corner of Escobar and Ferry streets, is now the Martinez Museum, a charming, white, two-story structure with a covered veranda and double-gabled roof.

From Marina Vista and Escobar streets, turn north on either Ferry or Berrellessa streets to reach the East Bay Regional Park District's Martinez Regional Shoreline. Its picnic tables and shorefront benches offer attractive places to rest along your Ridge Trail route. Friends and family could join you here for a picnic or snack and a chance to watch the waterfowl on ponds or the ships and pleasure boats that ply the swift waters of Carquinez Strait. A former ferry dock that is now used as a fishing pier might intrigue anglers.

When you leave this excellent shoreline park, follow Marina Vista westward past the old, wood-sided Southern Pacific railroad station to the newly built Amtrak station. Then turn left (southeast) on Berrellesa; after two blocks, go right (west) on Escobar. Turn right again at Talbart Street after two more blocks and ascend past small homes of Victorian and early 20th century vintage. Three blocks farther, at Foster Street, veer left onto Carquinez Scenic Drive and pass cemeteries on the right and left. William Smith, son-in-law of Don Martinez, is buried in Alhambra Cemetery, on the right. After you pass Rankin Park on the left, watch for the entrance to the East Staging Area of Carquinez Strait Regional Shoreline, where this segment of the Bay Area Ridge Trail ends.

The next Bay Area Ridge Trail segment continues southeast from this staging area to the John Muir Historic Site. (See *Carquinez Strait Regional Shoreline to John Muir National Historic Site.*)

When the new Benicia-Martinez bridge bicycle and pedestrian lanes are completed, Ridge Trail and Bay Trail users will be able to travel along several continuous segments of trail in Solano County and cross the bridge to join this trail in Martinez and others in Contra Costa County.

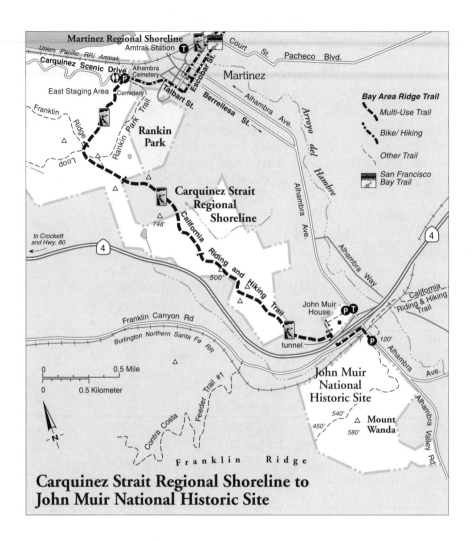

Bay Area Ridge Trail

Multi-Use Trail

Bike/ Hiking

Other Trail

San Francisco Bay Trail

Carquinez Strait Regional Shoreline to John Muir National Historic Site

CARQUINEZ STRAIT REGIONAL SHORELINE TO JOHN MUIR NATIONAL HISTORIC SITE
From East Staging Area to Visitor Center

Length: 3 miles

Accessibility: Hikers, equestrians, bicyclists

Regulations: Open 8 a.m. to ½ hour after sunset. Dogs on leash in staging area; under voice control in open space.
John Muir National Historic Site—Open Wed. to Sun., 10 a.m. to 4:30 p.m. Entrance fee.

Facilities: Restrooms at Carquinez Strait Regional Shoreline, East Staging Area; water and restrooms at John Muir National Historic Site.

R OAM ROLLING RIDGELANDS in northern Contra Costa County on the old California Riding and Hiking Trail, a round-the-state trail system planned in the mid-1900s. One of the few remaining segments, this route follows wide, unpaved service trails along the exposed ridge south of the Carquinez Strait and ends in the Alhambra Valley of Martinez, where you can visit John Muir's home. The first and last legs of the trail are short and steep.

Getting There

By Car

North trailhead, Carquinez Shoreline, East Staging Area: From I-80 or I-680 in Contra Costa County take Hwy. 4 (John Muir Pkwy) to Martinez. Take Alhambra Ave. exit and go 1.75 miles north through Martinez, turn left on Escobar, right on Talbart, and then veer left on Carquinez Scenic Dr. Just after cemeteries, turn left into East Staging Area.

South trailhead, John Muir Site: Follow directions above to Alhambra Ave. exit. Turn north on Alhambra Ave. and immediately look for John Muir National Historic Site on your left at 4202 Alhambra Ave. Limited parking on site. Additional parking at southwest corner of Alhambra Ave. and Franklin Canyon Rd. with access to the trail from Franklin Canyon Rd. through a tunnel under Hwy. 4.

 By Bus

Contra Costa County Connection bus 116 to Alhambra Ave. and Marina Vista and to Alhambra Ave. and Franklin Canyon Rd. from BART stations daily except Sundays.

On the Trail

The original name for this valley, derived from an 1842 land grant, was *Cañada del Hambre y las Bolsas del Hambre*, the Valley of Hunger. It was renamed Alhambra Valley when Mr. and Mrs. Strentzel, parents of John Muir's wife, settled here in the 1880s.

 Hikers, equestrians, and **bicyclists** begin this trip from the East Staging Area (also known as the Nejedly Staging Area); head uphill toward the East Bay Regional Park District's green gate, emblazoned with a prominent Bay Area Ridge Trail sign. (An alternate route through adjoining Rankin Park takes off to the left behind the uppermost picnic table.) Close the gate to the EBRPD Trail and take the path that cuts across a wide flat. You soon enter a glade of bay and buckeye trees, where toyon and poison oak grow in the understory.

You begin a steady ascent through oak woodlands, beside a seasonal creek, and gain over 500 feet in elevation in less than half a mile. You emerge into grasslands on a couple of switchbacks, but soon return to shaded woodland. In winter, you may find burnished, brown buckeye balls (seedpods) and deer or bobcat prints on the trail. In spring, you may see the long, wavy leaves of soap plant promising evening blooms of delicate, bluish-white flowers on tall stalks. After a series of three steep pitches, followed by short, level stretches, you reach a gate at the Franklin Ridge Loop Trail. If you detour to the right and circle the knoll, you'll find picnic sites overlooking the strait and a view west of Mt. Tamalpais.

To proceed southeast on the Ridge Trail, bear left at the gate; at the next fork, take the graveled road on the right and descend into a saddle between grassy, rounded hilltops. A pastoral scene of or-chard, windmill, and water tank lies in the valley to your left, remi-niscent of the farming that flourished in this area when John Muir and his family lived here.

Your route ahead rises to grass-covered hilltops followed by dips into hollows of evergreen oaks. Enjoy views from the hilltops: on your left, the Carquinez Strait, Benicia-Martinez Bridge, and the Navy's mothball fleet in Suisun Bay; the Benicia foothills rise across the strait, crossed by another leg of the Ridge Trail. (See *Vallejo-Benicia Buffer.*)

View of Martinez Bridge.

Kestrels may flutter overhead, while red-tailed and northern harrier hawks ride the updrafts, each bird searching for prey. Orange poppies and blue-eyed grass brighten the trail in spring.

You go through another gate, beyond which you are on an EBRPD trail easement through private property. Signs remind you to stay on the trail. A Ridge Trail sign directs you right, past a brown barn; a yellow house is on your left. You soon reach the trip's highest point. Mt. Diablo's twin summits loom ahead and are in sight for the rest of the trip; the view is fine at sunset, when a soft, pink glow cloaks the mountain. From the next hilltop you can see south to a succession of gently rounded hills that rise above tree-filled canyons. Franklin Ridge tops the canyon of the same name; Edward Franklin lived in the canyon from 1853, when he bought a portion of the Ignacio Martinez estate, until 1875. You cross under tall transmission towers and powerlines here.

Follow a Bay Area Ridge Trail sign that directs you onto a narrow, paved road into a tight canyon. Where the paving veers right, you continue straight ahead on a dirt trail; the town of Martinez lies below. From the top of a steep hill, you make a quick descent on a Caltrans easement above Highway 4, the John Muir Parkway. (Bicyclists should dismount.) The trail ends at a fenced cross trail, where you can go left to the John Muir Historic Site. To reach the southern trailhead of this Ridge Trail route, turn right and continue on the California Riding and Hiking Trail through a tunnel under the John Muir Parkway. At Franklin Canyon Road, turn left (east) to reach the parking area at Alhambra Avenue, where you could have a shuttle waiting. If not, your route back to the East Staging Area will afford fine views west, north, and east.

The next Bay Area Ridge Trail segment begins southwest across the Contra Costa County hills in the Sobrante Ridge Regional Preserve. (See *Sobrante Ridge Regional Preserve.*)

John Muir National Historic Site

Stop at the John Muir National Historic Site to learn more about the life of the father of our National Park System. At the visitor center, you can watch a video about his life, from his childhood in Wisconsin to his trip in Yosemite with President Theodore Roosevelt. Visit the Muir family Victorian house and grounds, with orchards, barns, and the old Vicente Martinez adobe.

Although John Muir's real love was the Sierra Nevada, he often wandered these hills with his daughters and set aside a special hilltop for evening strolls with them. Muir surely would have appreciated the Bay Area Ridge Trail Council's effort to join Bay Area open space with a regional ridgeline trail. As he wrote, "Everybody needs beauty as well as bread, places to play in and pray in where Nature may heal and cheer and give strength to body and soul alike."

From the desk in his study, Muir wrote many of the books and articles that inspired political action to save wildlands and wildlife. He helped establish a national conservation policy, reflected today in environmental legislation and in our excellent National Park System.

SOBRANTE RIDGE REGIONAL PRESERVE
From Pinole Valley Park to Conestoga Way

Length: 2.2 miles plus 1.2 miles on connector trail from Pinole Valley Park; 0.7 miles on connector trail from Coach Drive

Accessibility: Hikers, equestrians, bicyclists

Facilities: Water, restrooms, and phone at Pinole Valley Park; water at Coach Drive.

C LIMB TO HIGH GRASSLANDS and shaded woodlands on a narrow, shady trail from Pinole Valley Park that gains 640 feet in the first mile; on cool days, take the exposed alternate trail from Coach Drive for a easier climb of 200 feet in 0.7 mile. On the wide, partially shaded ridgetop trail, you'll take in remarkable views of the mountains that ring the bay; the narrow southern leg descends 320 feet in less than a mile.

Getting There

Northern trailhead at Pinole Valley Park: From I-80, turn east on Pinole Valley Rd., go about 1.5 miles to park entrance on right and park near playing field. Follow signs across creek and pass through picnic area to trail entrance at base of hill.

Southern trailhead at Conestoga Way: From I-80, in San Pablo take San Pablo Dam Rd., go 4 miles to Castro Ranch Rd., and turn left (northeast). Go about 1 mile, turn left on Conestoga Way, and in 0.1 mile look for trail entrance on left. Park on street.

Southern trailhead at Coach Dr: Follow directions above to Conestoga Rd., continue past trail entrance about 0.25 mile and turn left

169

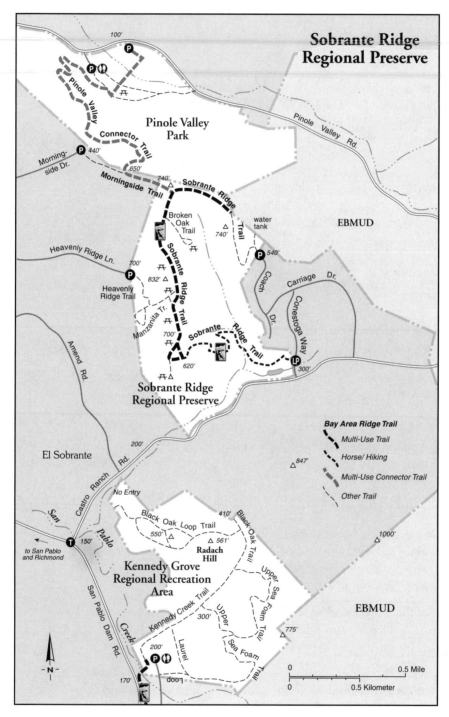

Sobrante Ridge Regional Preserve

100'

Pinole Valley

Connector Trail

440'

650'

Morningside Dr.

Morningside Trail

740'

Sobrante Ridge

Pinole Valley Park

Pinole Valley Rd.

Broken Oak Trail

740'

water tank

EBMUD

Heavenly Ridge Ln.

700'

832'

Sobrante Ridge Trail

540'

Coach Dr.

Carriage Dr.

Heavenly Ridge Trail

Manzanita Tr.

700'

Sobrante Ridge Trail

Conestoga Way

Sobrante

620'

300'

Sobrante Ridge Regional Preserve

Amend Rd.

200'

El Sobrante

Castro Ranch Rd.

No Entry

847'

Bay Area Ridge Trail

Multi-Use Trail

Horse/ Hiking

Multi-Use Connector Trail

Other Trail

San Pablo

150'

to San Pablo and Richmond

Black Oak Loop Trail

410'

550'

561'

Black Oak Trail

1000'

Radach Hill

Kennedy Creek Trail

Upper Sea Foam Trail

Kennedy Grove Regional Recreation Area

San Pablo Dam Rd.

300'

Upper Sea Foam Trail

775'

EBMUD

Creek

200'

Laurel Trail

-N-

170'

doo'

0   0.5 Mile

0   0.5 Kilometer

(southwest) on Carriage Dr. Turn right (north) on Coach Dr. and continue to its terminus and off-street parking.

On the Trail

As of this writing, this trip's official route begins in Pinole Valley Park on the Pinole Valley Connector Trail; it joins the main Bay Area Ridge Trail route on the Sobrante Ridge Trail, which ends at Conestoga Way. (You can also reach the northeast leg of the main Ridge Trail route from Coach Drive on a shorter, sunnier climb to the ridge.) A future Ridge Trail extension northeast will cross East Bay Municipal Utility District lands to connect this trail with the Carquinez Regional Shoreline-John Muir Historic Site segment.

Leftover Land

Sobrante Ridge Preserve's 277 acres cover part of the land grant that was deeded to Juan José Castro by the Mexican government in 1841. It was probably named *Sobrante,* meaning *leftover* or *surplus,* because of its position between two other land grants. After the break-up of Castro's rancho, several owners used the property. One owner, Cutter Labs, used it as pasture land for horses and cows used in the manufacture of vaccines. A later owner deeded the present ridgetop and lands on its east side to the East Bay Regional Park District in return for permission to develop on the lower western slopes.

Hikers, equestrians, and **bicyclists** begin at the parking area at Pinole Valley Park and wend your way past the playing fields and restrooms to a picnic area in a dense grove of bay trees. The park office is in a white Victorian-style building on your left, by the picnic area. Beyond the picnic tables, a narrow, multi-use trail zigzags uphill through oak and bay woodlands; ferns drape the banks and dainty white woodland stars and yellow buttercups bloom in the low underbrush. Farther uphill, the trail emerges from the woods to sunny clearings with swaths of wildflowers.

At the top of the ridge, you turn left (east) to merge with the Morningside Trail and continue into the preserve. (The 0.24-mile Morningside Trail originates at Morningside Drive in Pinole.) You soon join the Sobrante Ridge Trail on the 700-foot ridgetop and proceed a few feet east to meet the northeastern leg of the alternate trail from Coach Drive. Bear right (south) here on the wide, unpaved service road, bordered by scattered oak woodlands. Shortly

you reach a clearing and picnic table, where you can see Mt. Tamalpais on the left (west) and forested San Pedro Mountain to its right.
If the day is clear, Mt. Burdell is visible in the north (traversed by
another Bay Area Ridge Trail segment). To the northeast lies the
proposed route to the John Muir site and beyond is Suisun Bay.

Sheep in Sobrante

One late-spring day, when the author and a friend first hiked this trail, they saw
a small trailer parked here and a low, temporary, wire pen. A brownish cloud
was moving slowly up the hillside above Coach Drive. At first thinking it must be
dust, they realized there was no wind and looked more closely: it was a flock of
sheep, tended by a herder who lived in the trailer and the dogs who occupied
the pen. They walked toward the flock and saw that the sheep "mowed" the tall
grass as they moved ahead of the shepherd. At night, the "fire-prevention team"
remained inside a movable plastic fence, topped by a low-voltage electric wire.

As you continue south along the main trail, look to your left for
the Broken Oak Trail that leads to a picnic table on a shady knoll;
the trail then plunges downhill to a cluster of picnic tables in a high
canopy of majestic oaks, one of which gives the area its name. This
0.28-mile side trip makes a fine lunch stop on a hot day.

The Sobrante Ridge Trail gently undulates over the grasslands;
clearings along the way bring ever more expansive views of the
North Bay, and picnic tables attest to the popularity of this ridge,
despite the uphill trip to reach it. As you round the east side of the
preserve's highest point (an unnamed 832-foot knoll), elderberry
and toyon bushes and oak trees shade your route.

Side Trip on the Manzanita Trail

Sidetrack on the short Manzanita Trail loop to see the endangered Alameda
manzanita. Despite the steep slope and poor soil, this manzanita thrives on this
west-facing slope because of the frequent fog that blows in from the bay. Splendid specimens of native spring flowers also flourish in the Sobrante Ridge grasslands, on soil that many non-native species can't tolerate.

The double summits of Mt. Diablo are visible in the east, behind the nearer Oursan Ridge, covered in tight rows of houses. The
main trail trends downhill, forks, and forms a small loop. Although

not marked as one-way, for safety's sake, users should take the right-hand (west) segment and return on the left-hand (east) leg. Follow the right-hand trail to a 620-foot knoll and yet another picnic table.

Return to the main trail from the knoll and follow the loop trail to the right to the base of a high powerline tower.

Bicyclists must turn left on the east side of the loop and retrace your route north across the ridgetop to the trailhead.

Hikers and **equestrians** turn right on the final leg of this trail, to Conestoga Way. Descend the narrow 0.67-mile trail across an open slope on a contoured reach; then curve into the head of a shady ravine, under a canopy of oak and bay trees. In late summer and fall, the trail surface is covered with spent leaves and can be slippery. You then round the brow of a hill and drop into the willow-filled creekbed that drains into the wildlife refuge pond on the preserve's southeast corner. Climb out of this canyon and finally drop down to the short paved trail that leads to Conestoga Way.

The next leg of the Bay Area Ridge Trail starts in Kennedy Grove, on the other side of San Pablo Ridge. (See *Kennedy Grove to Inspiration Point.*)

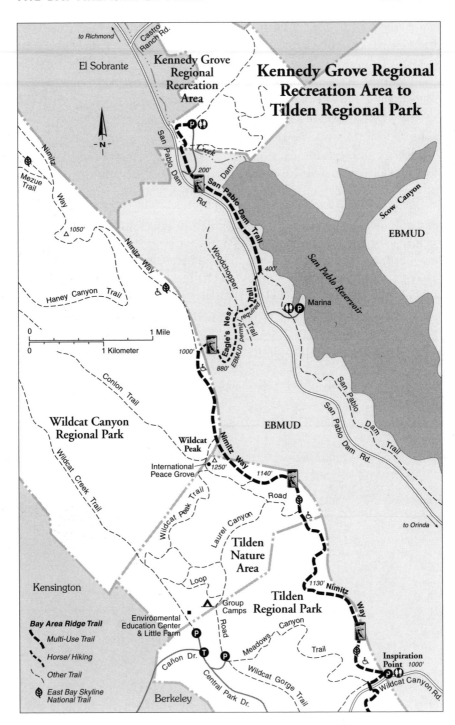

Kennedy Grove Regional Recreation Area to Tilden Regional Park

KENNEDY GROVE TO TILDEN REGIONAL PARK
From the Grove to Inspiration Point

Length: 4.4 miles

Accessibility: Hikers, equestrians, bicyclists, wheelchair users

Regulations: Kennedy Grove Regional Recreation Area, Wildcat Canyon and Tilden regional parks— Open 5 a.m. to 10 p.m., or as posted. Dogs on leash in parking lots, at picnic sites, and on lawns; under voice control on Nimitz Way. Fee for dogs and parking at Kennedy Grove.
San Pablo Reservoir Recreation Area—Old San Pablo Dam Road (on reservoir's west shore) open sunrise to 1 hour before sunset. No swimming in reservoir.
Eagle's Nest Trail—EBMUD Trail use permit required for hikers and equestrians. No dogs. No bicycles. Open sunrise to 1 hour before sunset. Cattle grazing, close gates behind you.

Facilities: Water, restrooms, and phone at Kennedy Grove; restrooms at Inspiration Point, Tilden Regional Park; water and restrooms at Steam Trains, Tilden Regional Park.

F ROM SHADY EUCALYPTUS GROVE to narrow shoreline path to wide ridgetop trail, this route passes diverse landscapes and takes in far-flung views of the Bay Area. You'll climb 810 feet on wide EBMUD trails through grasslands to San Pablo Ridge and then follow the paved ridgecrest trail to Inspiration Point.

Getting There

By Car

North trailhead, Kennedy Grove: From I-80 in Richmond area, take San Pablo Dam Rd. exit. Go east 4 miles to park entrance on left, 0.5 mile south of Castro Ranch Rd.

From Berkeley, Oakland, Orinda and Walnut Creek area, take Hwy. 24 to Orinda exit and turn north on Camino Pablo, which becomes San Pablo Dam Rd. After passing San Pablo Dam Recreation Area, continue 1 mile to Kennedy Grove entrance on right.

Southern trailhead, Inspiration Point: From Hwy. 24, take Fish Ranch Rd. exit. Go 1 mile and turn right on Grizzly Peak Blvd. Pass Lomas Cantadas Rd. and turn right on South Park Dr. after 1.3 miles. Go 1.5 miles to Wildcat Canyon Rd. and turn right. Follow it for about 1.5 miles to large parking area on left at Inspiration Point.

When South Park Dr. is closed to motor vehicles during the salamander migration season (November to March), continue on Grizzly Peak Blvd. to Golf Course Dr. Turn right, pass the clubhouse, and turn right again on Shasta Rd. Turn right on Wildcat Canyon Rd. and continue about 1.6 miles to Inspiration Point.

From I-80 in Berkeley, take University Ave. exit, and head east for 2 miles to Oxford St. (border of the U.C. campus). Turn left (north) on Oxford and after a few blocks turn right (east) on Rose. Go one block, turn left (north) on Spruce and continue to Grizzly Peak Blvd. Cross Grizzly Peak and veer right (east) on Wildcat Canyon Rd. Continue about 3 miles to Inspiration Point.

By Bus

AC Transit 69 and 71 to San Pablo Dam Rd. at Castro Ranch Rd. daily. 67 to Tilden Park weekends and holidays.

On the Trail

Hikers, equestrians, and **bicyclists** start this trip in Kennedy Grove. Head west from the main parking area toward the spacious lawns and eucalyptus groves. Past the Senior Center, at the south edge of the next parking area, a small Bay Area Ridge Trail sign marks a trail entrance on your left. Turn here and go downhill beside an intermittent stream; cross San Pablo Creek, easily forded except after heavy rains. Then bear left and reach Kennedy Grove's entrance road. Across the road, you go through a gate and enter

Equestrian on Nimitz Way.

Rancho El Sobrante

This trip takes you through lands that were once part of the 17,754-acre Rancho El Sobrante, granted to Juan José and Victor Castro in 1841. The rancho consisted of unclaimed lands between other established ranchos, hence its name "the left-over place". The Castros maintained a flourishing ranch, grazed cattle on the surrounding hillsides, and shipped hides and tallow via bayside ports.

By the 1870s, the Castros were beset by struggles with squatters and newly arrived settlers over legal rights to the land. A settlement granted the Castros only a small portion of the former rancho, however, they and their heirs continued operations on the land into the 1980s. Modern-day place names nearby—Castro Ranch Road, El Sobrante, and Sobrante Ridge—remind us of these early landowners.

EBMUD land. Climb up the west side of San Pablo Dam to Old San Pablo Dam Road, now an unpaved trail, and follow it top of the dam.

Continue on Old San Pablo Dam Road, along the reservoir edge. You have glimpses of the water and Sobrante Ridge above it. **177**

California and Nevada Railroad

Look for a boulder with a bronze plaque on the lawn just off the paved parking area. The plaque recounts the history of the California and Nevada Railroad, a wood-burning, narrow gauge train that ran through this valley in the 1890s. The train carried freight and farm products between Orinda and Oakland, and introduced picnickers and vacationers to recreation sites along San Pablo Creek. The railroad was plagued by washouts in winter, dust in summer, and continual financial problems; it never reached Nevada. Today's picnickers can see the wide swath of the train's former roadbed between the rows of eucalyptus trees in Kennedy Grove. The 0.33-mile Kennedy Loop Trail that encircles the upper lawn passes picnic sites named for stops on this historic railroad.

San Pablo Dam

Built as a water supply for the growing population in Berkeley and surrounding areas, San Pablo Dam impounds the waters of San Pablo Creek. It was constructed by Anthony Chabot, who used hydraulic mining techniques to whittle away hillside rock and soil and sluice it to the dam site. The dam project began in 1916 and was completed in 1921, although the reservoir stood empty during many drought years. It wasn't until an aqueduct brought water from the Mokelumne River in 1936 that the reservoir reached capacity; it now stretches southeast for 3 miles.

In the 1970s, the reservoir was drained to rebuild the dam according to modern earthquake standards. Archaeologists found Native American artifacts in shell mounds and graves, clues to native settlements in the San Pablo Creek valley. By 1810, most indigenous people from this area had been relocated to Mission San José; the few who remained to work on the Castro ranch died of pneumonia in 1850.

Archaeologists also found former farm sites of early American settlers. Before the dam was built, ranchers ran both dairy and beef cattle, grew hay, and raised goats in this valley. Several dairies flourished, notably the Scow Dairy, for which Scow Canyon (due east of Kennedy Grove) is named, and the Varsity Creamery.

Pass the road to the Oaks Picnic Area on your left and veer right, uphill. At a log gate beside San Pablo Dam Road, bear left and follow the road shoulder for 0.2 mile to a crosswalk. On the other side of the road, a gate leads into EBMUD watershed lands on the east side of San Pablo Ridge. Turn around here for a view of the reservoir's recreation complex, where visitors can enjoy picnicking, fishing, and boating.

Hikers and **equestrians** join the 0.9-mile Eagle's Nest Trail on the other side of the gate. Cross the Woodchopper Trail, veer left and then right almost immediately. From here the trip to the top of San Pablo Ridge traces a wide fire trail through eucalyptus groves and open grasslands. The eucalyptus trees were planted here and all over the Berkeley and Oakland hills around 1910. Originally planted for use as building material, the soft wood of eucalyptus proved useless for lumber, and the trees were never harvested.

Where the trail makes a wide swing to the right, you can look across the lake to identify landmarks. Sobrante Ridge rises from the east shore; little streams named for early settlers, including Sather and Dutra, flow through hillside canyons into the south end of the lake. You can see the Nunes Ranch in Scow Canyon, in operation since 1914; one of its original ranch buildings still stands.

When you reach the ridgetop, go through a gate into Wildcat Canyon Regional Park. Turn left (south) on Nimitz Way, named for World War II Admiral Chester Nimitz, who walked here daily in his retirement and scattered wildflower seeds. This paved multi-use trail is part of the 31-mile East Bay Skyline National Recreation Trail and also the Bay Area Ridge Trail. It runs for 4 miles along the crest of San Pablo Ridge, from a former Nike site northwest of here, to Inspiration Point.

You have remarkable views from this trail: San Francisco lies directly west across the bay; Mt. Tamalpais rises north of the Golden Gate; the Richmond-San Rafael Bridge crosses the northern bay, joining Marin and the East Bay; Pinole and Hercules peaks lie in the northwest; and due east, Mt. Diablo's 3849-foot summit rises above the surrounding plain.

Continue south along Nimitz Way. Pass the Conlon Trail (see side trip to Wildcat Peak) and continue to the Laurel Canyon Trail,

---

Side Trip to Wildcat Peak

Hikers can make a short side trip to Wildcat Peak from Nimitz Way for views of the Golden Gate and a visit to the International Peace Grove. Turn left on the Conlon Trail and climb to meet the Wildcat Peak Trail. Follow it to Wildcat Peak, where the vista point, enclosed by a double semi-circle of low rock walls, and grove were established by Rotary International and EBRPD. The grove and vista point offer the opportunity to contemplate the significance of friendship across the waters beyond the Golden Gate. Return to Nimitz Way.

---

where another side trip would lead you to the Sequoia Grove, planted by the Berkeley Hiking Club.

On the last half a mile of your trip on Nimitz Way, as you near Inspiration Point, you'll be in the company of casual walkers, hikers, bicyclists, roller-bladers, neighbors walking their dogs, and parents pushing strollers. Signs warn those on wheels to reduce their speed and call out before passing. Benches spaced conveniently along the way invite you to rest and enjoy the passing parade. Occasionally you can see Vollmer Peak, a high point on the Bay Area Ridge Trail route southeast through Tilden Regional Park.

Soon you skirt the stone pillars at the end of Nimitz Way and reach Inspiration Point viewpoint and parking area. Below you lies San Pablo Reservoir, nestled between the rounded hills of San Pablo and Sobrante ridges. At the far north end of the lake lies Kennedy Grove; a 4.4-mile, mostly downhill trip will return you to your starting point there. The Inspiration and Lakeview trails downhill (east) connect with the Old San Pablo Dam Road for an alternate route back to Kennedy Grove.

If you have a car shuttle waiting here, drive east down Wildcat Canyon Road for a bit more history. On the northeast corner of the junction with San Pablo Dam Road remain the scant foundations of a hotel. Rancher and former army general Theodore Wagner built the hotel to serve passengers on the California and Nevada Railroad. Wagner's fine home is now the rural campus of John F. Kennedy University (southeast of this intersection). General Wagner surveyed and built Wildcat Canyon Road in 1889, though it was not paved until 1930.

If you are continuing on the Bay Area Ridge Trail, see the description of the next segment on the following pages for *Tilden Regional Park to Redwood Regional Park.*

TILDEN REGIONAL PARK TO REDWOOD REGIONAL PARK
From Inspiration Point to Skyline Gate

Length: 9.3 miles

Accessibility: Hikers, equestrians, bicyclists

Regulations: Tilden, Sibley, and Huckleberry Regional Preserves—Open 5 a.m. to 10 p.m. Dogs on leash.
EBMUD lands—No dogs or bicycles.
EBMUD permit not required.

Facilities: Restrooms at Inspiration Point; water, restrooms, and phone at Steams Trains at Lomas Cantadas Rd.; water and restrooms at Sibley Regional Volcanic Preserve; water, restrooms, and phone at Redwood Regional Park.

CLIMB TO DRAMATIC VIEWS from San Pablo Ridge, descend to wooded streamsides, and traverse open grasslands: this challenging trip along the spine of the East Bay Hills crosses varied landscapes on trails that range from wide and rocky service roads to duff-covered narrow paths. You'll find sheltered, tree-covered sections and exposed, breezy segments, and often encounter fog that rolls in from the Golden Gate. You'll gain and lose considerable elevation in short stretches—a 860-foot gain in Tilden Park and a 600-foot loss in Sibley Preserve.

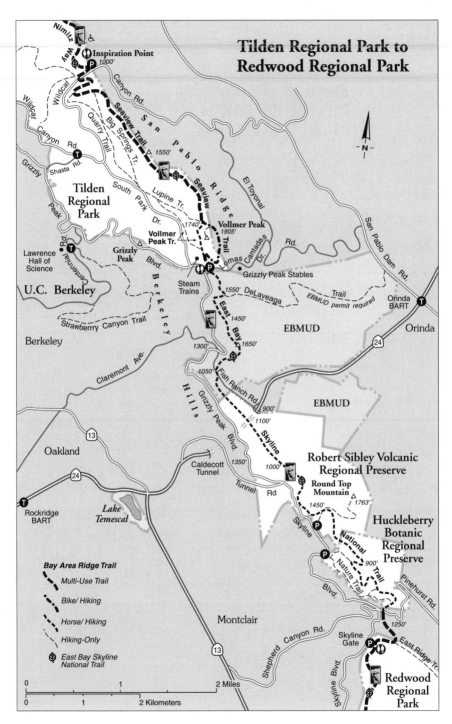

Tilden Regional Park to Redwood Regional Park

Inspiration Point
1000'

Nimitz Way

Wildcat Canyon Rd.

Canyon Rd.

Seaview Trail

Big Springs Tr.

Quarry Trail

△ 1550'

Lupine Tr.

San Pablo Ridge

Seaview Trail

El Toyonal

Wildcat Canyon Rd.

Grizzly Peak

Shasta Rd.

Tilden Regional Park

South Park Dr.

1740'

Vollmer Peak
1905' △

Vollmer Peak Tr.

Tomas A. Cantadas Dr.

Grizzly Peak Stables

San Pablo Dam Rd.

Lawrence Hall of Science

Centennial Dr.

Grizzly Peak

Berkeley Blvd.

Steam Trains

1550' DeLaveaga

Trail
EBMUD permit required

Orinda BART

U.C. Berkeley

Strawberry Canyon Trail

East Bay

1450'

EBMUD

Orinda

Berkeley

Claremont Ave.

1300'

1650'

1050'

Fish Ranch Rd.

24

900'

EBMUD

Hills

Grizzly Peak Blvd.

1100'

Skyline

Oakland

13

Caldecott Tunnel

1350'

1000'

Robert Sibley Volcanic Regional Preserve

Round Top Mountain
△ 1763'

24

Tunnel Rd.

Rockridge BART

Lake Temescal

1450'

Skyline

Huckleberry Botanic Regional Preserve

Skyline

National Trail

Nature Trail

900'

Pinehurst Rd.

Blvd.

Montclair

13

Shepherd Canyon Rd.

Skyline Blvd.

1250'

Skyline Gate

East Ridge Tr.

Redwood Regional Park

Bay Area Ridge Trail

Multi-Use Trail

Bike/ Hiking

Horse/ Hiking

Hiking-Only

East Bay Skyline National Trail

0   1   2 Miles

0   1   2 Kilometers

Getting There

By Car

North trailhead, Inspiration Point: From Hwy. 24, take Fish Ranch Rd. exit. Go 1 mile and turn right on Grizzly Peak Blvd. Pass Lomas Cantadas Rd. and turn right on South Park Dr. after 1.3 miles. Go 1.5 miles to Wildcat Canyon Rd. and turn right. Follow for about 1.5 miles to large parking area on left at Inspiration Point.

When South Park Dr. is closed to motor vehicles during the salamander migration season, November to March, continue on Grizzly Peak Blvd. to Golf Course Dr. Turn right, pass the clubhouse, and turn right again on Shasta Rd. Turn right on Wildcat Canyon Rd. and continue about 1.5 miles to Inspiration Point.

From I-80 in Berkeley, take University Ave. exit and head east for 2 miles to Oxford St. (border of the U.C. campus). Turn left (north) on Oxford and after a few blocks turn right (east) on Rose. Go one block, turn left (north) on Spruce and continue to Grizzly Peak Blvd. Cross Grizzly Peak and veer right (east) on Wildcat Canyon Rd. Continue about 3 miles to Inspiration Point.

South trailhead, Skyline Gate: From Hwy. 24 take Fish Ranch Rd. exit. After 1 mile, turn left onto Grizzly Peak Blvd. Continue to Skyline Blvd. and turn left. Continue 0.1 mile past Shepherd Canyon Rd. to Skyline Gate parking area on left (east) side of Skyline Blvd.

By Bus

AC Transit 67 serves Tilden Regional Park—weekends and holidays schedule and destination different from weekdays.

On the Trail

This 9.3-mile section of the Ridge Trail is part of the 31-mile East Bay Skyline National Recreation Trail (EBSNR Trail), also known as the Skyline Trail, which forms the backbone of a vast trail network in the East Bay. The Skyline Trail traverses East Bay Regional Park District and East Bay Municipal Utility District lands, from Wildcat Canyon Regional Park in Richmond to Cull Canyon Recreation Area in Castro Valley. Signposts display the Bay Area Ridge Trail logo as well as the EBSNR Trail symbol.

Two trailheads en route make it possible to divide this 9.3-mile trip into shorter sections—at Lomas Cantadas Road near the Steam Trains overflow parking lot (3 miles from Inspiration Point) and at **183** the Sibley Regional Volcanic Preserve parking area (3.4 miles from Lomas Cantadas Road).

Inspiration Point to Lomas Cantadas Road

From the trailhead at Inspiration Point, you have impressive views of rolling hills and San Pablo and Briones reservoirs. You begin this trip from the west side of the parking area. Go around the stone gates to Nimitz Way and immediately turn left onto the Curran Trail. Pass the Meadows Canyon Trail on the right and then turn left on a narrow trail that leads uphill to Wildcat Canyon Road.

View from Inspiration Point.

Cross the road and pick up the broad, multi-use trail Sea View Trail, which climbs steadily to reach the vistas that its name promises. Panoramic views unfold at every step (if the day is clear): through the Golden Gate to the sea; San Francisco Bay and its surrounding cities; and our tallest mountains—Tamalpais, St. Helena and Diablo.

The Bay Area Ridge Trail route follows the Sea View Trail for 1.3 miles along San Pablo Ridge. This 1500-foot ridge was uplifted some ten million years ago by stresses on the nearby Hayward and Moraga faults. Pass two junctions with the Big Springs Trail. At

184

the Lupine Trail junction, bicyclists split ways with hikers and equestrians.

Bicyclists continue straight on the Sea View Trail. You'll have splendid views of the North Bay hills as you climb; at the trail's highest point, look east across the ridges and valleys of Contra Costa County to Mt. Diablo, which dominates the landscape. Continue around the northeast side of Vollmer Peak (1913′) and then descend to the Lomas Cantadas/Grizzly Peak Boulevard intersection. This marks the end of the signed Ridge Trail route for bicyclists.

At the Sea View/Lupine trails junction, **hikers** and **equestrians** turn right (south) on the Lupine Trail, marked BAY AREA RIDGE TRAIL AND EAST BAY SKYLINE NATIONAL TRAIL. (Be sure not to make a sharp right on the Arroyo Trail, which goes north from this junction.) Continue along a coyote bush-wild blackberry-tangled hillside below Vollmer Peak to a junction with the Vollmer Peak Trail, where you make a very sharp left turn uphill (east). Climb 200 feet on this rocky path and then veer right on the signed Bay Area Ridge Trail. (The Vollmer Peak Trail continues straight). Your narrow trail follows the contour of the steep hillside, through grasslands dotted with purple lupine and yellow mule ears in spring. Beyond a small bay-tree woods, you emerge at the Steam Trains overflow parking area. Pass through the parking area and meet the paved service road, where bicyclists rejoin the route; continue straight to reach the picnic area by the Steam Trains at Lomas Cantadas Road.

Lomas Cantadas Road to Sibley Preserve

The second segment of this trip, for **hikers** and **equestrians**, extends from Lomas Cantadas Road to the Sibley Preserve, a 3.4-mile trip. A narrow trail begins on the south side of the road and leads to a gate into EBMUD lands. Beyond the gate, the trail crosses a hillside carpeted with a variety of annual grasses and native, perennial bunchgrasses and offers views east of the Contra Costa hills. In an oak woodland, you pass the De Laveaga Trail, which descends east to Orinda. You veer right, again in grasslands. In this peaceful scene of ranches nestled in valleys and cows grazing on hillsides, you can easily forget the proximity of nearby urban centers.

The trail soon makes a zigzag descent next to Grizzly Peak Boulevard to Fish Ranch Road. Cross the road and pass through the gate to the well-marked Skyline Trail. (Please close the gate). You have come 1.45 miles from Lomas Cantadas Road.

185

Masses of poison oak and thistles border the narrow trail in some places, and fragrant sticky monkeyflower and cow parsnip blossom in spring and summer. As you head uphill to cross over the Caldecott Tunnel, you can hear the traffic on Highway 24 below, but near the top you will find a quiet, peaceful rest stop at a rustic bench in a mature oak woodland.

In an opening in these woods, proceed a few hundred yards along an old wagon road to a wooden gate on your right. Here you enter Sibley Volcanic Regional Preserve, and then continue 1.95 miles on the EBSNR Trail. Keep to the north side of a creek, under a canopy of large evergreen oaks, multi-trunked bays and tall big-leaf maples. The trail crosses a bridge over the creek and turns due south, along the west side of the creek. You join a wide fire road and gain 300 feet in elevation to reach the Sibley Preserve parking area and visitor center.

Sibley Preserve to Skyline Gate

The third segment of this Ridge Trail route, 2.9 miles, starts at the entrance to the Sibley Preserve. Take the narrow trail that begins just to the left (north) of the visitor center. Follow it 0.2 mile through pine forests to a junction with a gated road on your left. A side trip on the Round Top Loop Trail begins through this gate. Round Top is an extinct volcano that last erupted over nine million years ago. Deposits from this volcano underlie some of the ridges you traveled over along this Ridge Trail route. Pick up an explanatory brochure at the visitor center to learn about the exposed volcanic rocks in Sibley Preserve.

To continue on the Ridge Trail route along the Skyline Trail, cross the Round Top Loop Trail and the paved road to the water tank, and follow a narrow trail 0.16 mile through a fragrant pine forest. Then you cross another paved road, which leads to Round Top's 1763-foot summit, and arrive at the top of a steep, rocky hillside, where the other end of the Loop Trail comes in from the east. You descend a rugged, precipitous, south-facing hillside, where you may see the brittleleaf and the pallid manzanitas, found in only two places in the world.

At the bottom, you reach San Leandro Creek Canyon and enter the East Bay Regional Park District's Huckleberry Botanic Regional Preserve.

You cross San Leandro Creek on a defunct dam, under a dense cover of oak and bay trees grown spindly in their search for light.

Make a sharp right turn (west) and start uphill on the north-facing slope. (A preserve gate bars an old trail, not recommended, along the creek). Continue through this delightful, verdant section on a well-designed trail with a lush understory of ferns, ocean spray, and huckleberry. This preserve receives heavy winter rainfall and dense summer fogs. In the wet season, you may be crossing full-flowing rivulets coursing down the ravines.

At a junction about 200 yards on your uphill way, you make a sharp left turn (southeast); a gated trail goes straight, uphill, to the Huckleberry Preserve's parking area on Skyline Boulevard. Your trail follows the contour of the hillside through a damp oak-and-bay forest and then climbs steeply up and around the head of a ravine. When you reach a junction with the Huckleberry Preserve Nature Trail, go left on the EBSNR Trail and cross warmer slopes in an oak-and-madrone forest.

Shortly you reach Pinehurst Road at its junction with Skyline Boulevard. Cross Pinehurst and proceed south along the east side of Skyline Boulevard, looking to your left for a trail entrance. Climb steeply through a eucalyptus grove and continue over the hilltop to the junction with the East Ridge Trail in Redwood Regional Park. Turn right (southwest) on the East Ridge Trail, also the Skyline Trail, a broad service road. Continue about 0.25 mile to the Skyline Gate and the end of your trip. If you have a shuttle car waiting here, you can make this a one-way trip. Equestrians able to travel greater distances in a day than hikers can probably make this a round trip.

The next leg of the Bay Area Ridge Trail, an 8.3-mile trip, continues through Redwood Regional Park to Bort Meadow in Anthony Chabot Regional Park. (See *Redwood Regional Park and Anthony Chabot Regional Park.*)

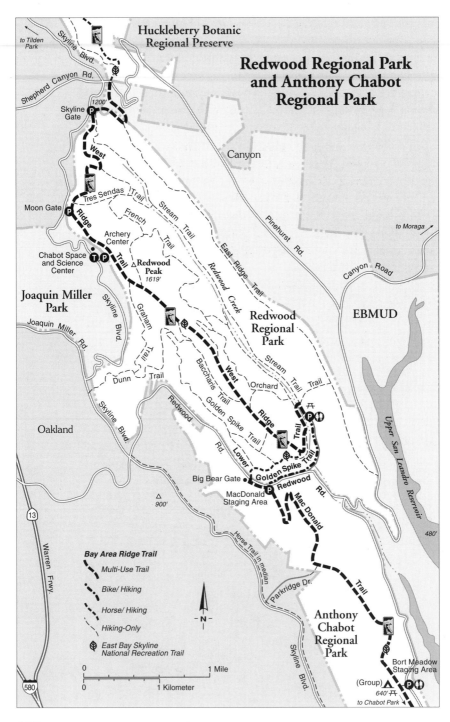

to Tilden Park

Skyline Blvd.

Shepherd Canyon Rd.

Huckleberry Botanic
Regional Preserve

**Redwood Regional Park
and Anthony Chabot
Regional Park**

Canyon

1200'

Skyline
Gate

West

Tres Sendas Trail

Moon Gate

Ridge

French

Stream Trail

Canyon

Pinehurst Rd.

to Moraga

Archery
Center

Chabot Space
and Science
Center

Trail

△ **Redwood
Peak**
1619'

Graham

East Ridge Trail

Redwood Creek

**Joaquin Miller
Park**

Joaquin Miller Rd.

Skyline Blvd.

Trail

Redwood
Regional
Park

EBMUD

Canyon Road

Dunn   Trail

Bacharis Trail

West

Orchard

Stream Trail

Trail

Ridge

Oakland

Skyline Blvd.

Redwood   Rd.

Golden Spike Trail

Trail

Lower

Big Bear Gate

Golden Spike Trail

Redwood

Rd.

Upper San Leandro Reservoir

480'

△
900'

MacDonald
Staging Area

Mac Donald

13

Warren Frwy.

Bay Area Ridge Trail

Multi-Use Trail

Bike/ Hiking

Horse/ Hiking

Hiking-Only

East Bay Skyline
National Recreation Trail

Horse Trail in median

Parkridge Dr.

Trail

Skyline Blvd.

-N-

**Anthony
Chabot
Regional
Park**

0   1 Mile
0   1 Kilometer

(Group) △   640'
to Chabot Park

Bort Meadow
Staging Area

580

REDWOOD AND ANTHONY CHABOT REGIONAL PARKS
From Skyline Gate to Bort Meadow

Length: 8.3 miles

Accessibility: Hikers, equestrians, bicyclists

Regulations: Redwood and Anthony Chabot regional parks—Open 5 a.m. to 10 p.m. or as posted. Dogs on leash.

Facilities: Water, restrooms, and phone at Redwood Regional Park; restrooms at MacDonald Staging Area, Chabot Regional Park; water and restrooms at Bort Meadow, Chabot Regional Park.

F OLLOW THE EAST BAY SKYLINE National Recreation Trail along the ridgeline of the East Bay hills to a broad valley, taking in views of rolling Contra Costa County ridges. You'll travel wide trails through second-growth redwoods, descend into a wooded canyon, and climb to open grasslands. Forested segments provide relief from warm sun or fog on open ridgetops. Elevation gain/loss on this route is 700 feet/1200 feet.

Getting There

By Car

North trailhead, Skyline Gate: From Hwy. 24, take Fish Ranch Rd. exit. After 1 mile, turn left onto Grizzly Peak Blvd. Continue to Skyline Blvd. and turn left. Continue 0.1 mile past Shepherd Canyon Rd. to Skyline Gate parking area on left (east) side of Skyline Blvd.

South trailhead, Bort Meadow Staging Area (Big Trees): From Hwy. 13 in Oakland, take Redwood Rd. northeast. At the Pinehurst Road junction, veer right and continue on Redwood Rd. for 2 miles to Bort Meadow Staging Area on south side of road.

By Bus

AC Transit bus 46 to Skyline Blvd. at Roberts Recreation Area, weekends only and 60 to Moon Gate.

California's Biggest Redwoods

Redwood Regional Park was once the site of a magnificent redwood forest; some trees measured more than 20 feet in diameter, larger than the greatest redwood of the North Coast. Ships that entered the Golden Gate, sixteen miles away, are said to have used two of the tallest trees to steer their course across San Francisco Bay.

This majestic redwood forest was part of early 19th century Spanish land grants. Sadly, between 1840 and 1860, with the rapid growth of Bay Area cities—San Francisco, Oakland, Benicia, and Martinez—it was felled to the last tree; even the tree stumps were rooted out for firewood. After the 1906 earthquake, young redwoods that had sprouted from the remaining stumps were cut to rebuild devastated buildings. Today, all the redwoods in the park are second- or third-growth, although some trees tower above the ridges, reaching 100-foot heights. Former mill sites for the logging operations serve as picnic areas in the park.

On the Trail

This segment of the Bay Area Ridge Trail route continues southeast on the EBRPD's 31-mile East Bay Skyline National Recreation Trail (EBSNR Trail). **Hikers**, **equestrians**, and **bicyclists** begin this trip from Skyline Gate on the West Ridge Trail. The wide, level path is frequented by a variety of trail users—strollers, bicyclists, runners, and local residents escorting their toddlers or walking their dogs. The first half a mile is exposed, although oaks, madrones, pines, and eucalyptus trees fill the canyon below. After rains, a rivulet trickles down an assemblage of smooth, sandstone boulders.

Beneath the first clump of redwoods, the trail surface is sprinkled with soft duff, composed of redwood branchlets and small cones. These tall, second-growth redwoods, intermixed with luxuriant bay trees, support an understory of ferns and shade-loving white and blue wildflowers in spring.

You round a bend and pass the French Trail on the left, about half a mile from the trailhead. If the day is very hot, the French Trail offers a cool, though longer, route for hikers and equestrians; it follows the canyon wall midway between the high West Ridge Trail and the Stream Trail on the canyon floor.

After another 0.5 mile on the West Ridge Trail, you pass the Tres Sendas Trail on the left, a footpath that descends into the canyon to join the French Trail. Soon you pass a short spur on your right that leads to the Moon Gate at Skyline Boulevard and begin a steady climb around the flank of a hill dominated by communications equipment and a water tank. At the outer edge of the flank is a bench overlooking some of Redwood Regional Park's 2,000 acres north and east of here.

For the next half a mile the trail goes through an extensive eucalyptus forest. You may wonder about the origin of these trees: in the early 1900s, a real-estate developer planted vast eucalyptus forests in the Oakland hills, planning to use the wood for lumber; he also built Skyline Boulevard to take investors to his project. However, his timber-harvesting scheme was ill-fated, as eucalyptus wood turned out to be financially unprofitable. The trees were also ecologically disastrous: the fast-growing and invasive eucalyptus, an import from Australia, inhibits the growth of native plant species, such as redwood and oak trees.

Despite the dense, shaggy eucalyptus forests, some native plants spring up in the tangle of litterfall. You will see robust toyon bushes on the hillside and wild huckleberry bushes in moist ravines. You can recognize the huckleberries by their small, shiny green, oblong leaves on long, graceful branches; in late summer, you may see their blue-black berries, much-favored by deer and blue jays. You'll pass seven maple trees to the right of the trail, planted on Arbor Day, 1986, to commemorate the seven astronauts lost on the *Challenger*. A wooden plaque marks the site.

You cross the entrance road to the new Chabot Space and Science Center and continue on the West Ridge Trail below the center. If you have time, stop in to see the exhibits and take a tour; if not, you will surely want to plan a visit. Cross another paved road and pass the Archery Center. Fog moisture drips from redwood trees along this wide, shady path and keeps it damp and cool. A fence lines the trail, its massive redwood posts draped with thick, green moss. About 2 miles from the trailhead, you reach inviting picnic facilities at Redwood Bowl, an open expanse on your left.

At the far end of Redwood Bowl, you meet the Graham Trail and bear left (east) to stay on the West Ridge Trail. (The Graham Trail leads off right to the swimming-pool complex, children's play equipment, and picnic tables in the Roberts Recreation Area.) In 500 feet, the Peak Trail branches left on a 0.2-mile climb to 1619-foot Redwood Peak, the highest point in Redwood Regional Park. You continue on the Bay Area Ridge Trail route, still on the long ridge on the west side of the park. Following the ridgeline on a bare sandstone surface, this wide trail marks the limits of chaparral on the west and forest on the east. Best taken during the cool hours of a hot day, this trail's southwest-facing orientation is most welcome on cool but sunny winter days.

You pass the north and south ends of the Baccharis Trail on your right, as well as several trails that head into the redwood canyon on your left. The Orchard Trail drops into the canyon and meets Redwood Creek just east of the Orchard and Old Church picnic areas. In the 1920s settlers built small homes and a church, and planted orchards in the cut forests. Some of their fruit trees still send out fragrant blossoms in spring.

Before long, the chaparral slopes on your left give way to a dense mixed woodland of oak, madrone, bay, and occasional redwood. You may see deer bounding across the trail or hear them crashing in the woods. The West Ridge Trail descends steeply.

Hikers and **equestrians** leave the West Ridge Trail here and turn right (south) on a short spur trail, just before the West Ridge Trail makes a wide arc to the left (north). The spur trail joins the narrow Golden Spike Trail for a pretty trip through the woods, across a rivulet, and down the hillside to the Lower Golden Spike Trail. Here you swing left and emerge in a clearing (probably the site of a former settler's home), marked by exotic plantings, several sizable redwood trees, and a plank bridge across Redwood Creek

Cross Redwood Road and veer left on the lovely, shady Big Bear Trail through Redwood Canyon; you are now in Anthony Chabot Regional Park. In spring, white plum blossoms glow among the dark conifers at the creekside. In summer, their deep purple leaves add contrast to the various greens of maples, sycamores and bay laurels.

Bicyclists stay on the West Ridge Trail, past the hiker/equestrian spur trail, and reach the park entrance road. Cross a stone bridge at the Fishway Interpretive Site and ride south on the entrance road.

Plank bridge across Redwood Road.

Turn right (west) on Redwood Road, and continue about 0.3 mile to the MacDonald Gate Staging Area.

Redwood's Native Trout

Explanatory plaques at the Fishway Interpretive Site tell the story of a unique species of rainbow trout, *Salmo Iridia*. Descendants of the pure native strain of the original rainbow trout, these fish are found only in Redwood Creek. They migrate from a downstream reservoir up the creek to the park; a Denil Fishway near the park's Redwood Road entrance helps the trout reach their spawning grounds further upstream. Because the fish are the subject of scientific studies, fishing is not permitted anywhere in Redwood Creek.

Hikers, equestrians, and **bicyclists** meet again at the MacDonald Gate Staging Area to begin the second half of this trip, through 4927-acre Anthony Chabot Regional Park. The park was named for a pioneer Californian who built an earth-fill dam across San Leandro Creek to form Lake Chabot. Long before Chabot's time, the Ohlone people lived in these hills, fished the streams, hunted small game, gathered acorns, and dug bulbs for food.

Begin your 3.2-mile trip through Anthony Chabot Park on the MacDonald Trail, another segment of the EBSNR Trail. Climb steeply on the wide, dirt park service road through oak woodlands to the park's central ridge; pause to look back northwest into wooded Redwood Canyon and over the vast public lands you have traversed. Just before the crest of the ridge, turn left on a little side trail that leads to a vista point. From a bench in this pleasant, shady spot you can see across a deep canyon to the opposite ridge where Pinehurst Road swings northwest. The town of Moraga lies beyond, and Mt. Diablo, the central survey point for Northern California, towers above the ridges and valleys of the East Bay.

Return to the MacDonald Trail, which travels just below the ridgetop, through grassland and chaparral. In 1 mile the trail arcs right and passes a junction with the Parkridge Trail; this trail begins at the park's south boundary and crosses a narrow, transverse ridge that divides two drainages—the eastern one feeds Chabot park's Grass Valley Creek.

You bear left on the MacDonald Trail and round a small knoll graced by a few oak trees and many wildflowers in spring. This trail continues for another 1.7 miles along the southwest-facing ridge, with no tree cover, so plan to take it in the cool hours. On the ridge-crest above you, a fringe of oak trees grows; coyote bush (*baccharis*) gains a toehold on the grassy slope below you. Stay on the main park service road past many informal trails that branch off of the MacDonald Trail.

Before long, you begin to see the grassy valley and tall trees of Bort Meadow. Please stay on the trail to the green gate. The Bort Meadow Staging Area, the end of this Bay Area Ridge Trail segment, is about 500 yards beyond the green gate. To reach the staging area and parking lot, turn right on the trail that goes down to the valley. Then turn right again to find picnic tables, barbecues, water, and restrooms in Bort Meadow.

You can have a shuttle car waiting here to return to the Skyline Gate or to drive east on Redwood Road to family campsites in Anthony Chabot Park. (Use the Marciel Gate entrance to reach camping areas.) Group camping can be arranged for Bort Meadow (see sidebar at beginning of this trip).

If you are continuing on the Ridge Trail route another 3.5 miles to Anthony Chabot campsites, head east on the Grass Valley Trail or the Brandon Trail. (See *Anthony Chabot Regional Park, Bort Meadow to Chabot Staging Area.*)

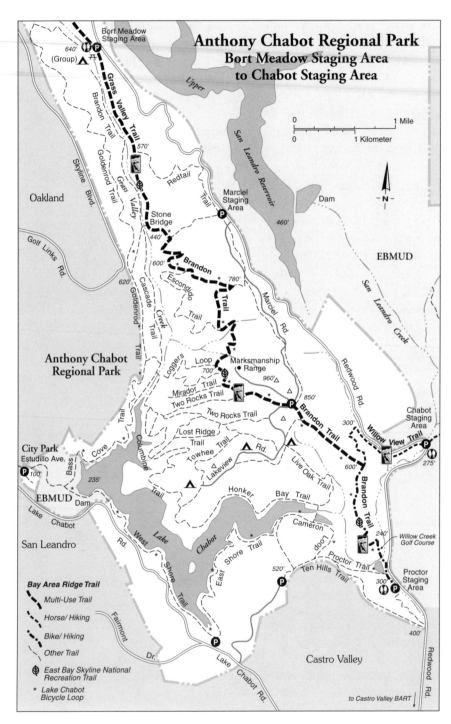

Anthony Chabot Regional Park
Bort Meadow Staging Area
to Chabot Staging Area

Bort Meadow
Staging Area

640'
(Group)

Oakland

Golf Links Rd.

Skyline Blvd.

Brandon Trail

Grass Valley Trail

Goldenrod Trail

570'

Redtail Trail

Stone Bridge
440'

600'

620'

Cascade Creek Trail

Goldenrod Trail

Anthony Chabot
Regional Park

Escondido Trail

Brandon Trail

780'

Loggers Trail

Loop
700'

Mirador Trail

Two Rocks Trail

Cove Trail

Columbine Trail

Two Rocks Trail

Lost Ridge Trail

Towhee Trail

Lakeview Trail

City Park
Estudillo Ave.

100'

235'

EBMUD

San Leandro

Lake Chabot Rd.

West Shore Trail

Lake Chabot

Dam

Marksmanship
Range
960'

850'

Brandon Trail

300'

Rd.

Live Oak Trail

Honker Bay Trail

Cameron

East Shore Trail

520'

Ten Hills Trail

Loop

Proctor Trail

San Leandro Reservoir

Upper

San Leandro Creek

Marciel
Staging
Area

460'

Dam

EBMUD

San Leandro Creek

Redwood Rd.

Chabot
Staging
Area

Willow View Trail

275'

600'

Brandon Trail

240'

Willow Creek
Golf Course

300'

Proctor
Staging
Area

400'

Redwood Rd.

Castro Valley

to Castro Valley BART

Bay Area Ridge Trail

Multi-Use Trail

Horse/ Hiking

Bike/ Hiking

Other Trail

East Bay Skyline National
Recreation Trail

★ Lake Chabot
Bicycle Loop

0 _____ 1 Mile

0 _____ 1 Kilometer

N

ANTHONY CHABOT
REGIONAL PARK
From Bort Meadow
to Chabot Staging Area

Length:	6.1 miles
Accessibility:	Hikers, equestrians, bicyclists
Regulations:	Open 5 a.m. to 10 p.m. or as posted. Dogs on leash.
Facilities:	Water and restrooms at Bort Meadow; water and restrooms at Chabot Staging Area.

EXPLORE THE LITTLE-TRAVELED LANDS of Chabot Regional Park. Your trail runs through a long, grassy valley beside a willow-lined creek and climbs gradually through eucalyptus forests to the ridgetop, a 340-foot elevation gain. Take in sweeping views to the east and then zigzag down 620 feet in the last 1.2 miles. Mostly on wide service trails, this route offers half sun and half shade.

Getting There

North trailhead, Bort Meadow Staging Area (Big Trees): From Hwy. 13 in Oakland, take Redwood Rd. northeast. At the Pinehurst Road junction, veer right and continue on Redwood Rd. for 2 miles to Bort Meadow Staging Area on south side of road.

South trailhead, Chabot Staging Area: From I-580 eastbound, take Redwood Rd. exit and turn left (north), passing under freeway. Continue on Redwood Rd. about 3 miles. After the road narrows, pass the Willow Park Golf Course on your left. Where Redwood Rd. makes a hairpin turn to the left, the entrance to the Chabot Staging Area is on your right.

From I-580 westbound take Castro Valley Blvd. exit and continue west on it to Redwood Rd. Turn right (north) and follow directions above.

 Bicycle trailhead, Proctor Staging Area: Follow directions for Chabot Staging Area above, but after going 2 miles on Redwood Rd., watch for Proctor Staging Area on left.

From Ranchland to Parkland

Once the 525-acre Grass Valley Ranch, this area was purchased by the East Bay Regional Park District in 1951 and called Grass Valley Park. Today it is part of 4,927-acre Anthony Chabot Regional Park. Later additions to today's park included the lands of Don Luis Maria Peralta and Don Guillermo Castro, who raised cattle to sell the hides for leather. In the 1860s, Don Castro's accumulated gambling debts led to the sale of his lands, which were later subdivided and sold to American beef cattle ranchers. As the Bay Area population grew, these lands became valuable watershed and were eventually consolidated into the East Bay Municipal Utility District. The EBRPD now leases the Lake Chabot area from EBMUD and makes it available for public recreation.

On the Trail

 From the Bort Meadow Staging Area, **hikers**, **equestrians**, and **bicyclists** take the gated service road that descends from the parking area (hikers can take the foot trail west of the parking area to the trail junction). At the bottom of the paved road, you can go right (north) about a quarter of a mile to visit Bort Meadow, a picnic and group camping area enclosed by high ridges and rimmed by tall eucalyptus and young redwood trees.

The Bay Area Ridge Trail route goes left (south) through Grass Valley on the Grass Valley Trail, a segment of the East Bay Skyline National Recreation Trail. For the next mile, the trail traverses the east side of the valley, bordered by the willow-lined Grass Valley Creek and chaparral slopes. Across the creek, the Brandon Trail runs parallel to the Grass Valley Trail. The trails converge at the stone bridge at the south end of the valley. Cattle often graze on or near the trail; even if you don't see them, heed the signs asking you to close gates. On the eastern ridge, powerline towers are perches for indigenous creatures—red-tailed hawks, which search the grasslands for rodents on broad, flat wings, and turkey vultures, whose wide, V-shaped wings and wobbly flight distinguish them from the hawks.

You pass the Redtail Trail on the left, just 1 mile from the trailhead. Then the valley narrows and your trail edges closer to the creek; you enter a eucalyptus grove, where coyote bush and young redwoods grow among the trees. The eucalyptus forests in this park were planted in the 1910s by the People's Water Company of Oakland; they spread rapidly and greatly altered the ecology of the hills. Severe freezes in the last 25 years turned the eucalyptus brown, but these hardy trees still survive. If you pass through eucalyptus groves on a foggy or rainy day, you will probably notice the trees' characteristic menthol fragrance.

Soon the Grass Valley and Brandon trails meet at the stone bridge, where the Grass Valley Trail terminates and the Brandon Trail crosses to the east side of the valley. Take a moment to walk out on the bridge to admire its huge sandstone block construction. Downstream from the bridge, Grass Valley Creek courses southeast through a tight canyon to reach Lake Chabot.

Now Ridge Trail users follow the Brandon Trail uphill as it gently climbs into the heads of ravines and around bends. This wide park service road is part of the well traveled Lake Chabot Bicycle Loop. In about a quarter of a mile, you pass an old trail that takes off left, but you continue on the broad Brandon Trail through the eucalyptus forest. In spite of the eucalyptus' dominance, the trail is edged with blackberries, ferns, and seasonal blossoms—inconspicuous creamy-white miner's lettuce and white, four-petaled milkmaids early in spring. In sunny areas, you may see the white clusters of Fremont lilies atop their long stalks and the vibrant orange hues of California poppies. Ubiquitous poison-oak plants explode each spring with shiny green, three-lobed leaves. In fall, you can easily recognize poison oak by its brilliant red and orange leaves. At any time of the year, this plant should be avoided.

Almost a mile from the stone bridge, you pass the right-branching Escondido Trail and continue straight (east) on the Brandon Trail as it curves into canyons and rounds shoulders of the hillside. The prints of many trail users mark the sandy surface of the trail—the corrugated tread of athletic shoes, the continuous pattern of bicycle tires, U-shaped prints of equestrians' steeds, spindly, three-toed bird prints, and the paw prints of many animals. If you look closely, you may see the sinuous track of a snake's passage. After you pass the other end of the Escondido Trail and make a deep sweep into the back of a ravine, you begin to hear rifles cracking in the forest. Unnerving as the noise may be, these weapons are contained in a marksmanship range.

You emerge from the shade of the eucalyptus groves to a south-facing, sloping grassland. Continue through grasslands on the Brandon Trail, past the Logger's Loop, Mirador, and Two Rocks trails to Marciel Road. Across Marciel Road, you'll find a parking area and restrooms. (If you plan to camp in the park, take the Towhee Trail right [south] to reach the campground kiosk.)

Continue on the Bay Area Ridge Trail route; after less than a quarter of a mile, you will find some trailside boulders—good perches for lunch or views northeast across two canyons to Dinosaur Ridge, the highest point of the next Ridge Trail segment. On clear days, the ridge's distinctive white rock is visible from here, almost 2 miles away. Beyond is an impressive vista of the East Bay's seemingly endless succession of rugged ridges.

When it's time to move on, start down the ridgetop trail flanked by evergreen oaks, toyon, and coyote bush.

On the Brandon Trail, immediately past the Willow View Trail, **bicyclists** curve right sharply. Continue downhill on the Brandon Trail for another 1.6 miles to the Proctor Staging Area, the end of the Ridge Trail route for bicyclists.

On the left, the Willow View Trail begins beside a bench in the shade of a beautiful evergreen oak tree. **Hikers** and **equestrians** descend this trail into the woods on the east side of the ridge. You wind along the canyonside under oaks and madrones and pass huge sandstone outcrops decorated with feathery moss and high trail banks festooned with ferns. The trail drops over 200 feet in 0.3 mile and then travels upstream along a little tributary of San Leandro Creek. You cross the tributary and then follow it downstream for another 0.3 mile. This trail, delightfully cool on a hot day, might be muddy after heavy winter rains.

A canopy of bushes and trees shields the trail from Redwood Road, which runs along the bank above this section of the Willow View Trail. An old fence post entwined with wild cucumber vines, a remnant of former ranching days, is on the right side of the trail. A little farther down the trail lies a jumble of smooth-edged, lichen-encrusted boulders under overarching oak and bay trees, from which you can watch the golfers on adjacent Willow Park Golf Course.

Continue on the Willow View Trail north, through a damp, woodsy flat; in early spring, a fabulous garden of three-petaled trillium flowers blossom in shades of pink, mauve, and burgundy. These plants are worth a special trip to see. In the midst of this garden, the Bay Area Ridge Trail arcs right at a fork in the trail; it then crosses the creek and goes under Redwood Road. (After heavy rains, take the left trail out to Redwood Road.)

The Chabot Staging Area, on the other side of the road, is the end of this Bay Area Ridge Trail segment for **hikers** and **equestrians**.

See *East Bay Municipal Utility District Lands to Independent School* for the continuation of the Bay Area Ridge Trail.

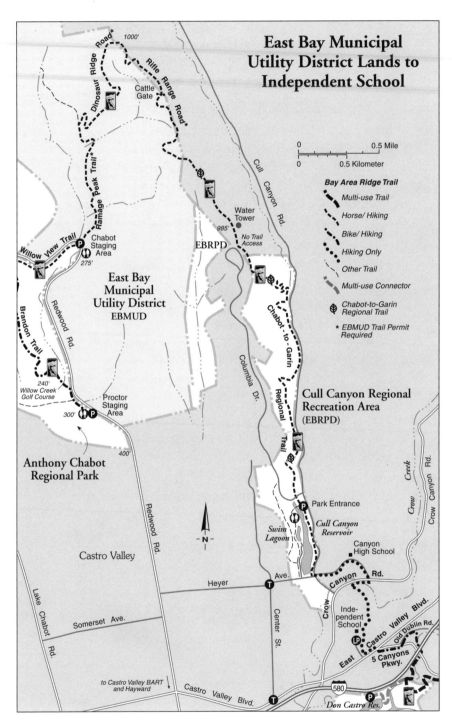

East Bay Municipal Utility District Lands to Independent School

Dinosaur Ridge Road*

1000'

Rifle Range Road*

Cattle Gate

Ramage Peak Trail*

Cull Canyon Rd.

Water Tower

985'

No Trail Access

EBRPD

Willow View Trail

Chabot Staging Area

275'

Chabot-to-Garin Regional Trail

East Bay Municipal Utility District EBMUD

Brandon Trail

Redwood Rd.

Columbia Dr.

240'
Willow Creek Golf Course

Proctor Staging Area

300'

400'

Anthony Chabot Regional Park

Cull Canyon Regional Recreation Area (EBRPD)

Castro Valley

Redwood Rd.

Crow Creek

Crow Canyon Rd.

Park Entrance

Swim Lagoon

Cull Canyon Reservoir

Canyon High School

Crow Canyon Rd.

Heyer   Ave.

Center St.

Lake Chabot Rd.

Somerset Ave.

Independent School

East Castro Valley Blvd.

Old Dublin Rd.

5 Canyons Pkwy.

to Castro Valley BART and Hayward

Castro Valley Blvd.

580

Don Castro Res.

- N -

Scale:
0 — 0.5 Mile
0 — 0.5 Kilometer

Bay Area Ridge Trail
Multi-use Trail
Horse/ Hiking
Bike/ Hiking
Hiking Only
Other Trail
Multi-use Connector

Chabot-to-Garin Regional Trail

* EBMUD Trail Permit Required

EAST BAY MUNICIPAL UTILITY DISTRICT LANDS TO INDEPENDENT SCHOOL
From Chabot Staging Area and Cull Canyon Regional Recreation Area to Independent School

Length: 8.4 miles (7.2 miles from Chabot Staging Area to Cull Canyon Recreation Area; 1.2 miles from Cull Canyon to Independent School)

Accessibility: Hikers, equestrians

Regulations: EBMUD trails from Chabot Staging Area to the water-tank clearing—No dogs or bicycles. EBMUD permit required.
EBRPD trail through Cull Canyon Regional Recreation Area to Independent School—Open dawn to dusk. Dogs on leash. No bicycles. No permit required.

Facilities: Restrooms at Chabot Staging Area; restrooms and water at Cull Canyon Regional Recreation Area.

A LONG RAMBLE through rolling grasslands arrives at a popular swimming, fishing, and picnicking site. This exposed route begins with a steady, 2-mile and 920-foot ascent on a path through oak woodlands. You arrive at 360-degree views from Dinosaur Ridge and follow wide service roads along a rolling ridgetop, through cattle-grazed lands with little shade, and then descend to Cull Creek. From Cull Canyon Regional Recreation Area, hikers can continue on a shadier trail past new subdivisions. Elevation loss is 1000 feet.

Getting There

North trailhead, Chabot Staging Area: From I-580 eastbound, take Redwood Rd. exit and turn left (north), passing under the freeway. Continue on Redwood Rd. about 3 miles. After the road narrows, pass the Willow Park Golf Course on your left. Where Redwood Rd. makes a hairpin turn to the left, the entrance to the Chabot Staging Area is on your right.

From I-580 westbound take Castro Valley Boulevard exit, continue west on it to Redwood Rd. Turn right (north), following directions above.

South trailhead, Cull Canyon Recreation Area: From I-580 eastbound, take Center St. exit and go north on Center St. Turn right (east) on Heyer Ave., turn left (north) on Cull Canyon Rd., and then turn left into recreation area parking lots.

From I-580 westbound, take Castro Valley exit, turn left (west) on East Castro Valley Blvd., and then go right (north) on Crow Canyon Rd. After 0.6 mile, turn left (northwest) onto Cull Canyon Rd. and proceed to recreation area.

South trailhead, Independent School: From I-580 eastbound, take Crow Canyon Rd. exit, cross over freeway, turn right on East Castro Valley Blvd., cross Crow Canyon Rd., and turn left on Independent School Rd. Park outside school gates on cul-de-sac.

Westbound, take East Castro Valley Blvd. exit, turn right on it, and then left on Independent School Rd.

On the Trail

With your EBMUD permit in hand, **hikers** and **equestrians** leave the east side of the Chabot Staging Area and go a few paces along a graveled road to EBMUD's Ramage Peak Trail entrance on your right. Also well-marked as the Bay Area Ridge Trail, this path leads into a shady glade, then winds uphill through oak woodlands on the east side of San Leandro Creek canyon.

About 0.75 mile from the trail entrance, you drop into the Tamler Memorial Redwood Grove, dedicated to the father of Lou Tamler. Lou supervised the Conservation Corps crew that built this trail.

In another 0.25 mile the Bay Area Ridge Trail route veers right (east) on Dinosaur Ridge Road, a wide ranch road. After a couple of zigzags under the powerlines, the trail heads straight up the nose of a bare hillside. An elevation gain of 480 feet in less than half a mile promotes frequent stops to enjoy views back across San Leandro Creek canyon and the forested ridges of Anthony Chabot Regional Park to San Francisco Bay.

Partway up, the trail curves around a knoll and levels off a bit; it then dips into a saddle before beginning another ascent. Looking ahead to the heights of Dinosaur Ridge, you see large white protrusions on the rounded mountaintop; regularly spaced and jagged, they stretch across the summit. From here it's unclear what they might be.

About 2 miles from your start, at a trail junction just below the summit, a Bay Area Ridge Trail sign points east, and wisely avoids an old ranch road that leads directly uphill; you follow the Ridge Trail route around to the east flank.

Side Trip to Dinosaur Ridge

The 0.2-mile side trip to the summit of Dinosaur Ridge is a worthwhile detour that reveals the derivation of the ridge's name. Turn left where the Bay Area Ridge Trail turns right (south) to join Rifle Range Road and climb gently on a short path to the ridge. The jagged protrusions indeed look like the protective plates or fins of a giant dinosaur; a closer look discloses white seashell fossils embedded in the rocks. Probably uplifted from the ocean floor during some ancient folding/faulting process, these rocks remained when softer materials eroded away.

From the top of Dinosaur Ridge you have around-the-compass views of the Bay Area—west to the Golden Gate guarded by Mt. Tamalpais, north to Mt. St. Helena, east to ridge after ridge of open space lands capped by Mt. Diablo, and south to Mt. Umunhum and Loma Prieta. To the southeast, your trail undulates along the ridgetops toward Cull Canyon.

The Ridge Trail turns right (south) on Rifle Range Road, which you follow for about a mile, past grazing cattle. Although oak and bay trees fill the canyons below the trail, only a few offer shelter on this west-facing slope. However, wildflowers, including lupine, wild cucumber, and Indian paintbrush, bloom in an extravagant display of color in springtime.

Turn left (east) where the Bay Area Ridge Trail leaves Rifle Range Road, and follow a short connector trail uphill to a green cattle gate. (Be sure to close the gate.) Beyond this gate turn right (south) beside an electric cattle fence. For a little more than a mile you are on an easement through private land. (Please stay on the trail and respect private property rights.) Your views open up eastward: steep-sided ridges clothed in spring green or summer gold, canyons filled with dark green oak and bay trees, and Mt. Diablo's pyramid in the distance.

Poppy and fossils on Dinosaur Ridge.

You pass through two more green gates, with shy cattle clustered nearby at watering troughs and salt licks, and enter a broad clearing behind a subdivision surmounted by a water tank. This is the EBMUD/EBRPD boundary and the north end of the Cull Canyon Regional Recreation Area; you have come 4 miles from Chabot Staging Area. You cross the clearing and descend into a beautiful forest on the Chabot-to-Garin Regional Trail. Wide-branched, symmetrically shaped specimen oaks stand at several switchbacks, immense bay trees grow around sandstone boulders, and shady stream canyons indent the steep hillside. On warm days, you will be pleased to plunge into these east-facing woods. Trailside gardens of blue hounds' tongue, blood-red trillium, and white milkmaids are early spring treats. Later in the year wild roses show their pink blossoms, and in the fall, white snowberries hang on bare-branched shrubs.

About halfway throught this trip, you step out onto a knoll with views over Cull Canyon. Here the trail becomes a wide, bare path through a pygmy forest of coyote bush. On a grassy shoulder between two forested canyons, you can find sunny picnic places or sheltered rest stops under wide-spreading oaks. You'll also find yellow suncups, blue-eyed grass, and blue brodiaea blooming beside and along the trail when in season. You then plunge back into the forest and zigzag down the mountain to steep-sided Cull Creek and the sounds of frogs croaking and birds singing. The creek is easily forded on rocks at low water, but it may be more difficult to cross in the wet season.

A surprise awaits on the other side of the creek—fluffy-furred, thin-legged, steely-eyed llamas grazing in a pasture. A charming Victorian house across the pasture brings reality to a momentary illusion of the high Andes. These sure-footed Andean creatures make fine pack animals for local mountains too.

The trail gently undulates along Cull Creek for about a mile, up and down its high, fern-draped banks, back into ravines to cross intermittent streambeds, through a flowery meadow, and again into the woods. The creek is diverted through a huge culvert under Columbia Drive; hikers and equestrians follow a path through the culvert as well, to enter Cull Canyon Regional Recreation Area.

Just over 7 miles from Chabot Staging Area, Cull Canyon provides opportunities to swim and fish in the lake and to picnic at tables beside it. This popular recreation area is an attractive place to spend a few hours with friends who could meet you here after your trip.

The Bay Area Ridge Trail continues a short distance south to Independent School, for hikers only. **Equestrians** can ride back to the Chabot Staging Area from Cull Canyon Regional Recreation Area, for an approximately 14-mile round trip. Or they can have a horse-trailer waiting in the unpaved parking area at Cull Canyon Recreation Area.

To continue to Independent School, **hikers** follow the lake's east shore for about half a mile on a path bordered by tall willow trees. To the tune of ducks quacking and red-wing blackbirds singing in the dense rushes, you continue until the trail rises to the side of Cull Canyon Road. At Heyer Avenue you cross Cull Canyon Road at the stoplight, and then proceed uphill along the south side of Canyon School Road. The Bay Area Ridge Trail route stays on the road's unpaved shoulder to the crest of the hill, then descends on an asphalt service road to Crow Canyon Road. Turn right on Crow Canyon Road and head downhill to a stoplight. Cross the road and bear right; cross a side street on your left and in a few paces enter a woodland trail on your left. Under arching oaks, this trail ascends the sheer side of the fern-draped canyon of Cull Creek.

As the trail climbs steadily, the woodland thins out. Now you see straight down to homes along the creek and above to fences, some quite elaborate, enclosing manicured gardens of an adjoining subdivision. After a last little rise, the trail edges Independent School's fenced playground and emerges at a cul-de-sac, the trail's end.

Since the trip back to Chabot Staging Area is more than 8 miles, hikers might prefer to avoid the long round trip by having a shuttle car waiting at the cul-de-sac near Independent School.

The next dedicated segment of the Ridge Trail begins here at Independent School. (See *Independent School to Five Canyons.*)

INDEPENDENT SCHOOL
TO FIVE CANYONS
From Independent School through
Don Castro Regional Recreation
Area to Five Canyons

Length: 5.4 miles round trip from Independent School
4 miles round trip from Don Castro Regional
Recreation Area

Accessibility: Hikers, equestrians, bicyclists

Regulations: Dogs on leash. Observe private property.

Facilities: Restrooms, water, and phone at Don Castro
Recreation Area.

F OLLOW CITY STREETS, a creekside path under a shady canopy, and trails through gently contoured grasslands to high meadows with 360-degree views of East Bay ridges and canyons. Most of this trip is in full sun.

Getting There

By Car

Independent School: From I 580 eastbound, take Crow Canyon Rd. exit, cross over freeway, and turn right on East Castro Valley Blvd. Cross Crow Canyon Rd. and turn left on Independent School Rd. to limited parking outside school gates on street.

From I-580 westbound, take East Castro Valley Blvd. exit, turn right on it, and then left on Independent School Rd.

Don Castro Recreation Area: From I-580 eastbound, take Center St. exit in Castro Valley. Go right on Center, left on Kelly, and then left on Woodroe to park entrance. Park at Ridgetop Picnic Area.

From I-580 westbound, take Castro Valley exit and go west on E. Castro Valley Blvd. Turn left on Grove, left on Center, left on

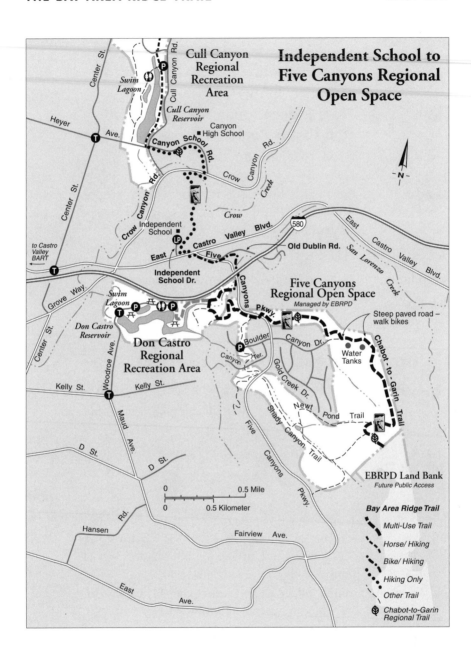

Independent School to
Five Canyons Regional
Open Space

Kelly, and then left on Woodroe to park entrance. Park at Ridgetop Picnic Area.

By Bus

Accessible from BART daily and AC Transit bus 95 hourly.

On the Trail

Hikers and **bicyclists** can begin this 2.7-mile (one-way) trip near the gate to Independent School and follow city streets east to Five Canyons Parkway, or do a 2-mile (one-way) trip that starts at the Ridgetop Picnic Area in Don Castro Regional Recreation Area. Equestrians begin this segment at the Recreation Area. (See *Getting There* directions to Don Castro and begin reading from Don Castro Recreation Area.)

Independent School to Don Castro Regional Recreation Area

As you leave the Independent School gate, **hikers** and **bicyclists** turn left (east) on East Castro Valley Boulevard. Stay on the north sidewalk until after crossing Jensen Road; then cross East Castro Valley Boulevard at the stop light and entrance to Five Canyons Parkway. Cross Five Canyons Parkway at the crosswalk and shortly

San Lorenzo Creek.

veer left onto Old Dublin Road. On a short descent along this narrow paved road, look for a trail on the right, which drops down to the first of three bridges over San Lorenzo Creek that you will cross on this trip. Swollen by Eden and Palomares creeks, this stream flows full and swift in winter, but becomes a gentle trickle in summer. Turn right (west) on the other side of the bridge and go under the high, arched span of I-580. Continue above the creek on a narrow paved road under the shade of willows and oaks to a second bridge, beyond which your quiet route runs adjacent to, but below I-580.

At the third and last bridge, the trail and creek widen as they approach the lake at Don Castro Regional Recreation Area. Beyond this bridge, a spur trail goes right, uphill, to parking, picnic tables, barbecues, water, phone, restrooms, fishing and swimming at Don Castro Recreation Area.

Don Castro Regional Recreation Area to Five Canyons Regional Open Space

From Don Castro, **hikers**, **equestrians**, and **bicyclists** descend a wide, steep trail that bends northeast along San Lorenzo Creek. Cross a bridge over the creek and go left uphill on a wide, rocky trail under a canopy of oaks, bays, and eucalyptus. When you reach a paved road, go left on it and watch for a trail entrance on the right, which is just beyond a rest area on the left. Framed by a semi-circle of large boulders and shaded by a canopy of live oaks, it is a pleasant place to listen to birdsong while enjoying a little rest.

This narrow trail climbs switchbacks up a steep, grassy hillside dotted with spring wildflowers. At Five Canyons Parkway, continue right and uphill on the sidewalk (equestrians use gravel path next to the sidewalk), to a crossing that leads to a trail along the south side of a swale and drainage area below the houses in the Five Canyons development. After crossing a concrete drainage ditch, your ascent becomes steeper and quite rocky, but is festooned with springtime blossoms of deep purple lupines and bright orange poppies.

Shortly you go through an EBRPD gate and traverse a hillside trail to a very steep paved road that leads to two immense EBMUD water storage tanks. Pass through another EBRPD gate and take in ridgetop views: the Bay Area Ridge Trail route through Contra Costa County lies to the north and west, and a future route to Garin Park lies to the southeast.

You now wander southeast on the ridge above Palomares Creek Canyon, through gentle, open grasslands with 360-degree views of

East Bay hills, canyons, forested ridges, and burgeoning subdivisions. Past isolated trees sprouting from jumbled outcrops and stock ponds for thirsty cattle and local wildlife, you turn right and make a short descent to end your trip at another green gate. Retrace your steps to your starting point, either Independent School or Don Castro Recreation Area. Someday in the future this Ridge Trail trip will be extended across the intervening hills and valleys to Garin Park.

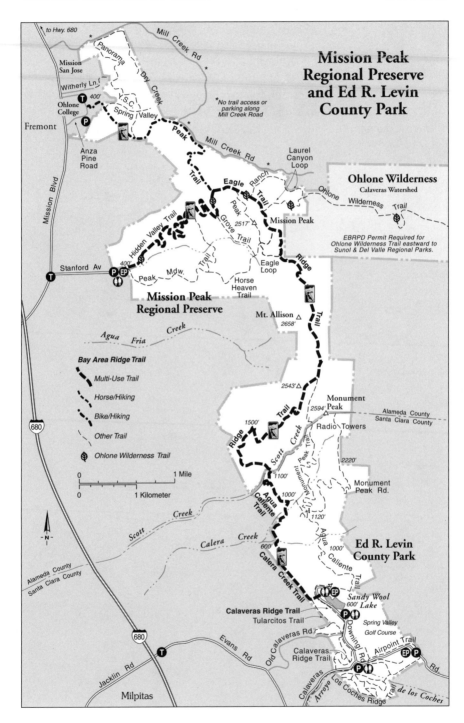

**Mission Peak
Regional Preserve
and Ed R. Levin
County Park**

Ohlone Wilderness
Calaveras Watershed

EBRPD Permit Required for
Ohlone Wilderness Trail eastward to
Sunol & Del Valle Regional Parks.

**Mission Peak
Regional Preserve**

Bay Area Ridge Trail

Multi-Use Trail

Horse/Hiking

Bike/Hiking

Other Trail

Ohlone Wilderness Trail

0 ———— 1 Mile

0 ———— 1 Kilometer

**Ed R. Levin
County Park**

Calaveras Ridge Trail
Tularcitos Trail

*Sandy Wool
600' Lake*

*Spring Valley
Golf Course*

Calaveras
Ridge Trail

Milpitas

MISSION PEAK REGIONAL PRESERVE AND ED R. LEVIN COUNTY PARK
From Ohlone College to Sandy Wool Lake

Length: 10.4 miles

Accessibility: Hikers, equestrians, bicyclists

Regulations: Mission Peak Regional Preserve—Open 5 a.m. to 10 p.m. or as posted. May be closed during extreme fire-danger periods. Dogs under voice control in open-space areas. Ed R. Levin County Park—Open 8 a.m. to dusk. Dogs prohibited on all trails; allowed on 6-foot leash in designated areas. Entrance fee on weekends. Cattle grazing along entire trail; close gates behind you.

Facilities: No drinking water anywhere on trail; water, restrooms, and phone at Ohlone College and Stanford Ave. Staging Area; chemical toilet at Hidden Valley/Peak Trail junction; water, restrooms, and phone at Ed Levin Park.

CLIMB THROUGH HIGH GRASSLANDS past three lofty peaks that top a rugged ridgeline. You'll have views of rippling hills, tree-filled canyons, and bayshore marshlands from these exposed and often windy trails.

Get an early start to do the bulk of the 2220-foot elevation gain before the day warms and to watch the sun rise above the fog-shrouded peaks, illuminating the landscape with an ethereal glow. With a 1920-foot elevation loss, you'll encounter some very steep segments in the final 4-mile descent to a pretty lake in a quiet valley. The side trip to Mission Peak's summit is on a narrow, steep, and rocky trail.

Getting There

 By Car

North trailhead, Ohlone College: From I-680 in Fremont, take Washington Blvd. exit and turn east. Go right (south) on Mission Blvd. and turn left on Anza Pine Rd. to Ohlone College parking. Weekends and holidays, parking free in college lots. When college is in session, obtain parking permit for small fee at vending machines in Lot D or H, and park in any lot.

Alternate north trailhead and equestrian staging area: In Fremont, take Mission Blvd. to Stanford Ave. Turn east and continue to parking at end of road.

South trailhead, Ed Levin Park: From I-680 in Milpitas, take Calaveras Rd. exit and continue east to park entrance. Turn left on Downing Rd. and continue to parking at Sandy Wool Lake. Find trailhead by the hang-glider landing zone across from parking area. Equestrian staging area near Sandy Wool Lake.

 By Bus

AC Transit lines 24 and 28 daily and 37 Monday through Saturday to Ohlone College. Lines 22 and 28 daily to Mission Blvd./Stanford Ave. intersection.

On the Trail

Hikers and **bicyclists** begin this trip from the parking area at Ohlone College on the southern leg of Anza Pine Road. Cross the road and pick up the adjoining, paved Ohlone Trail. Follow it uphill, turn right (east), and go past the swimming pool, where a dirt service road leads to the green gate into Mission Peak Regional Preserve. (There are many gates on this hike, each of which should be shut after you.)

Take the Peak Trail, the wide service road on your right (south), where a signpost bears a Bay Area Ridge Trail logo. The trail heads uphill under a string of powerlines, and views of the South Bay and its urban fringe unfold as you climb steadily around the west side of a 1000-foot hill.

Continue uphill past a small cave carved into the limestone bank and bend north around the shoulder of the hill above a tree-canopied creek canyon. For the next half a mile, you climb through

Mission San José de Guadalupe

This entire trip takes place on lands once part of Mission San José de Guadalupe. In 1797, Spanish colonizers established the mission at the base of Mission Peak, near the site of a Native American village, Oroysom. At its height, the mission held lands from Oakland to Coyote Hills and from the bay to Mt. Diablo.

Originally built of wood with thatched roofs, the mission church and outbuildings were later reconstructed with adobe walls and tile-covered, hewn redwood roof beams. Orchards, vegetable gardens, and promenades surrounded the mission, and extensive vineyards flourished at 400 to 500 feet on the rolling hills. On the upper hills, large herds of cattle ranged, said to number some 12,000 head. After the Mexican government took over Alta California and following the arrival of the Anglos in 1849, the mission complex fell into disrepair; the buildings were further damaged by the 1868 earthquake.

Today, the refurbished mission church and a museum lie just north of Ohlone College and the campus occupies some of the former mission gardens, promenades, and orchards. Mission Boulevard, which you followed to reach the college, approximates the trail that the Spanish explorers and mission padres traveled between the Santa Clara and San José missions. Some of the gnarled, gray-leafed olive trees lining the route remain from the mission plantings.

When the advance guard of mission founders chose this site, they noted it was "beside a perennial stream, found good tillable soil, . . . lime deposits and a rock formation called hewing stone, suitable for construction." You'll still see these features today along the Bay Area Ridge Trail route.

---

a narrow pass between high, rounded hills; in early spring, masses of shiny, yellow-faced buttercups and luminous, purple lupines cover these grasslands. In a basin at the top of the rise, a seasonal cattle pond sits among three hills; you might see swallows and red-wing blackbirds here also.

Bear right under evergreen oak and bay trees to follow the Peak Trail. As you pass through this shady glen, small rabbits may dart across the trail and tiny quail skitter into the bushes while a sentinel parent cries its warning call from a nearby fence post. When you emerge from the woods, your vista northeast takes in the grassy hills and tree-filled canyons that form the drainage of Mission Creek, which once powered the grist mill at Mission San José.

Now on a graveled service road, you begin a gradual climb up the north shoulder of Mission Peak. Young trees crowd into little clefts in the north-facing hillside, promising future shade on these open slopes. In springtime, watch for the hairy, curled necks of white phacelia peeking out of narrow crevices in a jumble of lichen-splashed rocks. Masses of yellow fiddlenecks crowd the surrounding fields. The shear, scarred west face of Mission Peak appears above you, dropping abruptly to the valley below.

Equestrians join **hikers** and **bicyclists** in a sometimes windy saddle, where the Hidden Valley Trail meets the Peak Trail. The 2.7-mile Hidden Valley Trail begins from the Warm Springs Staging Area at the preserve's Stanford Avenue entrance and is the official equestrian route for this segment of the Ridge Trail; part of the Ohlone Wilderness Trail, it is a good hiker and bicyclist route as well. Drainage from Mission Peak and the surrounding high plateau flows into Agua Caliente Creek, which runs down the west side of Hidden Valley. In the Spanish era, an aqueduct carried warm water from this creek to Mission San José for laundering and bathing.

Hiker Side Trip to Mission Peak

Hikers have two options for a short detour to the summit of 2517-foot Mission Peak; whichever one you choose, do not fail to make the less-than-half-mile ascent. From the Eagle/Peak trails junction, hikers can stay right (south) on the Peak Trail to climb the eroded, rocky flank of Mission Peak. Or, follow the Eagle Trail around the peak's east side; veer right at the second Eagle/Peak trails junction to ascend the peak's south flank.

If the day is clear, you'll have views of prominent peaks around the Bay Area— west from Loma Prieta and Black Mountain to Mt. Tamalpais, north to Mt. Diablo, and south to Mt. Hamilton. On a tall post a few feet north of the summit, directional sighting holes point to other important Bay Area landmarks. Just below you, on Mission Peak's craggy face, you occasionally see a herd of feral goats leaping from rock to rock.

Rejoin bicyclists and equestrians on the main Bay Area Ridge Trail route to Ed Levin Park.

Veer left (east) at the Hidden Valley/Peak trails junction and go 0.25 mile to the Eagle Trail. Veer right to follow the Eagle Trail around the peak's east side; from a high, grassy plateau filled with spring wildflowers, the Laurel Canyon Trail branches off to the park boundary. (Trail users with EBMUD permits can follow the Ohlone Wilderness Trail 25 miles east to Del Valle Regional Park, across San Francisco Watershed lands and the beautiful, rugged Sunol and Ohlone Regional Wilderness preserves.)

Follow the fence line across high grasslands to a green gate. Pass through the gate to a wide trail that heads southeast toward an array of antennae on the distant peaks. On a gradual climb, the trail passes remnants of ancient rock walls of uncertain origin, possibly predating the Ohlone period. The Spanish recorded that the hills "abounded in rocks which could be easily transported" to building sites. Here too are some of the springs the Spanish reported.

On the Hidden Valley Trail in Mission Peak Preserve.

Beyond a private road on the right, you curve around the east side of 2658-foot Mt. Allison, the highest point on this three-peak trip. To the east you may see the Ohlone Wilderness Trail on the west face of 3817-foot Rose Peak on Valpe Ridge.

Shortly you enter the land acquired in 1992 from the Wool family, whose ranch lies off to the left. Mr. E. O. (Sandy) Wool, a prominent 1900s rancher, once farmed the valley in Ed Levin Park, where the lake now bears his name. This 400-acre acquisition provided the link between Mission Peak Regional Preserve and Ed Levin Park in Santa Clara County.

For more than a mile you travel through a high valley between Mt. Allison and Monument Peak, both bristling with tall radio and TV towers—a veritable communications village or giant pincushion. Ignore all roads leading to these towers and head due south. The trail then trends west and surmounts a small rise, where a view of the bay unfolds below you. In the South Bay, you'll see the salt ponds, tinged shades of blue-green to rosy lavender, and the marshes, sloughs, mud flats, and open waters of Don Edward's San Francisco Bay National Wildlife Refuge. Due west, Jarvis Landing, an important grain and hide shipping port in the 1800s, was located on the shoreline. Now, the expanding communities of Fremont, Milpitas, and Newark stretch from the foothills to the bay, yet more than 4000 mountainside acres through which the Bay Area Ridge Trail travels remain in public open space.

Over the next 4 miles, you lose 2000 feet in elevation as you descend a wide ranch road on the steep prow of the East Bay hills. Caught between the Hayward and Calaveras faults, these hills were uplifted through the eons by fault movement. Rocky knobs dotting the hillsides are remains of sedimentary deposits formed as the Pacific Plate slid northward along the edge of North America some 15 million years ago.

A multi-trunked bay tree grows in a heap of boulders at a wide switchback, casting welcome shade on a southwest-facing slope. Although the steepness of the trail requires your close attention, pause occasionally to glance skyward for turkey vultures and red-tailed hawks wheeling on the updrafts, or for the golden eagles known to soar over these still-wild lands.

Spring wildflowers bloom in rainbow hues, from magenta redmaids and frilly pink checkerblooms to yellow buttercups, tiny baby blue eyes, and tall purple brodiaea. Great swaths of orange California poppies glow on south-facing hillsides. By early summer, the drying grasses turn golden, contrasting with the dark green oaks that fill the lower canyons, nourished by Agua Fria, Toroges, Scott, Calera and other small, unnamed creeks.

You continue to descend the rounded shoulders of the hills and reach the wooded banks of Scott Creek, the Alameda/Santa Clara County boundary and the entrance to Ed R. Levin Park. In Levin Park, the Bay Area Ridge Trail follows the Agua Caliente Trail past a catch basin for watering cattle and reaches Calera Creek in about half a mile. Lofty sycamore trees line the creekside, their gray-and-white-patterned bark mimicking the shades of the limestone deposits for which this creek is named. The Spaniards, and later the Mexican settlers, burned this stone in kilns to make mortar and whitewash for their adobes.

Go straight to follow the wide Calera Creek Trail to Sandy Wool Lake, 2.1 miles ahead. Now on a less-precipitous route, you cross Calera Creek and stay close enough to its banks to hear the rushing water and to appreciate the afternoon shade from trees along the trail.

You leave the main creek and ford a tributary of Calera Creek in a meadow filled with brilliant yellow mustard in spring. An early settler remarked that the mustard stalks were so strong that "ground squirrels climbed them to get a better view."

The trail hugs a fence surrounding former Minnis Ranch fields, which Santa Clara County purchased in 1967 for Ed Levin Park. These lands were once part of the Tularcitos Ranch ("little tules"), granted to José Higuera in 1821 by Pablo Vicente de Sola, the last Spanish governor of Alta California.

After passing a fenced, private development of homes surrounding a golf course and a pond, continue to a paved road heading left. Continue on the Calera Creek Trail across this road and go through a gate to an unpaved path that follows the fence line for 0.25 mile. At the next gate, you turn left and descend to yet another gate at the park road.

You have skirted a landing field where, especially on weekends, brightly colored hang-gliders alight after their flight from Monument Peak. Just beyond are the picnic tables and greensward beside the blue waters of Sandy Wool Lake, a cool, refreshing finishing point. It was at this pretty picnic area on April 24, 1993, that Bay Area Ridge Trail volunteers celebrated the completion of this long-planned regional trail.

As you plan your trip, you might arrange with friends to meet you here for a picnic and a car shuttle after your exhilarating ridgetop trek. Although hikers would probably eschew a round trip, stalwart bicyclists and equestrians with an early start could make this a 20-mile trip, although the return entails considerable elevation gain.

The next Bay Area Ridge Trail segment begins about 8 miles south at Alum Rock Park in San Jose. (See *Boccardo Trail Corridor.*)

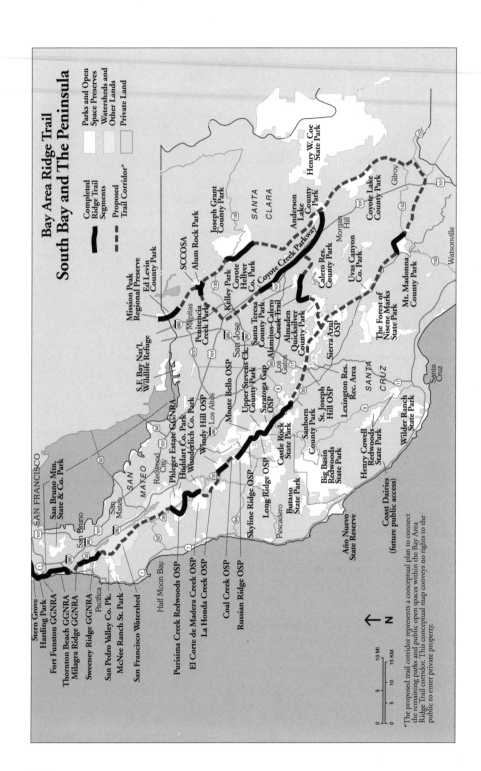

Bay Area Ridge Trail
South Bay and The Peninsula

Completed Ridge Trail Segments

Proposed Trail Corridor*

Parks and Open Space Preserves

Watersheds and Other Lands

Private Land

SAN FRANCISCO

Stern Grove
Harding Park
Fort Funston GGNRA
Thornton Beach GGNRA
Milagra Ridge GGNRA
Sweeney Ridge GGNRA
Pacifica
San Pedro Valley Co. Pk.
McNee Ranch St. Park
San Francisco Watershed

San Bruno Mtn. State & Co. Park

San Bruno

Half Moon Bay

Purisima Creek Redwoods OSP
El Corte de Madera Creek OSP
La Honda Creek OSP

Coal Creek OSP
Russian Ridge OSP

Phleger Estate GGNRA
Huddart Co. Park
Wunderlich Co. Park
Windy Hill OSP

Redwood City
San Mateo

SAN MATEO

Skyline Ridge OSP
Long Ridge OSP
Castle Rock State Park

Pescadero

Butano State Park

Año Nuevo State Reserve

Coast Dairies
(future public access)

Big Basin Redwoods State Park

Henry Cowell Redwoods State Park

Wilder Ranch State Park

Santa Cruz

SANTA CRUZ

Sanborn County Park

St. Joseph Hill OSP
Lexington Res. Rec. Area

Los Altos

Monte Bello OSP

Upper Stevens Creek County Park

Saratoga Gap OSP

Los Gatos

San Jose

Santa Teresa County Park

Alamitos-Calero Creek Trail

Almaden Quicksilver County Park

Sierra Azul OSP

The Forest of Nisene Marks State Park

Mt. Madonna County Park

Watsonville

Morgan Hill

Uvas Canyon Co. Park

Calero Res. County Park

Coyote Lake County Park

Gilroy

Anderson Lake County Park

Henry W. Coe State Park

SANTA CLARA

Coyote Creek Parkway

Coyote Hellyer Co. Park

Kelley Park

Milpitas
Penitencia Creek Park

S.F. Bay Nat'l. Wildlife Refuge

Ed Levin County Park

Mission Peak Regional Preserve

SCCOSA
Alum Rock Park

Joseph Grant County Park

N

0   5   10 Mi
0 5 10 15 KM

*The proposed trail corridor represents a conceptual plan to connect the remaining parks and public open spaces within the Bay Area Ridge Trail corridor. This conceptual map conveys no rights to the public to enter private property.

222

THE SOUTH BAY & PENINSULA

The eastern foothills rise beyond Coyote Creek's lush streamside vegetation.

BOCCARDO TRAIL CORRIDOR
From Alum Rock's Todd Quick Rest Area to a High Valley

Length: 6 miles round trip (includes 3 miles round trip to Todd Quick, 2.4 miles round trip to end of trail, and 0.6 mile round trip extension to summit)

Accessibility: Hikers, equestrians, bicyclists

Regulations: Open daily 8 a.m. to ½ hour after sunset. No dogs. Parking fee.

Facilities: Water, restrooms, and phone.

C LIMB TO A SECLUDED VALLEY surmounted by a high, rounded hill on the east side of the Santa Clara Valley for a birds-eye view of nearby San Jose that expands to include all the South Bay and the peninsula. The trail winds up a southwest-facing, grassy hillside, gaining about 1000 feet in elevation. This round trip is best done with an early start on cool spring days or mid-day in winter when skies are clear after rains.

Getting There

By Car

At this writing, the only access to the trail is from Alum Rock Park's Penitencia Creek Rd. entrance. From I-680 in east San Jose, take McKee Rd. east, turn left (north) on White Rd. and then right (east) on Penitencia Creek Rd. Continue past Dorel Dr. on left and go 0.2 mile to unpaved parking area.

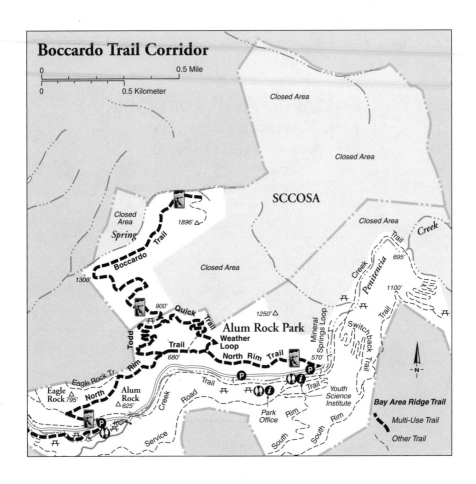

Boccardo Trail Corridor

0   0.5 Mile

0   0.5 Kilometer

Closed Area

Closed Area

SCCOSA

Closed Area

Closed Area

Creek

Spring

1896' △

Boccardo   Trail

Closed Area

1300'

900'

Quick   Trail

1250' △

Todd   Trail

Alum Rock Park

Weather Loop

North Rim Trail

680'

570'

Eagle Rock Tr.

North   Rim

Trail

Eagle Rock 795' △

Alum Rock △ 625'

460'

Creek   Road

Park Office

Service

South   Rim

South   Rim

Mineral Springs Loop

Penitencia   Trail

Creek

Creek

695'

1100'

Switchback   Trail

Trail

Youth Science Institute

Bay Area Ridge Trail

Multi-Use Trail

Other Trail

-N-

By Bicycle

Take Mabury Rd. east, turn left (north) on White Rd. and then turn right (east) on Penitencia Creek Rd., where there are bike lanes and an off-road path. Follow directions for cars to parking, but continue to the paved road entrance and watch for first concrete and rock bridge, take it through the former quarry, and join the Creek Trail.

By Bus

VTA to Piedmont and Penitencia Creek Rd. and to Penitencia Creek Rd. and Toyon entrance on Alum Rock Rd.

On the Trail

The Boccardo Trail Corridor is the first Santa Clara County Open Space Authority site to open to the public and the Boccardo Trail is its first Bay Area Ridge Trail segment. The property is adjacent to the north side of Alum Rock Park at the Todd Quick Loop Trail rest area. Since there is no outlet on the north side of Boccardo, this is a 6-mile round trip that combines the Alum Rock Park trip with a round trip on the Boccardo Trail.

All trail users start on the Creek Trail in Alum Rock Park and continue on the North Rim Trail to the Todd Quick Trail rest area, a one-way trip of 1.5 miles. After pausing here, perhaps to enjoy a snack at the picnic table under the eucalyptus trees, go through the green gate on your right and step onto the wide, new Boccardo Trail. You'll find explanatory panels and a map on the information boards. A sandstone boulder here is embedded with a dedication to the Boccardo family, who helped fund the purchase of this beautiful, open ranchland. Take a few steps beyond to glimpse the high, grassy hill that shields the secluded valley on its north side. (Its rounded, 1896-foot summit affords fabulous views of the mountains, valleys, and cities of the South Bay and peninsula, as well as some prominent peaks of the North Bay.)

The trail swings left and quickly bears right on a short but steep climb. You reach a level area on your right, probably a slump from the side of the high hill, long since settled; note the hill's concave face. A horse watering trough sits beside the trail and a dense grove of oaks lies off-limits to the right. As the author and friend approached this flat, a doe and her fawn appeared, pausing to assess

227

our potential threat. Then, sedately and gracefully, they disappeared among the trees.

After a pause here to appraise your uphill route, bear right (northeast) on the wide service road and continue past lush stands of tall, yellow-flowered mustard. In spring, you may hear the cheery, lilting song of red-winged blackbirds calling to their mates from perches on the mustard. These glossy black birds with brilliant red shoulder patches will accompany you most of the way uphill, flitting across your path to nests in the oak trees. Listen, too, for the meadowlarks' trilling song from their nests hidden in the grass.

After rounding a bend, you traverse a south-facing shoulder of the hill to reach a small, grassy promontory. Here you have your first view of the South Bay scene, growing more extensive as you quickly gain altitude. A patch of oaks, both coast live oak and deciduous blue oak, grace the hillside to your left as you curve around the top of a west-facing prominence on a long, rounded ridge (sometimes called a hogback).

On an eastern reach, you begin a steady, uphill climb. On your right, the hill rises abruptly; on your left, a sheer bank clothed with trees drops into a tight ravine. Spring wildflowers bloom in abundance on either side of the trail. Golden poppies and yellow mule-ears stand tall and bright, but you may need to search for the reddish-purple tomcat clover among the grasses; lupine and blue-eyed grass complete the show. Later in spring, you may find yellow mariposa lilies waving on tall stems, intermixed with deep blue brodiaea. In summer and fall, this route is redolent with the fragrance of California sagebrush, the two-to-three foot, gray bush commonly found here and on many west- and south-facing California hills.

A few openings in the cluster of trees reveal a tiny, unnamed stream in the ravine, a tributary of Penitencia Creek and no doubt the water source for the deer and other wildlife that make their homes in these hills. (Thanks to SCCOSA for preserving their terrain.)

Soon the oak, bay, and buckeye forest becomes more dense and covers both sides of the trail, forming a veritable tunnel for a brief stretch. Look for small, white-petaled woodland stars waving on tall, slender stems and red shooting stars clustered among the ferns and mosses on the high, moist right bank. Shortly, you bear east and leave the canopy of trees to emerge in a valley where, in early spring, shiny buttercups paint the hills yellow. Off to your left, a carpet of brilliant orange poppies covers a west-facing slope. In summer and

View from Boccardo Trail.

fall, these hills take on the California "golden" hue of drying oat grass.

One hundred yards ahead is the end of the Ridge Trail segment in the Boccardo Trail Corridor. Before you start back, however, be sure to take the new, well-designed trail on your right for a 0.3-mile trip to the summit. It heads due east, then makes a switchback going west above a clump of venerable buckeye trees. At the next switchback stands another majestic buckeye whose bare limbs seem stained by rusty lichen. Beyond this turn, you round the east side of the hill, climbing gradually southwest to reach the summit. Fierce spring winds can blast Bay Area summits, so hang on to your hats and bring a warm jacket. Interpretive plaques at trail's end point out what you can see from the top: north to San Francisco, with Mt. Tamalpais rising beyond it, and south to Mt. Hamilton, topped by its observatories. West lie the Santa Cruz Mountains surmounted by Loma Prieta and Mt. Umunhum. At your feet is the trail you just climbed and the tree-filled canyon of Alum Rock Park. On the broad bay plain, the sprawling metropolis of San Jose stretches south to Coyote Valley and north to the edge of San Francisco Bay. If the day is very clear, you can discern the salt ponds at bay's edge and watch them change from blue to pink as the brine is pumped from the west to the east side of the bay.

The strong winds that often sweep this hill offer challenges to raptors. Red-tailed hawks are commonly seen here soaring overhead in search of small rodents and snakes. Updrafts provide the loft these big birds need to glide on their 3-to-6-foot wingspan. Sometimes they fly below the summit; you can identify a red-tail by its rusty-red tail feathers. Other "frequent flyers" include turkey vultures and red-shouldered hawks; an occasional golden eagle also soars here.

After savoring the summit views, stop often on your descent to look into the steep, rugged canyons of Penitencia Creek and Arroyo Aguague. The Penitencia rises in the hills east of Alum Rock Park and the Arroyo Aguague flows north from the heights of Joseph Grant County Park to join the Penitencia at the northeast end of Alum Rock's Creek Trail.

It's all downhill from here to the Todd Quick rest area and on to the west entrance of Alum Rock Park. As you leave the park, you will follow Penitencia Creek for several miles along a tree-lined route. It meanders through eastern San Jose, passes schools and playing fields, is held back in percolation ponds, pauses in pools in Penitencia Creek Park, and eventually joins Coyote Creek to flow with it to San Francisco Bay.

ALUM ROCK PARK
From Penitencia Creek Road to Todd Quick Rest Area

Length: 3.1 miles round trip

Accessibility: Hikers, equestrians,bicyclists, wheelchair users

Regulations: Open daily 8 a.m. to ½ hour after sunset. No dogs. Parking fee.

Facilities: Water, restrooms, and phone at visitor center and picnic areas throughout park.

FOLLOW WIDE PATHS and paved service trails along the park's north hillside and climb the narrow, well-graded Todd Quick Trail to views of wooded Penitencia Creek canyon. This south-facing slope is especially pleasant on sunny winter or early spring days or on a summer evening. Loop back on the Creek Trail and visit remnants of the park's days as a popular spa and recreation area in the early 1900s. You'll gain and lose 960 feet in elevation.

Getting There

By Car

At this writing, the only access to Alum Rock Park is from the Penitencia Creek Rd. entrance. From I-680 in east San Jose, take McKee Rd. exit and head east. Turn left (north) on Toyon Ave. and then right (east) on Penitencia Creek Rd. Bear right after passing Dorel Dr. on left and go 0.2 mile to unpaved parking area where Ridge Trail begins. For additional parking, continue 200 yards to park entrance road on right and proceed to several parking areas at picnic sites and visitor center. You can access the Creek Trail from these parking areas also.

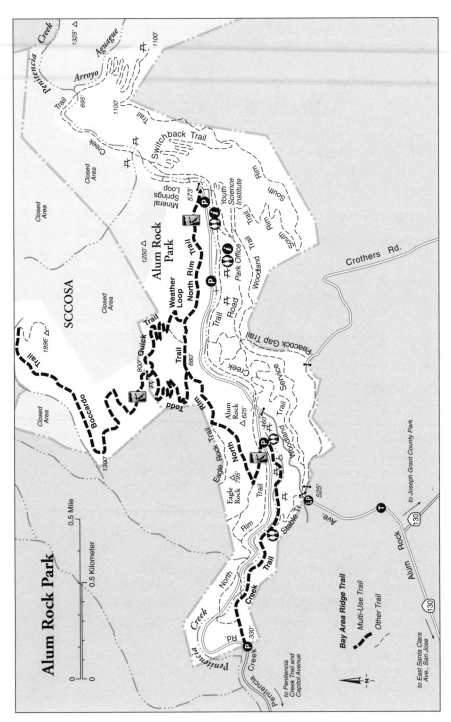

Alum Rock Park

By Bicycle

Take Mabury Rd. east, turn left (north) on White Rd. and then turn right (east) on Penitencia Creek Rd. Follow directions for cars to parking, but continue to the paved road entrance and watch for first concrete and rock bridge, take it through the former quarry, and join the Creek Trail. Note: there are bike lanes and an off-road path on Penitencia Creek Rd.

By Bus

Valley Transit Authority (VTA) to Piedmont and Penitencia Creek Rd. and to Penitencia Creek Rd. and Toyon entrance on Alum Rock Rd.

On the Trail

Since there is no entrance to the park's northernmost point at the Todd Quick Rest Area at this writing and the main park entrance is temporarily closed due to serious landslides, this trip is written from the park's west entrance on Penitencia Creek Road.

From the parking area on Penitencia Creek Road, **hikers**, **equestrians**, and **bicyclists** begin on the Creek Trail, on a series of railroad-tie steps that climb to a broad plain of a former quarry. Excavated for rock to expand the San Jose Airport in the 1960s, the site is now leveled and newly planted with native trees, and is an attractive entry to the broad Creek Trail, a designated National Recreation Trail.

Wheelchair users begin on the park road and cross the first bridge to join the Creek Trail through the refurbished quarry.

Head east on the paved trail along Penitencia Creek, under a canopy of buckeye, bay laurel and willow trees. Seasonal wildflower displays, several varieties of fern, and low shrubs crowd the banks on the trail's south side.

Continue past the Eagle Rock Picnic Area and its parking lot and cross the entrance road to a trail. Go a few feet uphill to a trail junction; the Creek Trail turns right, but you bear left on the North Rim Trail, which shortly turns right, uphill. After 0.3 mile on the North Rim Trail, bear right at a fork and then right again, to continue on the broad trail. (Two left turns take you to Eagle Rock and a scenic overlook—a worthwhile destination itself.)

Alum Rock Steam Railroad

At a sharp bend in the trail after 0.75 mile, note the remnants of large concrete pillars that once supported the Alum Rock Steam Railroad. From 1890 to 1911, when it was destroyed by heavy floods, the railroad ferried passengers between downtown San Jose and Alum Rock Park, then a popular health spa and recreation area. Mount the steep steps on your right to a platform on the former roadbed, where a plaque commemorates Richard H. Quincy, a San Jose wood and coal dealer who promoted the railroad. You'll also have a view of Eagle and Alum rocks, two large volcanic outcrops, and be able to trace the verdant, tree-lined path of Penitencia Creek through the canyon.

From the gently undulating trail, you can look east up the wooded canyon of the Penitencia to its hidden junction with the Arroyo Aguage, a lively stream that originates father south, in the heights of Joseph Grant County Park.

Scattered clumps of evergreen and deciduous oaks shade the way and offer cover for a few picnic tables. Watch for the left-branching Todd Quick Loop Trail and follow it uphill on a comfortable grade, passing more clumps of oaks and the remnants of a former dwelling. At the apex of the trail, tucked under tall eucalyptus trees, a picnic table makes a good rest stop at the park's northern boundary. Pause here to enjoy the views of San Jose, the southern Bay Area, and high points of the Santa Cruz Mountains—Mt. Umunhum and Loma Prieta. Uphill from this rest stop is the new Boccardo Trail in the adjacent holding of the Santa Clara County Open Space Authority (SCCOSA). (See *Boccardo Trail Corridor*.)

To continue on the current segment, follow the trail downhill through grasslands dotted with clusters of wind-gnarled buckeye trees. The trail criss-crosses a small arroyo that nourishes these buckeyes and the nearby tall light blue ceanothus shrubs (the very fragrant California lilac). At the first trail junction, you could bear right to return to the parking area on the North Rim Trail; to make a loop, bear left and circle the east side of the Weather Loop. (Rangers use this area to take weather measurements.) At the next junction, veer left (east) on the North Rim Trail, go 0.45 mile, and then descend to the large parking area at the eastern terminus of the park road.

On the south side of the road, cross the creek on one of the park's ornate 1930s bridges, its balustrades faced with fossil rocks taken from the creek bed. You can visit other remnants of the park's early days, such as the mineral baths upstream and the classic structure that encloses the park's only potable spring, just downstream. Turn right (west) on the Creek Trail and stop at the visitor center to see photos of the park's heyday: mineral baths, an indoor swimming pool, a tea garden, a grand restaurant, and even a dance pavilion, made this a popular recreation area in the early 20th century.

To finish the loop back to the trailhead, follow the sycamore-shaded Creek Trail downstream past several picnic areas and a children's playground to the park's western end at Penitencia Creek Road. The next Ridge Trail segment begins in *Joseph D. Grant County Park*, just 10 miles south of Alum Rock Park on the Mt. Hamilton Road.

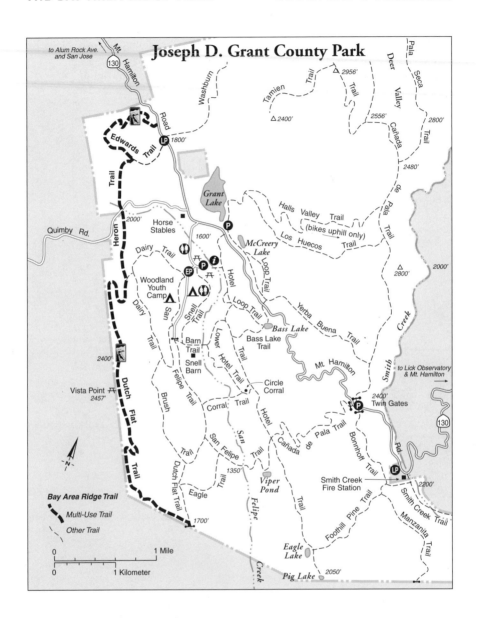

Joseph D. Grant County Park

to Alum Rock Ave.
and San Jose

Mt. Hamilton

130

Washburn

Edwards Trail

LP 1800'

Grant Lake

Heron Trail

Quimby Rd.

2000'

Horse Stables

1600'

Dairy Trail

Woodland Youth Camp

EP

P

Dairy Trail

2400'

San Trail

Snell Trail

Vista Point 2457'

Brush Trail

Felipe Trail

Barn Trail

Snell Barn

Lower Hotel Trail

Corral Trail

Dutch Flat Trail

San Felipe Trail

Eagle Trail

1350'

1700'

Tamien Trail

△ 2400'

△ 2956'

Halls Valley Trail
(bikes uphill only)

McCreery Lake

Los Huecos Trail

Loop Trail

Loop Trail

Hotel Trail

Bass Lake

Bass Lake Trail

Yerba Buena Trail

Circle Corral

Hotel Trail

San Felipe Trail

Viper Pond

Cañada de Pala Trail

Mt. Hamilton

Deer Valley

Pala Seca Trail

2556'

2800'

2480'

2800'

△ 2800'

2000'

Smith Creek

Cañada de Pala Trail

to Lick Observatory
& Mt. Hamilton

2400'
Twin Gates

P

130

LP

2200'

Smith Creek Fire Station

Smith Creek Trail

Bonhoff Trail

Foothill Pine Trail

Manzanita Trail

Eagle Lake

Pig Lake 2050'

Felipe Creek

Bay Area Ridge Trail

— Multi-Use Trail

- - - Other Trail

0   1 Mile

0   1 Kilometer

N

JOSEPH D. GRANT COUNTY PARK
From Edwards Trail Gate on Mt. Hamilton Road to Dutch Flat Trail Gate at Park's Southwest Boundary

Length: 8.4 miles (includes 5.6 miles to southern boundary of park; 2.8 miles from southern boundary to return to main parking area)

Accessibility: Hikers, equestrians, bicyclists

Regulations: Open year round 8 a.m. to sunset. No dogs on trails; allowed in limited areas on 6-foot leash. Entrance fees on weekends and holidays, and on weekdays from one week before Memorial Day until one week after Labor Day. Fees for camping and for use of group picnic areas. Helmets mandatory for mountain bicyclists.

Facilities: Water, restrooms, and phone

TRAVERSE REMOTE OAK WOODLANDS and an ancient bay-tree forest to reach a 2457-foot vista point with outstanding views of the high peaks of the Coast Range. This segment traces the western boundary of 9522-acre Joseph D. Grant County Park on a broad trail, at times rocky and dusty, and gains 700 feet. Most of the route is in full sun, so plan an early start and carry plenty of water.

Getting There

From Hwy. 101 or Hwy. 680 in San Jose, take Alum Rock Ave. exit east. Go 2.5 miles and turn right on Mt. Hamilton Rd. Look for the Edwards Trail on the west side of the road after 6.5 miles, with a small roadside pullout for three or four cars on the east side. Do not block the gated entrance to a private road and the Washburn Trail. If you leave a car here, you will need to walk or ride 1.5 miles back to it after your trip. For additional parking, or to leave a shuttle car, continue 1.5 miles to the main park entrance, on the right. Park at any of several designated areas and return to the trailhead on Mt. Hamilton Road.

On the Trail

From the trailhead on Mt. Hamilton Road, **hikers**, **equestrians**, and **bicyclists** begin a fairly steady climb on the Edwards Trail, an old ranch road. In spring, you may meet grazing cattle along this trail, still used to tend cattle. Occasional monarch live oaks shade your route and blue lupines and large yellow mule ears bloom in spring. At one of several wide switchbacks you can look back over Hall's Valley to Joseph D. Grant's former ranch house complex. Beyond, the park's steep eastern hills rise from the valley and the domes of Lick Observatory on Mt. Hamilton glisten in the sun.

You soon pass a spring where cattle have trimmed the wide-spreading branches of a huge live oak. When you reach the highest point of this first 1-mile leg of your trip, you turn south, intersect the other leg of the Edward's Trail, and pass a small pond shaded by

Sun brightens the oak trees on a stormy day.

a stand of black oaks. Shortly, you turn right onto the Heron Trail and proceed under the powerlines for 0.6 mile to the green-gated crossing of Quimby Road and reassuring Ridge Trail signs. You will follow high powerlines for a good part of this trip.

Continue south on the undulating Heron Trail beyond Quimby Road; huge white oaks arch over the trail and bay trees and willows grow in shaded ravines. Quite unexpectedly, you dip into a dense, cool grove of very large and mature bay trees—one has 14 trunks growing from its central bole.

The Heron Trail ends at a junction with the Dairy Trail, on your left, and you continue your route to the south end of the park on the Dutch Flat Trail. After a wide swing to the right, your climb begins in earnest through a fine stand of black oaks—deciduous in winter, bronze-red in spring when getting their new leaves, and tawny-gold and orange in fall. You may find fox, bobcat, or snake tracks in the dust, and through openings in the woods, you see vast Hall's Valley, the centerpiece of this park. Grant Lake shimmers in the sunlight, and the park's many trails meander down the valley and up grassy hillsides indented by streamlets that nourish stands of oaks and sycamores.

On a steady climb toward the vista point, you pass through a couple of cattle gates and follow the fenced park boundary for the next few miles. Ducks swim in several water impounds for cattle, and birds swoop down for a drink. In this remote area, the dominant sounds are birds singing, hawks calling, and the wind in the trees. Lovely pinkish-white buckeye blossoms fill the spring air with their sweet scent.

From the 2457-foot vista point, Mt. Umunhum and Loma Prieta in the Sierra Azul, the southern portion of the Santa Cruz Mountains, dominate the western skyline, their summits often backed or obscured by fog. If you have lunch in your pack, sit at the picnic table here and note how well the two arms of the Coast Range mountains enclose the Santa Clara Valley. Look north from the dominant southern peaks in the outer Coast Range to Black Mountain, San Bruno Mountain, and Mt. Tamalpais.

You begin your descent on the Dutch Flat Trail through an avenue of deciduous black and valley oaks. In fall, the spent oak leaves carpet the trail and hillsides, their acorns crunch underfoot, and mistletoe hangs from branches. Three fallen giants lie in a ravine beside the trail, their bark riddled with woodpecker holes and their undersides inhabited by ground-burrowing creatures. The trail descends steeply through live oak/madrone woodland with a tangled understory of toyon, poison oak, and wild rose.

The vegetation changes to chaparral, and you soon reach the park's southern boundary. You are now at 1660 feet, almost 800 feet lower than the vista point. The Ridge Trail segment through Joseph D. Grant Park officially ends here. For an alternate route back to the park entrance, turn left on the Dutch Flat Trail and head due north. Continue through rolling grasslands past the Eagle Trail to the Brush Trail; bear right and then left on the San Felipe Trail.

Hikers and **equestrians** can follow the San Felipe Trail all the way back to the parking areas.

However, **bicyclists** must turn right (east) on the Corral Trail and cross San Felipe Creek to either the Lower Hotel Trail or the Hotel Trail to return to the parking area. From the Dutch Flat/Brush Trail junction to the parking areas the route drops another 150 feet in elevation with small gains and losses en route.

This last leg of the trip is quite spectacular in spring when the grasslands put on a brilliant display of yellow, purple, pink, and orange wildflowers. Hawks circle overhead in their never-ending search for rodents. You may see their favorite prey—a plentiful supply of ground squirrels—scurrying through the grasses or sounding their warning calls from upright positions by their burrows.

The next Bay Area Ridge Trail segment begins about 13 miles south at Yerba Buena Parkway north of Coyote Hellyer County Park in south San Jose. (See *Coyote Creek Parkway North.*)

COYOTE CREEK PARKWAY NORTH
From Coyote Hellyer Park to Metcalf City Park

Length: 6.3 miles

Accessibility: Hikers, bicyclists

Regulations: Coyote Hellyer and Parkway Lakes—8 a.m. to dusk. Dogs on maximum 6-foot leash. Entrance fee. No horses.
Coyote Creek Trail—Dogs on maximum 6-foot leash. No horses.
Shady Oaks and Metcalf parks—Open daylight hours.

Facilities: Water, restrooms, and phone at Coyote Hellyer Park; water, restrooms, and phone at Metcalf Park.

COYOTE CREEK TRAVELS 31 MILES from the Diablo Range to the San Francisco Bay. On this 6-mile Ridge Trail segment, you follow the creekbed beneath shady riparian cover and past remnants of the Santa Clara Valley's agricultural history to freshwater lagoons at Metcalf Park, habitat for many year-round and migratory birds species. The wide, paved trail travels a nearly level course.

Getting There

North trailhead, Coyote Hellyer Park: From Hwy. 101 in San Jose south of Fwy. 280 take Hellyer Ave. exit to west side of Hwy. 101 and then bear right (north). At park stop sign, continue straight ahead to parking beyond ranger station; or go left at park stop sign and then turn left to parking at Cottonwood Lake.

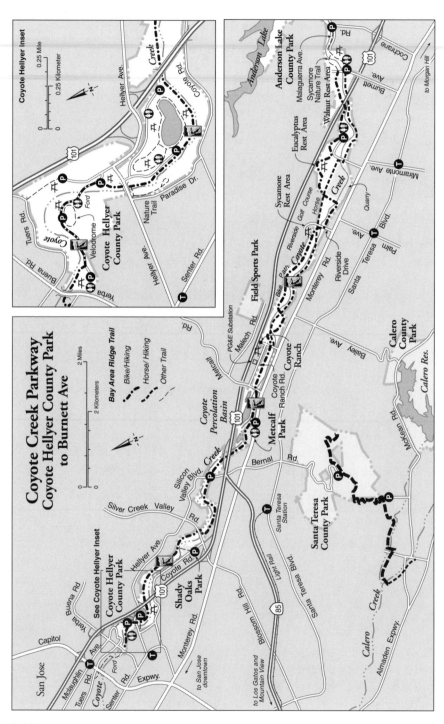

Coyote Hellyer Inset

0.25 Mile

0.25 Kilometer

0

Coyote Hellyer County Park

Coyote Creek Parkway
Coyote Hellyer County Park
to Burnett Ave

Bay Area Ridge Trail
Bike/Hiking
Horse/Hiking
Other Trail

2 Miles

2 Kilometers

0

San Jose

South trailhead, Metcalf Park: From Hwy. 101 in southeast San Jose, take Bernal Rd. exit. After 0.25 mile on Bernal Rd., take Monterey Rd. exit, and turn left (southeast) on Monterey Rd. At Metcalf Rd. make a U-turn and go 0.5 mile northwest to Metcalf Park staging area on right.

On the Trail

Begin at any of several parking areas in Coyote Hellyer County Park and take the paved **hiking** and **bicycle** trail under a leafy canopy of cottonwood, sycamore, and oak trees. A veil of poison-oak vines and elderberry bushes shields the creek here, but you can frequently peak through the vegetation to see the creekbed. In summer, very little water flows through the creekbed, but during winter storms it can be a raging torrent.

In Coyote Hellyer Park you pass picnic tables, lawns, and pretty Cottonwood Lake. When this section of the Ridge Trail was dedicated in October 1990, children lined up along the lakeshore to vie for its stocked trout and bluegill.

The trail follows the creek upstream as it curves east to dip under the Highway 101 bridge. Under tall cottonwoods, the creek flows through a wide, gravelly flat tangled with berry vines and reeds. Soon the trail rises to the bluffs high above the creek, where venerable oaks shade the way. These ancient oaks send their roots deep to tap the creek's underground moisture. White-barked, big-leafed sycamore trees and the cottonwoods, whose roots prefer a streamside location, grow closer to the water.

The trees, along with an understory of shrubs, grasses, and flowers, make a hospitable environment for trail users, as well as for birds, mammals, and reptiles. You will probably see swallows and blue jays flitting in and out of the trees and hear mourning doves and quail calling. At dusk you may see deer or smaller animals searching for food or going to the creek for a drink.

On your right, about 2 miles south from Coyote Hellyer Park, a wide, wooden plank bridge arches over the creek. Cross it to the City of San Jose's Shady Oaks Park, a pleasant place under the oak and pepper trees for your backpack lunch. In this neighborhood park you'll find acres of invitingly green turf, basketball courts, and young children's play equipment.

Return to the trail to meander for another mile under wide-spreading oaks, past a few truck gardens and unkempt walnut

Coyote Creek

From the air, Coyote Creek looks like a verdant, dark green serpent slithering through the Santa Clara Valley. The longest creek in Santa Clara County, it begins in the steep, rugged ridges of Henry W. Coe State Park. The creek flows north through the eastern foothills into the east side of the Santa Clara Valley; Coyote and Anderson lakes—Santa Clara Valley Water District reservoirs—temporarily slow its course. Coyote Creek is joined and enlarged by many tributaries, including Silver, Penitencia and Berryessa creeks, as it makes its way through a corridor of riparian vegetation to the salty waters of San Francisco Bay. The creek's fresh water empties into the complex system of sloughs and marshes in the Don Edwards San Francisco Bay National Wildlife Refuge.

Before European settlers arrived in the Santa Clara Valley, the Ohlone used trails along Coyote and other creeks to reach settlements of other tribes, with whom they traded shells, salt, cinnabar, arrowheads, and stone knife blades. Spanish explorers also followed the creek along Ohlone routes, keeping to high ground above the water's edge.

Early settlers in the valley built houses along Coyote Creek and used its water for their homes, farms, and orchards. Periodic floods destroyed many settlers' homes and inundated their crop lands. In the 1930s, the Santa Clara Valley Water District dammed the valley's major streams—Guadalupe, Los Gatos, Stevens, Calero, Los Alamitos and Coyote—in order to provide drinking and irrigation water, and reduce ground subsidence. They also built percolation ponds along some of the watercourses to recharge the groundwater supply.

In the 1970s, park planners, public officials, and interested citizens began planning recreation trails along creeks in the valley, the foothills and mountains, and beside the bay. The resulting Trails and Pathways Master Plan, adopted into the County General Plan by the Santa Clara County Board of Supervisors in November 1980, guided the development of a network of trails that would link city, county, and regional parks throughout Santa Clara County. Cities also integrated their trails plans with the county network. The trail we follow along Coyote Creek is the result of these city and county plans, formed in cooperation with the Santa Clara Valley Water District. Today, Coyote Creek's broad, tree-lined course provides a recreation corridor for the residents of urbanized Santa Clara Valley, as well as food, shelter, and a travel route for wildlife.

---

orchards. When you go under the large Silver Creek Valley Road bridge leading to an industrial park and new housing developments, you turn sharply right onto a former vehicular bridge. Now closed to motor vehicles, this bridge is the trail route to the creek's west side.

A staging area on the south side of Silver Creek Valley Road is another entrance to the Coyote Creek Trail. A paved path descends from the staging area to creek level, flanked by rangy sycamore trees whose mottled white trunks grow at odd angles. In the creekbed, tall reeds, cattails, and grassy thickets make good nesting sites for migratory and resident ducks and grebes.

You veer away from the creek and pass through an old prune orchard and then travel beside widely spaced oaks and tall black walnut trees. On the low eastern foothills across the creek there are still a few truck gardens and greenhouses. The trail follows the creek as it swings left, past acres of percolation ponds. During drought years, these ponds, which depend upon water from upstream reservoirs, may be dry.

Between the trail and the freeway to the west, a large floodplain is planted with orchards and bordered by a few houses. This still semi-pastoral setting is particularly delightful on a summer evening when sunset casts its slanting, golden light.

Before you reach Silicon Valley Boulevard, new commercial and industrial development fills the land between the Coyote Creek Trail and the freeway. Cross the road and continue south along the wide, shallow creekbed. A Caltrans riparian-habitat planting project was installed here to mitigate for wetlands lost during completion of the Highway 85 extension. Just beyond, the trail, protected by cyclone fencing, comes close to the freeway and then passes beneath it.

Soon you see the first Parkway Lakes percolation pond on your left. These ponds are the largest freshwater lagoons in the county, harboring many year-round and migratory bird species. Look for white egrets and terns, black cormorants, and blue-gray kingfishers as you travel the last part of this trail.

A large new subdivision on your right fills once-open land, but you can still look west to Santa Clara County's high peaks, Mt. Umunhum and Loma Prieta. You will find some magnificent ancient oak trees that still border the lakes and shade the Coyote Creek Trail as it meanders through Metcalf City Park.

The next Bay Area Ridge Trail segment, *Coyote Creek Parkway South*, continues another 7.7 miles south from Metcalf Road to the Anderson/Burnett Ranger Station.

The Bay Area Ridge Trail will someday lead south from Alum Rock Park along the ridges higher up on the eastern hills and cross over to a completed segment in Mt. Madonna County Park. But for

Coyote Lakes near Metcalf Road.

now, the Ridge Trail route encompasses the entire Coyote Creek Trail, one to treasure and travel often.

Another segment of the Ridge Trail begins 3.5 miles west of Metcalf Road in Santa Teresa County Park at the end of Bernal Road. (See *Santa Teresa County Park and Los Alamitos/Calero Creek Trail.*) This route will someday join Almaden Quicksilver County Park and continue on to MROSD's vast holdings in Sierra Azul Open Space Preserve.

COYOTE CREEK
PARKWAY SOUTH
From Metcalf City Park to
Burnett Ranger Station

Length: 7.7 miles

Accessibility: Hikers, bicyclists, equestrians, wheelchair users

Regulations: Dogs on maximum 6-foot leash.

Facilities: Water and restrooms at Burnett Avenue; water, restrooms, and phone at Model Airplane site.

TAKE A SHORT, CREEKSIDE STROLL through the broad Coyote Creek floodplain. You'll enjoy pleasant rest stops under large shade trees and awesome views of the nearby Coast Range. The entire route follows a level paved trail (with unpaved path for horses).

Getting There

North trailhead, Metcalf Park: From Hwy. 101 in southeast San Jose, take Bernal Rd. exit. After 0.25 mile on Bernal Rd., take Monterey Rd. exit, and turn left (southeast) on Monterey Rd. At Metcalf Rd. make a U-turn and go 0.5 mile northwest to Metcalf Park staging area on right.

South trailhead, Burnett Ranger Station: From Hwy. 101 in Morgan Hill, take the Cochrane Road exit west, continue 0.9 mile to Hwy. 82 (Monterey Hwy.) and then bear right. Go north less than 0.8 mile and turn right (east) on Burnett Ave. Continue to creekside parking at the end of the road. Alternatively, from Metcalf Park travel south on Hwy. 82 to Burnett Ave. and turn left.

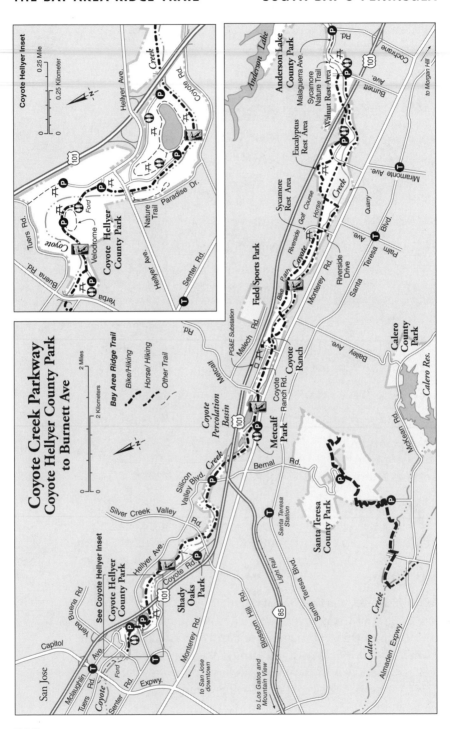

Coyote Hellyer Inset

0.25 Mile

0.25 Kilometer

Coyote Hellyer County Park

Anderson Lake County Park

Malaguerra Ave.

Sycamore Nature Trail

Walnut Rest Area

Eucalyptus Rest Area

Sycamore Rest Area

Field Sports Park

Coyote Ranch

Calero County Park

Calero Res.

Coyote Creek Parkway
Coyote Hellyer County Park
to Burnett Ave

Bay Area Ridge Trail
Bike/Hiking
Horse/Hiking
Other Trail

2 Miles

2 Kilometers

Coyote Percolation Basin

Metcalf Park

Santa Teresa County Park

See Coyote Hellyer Inset

Coyote Hellyer County Park

Shady Oaks Park

San Jose

Capitol

to San Jose downtown

to Los Gatos and Mountain View

South trailhead, Cochrane Rd.: From Metcalf Rd., continue south on Hwy. 82 to Cochrane Rd.; cross freeway and continue to parking on east side of creek.

On the Trail

All trail users head south from the parking area to the Metcalf Road pedestrian and bicycle bridge. Cross the bridge and turn right (south) onto the Creek Trail. This trail follows the willow- and blackberry-bordered creek closely, shifting back and forth between the east and west banks. At Coyote Ranch Road, you bear east, and just before the Coyote Ranch picnic area, the horse and hiker/bicyclist/wheelchair trails split and take separate routes on opposite sides of the creek.

You reach the Sycamore Rest Area midway through your trip, the first of three shady, attractive stops with picnic tables. This is a delightful lunch place where you can enjoy the lush creekside environment. As the name implies, tall, white-barked, big-leaved sycamores provide welcome shade on a hot summer day. These deciduous trees are shorn of their leaves in fall offering dappled sunlight as the weather cools.

Farther on, at the mini-airport for model airplanes, you might enjoy watching the planes take off and land, but perhaps not the buzz of their little motors. Beyond the airport, the trail skirts the golf course, often just below a landscaped, high berm. Shortly you pass under Highway 101 and reach the Burnett Avenue Ranger Station parking area. Across the creek, the Walnut Rest Area provides barbecues and picnic tables under a canopy of oak trees. This is a popular spot for anglers who try their luck in the rushing waters below the Anderson Dam outflow. If you have hiked or ridden your bike to this place, you might arrange for friends to meet you here for an evening barbecue beside the creek.

From here you have the choice of two segments of the Ridge Trail—northwest is the *Santa Teresa/Los Alamitos Creek Trail* and southwest is the *Mt. Madonna County Park* leg. The former is about 10 miles north, the latter about 16 miles south.

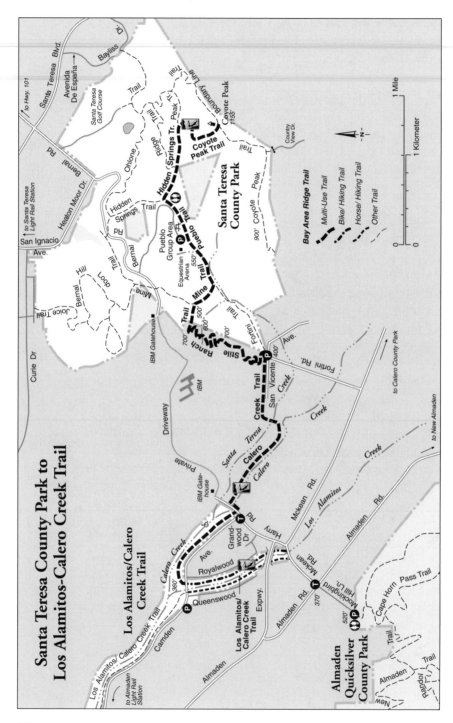

Santa Teresa County Park to
Los Alamitos-Calero Creek Trail

SANTA TERESA COUNTY PARK AND LOS ALAMITOS/CALERO CREEK TRAIL
From Pueblo Group Picnic Area to McKean Court/Harry Road Junction

Length: 6.3 miles (includes 2 miles round trip to Coyote Peak and 4.3 miles to McKean Court/Harry Road)

Accessibility: Hikers, equestrians, bicyclists, wheelchair users

Regulations: Open daylight hours. Dogs on leash.

Facilities: Water and restrooms at Pueblo Group Picnic Area, Santa Teresa County Park.

THE RIDGE TRAIL ROUTE branches east and west through Santa Teresa Park. Take a round trip trail east through high, oak-studded grasslands to Coyote Peak. Then head west on well-graded, exposed paths, past spring wildflower displays, serpentine outcrops, and Coast Range views; listen to the sound of running water on tree-lined, creekside trails. Finish on the wide, paved Los Alamitos/Calero Creek Trail through San Jose, partially shaded in late afternoon.

Getting There

By Car

East trailhead, Santa Teresa County Park: Take Hwy. 101 to Bernal Rd. exit, turn south and go 1.6 miles to park entrance. Continue 1 mile uphill on Bernal Rd. and turn left to Pueblo Group Picnic Area and parking.

West trailhead, Los Alamitos/Calero Creek Trail: In south San Jose, take Almaden Expwy. to Harry Rd., and turn right (south). In next

300 yards look for street parking on Harry Rd. or on adjacent McKean Ct.

Limited parking at west end of Stile Ranch Trail, reached by going south from Harry Rd. on McKean Rd. for 1.1 mile. Turn left (east) on Fortini Rd. and continue to its end.

By Bus

Santa Clara County Transit buses 67 and 68 to Santa Teresa Blvd./Bernal Rd. intersection daily; 13 to Harry Rd. daily.

Santa Clara Valley Parks

Santa Teresa Park is one of a cluster of three Santa Clara County parks in south San Jose—Santa Teresa, Almaden Quicksilver, and Calero Reservoir parks—which encompass 7400 acres in the narrowest part of the Santa Clara Valley. This Bay Area Ridge Trail trip begins in 1677-acre Santa Teresa County Park, at the southern end of the Santa Teresa Hills. Portions of these hills and some of the adjacent valleys were part of Joaquin Bernal's vast Rancho Santa Teresa. Bernal received the 9646-acre land grant as compensation for investigating mineral deposits in California. There were no productive mines in present-day park land, but Bernal and his family lived near here and ran cattle on these hills for many years.

On the Trail

The 2-mile round trip to 1155-foot Coyote Peak, the highest point in the park, begins from the Pueblo Group Picnic Area. A few yards uphill from the picnic area, turn left (east) on the Pueblo Trail. You soon turn right on the Hidden Springs Trail, and cross a bridge over an unnamed creek. For a short while, lovely, broad-branched oaks and spring-flowering buckeye trees shade your route. As you climb, however, the shade trees disappear. Pass the park's own Ridge Trail coming in on the left and very shortly turn right on the Coyote Peak Trail.

For the next half a mile, you follow the hillside up to and around the peak, with westward views to the wooded heights of the Santa Cruz Mountains. When the trail swings around to the south slope of the peak, take the left (northwest) turn to reach the summit, which offers sweeping panoramas of the Santa Clara Valley. This fertile land, once known as the Valley of Heart's Delight, the fruit bowl of America, has been developed with industrial plants, shopping malls and subdivisions. Yet, thanks to far-sighted citizens who many years ago voted funds for park acquisition, the county's foothill and mountain parks and its creekside and baylands parks preserve some of the valley's former characteristic environment. Now retrace your steps to the Pueblo Group Picnic Area and begin the next leg of your Ridge Trail trip.

Follow the Pueblo Trail west along the base of the rocky slope above the picnic area. Continue through the equestrian arena, unless some activity is in progress. On the far side of the arena, bear left (south) on the Mine Trail, which descends gently to Santa Teresa Creek, the small stream that drains the park's lush central meadow, now closed off for wildlife habitat protection.

Descend through a little valley, along the west side of the stream, bordered by a few oaks and many bay trees. The south-facing hillsides, punctuated by lichen-encrusted igneous rocks interspersed with gray sage bushes, come alive with blue brodiaea, orange poppies, and magenta clarkia after winter rains. Among the rocks you may see gray-green serpentine, the California state rock. According to the geologic maps, a small fault runs through this valley.

You curve north, away from the creek, and climb to a ridgetop where a clump of gnarled oak trees with small, leathery, dull-green leaves stands beyond the fence on your left. This native California tree, mostly found on serpentine soil, is known as the leather oak. You will see other specimens of leather oak as you traverse sections of this trail cut through serpentine rock.

The trail descends into a quiet, grassy swale, sprinkled with fine old valley oak trees and pierced by an intermittent stream. After you cross the stream, go left on the Stile Ranch Trail; the Mine Trail continues right. The Stile Ranch Trail weaves through the sloping grasslands at a very manageable grade. Then you follow well-graded switchbacks uphill through tall grasses, ungrazed for several years. In early morning or late afternoon, you may see deer going to drink from the stream in a little notch in the hills.

As you zigzag up an east-facing ridge on a trail cut through solid rock and lined with chunks of serpentine, you can appreciate the persistent, indefatigable volunteer trail builders' work. With the combined efforts of the County Parks Department, which funded the trail construction and now maintains it; the Trail Center, which directed the trail crews; and International Business Machines (IBM), which granted an easement over its land, this 1.6-mile Stile Ranch Trail was completed in 1991.

Volcanic rock along the Stile Ranch Trail.

As you dip into another valley among clumps of bunchgrass, light-pink-flowered buckwheat, and tall stalks of white yarrow, a couple of switchbacks take you to a plank bridge across a wash (dry in summer). Then you begin ascending an east-facing ridge, a veritable Persian carpet of multi-colored wildflowers in spring. Even in July this hillside glows with the magenta haze of Clarkia blossoms. A few oaks and an occasional bay tree offer shade in the late afternoon. When you reach a switchback, look east to see the white domes of the Lick Observatories atop Mt. Hamilton in the Diablo Range.

The trail levels at the top of the ridge and passes a couple of 6-foot-high sentinel rocks splashed with orange and red lichen. One rock set farther back from the trail could serve as a traveler's bench and rest stop to enjoy this remote oak-dotted grassland. You have a panoramic vista west of the Santa Cruz Mountains: Loma Prieta, the tallest mountain in this range, lies south of Mt. Umunhum, which you can identify by the tall structure on its summit. In the valley below, subdivisions and ranchettes are replacing the vineyards and orchards of yesteryear. Feeder roads in the valley bear former ranchers' names—Fortini and Rakstad, among others.

As you descend rapidly down numerous switchbacks, note a fine old rock wall that undulates uphill and down, defining an early boundary, which is now also delineated by a barbed-wire fence. Bluebird boxes hang from tall posts on the far side of the wall. This open, oak-studded grassland is typical habitat for the rusty-breasted Western bluebird, but rapid urbanization has decreased its natural nesting sites and reduced this beautiful bird's numbers. Yet it is known that bluebirds can be lured to nest in bird boxes.

When you reach the bottom of the hill, follow the trail between a double row of live oaks and go right (west). On the City of San Jose's Calero Creek Trail between the road and the fence, you head west for less than a quarter of a mile and cross a log barrier. Proceed along the base of the slope past wide fields, planted or plowed according to the season. Signs request that you stay out of these fields. (There is no outlet on the other side.)

Carry on for half a mile, then angle left (south) between two barbed wire fences. The trail dips down into the channel of intermittent Santa Teresa Creek, which drains the terrain through which you just traveled. This streamcourse is a cool, damp place under a tall canopy of trees—delightful on a hot day, but potentially difficult to cross after heavy rains.

On the other side of the stream, you pass a well-kept, fenced walnut orchard on the right and a small model-plane landing strip on the left. When you reach the next line of trees, veer right (west) and follow a wide track for half a mile beside Calero Creek. Accompanied by the sounds of running water, leaves rustling in the breeze, and birds singing in the trees, you wander along the creek bank sheltered by tall, white-barked sycamores and broad-branched oaks. Through openings in the understory of elderberry, poison oak, and wild roses, you can see the creek flowing toward its confluence with Los Alamitos Creek.

Your creekside ramble continues to Harry Road, where you cross the road, jog left on the bridge over the creek, and then turn right on the paved trail that meanders through a wide easement between the creek and Camden Avenue. Although the creek is completely hidden from view, its wooded corridor adds charm to the neighboring community.

Wheelchair users can join others on the paved Los Alamitos/Calero Creek Trail.

About 1 mile from Harry Road, Camden Avenue crosses Los Alamitos Creek, which joins Calero Creek just beyond. Here, at the confluence of the two creeks, in a wide half-moon-shaped easement, is a parking area on the site of a proposed park. Beyond here the City of San Jose's Los Alamitos/Calero Creek Trail extends 2.7 miles to Almaden Lake, a water sports/picnic park, from which a trail will someday follow the Guadalupe River to San Francisco Bay.

However, to continue on the Bay Area Ridge Trail from Camden Avenue south to the McKean Court/Harry Road junction, take one of the paths on either side of Los Alamitos Creek. These wide paths are built on raised levees between the generous creekbed and the adjoining subdivision roads and meander upstream for a mile, shaded by oaks, sycamores, and cottonwoods. Choose the paved

Egret watching for prey on Los Alamitos Creek.

Quicksilver Mining

Los Alamitos Creek originates in Almaden Quicksilver County Park, west of Santa Teresa Park in Santa Clara Valley. Long before Europeans settled in this valley, Native Americans traveled upstream along Los Alamitos Creek to gather cinnabar in the hills of today's Almaden Quicksilver Park. They crushed the rock to make the red pigment with which they decorated their bodies. Cinnabar, also known as quicksilver, came under high demand during the Gold Rush, and the park was the site of a large mining operation.

Cinnabar contains mercury, and residual mercury in the soil and streams is highly toxic. Some areas of the abandoned Almaden Quicksilver mines are closed to the public, and prominent signs along the trails warn that fish in the creek are contaminated by mercury and should not be eaten. Plans to expand the use of Almaden Quicksilver Park were delayed by the state while preventive measures to control toxicity took place, but many miles of park trails are now open to hikers, runners, and equestrians. In the near future, the Bay Area Ridge Trail route may extend to the park and continue west to join ridgeline trails in the Santa Cruz Mountains.

---

trail on the east side of the creek for shade in the afternoon on a hot day. Equestrians use the unpaved trail on the west side.

Continue on the creek trail as it dips under the broad span of the Almaden Expressway bridge. You will be joined on this last leg of the trip by children on bicycles, neighbors strolling or walking their dogs (on leash), runners, and parents teaching youngsters to ride bikes. For the time being, the Ridge Trail segment terminates at the intersection of McKean Court and Harry Road. You can retrace your route to Santa Teresa Park or have a shuttle car waiting at one of two parking areas along the route, either at Camden Avenue or at a limited-parking place at the foot of the Stile Ranch Trail on parklands off Fortini Road.

The next segment of the Bay Area Ridge Trail climbs to the crest of the Santa Cruz Mountains in southwestern Santa Clara County. (See *Mt. Madonna County Park*.)

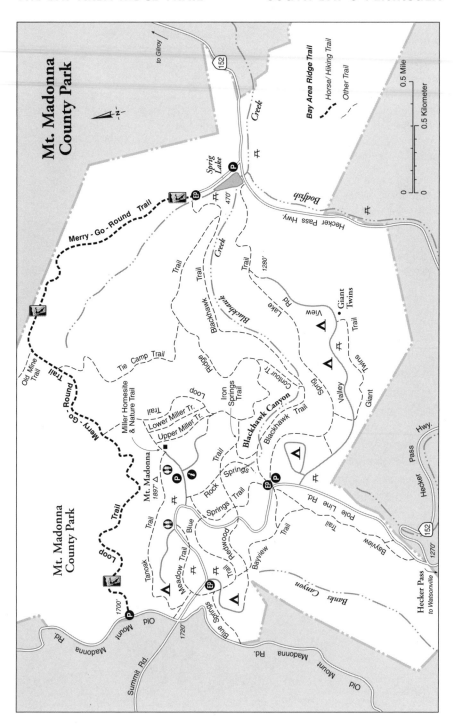

Mt. Madonna
County Park

to Gilroy

152

Sprig
Lake

Merry - Go - Round Trail

Bodfish

Creek

Hecker Pass Hwy.

Bay Area Ridge Trail
Horse/Hiking Trail
Other Trail

0.5 Mile
0.5 Kilometer

470'

Creek

1280'

Giant
Twins

View

Lake Rd

Blackhawk

Trail

Blackhawk

Trail

Trail

Tie Camp Trail

Ridge

Contour Tr.

Spring

Twins

Valley

Giant

Old Mine Trail

Merry - Go - Round Trail

Miller Homesite
& Nature Trail

Lower Miller Tr.

Upper Miller Tr.

Loop

Iron
Springs
Trail

Blackhawk Canyon

Blackhawk

Trail

Mt. Madonna
1897' △

Rock

Springs

Springs Trail

Pole Line Rd.

Trail

Bayview

Hecker

Pass

Hwy.

152

1270'

Mt. Madonna
County Park

Loop

Trail

Trail

Tanoak

Meadow Trail

Blue

Redwood Trail

Bayview

Banks Canyon

Hecker Pass
to Watsonville

Loop

1700'

Old Mount Madonna Rd.

Summit Rd.

Blue Springs

1720'

Mount Madonna Rd.

Old

MT. MADONNA
COUNTY PARK
From Sprig Lake Entrance
to Old Mt. Madonna Road

Length: 3.1 miles

Accessibility: Hikers, equestrians

Regulations: Open sunrise to ½ hour after sunset. No bicycles on trails. No dogs on trails; 6-foot leash or less in campground, in confined areas overnight. Entrance fee.

Facilities: Water, restrooms, and phone

AN UPHILL TRIP FROM lakeshore to redwood summit—you'll gain and lose 1250 feet and take in excellent views of southern Santa Clara County and the inner Coast Range mountains. The wide service road skirts an intermittent creek, crosses boulder-strewn grasslands, swings through chaparral and scrub-oak forest, and finishes in a cool, steep-sided redwood canyon. Before you reach the redwood-forested Loop Trail, the southeast-facing trail is mostly in sun.

Getting There

Sprig Lake trailhead, from the east: From Hwy. 101, take Hwy. 152 (Hecker Pass) west exit and follow signs through Gilroy. About 7 miles east of Hwy. 101, watch for Sprig Lake entrance on right.

Sprig Lake trailhead, from the west: From Hwy. 1 in Watsonville, take Hwy. 152 (Hecker Pass). Pass Pole Line Rd. at the summit and continue 3 more miles to Sprig Lake entrance on left.

Main park entrance, from the east: From Hwy. 101, take Hwy. 152 (Hecker Pass) west exit and follow signs through Gilroy. Go 10 miles to Pole Line Rd. at Hwy. 152 summit. Turn right (north) and proceed to park entrance.

Main park entrance, from the west: From Hwy. 1 in Watsonville, take Hwy. 152 (Hecker Pass) to Pole Line Rd. at summit. Turn left (north) on Pole Line Rd. and proceed to park entrance gate.

On the Trail

Starting from the east shore of Sprig Lake, **hikers** and **equestrians** head up the wide dirt road, under a shady canopy of tall oaks, buckeyes, and big-leaf maples beside an unnamed tributary to Blackhawk Creek. You can glimpse the small creek bouncing over its rocky bed through the tangled undergrowth well below the left side of the trail. On the right, perennial streams have cut canyons on a forested ridge.

After 0.3 mile, you come to a fork in the road where you go right on the Merry-Go-Round Trail; the Blackhawk Trail takes off left. A staging area offers a turn-around for horse trailers, a horse watering-trough, and a picnic table or two.

Go around the barrier to vehicle traffic on the Merry-Go-Round Trail and continue on the Ridge Trail route through a leafy corridor. Oaks and buckeyes predominate, but tall madrones search for sunlight and offer climbing posts for persistent poison oak and occasional native honeysuckle vines. After 0.1 mile on this trail, you reach a small grove of tall, second-growth redwoods; moss-covered rocks, old tree stumps, and lush redwood sorrel complete this patch of coastal redwood community.

After a short climb, you emerge in a bare opening between high banks, perhaps a borrow-pit for road repairs. You pass through grasslands below a west-facing ridge topped by mixed conifer forest. Back in a woodland of oak and willows, note two side trails on the right—one to a horse trough and another to a small meadow dominated by an ancient live oak. Early spring wildflowers at trail's edge—buttercups, some milkmaids, and lupines—will cheer you on this uphill leg; in summer and fall, bushy, yellow sticky monkey-flower and magenta clarkia brighten the trailside.

As the Merry-Go-Round Trail swings northwest and enters open grasslands, you may see a gate on the right that leads out of the park. Continue past the gate and then pass the right-branching Old

Mine Trail. Large boulders dot the grasslands, accented by a riot of orange poppies, yellow mule-ears, and blue lupines. To the west, near the terminus of the Ridge Trail, the Mt. Madonna summit is the southernmost high point of the Santa Cruz Mountains.

After 1.4 miles on the Merry-Go-Round Trail, the Tie-Camp Trail branches left. A cut log offers a shaded seat at the junction, under an oak of promising stature. Indeed, there was a Tie Camp along this trail, where redwoods were cut and shaped to form railroad ties. You continue on the Merry-Go-Round Trail's pebbly, fine black-gravel surface; as you ascend steadily with little shade, you'll realize the importance of starting early on a summer day. Your chances of garnering shade along the trail's edge are hampered by a drainage ditch, a vital ingredient in maintaining a good roadbed for service vehicles. In winter, the exposure to full sun is most welcome.

The chaparral plants found here—artemesia, sticky monkey-flower, toyon and honeysuckle—offer good forage for the birds whose call you may hear. Before long the trail narrows a bit, and live oaks reach over manzanita, toyon and other chaparral plants. Less than half a mile beyond the last junction, the Merry-Go-Round Trail ends and the Loop Trail forks straight ahead and left. To continue on the Ridge Trail route, you go straight on the Loop Trail.

Beneath the shade of oaks, tanoaks, bays, and madrones, this old logging road is pleasantly cool. The trail levels off and then, in a dramatic change in terrain and vegetation, descends slightly into a second-growth redwood forest. Note the horizontal ax cuts on huge redwood stumps. Loggers inserted boards into these cuts and then laid cross boards on top. Two hardy men stood on the cross boards, 8 to 10 feet above ground, and used a long, two-handled saw to cut through the gigantic trees. They always felled the tree uphill because it might have splintered in the longer fall.

As you follow the trail along a shelf that is cut into a high, steep, north-facing mountainside, you'll hear the sound of rivulets of water falling over sandstone boulders in the still forest. The moisture from rain and fog-drip promotes the growth of these second- and third-growth redwoods into a healthy forest. The forest exists today as a park for all to appreciate because of the foresight of Santa Clara County in purchasing this land.

Recent rains and high winds may clutter the trail with fallen limbs and twigs of redwood. Scattered eucalyptus trees, grown exceedingly tall in the forest's dense shade, yet accustomed to sunshine, are more likely to lose limbs and even topple.

261

The trail heads into deep ravines cut by intermittent streams, then swings out around the shoulders of the mountain. Drooping branches of wild roses and several kinds of ferns grace the hillsides above the trail. A few immense sandstone boulders accent the steep hillside, and others form jumbled streambeds for tumbling intermittent creeks. Shortly, look for a small shed on your left, backed by a 15-foot-high, moss-covered rock wall; another lower wall is on the other side of a lively stream. Henry Miller, cattle baron and former owner of this park, built these walls to protect his underground water tank and pumphouse; a steam engine pumped water hundreds of feet uphill to his mountaintop home. Today, the water serves as a backup supply for fire suppression.

A few minutes beyond the water tank you reach a gate that bars vehicle entry to this beautiful trail. Beyond the gate, Old Mt. Madonna Road, formerly the Old Watsonville Road, ends this segment of the Ridge Trail. From here, the next segment lies about 20 miles north in Santa Teresa County Park on the east side of the Santa Cruz Mountains. (See *Santa Teresa County Park and Los Alamitos/Calero Creek Trail.*)

If you have a car shuttle waiting for you, there is some room to park beside this old road for a return to Sprig Lake. Better still, have your friends meet you at one of the beautiful picnic sites in this 3500-acre mountaintop retreat. You can walk up this old mountain road through redwood groves of impressive girth and height and thickly carpeted with pink-blossomed, three-leafed redwood sorrel. At the corner of Old Mt. Madonna and Pole Line roads, the Meadow Trail parallels Pole Line Road, heading south to picnic areas among the redwoods. The Tan Oak Trail branches left from the Meadow Trail and wanders through the woods to park headquarters, picnic areas and the old Miller homesite.

To return to Sprig Lake parking by trail, take the Ridge Trail in reverse (downhill all the way) or try the well-designed, shady Sprig Lake Trail: follow the Tan Oak and Rock or Blue Springs trails to a wide opening in the woods about 1 mile south, just off Pole Line Road. The Sprig Lake Trail (hikers only) leads right and the Blackhawk Trail (hikers and equestrians) goes straight. You return to the west side of Sprig Lake, easily accessible to the east side where you started this trip.

SANBORN COUNTY PARK AND CASTLE ROCK STATE PARK
From Sunnyvale Mountain Picnic Area to Saratoga Gap

Length: 4.9 miles

Accessibility: Hikers, equestrians

Regulations: Open 8 a.m. to dusk. No dogs or bicycles on trails.

Facilities: None near trail

FOLLOW THE SKYLINE TRAIL along the ridgeline of two vast parks—Sanborn County Park and Castle Rock State Park. On the route of old Summit Road, you'll wind along the protected east side of the crest of the Santa Cruz Mountains, through forests of Douglas-fir, oak, and madrone; you'll pass impressive sandstone outcrops and vestiges of early homesteaders' orchards and dwellings. This level trip is ideal for warm days, entirely in shade on a trail that varies in width from wide to narrow.

Getting There

South trailhead, Sunnyvale Mountain Picnic Area: Take Skyline Blvd. (Hwy. 35) to Sunnyvale Mountain Picnic Area, 4.7 miles south of Saratoga Gap (at junction of Hwy. 35 and Hwy. 9), on east side of road.

North trailhead, Saratoga Gap: Take Skyline Blvd. (Hwy. 35) to Saratoga Gap, at the junction with Hwy. 9. Parking area 500 feet south of Saratoga Gap on east side of Skyline Blvd.; some spaces available at trailhead on northeast side of Hwy. 9.

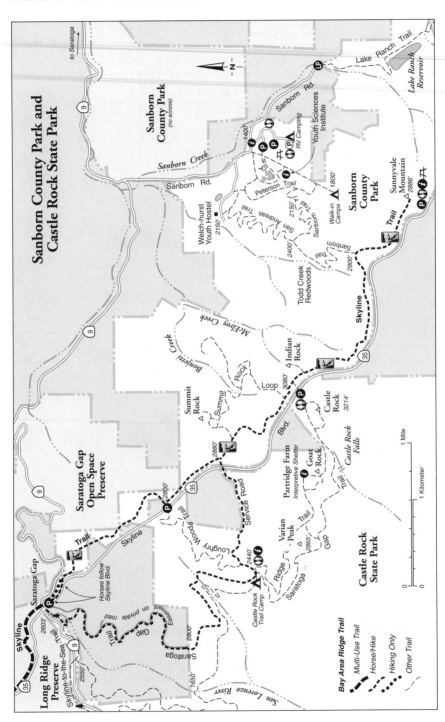

Sanborn County Park and Castle Rock State Park

Early Skyline Settlers

In the late 1800s, immigrants from mountainous regions of Europe settled these hillsides, set out orchards and vineyards, and built wineries. But the 1906 earthquake struck hard here, causing landslides and severe property damage. Eventually most of the hillside farms were abandoned. After Santa Clara County bought the parklands in the 1970s, the dwellings were removed, but some exotic plantings remain. As you follow the route of the old road joining their farms, imagine the hard work and tenacity required to carve out an existence on these steep hillsides far from the fertile Santa Clara Valley.

On the Trail

From the north side of the Sunnyvale Mountain Picnic Area, **hikers** and **equestrians** follow the Bay Area Ridge Trail as it skirts the edge of an overgrown orchard and heads northward on a wide, old farm road. Stay left at a fork in the trail and climb gently under a canopy of mature Douglas-fir trees. In a forest clearing, fragments of a sea captain's garden mark the former Seagraves' residence; beyond, on a clear day, you may see south across Monterey Bay to the Monterey Peninsula and its mountains.

Looking east to the Diablo Range from Indian Rock.

Back in forest, the trail descends to a shady redwood grove with two picnic tables beside a stone wall that flanked the now-closed entrance to the Seagraves' homestead. Beyond here the trail narrows and continues through a dense forest, into and around steep-sided canyons, the headwaters of streams named for early settlers—Todd, McElroy, and Bonjetti.

You soon pass the first of several wind- and water-eroded sandstone outcrops, uplifted over the millennia by folding and faulting along the San Andreas Rift Zone.

Keep left at the next junction and pass a few pear trees, temptingly adorned with fruit in fall. Many deer tracks in the dust of the trail, the sharp call of blue jays, and the chatter of squirrels in the trees attest to the presence of others who may enjoy this feast.

On a wide swing east around the shoulder of a ridge, you meet the Sanborn Trail, 1.2 miles from your starting point.

Side Trip to Todd Redwood Grove

Follow the Sanborn Trail to Todd Redwood Grove (0.3 mile), where a few venerable giants remain after the logging of the late 1800s. Further along the Sanborn Trail, you'll find backpack campsites, 1.6 miles downhill in Sanborn Park, and the Sanborn Hostel, set in a grove of majestic redwoods off the San Andreas Trail. The hostel, known as Welch-hurst, was built as a mountain retreat by former Santa Clara County Judge James Welch in the early 1900s. It is now on the National Register of Historic Places

Side Trip to Indian Rock

The best views are from Indian Rock, 1.2 gentle uphill miles from the Sanborn Trail intersection and 0.2 mile from the main trail. Rock-climbers and casual hikers clamber up on these exposed sandstone rocks, set among gnarled oaks and madrones, for east and south views over the Santa Clara Valley to the high points of the South Bay—Mt. Hamilton and Mission Peak. The dramatic drop-off on the east side of the rocks is a breathtaking 150 feet.

The Skyline Trail continues northwest, cut into the steep sides of Todd Creek canyon. Madrones and tanoaks intersperse the Douglas-fir forest, and you have occasional glimpses of the Santa Clara Valley.

Just past Indian Rock, you pass a sign for Castle Rock State Park, 3,000 acres of semi-wilderness mostly east of Skyline Boulevard on the steep west face of the Santa Cruz Mountains. Hiking trails lead to waterfalls, shady forests, extensive sandstone outcrops and a backpack trail camp (2.7 miles from the Skyline Boulevard parking area).

The Bay Area Ridge Trail route continues north on the Skyline Trail; you pass the south end of the Summit Rock Loop Trail, which descends into Bonjetti Creek Canyon, and then the north end of the loop trail, after curving around yet another settler's homesite.

Side Trip to Summit Rock

A short (0.2-mile) side trip takes you to Summit Rock, another huge sandstone outcrop. Veer right at the second junction of the loop trail. From perches some 20 feet off the ground, you'll have a hawk's-eye view of Sanborn County Park and Monte Bello Ridge to the north.

Bear left at the second junction of the Summit Rock Loop Trail and follow the wide, old roadbed northwest past some big mahogany-barked, broad-branched madrones.

When you pass between two boulders marking the trail entrance from a parking area near Skyline Boulevard, veer right, staying on a narrow ridge until you join the old Summit Road going north.

You leave Sanborn County Park and enter the 120 acres of Castle Rock State Park that lie on the east side of the Skyline ridge, formerly known as Loghry Woods. The Skyline Trail, now a narrow footpath, continues through mixed woodland, swinging around the east side of a 2920-foot rise.

Then, skirting a fenced, private inholding, you once again pick up old Summit Road, with tall, fragrant firs overhead, soft forest duff underfoot, and moss-covered rocks at trailside. Fern fronds and clumps of iris edge the trail, while fine-leafed ocean spray and hazelnut bushes often overhang it. In spring you may find blue hound's tongue blooming on tall stalks.

Equestrians can cross Skyline Boulevard (from the parking area marked by two boulders) to Castle Rock State Park and take the 1.5-mile Service Road Trail, then head north for 4.5 miles on the Saratoga Gap Trail. Or you can continue with hikers on the narrow path, but 0.3 mile before the end of the route, you must descend to

Skyline Boulevard on a cut-off to the left in order to circumnavigate one impassable stretch. Check with the Castle Rock ranger for details.

For the last 0.3 mile of this trip, **hikers** traverse a very steep hillside on a narrow footpath for hikers only. After crossing a couple of sturdy wooden bridges over gullies and passing some sizable sandstone boulders, you come to the Saratoga Gap parking area.

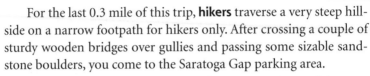

Hikers and **equestrians** meet at the Saratoga Gap parking area and continue on the next leg of the Bay Area Ridge Trail.

On the north side of Highway 9, the Bay Area Ridge Trail continues through the forests of Saratoga Gap Open Space Preserve, into Upper Stevens Creek County Park, and then on to the west-side ridgelands. (See *Saratoga Gap to Skyline Ridge Open Space Preserve*.)

For those who left cars at the Sunnyvale Mountain Picnic Area, it's time to turn around and make the trip southeast to your starting point or have a shuttle car waiting here for you.

SARATOGA GAP OPEN SPACE PRESERVE TO SKYLINE RIDGE OPEN SPACE PRESERVE
From Saratoga Gap to Horseshoe Lake

Length: 7.8 miles

Accessibility: Hikers, equestrians, bicyclists, wheelchair users

Regulations: MROSD Preserves—Open dawn to ½ hour after sunset. Dogs on leash in designated area of Long Ridge Open Space Preserve just north of Grizzly Flat entrance; maps available from MROSD office. Bicyclists must observe 15-mile-per-hour speed limit and wear helmets. Upper Stevens Creek County Park—Open 8 a.m. to sunset. No dogs. Helmets required for bicyclists.

Facilities: No water on route; restrooms at Horseshoe Lake parking area in Skyline Ridge OSP; water and phone at Saratoga Summit Fire Station (0.7 mile north of Saratoga Gap on west side of Skyline Blvd.).

T RAVEL THROUGH MOIST evergreen forests, oak-madrone woodlands, and high grasslands along the crest of the Santa Cruz Mountains. Stunning coast and bay views greet you on this Ridge Trail route through three MROSD preserves and one county park.

The trail roughly follows old Summit Road, a wagon route used by early settlers before Skyline Boulevard was built. Trail width and surface varies from a narrow path to a wide patrol road, soft in forests and along creekbeds, and firm and bare through grasslands. You'll gain and lose 400 feet in elevation, plus several ups and downs en route of 100 to 300 feet. Be prepared for wind and fog on

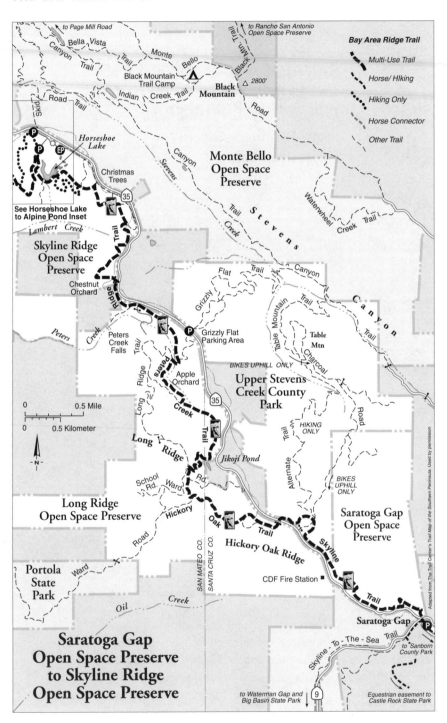

Bay Area Ridge Trail

Multi-Use Trail

Horse/ Hiking

Hiking Only

Horse Connector

Other Trail

to Page Mill Road

Bella Vista

Canyon   Trail

Monte

Bello

Black Mountain
Trail Camp

Indian   Creek Trail

Black
Mountain

2800'

Skyline   Road   Trail

P

P

EP

Horseshoe
Lake

Christmas
Trees

35

See Horseshoe Lake
to Alpine Pond Inset

Lambert Creek

Skyline Ridge
Open Space
Preserve

Chestnut
Orchard

to Rancho San Antonio
Open Space Preserve

Black Mtn Trail

Road

Canyon

Monte Bello
Open Space
Preserve

S t e v e n s

Waterwheel Creek Trail

Stevens

Creek

Ridge   Trail

Peters

Creek

Peters
Creek
Falls

Long

Ridge

Trail

Peters

Creek

Trail

Apple
Orchard

Flat

Trail

Grizzly

Grizzly Flat
Parking Area

P

35

Table Mountain Trail

Canyon

Charcoal

C a n y o n

Trail

Table
Mtn

BIKES UPHILL ONLY

Upper Stevens
Creek County
Park

Road

HIKING
ONLY

0   0.5 Mile

0   0.5 Kilometer

— N —

Long   Ridge

Jikoji Pond

School Rd.

Ward

Rd.

Alternate

Trail

BIKES
UPHILL
ONLY

Long Ridge
Open Space Preserve

Hickory

Road

Oak

Trail

Saratoga Gap
Open Space
Preserve

Portola
State
Park

Ward

Creek

SAN MATEO CO.

SANTA CRUZ CO.

Hickory Oak Ridge

CDF Fire Station

Skyline

Trail

Oil

Creek

Saratoga Gap
Open Space Preserve
to Skyline Ridge
Open Space Preserve

Saratoga Gap

Skyline - To - The - Sea   Trail

P

to Sanborn
County Park

to Waterman Gap and
Big Basin State Park

9

Equestrian easement to
Castle Rock State Park

Adapted from The Trail Center's Trail Map of the Southern Peninsula. Used by permission.

exposed ridgetops, and for heat on protected west- and south-facing slopes.

The Hickory Oak gate on Skyline Boulevard makes it easy to break this route into two trips—a shady, moderately level, 2-mile trip from Saratoga Gap to Long Ridge OSP, and a 5.8 mile trip from there to the Horseshoe Lake parking area in Skyline Ridge OSP.

Getting There

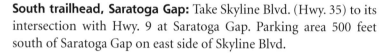

South trailhead, Saratoga Gap: Take Skyline Blvd. (Hwy. 35) to its intersection with Hwy. 9 at Saratoga Gap. Parking area 500 feet south of Saratoga Gap on east side of Skyline Blvd.

North trailhead, Skyline Ridge OSP, Horseshoe Lake: Take Page Mill Rd. to Skyline Blvd. (Hwy. 35), turn left (south), and go 0.75 mile to preserve entrance on west side of road.

On the Trail

Hikers, **equestrians**, and **bicyclists** enter Saratoga Gap OSP under a canopy of great oaks on the Skyline Trail. For the next 1.7 miles, you meander around bends and into hollows above a steep-sided canyon. With Douglas-firs towering overhead, you skirt massive wind- and rain-pocked sandstone outcrops. These rocks were probably uplifted when the Pacific Plate dipped under the North American Plate in the geologic processes that built these Santa Cruz Mountains eons ago.

Because the drop-off on your right is too sheer for farming or cattle-grazing, this mountainside has remained relatively untouched. The rather unusual California nutmeg tree, which you can recognize by its flat, prickly needles that distinguish it from Douglas-fir tree needles, is taking hold here. An old springhouse remains in a steep ravine below the trail. Fallen leaves from ancient madrones carpet the ground with shades of mauve, yellow and gold.

After reaching Upper Stevens Creek County Park, you swing east into a clearing and meet unpaved Charcoal Road. This historic road, once used for hauling charcoal that was made from trees here, descends through second-growth forests to Stevens Creek in Monte Bello OSP. Your trail continues northwest toward Skyline Boulevard, through an oak-madrone woodland.

Cross Skyline Boulevard to the Hickory Oak gate of Long Ridge OSP. After a short rise to the ridgetop, you head north on the Hickory Oak Trail, part of old Summit Road and now a MROSD patrol road, through a forest of the area's namesake—mature, widely spaced hickory oaks, also called canyon live oaks, some at least 5 feet in diameter. The canyon live oak bears dark green, prickly leaves that are powdery tan or gray underneath. Its acorns have a furry golden ruff around the cup, giving it yet another name, the golden cup oak. Regardless of your name preference, you will surely notice how well this species grows along the west side of the Skyline ridge.

Beyond the woods, the main Bay Area Ridge Trail route continues on the patrol road, but you can veer left on a narrow trail to the preserve's 2693-foot high point. Here more sandstone outcrops, lichen-splotched and weather-etched, stand near the lip of an abrupt decline into tree-filled Oil Creek canyon. From this vantage point, the panorama of successive forested ridges creased by wooded stream canyons is an uncluttered, pastoral scene to nourish your spirit.

Continue on the narrow trail around the shoulder of the knoll and zigzag downhill through the hickory and live-oak woods to loop back to the main Bay Area Ridge Trail route on the Hickory Oak Trail. You make several descents into broad swales and subsequent climbs to hilltop viewpoints. In spring and summer bright orange poppies nestle against boulders, and pink checkerblooms peek out from the grasses; in fall vinegary-smelling blue curls add trailside touches of color to this spectacular trip.

At the next junction, you ascend right, around a shoulder of the ridge, and the Hickory Oak Trail descends west to Portola Redwoods State Park on Pescadero Creek. You follow the ridgetop Long Ridge Trail to a junction with the Peters Creek Trail, the multi-use Bay Area Ridge Trail route for the next 1.7 miles, and turn right (east). (An alternate, 2.1-mile route continues along the ridge and down the Peters Creek Loop Trail; it meets the Ridge Trail route at the last Peters Creek crossing.) Your trail, the Peters Creek Trail, descends switchbacks through an oak forest to cross the earthen dam that holds back the waters of Peters Creek. On the dam's east side, turn left and follow the former wagon road, an avenue of welcome shade in summer and a moist trail under leafy arches in winter.

Past homesteaders' moss-covered fence posts and remnants of an apple orchard, you traverse a secluded valley where willow thickets mark the creek's course. Soon you and the creek arc right into a tight little canyon with delicate fern fronds draping the hillsides and exposed, gnarled tree roots growing around moss-covered boulders. After crossing the Peters Creek bridge, the Ridge Trail follows a connector trail between the Peters Creek crossing and the southern entrance to Skyline Ridge OSP. Parts of this 1-mile trail, open to hikers, bicyclists, and equestrians, adjoin private lands. Please respect fences, close gates, and observe trail directions. (After the Peters Creek bridge, you could make a gentle, 0.5-mile ascent to Long Ridge OSP's Grizzly Flat entrance on Skyline Boulevard; leave a second car here to shorten this trip.)

The connector trail terminates in Skyline Ridge OSP on a knoll overlooking a hillside orchard of widely spaced chestnut and walnut trees. If you come here in fall, you can buy harvested nuts from the orchard's former owners. The next leg of the Ridge Trail meanders downhill through the orchard, above a tributary of Lambert Creek under a canopy of overhanging trees. In spring, fronds of creamy Solomon's seal drape over moist, fern-clad banks and heavenly blue and light yellow irises bloom on erect stalks.

You pass an ancient oak with fire-scarred heart and are again on old Summit Road until you leave the woods. Then turn sharply left and watch for Bay Area Ridge Trail signs that guide you up and down hills on a graveled road bordering a Christmas tree farm. You pass straight, tight rows of conically pruned conifers on one side and a graceful, untamed native forest on the other. Beginning in early November, this farm, leased from MROSD, draws eager urbanites searching for the perfect Christmas tree. After a final uphill pitch on the graveled surface, pause to look across Stevens Creek canyon and the San Andreas Rift Zone to Monte Bello Ridge. Creased by tree-filled canyons, the rounded, grassy ridge is surmounted by 2800-foot Black Mountain, its summit marked by tall antennae.

From this viewpoint, the 0.6-mile **hikers-only** route angles left up to a ridgetop crowned by venerable, 3-foot-diameter Douglas-firs. Wend your way along the ridge under these magnificent trees for 0.2 mile and then abruptly descend switchbacks to Horseshoe Lake, the headwaters of East Lambert Creek, on a steep, oak- and fir-forested, west-facing slope.

Equestrians and **bicyclists** continue on the graveled road, a relatively level, wide route that curves around the northeast side of the ridge that the hiker's route traverses, and meet hikers on the east side of Horseshoe Lake.

Hikers and **bicyclists** proceed southwest around Horseshoe Lake to the dam; to reach the Horseshoe Lake trailhead and parking area from the dam, they take parallel routes on the west side of the lake, going north to the handicapped parking area. They then proceed uphill (northeast) on the same trail and cross a sloping meadow to the preserve's Horseshoe Lake north parking area.

Equestrians leave the hiker/bicyclist/equestrian junction on the east side of the lake and proceed north through woods of oak and buckeye to the equestrian parking area.

Before you leave Horseshoe Lake, note that the lake does indeed resemble an equine shoe, with arms wrapped around the base of a high, tree-thatched knoll. Home to red-wing blackbirds and several species of ducks, Horseshoe Lake is known to attract a pair of black-shouldered kites. These large white birds with black-tipped wings are often seen here searching the lakeshore for the frogs and water snakes that make up their diet.

You too can enjoy this scene by circling the lake on the foot trails that reach the picnic tables at the tip of the knoll above the lake. Here is a delightful spot to enjoy a knapsack lunch or snack and savor your experiences on this beautiful segment of the Bay Area Ridge Trail.

From the handicapped parking area, **wheelchair users** can take the gently graded Ridge Trail route along the lake's reed-lined west shore, cross the bridge over the dam on the south side, and then circle the wooded east side of the lake.

The next leg of the Bay Area Ridge Trail continues northward from the Horseshoe Lake parking areas. (See *Skyline Ridge and Russian Ridge Open Space Preserves.*) Adding this 4.8-mile trip, with a car shuttle at Russian Ridge, makes it possible for the trail user to spend a full day and 12.6 miles in the finest of coastal, mixed-evergreen forests and on untrammeled grasslands with unsurpassed views. A round trip from Saratoga Gap to Horseshoe Lake and back makes for an almost 16-mile excursion.

SKYLINE RIDGE AND RUSSIAN RIDGE OPEN SPACE PRESERVES
From Horseshoe Lake to Rapley Ranch Road

Length: 4.8 miles

Accessibility: Hikers, equestrians, bicyclists, wheelchair users

Regulations: Open dawn to ½ hour after sunset. No dogs. Bicyclists must wear helmets and observe 15-mile-per-hour speed limit.

Facilities: No water on route; restrooms at Horseshoe Lake parking area in Skyline Ridge OSP; restrooms at Russian Ridge OSP parking area.

ENJOY THE MIDPENINSULA'S FINEST VIEWS and most spectacular spring wildflower displays on these ridgeline trails through Russian and Skyline Ridge OSPs. Climb through open grasslands to high knolls on trails that vary in surface from duff-covered to gravelly or rocky, and in width from narrow (hikers only) to wide, paved and unpaved ranch roads. Expect gradual ridgetop elevation gains and loses. These exposed ridgetops can be foggy and windy; trails on south- and west-facing slopes offer only intermittent shade.

Getting There

South trailhead, Skyline Ridge OSP, Horseshoe Lake: Take Page Mill Rd. to Skyline Blvd. (Hwy. 35), turn left (south), and go 0.75 mile to preserve entrance on west side of road.

North trailhead, Russian Ridge OSP, Rapley Ranch Rd./Skyline Blvd.: Take Page Mill Rd. to Skyline Blvd. (Hwy. 35), turn right

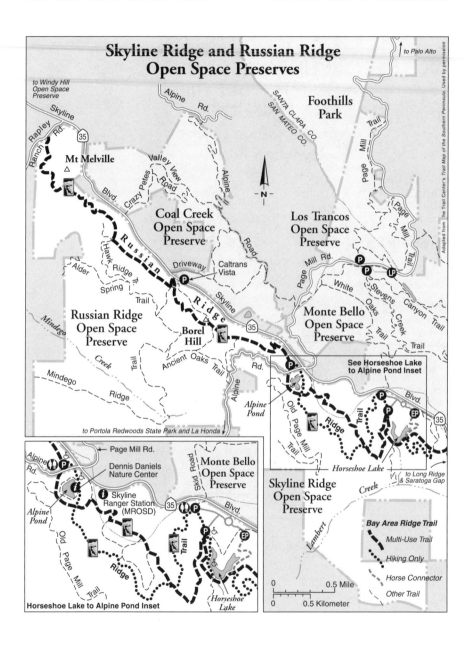

Skyline Ridge and Russian Ridge Open Space Preserves

to Palo Alto

Adapted from the Trail Center's Trail Map of the Southern Peninsula. Used by permission

to Windy Hill
Open Space
Preserve

Foothills
Park

Alpine Rd.

SANTA CLARA CO.
SAN MATEO CO.

Skyline

Rapley Ranch Rd.

35

Mt Melville

Valley View Road

Crazy Petes Blvd.

Alpine

Page Mill Trail

Coal Creek
Open Space
Preserve

Los Trancos
Open Space
Preserve

Page Mill Trail

Russian

Hawk Ridge Tr.

Alder

Spring

Trail

Ridge

Driveway

Caltrans
Vista

Road

Page Mill Rd.

White Oaks

P

P   LP

Skyline

Russian Ridge
Open Space
Preserve

Borel
Hill

Mindego

Creek

Monte Bello
Open Space
Preserve

Stevens Creek

Canyon Trail

Trail

35

Ancient Oaks Trail

Mindego

Ridge

Rd.

Alpine

P

See Horseshoe Lake
to Alpine Pond Inset

to Portola Redwoods State Park and La Honda

Alpine
Pond

Old Page Mill Trail

Ridge Trail

P

P

EP

35

Blvd.

Horseshoe Lake

to Long Ridge
& Saratoga Gap

Skyline Ridge
Open Space
Preserve

Lambert Creek

Horseshoe Lake to Alpine Pond Inset

Page Mill Rd.

Alpine Rd.

P

Dennis Daniels
Nature Center

i

i Skyline
Ranger Station
(MROSD)

Monte Bello
Open Space
Preserve

Skid Road

Alpine
Pond

Old Page Mill Trail

Ridge

35

Trail

P

P

P

EP

Blvd.

Horseshoe
Lake

Bay Area Ridge Trail

Multi-Use Trail

Hiking Only

Horse Connector

Other Trail

0   0.5 Mile

0   0.5 Kilometer

(north), and go 2.7 miles to roadside parking on west side of road at
Rapley Ranch Rd.

On the Trail

Wheelchair users can follow the gently graded trail around
Horseshoe Lake's west shore to the bridge over the dam on the
south side and then circle the wooded east side of the lake. The trail
around Alpine Pond is also accessible to wheelchairs from the
Alpine Road parking area.

Hikers begin this Ridge Trail segment on a different route than
equestrians and bicyclists. From the northwest parking area at
Horseshoe Lake, make a long, gradual ascent southwest on a steep,
grassy hillside above East Lambert Creek. In late spring, a striking
display of lemon-yellow mariposa lilies and blue brodiaea rise above
drying oat grass.

Look across Horseshoe Lake to its tree-topped knoll.

After 0.9 mile, swing around to the west side of the preserve and
walk through pungent chaparral punctuated by occasional small
oaks. From a dramatic parapet chipped out of a sheer sandstone
butte, a 180-degree sweep of forests, stream canyons, ridges, and
grasslands unfolds below you. On clear days, you can see the ocean,
and in almost any weather, you can find Butano Ridge, which forms

the western rampart above Portola Redwoods State Park and Pesca-dero and Memorial county parks. You can reach these parks from the Bay Area Ridge Trail via Ward Road in Long Ridge OSP, and someday Old Page Mill Road in Portola Redwoods State Park will connect to the Bay Area Ridge Trail through Skyline Ridge OSP.

The trail bends into folds of the mountain and traverses sloping grasslands for about half a mile and then enters a brief forested section, where great canyon live oaks flank the trail. A knoll above the Old Page Mill Road junction is the site of former Governor James Rolph's 1930s "Summer Capital," which was topped by a gold-painted, papier-mâché dome. "Sunny Jim" owned this land, as well as present-day Russian Ridge Open Space Preserve. Many years earlier, before the settlers arrived, the Ohlones came here to gather acorns, which they ground on nearby rocks.

Continuing on the Bay Area Ridge Trail, round the east side of reed-lined Alpine Pond, cross Alpine Road to the Russian Ridge OSP parking area, and rejoin the bicyclists and equestrians.

Bicyclists and **equestrians** leave the Horseshoe Lake parking areas (bicyclists use the northwest area, equestrians the northeast) and follow the marked routes down to the patrol road above the handicapped parking area at Horseshoe Lake. Here you go over a stile, veer right (south), and then bend northwest for a steep climb out of East Lambert Creek canyon. Cross the hikers' route and continue uphill (northwest) on an old, hard-surfaced, farm road through the preserve lands, now cleared of Christmas trees and re-planted with native oaks by volunteers. At Alpine Pond, use the trail on the west side and cross Alpine Road to the Russian Ridge OSP parking area.

From the north side of the parking area, **hikers**, **equestrians**, and **bicyclists** take the multi-use Ridge Trail route that zigzags up through grasslands toward 2572-foot Borel Hill. Although this hill was named for former owner Antoine Borel, a San Francisco banker and peninsula resident, the preserve's name commemorates a Russ-ian emigrant who lived east of the ridge from 1920 till 1950.

In years of ample rain, this ridge in springtime is a wondrous wildflower sight. On both sides of the trail as far as you can see, ex-travagant palettes of color sweep over the hillsides and knolls. Often beginning in January you will find perky Johnny-jump-ups turning their yellow-orange faces to the sun. Then goldfields, cream cups, orange poppies, pink checkerblooms, red maids, and blue lupines follow. These beautiful flower fields may approximate what John Muir saw on his trips across California.

After 0.7 mile, just before you reach Borel Hill, a fork in the trail invites you to veer left (northwest) and follow the gently graded, multi-use Bay Area Ridge Trail route around the west side of the ridge. From this trail you can look past the preserve's boundary to Mindego Hill, an ancient, extinct volcano. Beyond lies a succession of rounded, grassy hills creased by almost a dozen streams that join San Gregorio Creek on its way to the San Mateo coast. This west fork of the Ridge Trail descends to a cleft in the ridgeline from where the Mindego Ridge Trail goes right (east) to reach the Caltrans Vista Point on Skyline Boulevard, a convenient parking area where you could put a shuttle car.

However, to continue toward the Russian Ridge north boundary, make a slight jog (less than 0.1 mile) to the left (west) on the Mindego Ridge Trail and then turn right (northwest) on the Bay Area Ridge Trail. A short steep climb to a 2400-foot ridgetop will reward you with wonderful views of the Bay Area: north lie San Francisco and Mt. Tamalpais; across the bay is Mt. Diablo, and farther south of it are Mission and Monument peaks, where another Bay Area Ridge Trail segment traverses East Bay ridgetops; southeast beyond San Jose is Mt. Hamilton. If you look due south on very clear days, you can see the Santa Lucia Mountains rising beyond Monterey Bay.

After 0.5 mile on this top-of-the-world trail, look right for a Ridge Trail turnoff marked RAPLEY RANCH ROAD, where **all users** bear right; the Hawk Ridge Trail angles sharply left.

A 1.6-mile segment proceeds to the Skyline Boulevard/Rapley Ranch Road junction. Follow the old ranch fence line, curving around the south and east sides of another 2400-foot hill crowned by telephone-relay and electric-transmission-line towers. Abruptly you enter a woods of tall oak trees that shade both you and the low-growing shrubs of elderberry, hazelnut, gooseberry, and thimbleberry. As the trail straightens out on the north side of the hill, you pass a wooden platform, a perfect picnic site for your backpack lunch or early evening supper.

Continue north on a long, downhill switchback, under a canopy of broad-branching oaks with lichen- and moss-covered trunks. Looking back, note the transmission towers outlined against the sky contrasting with an earlier, but still operative, form of energy—a windmill. When strong ocean winds blow across this ridge, you can hear the powerline wires singing and the windmill paddles whirring.

A few more switchbacks carry you downhill, across a service road, and below a fascinating, glass-fronted, circular private home high above on the crest of the hill. In the wooded ravine far below the trail another windmill is set in a pretty garden. Follow the contour of the trail around a few curves midway between the woods and the ridgecrest; you pass great boulders splattered with lichen and bedecked with healthy patches of poison oak. In late summer the pearly everlasting's tufted, creamy flowers edge the trail cut into a steep hillside.

Looking west to Mindego Hill.

After passing through a little woods nourished by an intermittent stream, you skirt a small meadow, round a shoulder of the ridge with a close-to-vertical drop-off, and then enter another woods. At the preserve gate at Rapley Ranch Road, use the stile beside the brown pipe gate. On the left, note the barn with an electric fence, once used to pen a flock of sheep. Enjoy this picturesque, but off-limits, pastoral scene and carry on to the right for just 0.1 mile to roadside parking on Skyline Boulevard.

Someday the Bay Area Ridge Trail will bridge the short gap from here to Windy Hill Open Space Preserve. (See the following trip description.) In the meantime, plan a car shuttle at Skyline Boulevard or retrace your steps to the Alpine Road parking area. If you are making a round trip, try an alternate return route, using the Hawk Ridge, Alder Spring, and Mindego Ridge trails to reach the

Bay Area Ridge Trail going south.

WINDY HILL OPEN SPACE PRESERVE
From Upper Razorback Ridge to Top of Spring Ridge

Length: 3.2 miles

Accessibility: Hikers, equestrians, bicyclists

Regulations: Open from dawn to ½ hour after sunset. No dogs on Lost Trail or Connector Trail; dogs on leash on Anniversary Trail and top of Spring Ridge.

Facilities: No water; restrooms at picnic area.

FOLLOW THE WINDY HILL RIDGELINE, through a sheltered forest and across rolling grasslands, on a narrow footpath and broad wagon road. After initially descending 320 feet, you gradually gain 234 feet on a final short climb to the knobs of Windy Hill, a peninsula landmark. Expect sweeping views of the San Mateo Coast and the Santa Clara Valley. True to its name, strong winds are possible in this preserve, as is coastal fog.

Getting There

South trailhead, Upper Razorback Ridge: Take Skyline Blvd. (Hwy. 35) south 4.3 miles from La Honda Rd. (Hwy. 84) at Skylonda or north 3 miles from Page Mill Rd. Off-road parking for 6 cars at trail entrance.

North trailhead, Top of Spring Ridge, Gate 1 (WHO1): Take Skyline Blvd. (Hwy. 35) south 1.8 miles from La Honda Rd. or 5.5 miles north from Page Mill Rd. Ample off-road parking.

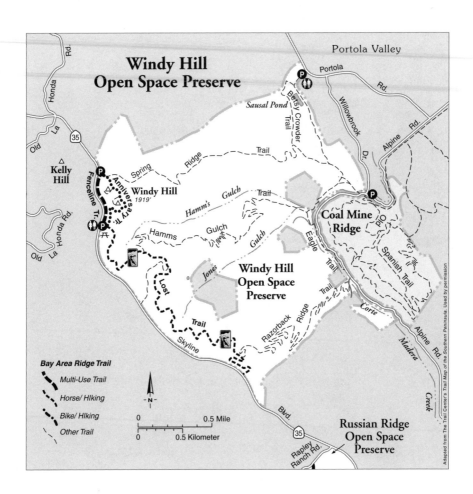

Windy Hill
Open Space Preserve

Portola Valley

Kelly
Hill

Windy Hill
1919'

Coal Mine
Ridge

Windy Hill
Open Space
Preserve

Bay Area Ridge Trail

 ━ ━ ━ Multi-Use Trail

 ‒ ‒ ‒ Horse/ Hiking

 • • • Bike/ Hiking

 ╱ ╱ ╱ Other Trail

—N—

0   0.5 Mile
├─┼─┼─┼─┼─┤
0   0.5 Kilometer

Russian Ridge
Open Space
Preserve

Adapted from The Trail Center's Trail Map of the Southern Peninsula. Used by permission.

Spring Ridge Picnic Area, Skyline Blvd.: Take Skyline Blvd. 2.3 miles south from La Honda Rd. or 4.9 miles north from Page Mill Rd.

On the Trail

Bicyclists' access to Windy Hill Preserve begins at Spring Ridge Picnic Area.

An MROSD sign and Bay Area Ridge Trail logo at the Razorback Ridge Trail direct **hikers** and **equestrians** left and downhill. Leaving the whir of Skyline Boulevard traffic behind, hikers and equestrians take the wide trail, an old farm road, through a mixed woodland where feathery moss and clusters of lichen decorate the trees. After 0.4 mile and a couple of zigzags on the steep hillside you reach the Razorback Ridge Trail, which branches right (east), downhill. You bear left on the Lost Trail, and for the next 1.7-miles, traverse the upper reaches of the preserve.

Head northwest on the Lost Trail, through a fir forest at approximately 1700 feet. You wind in and out of little ravines and cross headwaters of streams named for settlers who once farmed this mountainside. Water seeping from the hillside and onto the trail feeds the creeks that empty into perennial Corte Madera Creek on the lower east side of the preserve.

Primeval Redwood Forest

This mountainside was once part of a huge land grant known as Rancho El Corte de Madera, deeded to Maximo Martinez and Domingo Peralta in 1834 by Governor José Figueroa. Its Spanish name means "the wood-cutting ranch". As you travel through the forest, try to picture its former grandeur. Before the mid-19th century, redwood trees 8-10 feet in diameter covered the mountains above present-day Portola Valley and Woodside. These primeval redwood forests supplied the wood that built Mission Santa Clara and the Pueblo of San José. Severe logging for building Gold Rush San Francisco in the 1850s and a disastrous fire in the 1860s left hardly a tree standing here.

Today, a second-growth forest of Douglas-firs and redwoods flourishes in the 1130-acre Windy Hill Open Space Preserve. Some trees have grown to considerable girth, aided by natural springs, heavy rainfall, and coastal fogs that often shroud this ridgetop.

After 1.3 miles from the start, you emerge from the dense forest at the head of Jones Gulch. The former Lauriston estate, a forested private inholding, lies in Jones Gulch. In 1915, Herbert E. Law began to purchase land and eventually accumulated 627 acres of meadows, mountains and valleys. His holdings, known as Willow Brook Farm, included the magnificent villa, Lauriston, and acres of lath houses for his agricultural enterprises. In 1937, John Francis Neylan, a San Francisco attorney, purchased the estate. Subsequent owners, Ryland Kelley and partners, gave part of the estate to the Peninsula Open Space Trust (POST). Sold to MROSD in the early 1980s, this land became the original Windy Hill Open Space Preserve.

A rusty wheelbarrow chained to a tree recalls former days. Below the trail, now-rotting fence posts once marked boundaries of old ranches. High sandstone cliffs draped with ferns and berry bushes may have been the site of Herbert Law's quarry.

Hikers on Anniversary Trail.

Now you skirt a chaparral-clothed, south-facing flank of the mountain and cross a dirt access road from Skyline Boulevard. Bending west toward Skyline, you tread a boardwalk over a marshy area fed by springs that empty into Hamms Gulch. Where the trail that bears this settler's name turns right, you veer left along the edge of the gulch where several immense Douglas-firs cling to the hillside. The Hamms Gulch Trail zigzags downhill for 2.4 miles to a stone bridge over Corte Madera Creek and the ornate iron gates of the former Lauriston estate.

You continue on the Bay Area Ridge Trail route for another 0.4 mile to the picnic area. You pass Bob's Bench, named for the first executive director of POST, Bob Augsburger. A large wooden sign thanks contributors to the Windy Hill Loop Trail and the trail crews, under the direction of Jane Ames, who built the 8.4-mile loop trail up, down, and around this preserve.

Shortly you reach the picnic area next to Skyline Boulevard near the site of the pioneering Brown Ranch. Settlers Brown and his neighbor to the north, Orton, must have traversed the Lost Trail route you just followed. Until Skyline Boulevard was built in the 1920s, this old wagon road, known as the Ridge Road, stayed below the ridgecrest. From the picnic area, **all users** begin the northbound leg of this trip on the Anniversary Trail, but soon split ways.

Hikers continue on the Anniversary Trail where the Fence Line Trail branches left. The 0.75-mile Anniversary Trail was constructed with funds from POST to mark the tenth anniversary of the establishment of the Windy Hill Preserve. Gradually ascend the east side of the Windy Hill knobs and climb to the summit on one of the small side trails you pass. These treeless protrusions above the long sweep of grasslands descending to Portola Valley are prominent landmarks on the peninsula. On a clear day, they offer views of the entire Bay Area and the San Mateo coast. On a day true to its name, the 1917-foot summit can be a challenge to steady footing, yet a delight for kite flyers and model-glider enthusiasts. From the summit, it is a quick descent to the north parking area at the top of Spring Ridge, the end of this Bay Area Ridge Trail segment.

Equestrians and **bicyclists** leave the Anniversary Trail at the first swale and veer left on the Fence Line Trail. The trail, which heads north above Skyline Boulevard, offers splendid ocean views when the day is clear. They join the hikers at the top of Spring Ridge.

Since this is a short trip, hikers and equestrians may want to do the 6.4-mile round trip. If not, park a shuttle car at the picnic area or at the top of Spring Ridge and do the shorter trip. The next segment begins in Wunderlich Park, about 5 miles north of Windy Hill. (See *Wunderlich County Park to Huddart County Park.*)

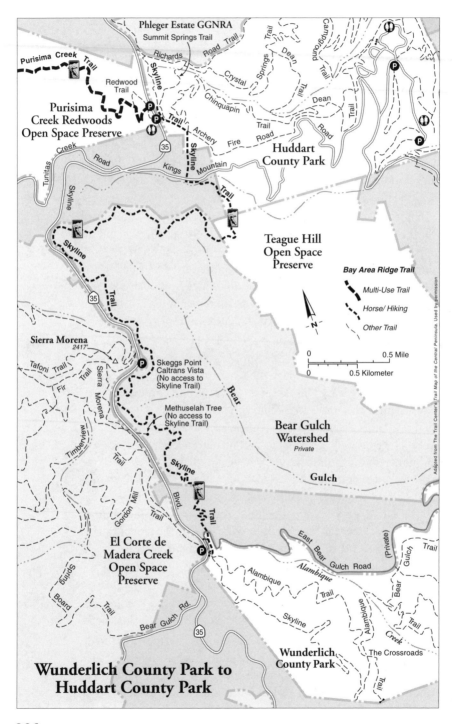

Phleger Estate GGNRA
Summit Springs Trail

Purisima Creek Trail

Redwood Trail

Purisima
Creek Redwoods
Open Space
Preserve

Richards Road Trail

Skyline Trail

Crystal Springs Trail

Dean Trail

Chinquapin Trail

Dean Trail

Campground Trail

Archery Fire Road

Huddart
County Park

Tunitas Creek Road

Skyline

Kings Mountain Trail

Skyline

Teague Hill
Open Space
Preserve

Bay Area Ridge Trail

Multi-Use Trail

Horse/ Hiking

Other Trail

N

0   0.5 Mile
0   0.5 Kilometer

Sierra Morena
2417'

Tafoni Trail

Fir

Sierra Morena Trail

Skyline Trail

Skeggs Point
Caltrans Vista
(No access to
Skyline Trail)

Methuselah Tree
(No access to
Skyline Trail)

Bear

Bear Gulch
Watershed
Private

Gulch

Timberview Trail

Gordon Mill Trail

Skyline Blvd.

Skyline Trail

El Corte de
Madera Creek
Open Space
Preserve

East Bear Gulch Road

(Private)

Trail

Bear Gulch

Alambique

Alambique Trail

Alambique Creek

Bear Gulch Trail

The Crossroads

Spring Board Trail

Bear Gulch Rd.

Skyline Trail

Wunderlich
County Park

Adapted from The Trail Center's Trail Map of the Central Peninsula. Used by permission.

Wunderlich County Park to
Huddart County Park

WUNDERLICH COUNTY PARK TO HUDDART COUNTY PARK
From Wunderlich West Gate to Purisima Creek Trailhead

Length: 5.8 miles

Accessibility: Hikers, equestrians

Regulations: Open 8 a.m. to sunset. No dogs. No bicycles.

Facilities: No water or restrooms along the trail; restrooms on Redwood Trail in Purisima Creek Redwoods OSP, across Skyline Blvd. from north trailhead at Huddart Park.

F OLLOW THE GENTLY GRADED SKYLINE TRAIL through redwood and Douglas-fir forests just below the crest of the Santa Cruz Mountains. You'll discover unusual spring wildflowers along one of the few remaining segments of the old California Riding and Hiking Trail, a trail system established in 1954. Take this easy, shaded trail on a summer day when you need a retreat from the valley heat.

Getting There

South Trailhead, Wunderlich Park: Take Skyline Blvd. (Hwy. 35) 3 miles north from La Honda Rd. (Hwy. 84) junction or 10 miles south from Half Moon Bay Rd. (Hwy. 92) junction. Limited parking on west side of Skyline Blvd. Trailhead is on east side of Skyline.

North trailhead, Huddart Park: Take Skyline Blvd. (Hwy. 35) 6.5 miles south from Half Moon Bay Rd. (Hwy. 92) or 6.5 miles north from La Honda Rd. (Hwy. 84) to parking at Purisima Creek trailhead on west side of Skyline Blvd. Trailhead is on east side of Skyline.

On the Trail

Hikers and **equestrians** begin this trail from the northwest corner of Wunderlich Park and quickly lose 100 feet in elevation on switchbacks through a redwood forest. You cross private Bear Gulch Road, then head north below a subdivision in the shade of redwoods and firs, grown tall since most logging ended here in the mid-1860s.

For the next 4 miles, you are on the upper slopes of the California Water Service Company watershed (formerly the Bear Gulch Water Company). You wind in and out of small ravines, often close enough to Skyline Boulevard to hear the murmur of traffic, but not so close that you cannot hear the calls of Steller's jays, the crested blue-black cousins of the blue (scrub) jays of the foothill woodlands.

On clear days, you'll catch occasional glimpses through the trees of the valley below, though fog often shrouds the view. In all weather, the forest in all its variety delights at every turn. Tall Douglas-firs are part of the new forest taking hold here after the logging of the 1800s. A contrast to the dark conifers is the light foliage of big-leaf maples growing in ravines where water is plentiful.

By the edge of the trail, blue hound's tongue bloom in early spring, followed by masses of Douglas iris in shades of lavender. In May you will find the bright, rose-red flower clusters of the uncommon Clintonia. The elegant, lacy-leafed, pink bleeding-heart nestles in damp ravines.

After traveling 1.5 miles along the trail, you will see old moss-covered stumps of the largest redwood trees, some 10 feet or more in diameter. These immense trees, some of which were 2000 years old, flourished in the heavy rainfall along the ridge—as much as 40 inches a year, with frequent fogs adding to the precipitation.

After rounding a wide curve in the trail below Skeggs Point, you come to a wooden bench and memorial plaque, dedicated by the local Sierra Club chapter to Clara May Lazarus, an ardent trail advocate. Here is a peaceful place for enjoying the forest's solitude.

You continue through forest and beside occasional meadows, flower-filled in spring, and skirt a few mountaintop homes. After a short climb, about 2.5 miles from Wunderlich Park, the trail veers east, bringing spectacular views south as far as Black Mountain in Santa Clara County. You follow a south-facing ridge through oak woodland and chaparral to Teague Hill Open Space Preserve, and

The Pulgas Redwoods

The size of the redwood stumps along this trail gives you an idea of the scale of the ancient forest. Known to the Spanish as the Pulgas Redwoods, the forest once covered the eastern slopes of the Santa Cruz Mountains above present-day Woodside and Portola Valley.

Note the horizontal slots in the stumps, cut about six feet from the ground, which held boards on which loggers stood to fell the trees. This whole forest was cut to supply redwood to build Gold Rush San Francisco. Oxen dragged the logs down the steep hills to sawmills; the wood was then taken to the port of Redwood City and sent up the bay on barges.

So great was the demand for wood that by 1870 hardly a redwood remained standing on this mountainside. Logging finally ceased here because the water of Bear Gulch Creek, formerly used in the sawmills, was needed for other uses—first to supply a grist mill and then for the growing communities in the valley.

then begin a gentle descent northwest through a redwood forest to Kings Mountain Road. Follow the footpath beside the road to a marked pedestrian crossing leading to Huddart Park.

The trail passes a large, private home on a hill and enters redwood forest again at a Huddart Park crossroads. The Bay Area Ridge Trail route, also the Skyline Trail, turns west on a graveled service road through open woodland and continues 0.3 mile to Skyline Boulevard, where this segment of the Bay Area Ridge Trail ends. The next segment of the Ridge Trail in Purisima Creek Redwoods Open Space Preserve begins across the road on the west side of Skyline Boulevard. (See *Purisima Creek Redwoods Open Space Preserve.*)

On the east side of Skyline Boulevard, the Skyline Trail continues north for almost 2 miles through Huddart Park and the Phleger Estate lands. One day, the trail may reach the north entrance of Purisima Creek Redwoods OSP.

From the Huddart Park northwest boundary, the Crystal Springs Trail descends 2 miles to a woodsy setting in the park where group campsites with picnic tables and restrooms are available for equestrian and hiker groups by reservation only. Here is a pleasant place to camp before continuing on to the next leg of your Ridge Trail trek.

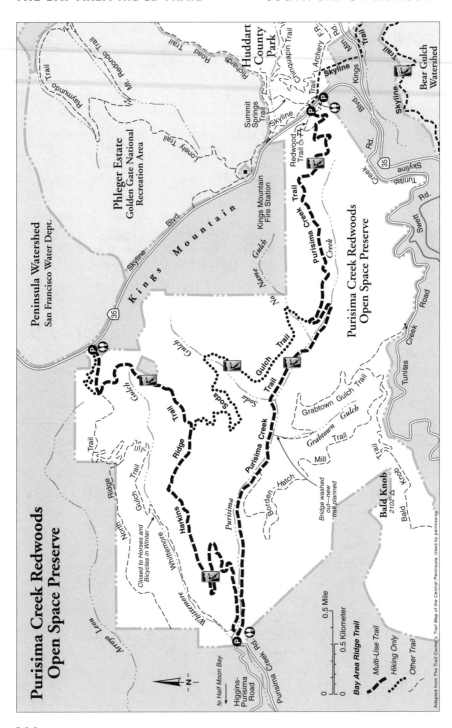

Purisima Creek Redwoods Open Space Preserve

Huddart County Park

Phleger Estate
Golden Gate National Recreation Area

Peninsula Watershed
San Francisco Water Dept.

Purisima Creek Redwoods Open Space Preserve

Bear Gulch Watershed

Kings Mountain Fire Station

Kings Mountain

Skyline Blvd.

Bald Knob
2102 △

to Half Moon Bay

Higgins-Purisima Road

0.5 Mile

0.5 Kilometer

Bay Area Ridge Trail
Multi-Use Trail
Hiking Only
Other Trail

Adapted from The Trail Center's Trail Map of the Central Peninsula. Used by permission.

PURISIMA CREEK REDWOODS OPEN SPACE PRESERVE
From Purisima Creek Trailhead to Preserve's North Entrance

Length: 5.7 miles, hikers
      7.7 miles, equestrians and bicyclists

Accessibility: Hikers, equestrians, bicyclists, wheelchair users

Regulations: Open dawn to ½ hour after sunset. No dogs.
      Helmets required for bicyclists, mandatory
      15-mph-speed limit.

Facilities: Restrooms at south and north ends of trail;
      no water.

F IVE TRAILS IN PURISIMA CREEK REDWOODS OSP link together for a challenging loop through forested canyons and over high ridges. You'll lose 1,000 feet in elevation in the first 2 miles and regain it on a steady climb out of the canyon. Summer fog sometimes bathes the forested areas, while the open, south-facing ridges may be hot.

Getting There

South trailhead, Purisima Creek Trailhead: Take Skyline Blvd. (Hwy. 35) 6.5 miles south from Half Moon Bay Rd. (Hwy. 92) or 6.5 miles north from La Honda Rd. (Hwy. 84) to parking at Purisima Creek trailhead on west side of Skyline Blvd. Disabled parking 0.1 mile farther south at head of Redwood Trail on west side of Skyline Blvd.

North trailhead, Purisima Creek Trailhead: Take Skyline Blvd. (Hwy. 35) 4.5 miles south from Half Moon Bay Rd. (Hwy. 92) or 8.5 miles north from La Honda Rd. (Hwy. 84) to large parking area on west side of road; equestrian trailer parking available.

On the Trail

Wheelchair users start from the head of the Redwood Trail and follow the well-graded path northwest through a beautiful redwood grove, where shade-loving wildflowers and shiny-leaved huckleberry shrubs thrive at trailside. Your path crosses the Purisima Creek Trail and continues 0.2 mile to a flat where a picnic table affords a place to have a snack and enjoy the forest view.

Hikers, equestrians, and **bicyclists** descend into a deep canyon on the Purisima Creek Trail under tall, second-growth redwoods and tanoaks. The trees in this 2511-acre preserve were heavily logged in the late 19th century. The forest scene here was very different from what you see now—loggers felled redwoods by hand, several streamside mills cut the wood into shingles, and oxen teams pulled wagons loaded with logs up the steep mountainside.

Logging continued sporadically into the 20th century, until MROSD completed its purchase of this land in 1984. Today, historic logging roads, linked by newly built footpaths, make fine trails.

The wide openings in the forest were once used as landings for the logs and are now springtime gardens of blue ceanothus, scarlet columbine, and the yellow blossoms of invasive Scotch broom. In fall, the brilliant yellow of big-leaf maples accents the forest greens.

After 1.8 miles of steady downhill on the Purisima Creek Trail, and 1000 feet elevation loss, hikers split ways from bicyclists and equestrians.

Equestrians and **bicyclists** continue downhill to the western terminus of the Purisima Creek Trail, losing 1630 feet in elevation. Then turn right, uphill, on the Harkins Ridge Trail.

Hikers turn right on the 2.5-mile, hikers-only Soda Gulch Trail, its secluded entrance marked by a Bay Area Ridge Trail sign on the right side of a hairpin turn. The trail follows the forested east side of No Name Gulch, where delicate springtime flowers abound. You cross a bridge over a tributary, and another over the main creek, and switch to the drier, south-facing slope. Tanoaks, cream bush, and even an evergreen oak or two flourish in this sunny zone.

You reach Soda Gulch and return to deep forest, where circles of second-growth trees surround redwood stumps 5 to 6 feet in diameter. One of the largest trees on the steep-sided trail is a towering, double-trunked redwood, whose scarred bark may indicate it was used to anchor cables for hauling logs uphill.

Shade-loving Clintonia thrives in Purisima Creek Redwoods.

A handsome wooden bridge crosses the upper reaches of Soda Gulch Creek, full in spring, though sometimes dry by fall. Now more than halfway along the Soda Gulch Trail, you again leave the moist redwood forest and begin to ascend open chaparral slopes. At a bend in the trail, you will find welcome shade under a lone, wide-spreading tanoak tree.

Turn right (east) when you reach the Harkins Ridge Trail junction and meet the equestrian/bicyclist route, 1.4 miles from the north parking area.

Hikers, **equestrians**, and **bicyclists** climb steeply on the wide Harkins Ridge Trail, formerly known as the Harkins Fire Road. Low chaparral and a scattering of trees line the trail, which veers left and levels off to cross over the headwall of Whittemore Gulch. Look west to the ocean to see breakers crashing on the beach near Half Moon Bay. Past sizable redwoods, clusters of Douglas fir, and abundant seasonal flowers, you come to the North Ridge Trail junction.

Hikers cross the wide North Ridge Trail to a well-graded footpath that zigzags up through a fir and tanoak forest. At one of the bends in the footpath, you can see other high points of the Santa

293

Cruz Mountains to the northwest—Montara Mountain, Scarper Peak, and the long central Cahill Ridge in the San Francisco Watershed. Soon you reach the parking area at the crest of the Skyline ridge, having regained the 1,000 feet in elevation you lost in Purisima Creek Canyon.

Equestrians and **bicyclists** veer right (east) and follow the North Ridge Trail to the parking area.

On a beautiful day in May 1989, this 5.7-mile segment and the one just south, Wunderlich County Park to Huddart County Park, were dedicated as the first Ridge Trail segments in San Mateo County. The occasion was marked by speeches congratulating all trail advocates and volunteers. There were hikes and rides on both legs of the Bay Area Ridge Trail, followed by refreshments for all.

From the northern terminus of this trail all the way to Sweeney Ridge, there is a 16-mile gap in the Bay Area Ridge Trail route. Negotiations for use of a graveled service road on Cahill and Fifield ridges in the San Francisco Watershed are continuing. See *Sweeney Ridge to Milagra Ridge* for the next dedicated segment.

SWEENEY RIDGE TO MILAGRA RIDGE— GOLDEN GATE NATIONAL RECREATION AREA
From Portola Gate to Milagra Ridge Gate

Length: 7 miles from Sneath Lane trailhead, 7.6 miles from Mori Ridge trailhead (includes round trip to Portola Gate from Discovery Site, and then north to Milagra Ridge gate)

Accessibility: Hikers, equestrians, bicyclists

Regulations: Sweeney Ridge—Open 8 a.m. to ½ hour after sunset. Dogs on leash only.
Skyline College—Open during college hours. No dogs. Bicyclists use campus roads.

Facilities: Toilet at Nike site on Sweeney Ridge; water, restroom, and phone at vista point on west side of Skyline College campus.

A TREK ALONG THE 1000-ACRE RIDGETOP visits the San Francisco Bay Discovery Site, unique coastal plant communities, and the Skyline College campus, and offers sweeping views of the coast and mountains. The long, rounded Sweeney Ridge, separating north peninsula bayside and coastal communities, was slated to become I-380—the route from Highway 101 to Highway 1— until the Golden Gate National Recreation Area purchased it in 1982. The exposed ridge can be windy, foggy, or hot, and is subject to sudden changes in weather.

Choose from two trailheads, on the east and west sides of the ridge: you'll gain 550 feet from the Sneath Lane trailhead, and 850 feet from the Mori Ridge trailhead. The trail from Sneath Lane to the Nike site is a paved road; all other trails are wide and unpaved.

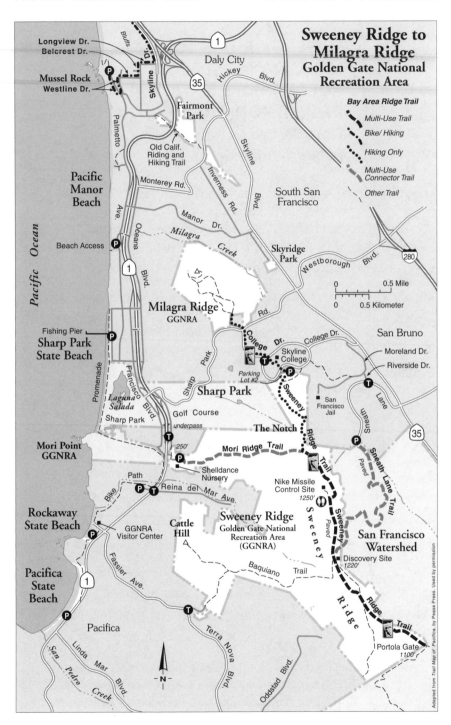

Sweeney Ridge to Milagra Ridge
Golden Gate National Recreation Area

Bay Area Ridge Trail

Multi-Use Trail

Bike/ Hiking

Hiking Only

Multi-Use Connector Trail

Other Trail

Longview Dr.
Belcrest Dr.

Mussel Rock
Westline Dr.

Daly City

Fairmont Park

Old Calif. Riding and Hiking Trail

Monterey Rd.

Pacific Manor Beach

Beach Access

South San Francisco

Skyridge Park

Westborough Blvd.

0   0.5 Mile
0   0.5 Kilometer

Milagra Ridge
GGNRA

San Bruno

Moreland Dr.
Riverside Dr.

Fishing Pier

Sharp Park State Beach

Skyline College

Parking Lot #2

Sharp Park

San Francisco Jail

Sneath Lane

Laguna Salada

Golf Course

Sharp Park

underpass

The Notch

Mori Point
GGNRA

250'

Mori Ridge Trail

Sheldance Nursery

Nike Missile Control Site
1250'

San Francisco Watershed

Rockaway State Beach

GGNRA Visitor Center

Cattle Hill

Sweeney Ridge
Golden Gate National Recreation Area
(GGNRA)

Discovery Site
1220'

Pacifica State Beach

Fassler Ave.

Baquiano   Trail

Pacifica

Terra Nova Blvd.

Oddstad Blvd.

Portola Gate
1100'

Linda Mar Blvd.

San Pedro Creek

- N -

Pacific Ocean

Palmetto

Oceana

Francisco Blvd.

Promenade

Bike

Path

Reina del Mar Ave.

Manor Dr.

Milagra Creek

Inverness Rd.

Skyline Blvd.

Hickey Blvd.

Skyline Dr.

Bluffs

College Dr.

Sneath Lane Trail

Sweeney Ridge Trail

Adapted from Trail Map of Pacifica, by Pease Press. Used by permission.

Getting There

By Car

South trailhead, Portola Gate: Not accessible by car, except on some guided GGNRA hikes.

Sneath Lane trailhead: From Skyline Blvd. (Hwy. 35) in San Bruno, go west on Sneath Lane to off-street parking at gate.

Mori Ridge trailhead: Going north on Hwy. 1 in Pacifica, pass Reina del Mar Ave., and turn abruptly right into the Shell Dance Nursery. Continue past nursery buildings to parking at end of dirt road.

Going south on Hwy. 1 in Pacifica, make a U-turn at Reina del Mar Ave. and go north, following directions above.

Skyline College: From Skyline Blvd. (Hwy. 35) in San Bruno, go west on College Dr., turn left at college entrance, and proceed to parking lot 2. Several spaces reserved for GGNRA trail use.

North trailhead, Milagra Ridge: From Hwy. 1 or from Skyline Blvd. (Hwy. 35), take Sharp Park Rd., turn north on College Dr. Extension N. and continue to roadside parking at Milagra Ridge gate.

By Bus

SamTrans 20J and 21B to Skyline College weekdays and 30B daily except Sunday. SamTrans 32P to Sneath Lane/Monterey Dr. intersection weekdays. SamTrans 10S daily except Sunday and 1L daily on Hwy. 1 to Westport Dr. or Reina del Mar Ave. near Mori Ridge trailhead in Pacifica.

On the Trail

This segment of the Bay Area Ridge Trail has no southern entry point. Therefore, your trip begins with an ascent from Sneath Lane in San Bruno or from Mori Ridge in Pacifica to the Discovery Site; you then go south and/or north on the Sweeney Ridge Trail. Equestrians begin from the private Park Pacific Stables to reach the Sweeney Ridge Trail.

To start from the bayside, **hikers** and **bicyclists** go around the locked gate at the end of Sneath Lane and pick up the paved road that climbs through a dense growth of chaparral and coastal scrub. The trail curves into ravines and rounds shoulders of the ridge. A rich variety of native shrubs—red-berried toyon, cream-colored

297

Queen Anne's lace, coyote bush, arroyo willows, elderberry bushes, and blue-blossomed California lilac—border the route. In springtime, scarlet and yellow columbines, orange poppies, and lavender yerba santa brighten your way.

At the crest of the ridge, the paved trail veers right (north), but you turn left to reach the Portolá Discovery Site. Almost immediately, you pass the right-branching Baquiano Trail, named for Portolá's scout, Sergeant José Francisco Ortega, who was the first European to see San Francisco Bay. This trail crosses private property at its western end and is open only to occasional ranger-led walks.

Continue a short distance beyond the Baquiano Trail to the Portolá Discovery Site on a 1200-foot knoll on your left, on the east side of the trail. Two monuments commemorate the sighting of San Francisco Bay on November 4, 1769 by Don Gaspar de Portolá's men. A bronze plaque on a weathered serpentine boulder on the left states that the men first saw the bay while searching for a land route to Monterey Bay. On the right (south) side of the knoll, a monument shows the outlines and names of the Bay Area's major peaks etched on a black granite cylinder. Among the peaks shown are Mt. Tamalpais, Mt. Hamilton, Mt. Diablo, San Bruno Mountain, and Montara Mountain.

Portolá's men would have seen these same Bay Area peaks and ridges from this knoll. The commission was traveling north to establish a colony in Monterey to thwart British and Russian settlements in Alta California. Not until after Portolá's journey, when other expeditions recorded the vastness of the bay's waters, did the Spaniards realize the importance of their find. They then charted the extensive harbor and, in 1776, established their northern colony in present-day San Francisco on the shores of that bay.

Discovery Site South to Portola Gate

To reach the boundary between Sweeney Ridge and the San Francisco Watershed lands at the Portola Gate, you can make a 2.4-mile round trip south from the Discovery Site on the Sweeney Ridge Trail. It takes you past luxurious clumps of Douglas iris, beautiful blue or creamy-white blossomed in May, and beside a few springs seeping from winter to early summer. You can locate the springs in summer by the patches of sedges and tall grasses that prosper in the damp soil of the seep. Along this trail in late summer, you may be lucky enough to see, half-concealed under the shrubs, tall, slim flower stalks clustered with whitish-green blossoms—one of California's native orchids.

Enroute to the Portola Gate, you pass the horse trail that leads to private stables in Pacifica outside the Sweeney Ridge property. **Equestrians** use this route to reach the Sweeney Ridge Trail and then go north to the Discovery Site or south to the Portola Gate.

Toward the south end of the Sweeney Ridge Trail, crinkly-leaved ceanothus (California lilac) and orange-flowered twinberry have grown tall enough to provide a hedge and a modest but welcome windbreak. The vegetation soon opens up in a clearing at the watershed boundary, and a high fence and restrictive signs bar travel beyond the Portola Gate. However, the GGNRA rangers and Bay Area Ridge Trail docents frequently offer public nature hikes and discovery walks in the watershed. Management requires advance reservations and a fee for these events; contact the Bay Area Ridge Trail office in San Francisco. Retrace your steps to the Discovery Site.

Rift Zone Lakes

On clear days, you can see three long lakes that fill the linear valley at the east base of the ridge, San Andreas Lake and the Crystal Springs lakes, from north to south. The linear valleys continue further south, though they aren't dammed for water storage. On a visit to California in the 1890s, Andrew Lawson, a pioneering geologist, recognized these linear valleys as typical of a rift zone and after the 1906 San Francisco earthquake, named the great California earthquake fault for the valley containing the northernmost lake, the San Andreas Fault.

Water from the Hetch Hetchy Reservoir in the Sierra Nevada is transported through huge pipes to be stored in these lakes, and is then purveyed to more than a million users in San Francisco and on the peninsula. Local water runoff from the east side of Sweeney Ridge and those ridges to the south, Fifield and Cahill, also stored in these lakes, amounts to less than 5 percent of the drinking water supplied by the San Francisco Water Department to its patrons.

North to Skyline College

From the Discovery Site, **hikers, equestrians,** and **bicyclists** follow the paved service road with yellow fog line past defunct buildings of a former Nike site—the highest point on the ridge at 1250 feet. As the trail swings west around the buildings, views of Mt. Tamalpais, Wolf Ridge in the GGNRA Marin Headlands, San Bruno

Mountain, and the beautiful bay open up. Even when fog lies in the valleys, the peaks might be visible, giving you the feeling of overlooking a vast, misty sea, pierced by isolated islands.

Soon the Sweeney Ridge Trail meets the Mori Ridge Trail, the coastside connector from Pacifica. The Mori Ridge Trail gains 850 feet in elevation in 1.3 miles, in a series of steep pitches that alternate with more gentle climbs. It offers magnificent views of the coast, from San Pedro Point in the south to the tip of Point Reyes Peninsula in the north. In the southwest, Montara Mountain's long sweep to the sea stands dark against the sky, its many antennae piercing the blue. Diverse species of coastal scrub cover the hillside along the Mori Ridge Trail—from pungent sage to aromatic coyote mint. The moist ocean air enhances and intensifies the color of the plants' blossoms, particularly the blue-flowered lupine and the bushy yellow lizardtail. Crimson stalks of Indian paintbrush glow among the wind-sculpted coyote bush and California coffeeberry.

From the Mori Ridge/Sweeney Ridge trails junction, **bicyclists** and **equestrians** return to their starting points.

Hikers veer right (northeast) at the junction, to follow the Sweeney Ridge Trail to Skyline Community College and on to Milagra Ridge. Dedicated on October 12, 1996, the Ridge Trail route from here descends a very steep ravine known as "The Notch." Broad steps defined by rope hand rails strung through pressure-treated posts offer a safer grade and protect native plants that host the endangered Mission Blue butterfly.

On the other side of the steep ravine, you traverse a high ridge with views of the coastline. On clear days, you'll see waves crashing against the rocky cliffs and lapping at the sandy beaches. At your feet is evidence of the geologic beginnings of this land. A trained eye will distinguish Franciscan Formation rocks such as greenstone (a rounded basalt), some sandstone, and a red chert. White patches you may see on some rocks are remnants of the Calera limestone, which is found in abundance in the Rockaway Quarry just west of here. These Franciscan rocks formed under water, then were stressed and modified through the ages by action deep within the earth's crust and along the San Andreas Fault.

The Bay Area Ridge Trail descends from the ridge to parking lot 2 at Skyline College. Cross the lot and go down 78 broad steps through a tall conifer forest. Then cross the road to a pretty plaza, its left side sheltered by mature cypress trees in huge planters. On

View of coastline from "The Notch."

a large campus map, you can note the route through the inner campus.

Proceed through the plaza to the bookstore, turn left (west), mount a series of steps, and pass the north side of Buildings 1 and 2. Between these buildings is another tree-filled plaza where the dedication of the Skyline College Ridge Trail Connection took place. Skyline College marked its 25th Anniversary by celebrating the completion of this important link between Sweeney and Milagra ridges and the opening of the first Bay Area Ridge Trail segment to pass through a college campus. Continue past this plaza, pausing at the north corner of Building 1 to read a bronze plaque commemorating Skyline College's dedication on May 17, 1970. Then turn right (north), pass Building 7, and cross the street to a bus stop, which is often crowded with children, college students, and Bay Area Ridge Trail travelers.

North to Milagra Ridge Gate

Bay Area Ridge Trail directional arrows placed high on lamp-posts and street signs mark the route from here. Go around the corner and veer right (north) on sidewalks beside College Drive. Shortly the Ridge Trail route shifts a few feet east onto parallel Ysabel Drive and continues north to Sharp Park Road. Crosswalks at

301

stoplights take you to the opposite side of the street, where you use the road past a residential complex to continue north to the Milagra Ridge gate. You could park a shuttle car here or leave one at parking lot 2 on the college campus. A few places on the south side of this lot are reserved for those using the trail.

Negotiations are underway to complete a short gap between the northwest end of Milagra Ridge Preserve and city streets in Pacifica. For now, you can take a brisk round trip along the trail that traverses the ridgetop to the end of the preserve. Due to revegetation efforts by the National Park Service, once-rampant pampas grass is gone, the lupine plant that is host to the Mission Blue butterfly is being protected, and new plants native to this region are being set out. On crisp, clear days, the fabulous views of ocean and coastline are well worth a trip on this ridge.

Retrace your route along College Drive North to parking lot 2 at Skyline College, or have a shuttle car waiting to take you to Sneath Lane or Mori Ridge parking areas.

The next segment of the Bay Area Ridge Trail begins at Mussel Rock in Daly City, about 5 miles north of Milagra Ridge. (See *Mussel Rock to Fort Funston.*)

MUSSEL ROCK TO FORT FUNSTON—GOLDEN GATE NATIONAL RECREATION AREA
From Vista Point through Daly City Neighborhoods and from Hang-Glider Viewing Deck over Sand Dunes

Length: 2.9 miles through Daly City neighborhoods
2.4 miles round trip through Fort Funston

Accessibility: Hikers, equestrians, bicyclists

Regulations: Daly City—Open during daylight hours. Dogs on leash.
Fort Funston—Open sunrise to sunset. Dogs on leash. Pick up pet litter.

Facilities: Water, restrooms, and phone at Fort Funston.

HERE ARE TWO COASTAL TRIPS along the Bay Area Ridge Trail. On the southern segment, take in impressive views from Mussel Rock and then travel north on city streets to Palisades Park in Daly City. From the northern trailhead, follow a sandy trail over dunes and through coastal scrub from Fort Funston to Thornton Beach State Park. These exposed bluff-tops offer no shade and can be breezy and foggy. You'll gain 550 feet in elevation in the first 0.75 mile from Mussel Rock and lose 200 feet along the Dunes Trail from Fort Funston.

Getting There

By Car

South trailhead, Mussel Rock: Going south, take Skyline Blvd. (Hwy. 35) to Westmoor Ave. in Daly City and turn right (west). Immediately turn left (south) on Skyline Dr., continue 1.75 miles to Belcrest Ave. and turn right. Go 4 blocks to Westline Dr., turn left

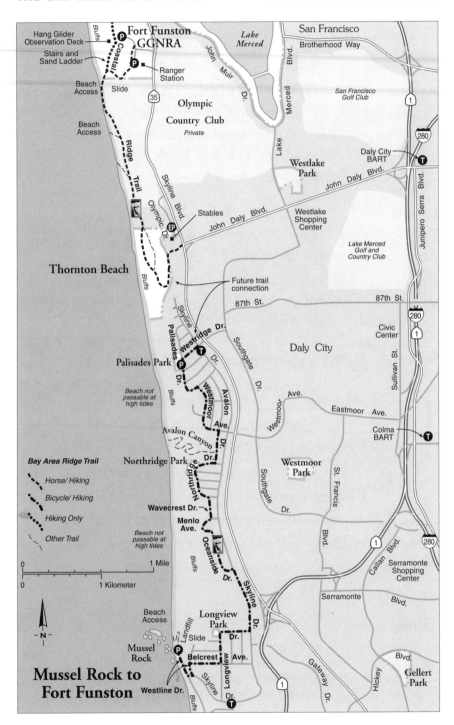

Hang Glider
Observation Deck

Fort Funston
GGNRA

San Francisco

Lake
Merced

Brotherhood Way

Stairs and
Sand Ladder

Ranger
Station

Beach
Access

Slide

San Francisco
Golf Club

Olympic

Country Club
Private

Beach
Access

Daly City
BART

Westlake
Park

John Daly Blvd.

Stables

John Daly Blvd.

Westlake
Shopping
Center

Thornton Beach

Lake Merced
Golf and
Country Club

Future trail
connection

87th St.

87th St.

Daly City

Civic
Center

Palisades Park

Beach not
passable at
high tides

Avalon Canyon

Northridge Park

Eastmoor Ave.

Colma
BART

Westmoor
Park

Bay Area Ridge Trail

Horse/ Hiking

Bicycle/ Hiking

Hiking Only

Other Trail

Wavecrest Dr.

Menlo
Ave.

Beach not
passable at
high tides

Serramonte
Shopping
Center

0   1 Mile

0   1 Kilometer

Serramonte

Beach
Access

– N –

Longview
Park

Slide

Mussel
Rock

Belcrest Ave.

Mussel Rock to
Fort Funston

Westline Dr.

Gellert
Park

and then go right to continue north to entrance road of Mussel Rock parking area.

Going north, take Hwy. 1 to Manor Dr. exit in Pacifica, turn left at first stop sign, go two blocks, turn left on Manor Dr., and cross highway. Immediately turn right onto Palmetto Ave. and continue for almost 1 mile to Westline Dr. in Daly City. Turn left on Westline Dr. and then veer left on entrance road to Mussel Rock parking area.

North trailhead, Fort Funston: Going south on Skyline Blvd. (Hwy. 35) towards Lake Merced, go 0.1 mile past John Muir Dr. and turn right (west) into Fort Funston. At fork in road, bear right and continue to extensive parking area. Sunset Trail entrance on north side of parking area near hang-glider viewing deck on bluff above beach.

Going north on Skyline Blvd. (Hwy. 35), make a U-turn at John Muir Dr. and go south on Skyline Blvd. 0.1 mile, turn right (west) into Fort Funston, and follow directions above.

When leaving Fort Funston, autos and bicycles must turn right. To go north, continue south on Skyline Blvd. to John Daly Blvd. and make a U-turn.

Equestrian trailhead: Going south, take Skyline Blvd. (Hwy. 35), turn right (west) on Olympic Way and proceed south to stables and equestrian parking.

Going north, take Skyline Blvd. (Hwy. 35) to John Muir Dr., make a U-turn, and follow directions going south as above.

By Bus

SamTrans 1L from Daly City BART Station serves Palmetto/Westline intersection daily. SamTrans 10S serves Daly City and Pacifica daily except Sunday from Serramonte Shopping Center.

On the Trail

North through Daly City

Before setting off, walk from the Mussel Rock parking area to an opening in the fence where a short trail leads to a small vista point high above the ocean. Just offshore lie several jagged, rocky islets, the largest of which, topped by a navigational marker, is Mussel Rock. These small, offshore islands, inhabited by black-coated, long-necked cormorants, present both a formidable boating hazard and a tempting destination for fishermen and adventurers. One islet is accessible by foot at low tide, but getting there is exceedingly dangerous because of erratic wave patterns off this coast. The San Andreas Fault enters the Pacific Ocean at Mussel Rock, to reappear on the Point Reyes Peninsula.

Look south along the gentle curve of beaches and rocky shoreline beyond the Pacifica pier to see Point San Pedro jutting into the sea. Just east of Pacifica lies the rounded flank of Sweeney Ridge in the 74,000-acre Golden Gate National Recreation Area, where another segment of the Bay Area Ridge Trail traverses the 3-mile-long ridgeline.

Fort Funston lies to the north, and beyond, San Francisco's Ocean Beach stretches all the way to the Golden Gate. On a very clear day, the Marin Headlands and Point Reyes are visible farther north. Twenty-five miles offshore, the Farallon Islands stand guard, beyond the narrow entrance to San Francisco Bay.

Landward and immediately north of the vista point in a deep canyon, a former dumpsite has been replaced by the refuse transfer station housed in the large concrete building above the parking area. This canyon developed when heavy winter storms washed out great chunks of coastal bluffs.

Almost hidden, north of the canyon on a shelf midway between the cliffs and the ocean, lies more testimony to the relentless force of Pacific Ocean storms. The northern leg of the Ocean Shore Railroad ran along this coast from 1907 until its demise in 1920. Although planned to connect San Francisco and Santa Cruz, the tracks never bridged the gap south of Half Moon Bay between Tunitas Creek and Davenport Landing. However, passengers were transported by Stanley Steamer on a scenic ride across the unfinished section. Your Bay Area Ridge Trail trip approximates the old railroad route north on a safer alignment.

After orienting yourself at the vista point above Mussel Rock, **hikers** and **bicyclists** go back along the entry road to the first corner, where Westline Drive curves north. Turn left (east) on Westline. Hikers use the sidewalks on the left side of the street; bicyclists ride on the street. After just one block, turn right on Belcrest Avenue. Then go left (north) on Longview Drive. In three blocks you come to Longview City Park, where you'll find attractive benches. Follow Longview Drive as it curves right (east), around the corner.

At each intersection on this trip, a Bay Area Ridge Trail marker on a signpost tells you which way to turn. For most of the trip north through Daly City, houses sit between you and the bluffs. However, occasional openings between the houses and three cliff-top city parks offer ocean views. In this Daly City neighborhood each home has its plot of lawn, often graced with small, rock-bordered flower beds of ferns and roses and accented by a palm tree.

At Skyline Drive, turn left and follow it north. When you pass a water tower on the right at Fog Cap 3, you've reached the summit of your invigorating climb and it's downhill from here to the end of the first trip on this Ridge Trail segment.

There are a few benches and remnants of playing fields at Daly City's Northridge Park, but storm damage has taken out much of this park. On balmy days, neighborhood residents still relax in protected, sunny areas. Each of the city parks you pass has fencing and hedges atop the bluff and breaks in the hedges afford sea views. Even when it's foggy, the sound of the surf reminds the visitor of the ocean's incessant action below the cliffs.

Disastrous winter storms took out cliffs and rendered cliffside houses unsafe just beyond Northridge on Avalon Drive. Gone are those houses, but you can walk on the east side of the street and look out to sea.

This first section ends at Palisades Park at the corner of Palisades Drive and Westridge Avenue. You can return to Mussel Rock on foot or bike or have a shuttle car waiting on Palisades Drive by the park.

South from Fort Funston

Hikers begin the second part of this Bay Area Ridge Trail segment at Fort Funston. From the parking area, walk seaward to the viewing deck to survey your coastal route south and watch the flotilla of hang-gliders on the wing or parked immediately adjacent to this deck. Return to the west edge of the parking area and take a trail that starts just left (south) of the hang-glider staging area. You make a dramatic descent from the bluff top to the dunes on a unique sand-ladder staircase, which is edged by a sturdy rope strung between 4×4 posts.

When you reach the sand dunes, bear left (south) with the sight and sound of the waves nearby. A few Bay Area Ridge Trail signs mark the route through a network of trails. In general, keep to the trail on top of the dunes, or if the tide is out, you can walk along the beach. Even from the dunes, you see shorebirds searching for sand

Mussel Rock from Fort Funston, with
Montara Mountain in the distance.

crabs, grebes and terns diving for fish, and several kinds of seagulls resting on the sand. Overhead hang-gliders and paragliders join long lines of pelicans riding the winds. At any time of the year, a few wildflowers accent your way, but in spring the display of scarlet Indian paintbrush, lavender sea daisies, yellow lizardtail, and purple sand verbena makes this a colorful trip.

When the fog hangs over the shore, there is a sense of solitude here, broken only by the shrieks of gulls. When coastal breezes sweep in and the surf crashes on the beach, the closeness to nature's power makes this almost a wilderness experience. And on clear, sunny days with the glint of sunshine on the breaking waves, with flocks of shorebirds searching for clams, and with warm sand underfoot, this is truly a glorious place to be.

Shortly, the Bay Area Ridge Trail traverses an easement granted to the GGNRA by the Olympic Club. Along this stretch, look for a paragliders' launching site on a leveled-off sand dune. From the launching site, these aerial adventurers rise above the beach, floating, suspended by ropes from a longitudinal sliver of double-layered, multi-colored parachute cloth.

As you rise to the crest of a long, high dune between a ravine and the shore, you approach a clump of windswept pine and cypress trees. Just before the trees, a sign directs you left down into the ravine and then another points right to two picnic tables in the lee of this high dune. These tables, the ravine, and the battered cliffs above you are all that remain of the former Thornton State Beach development, yet another example of the turbulent power of the sea.

Continue south on this sandy trail, up and down the dunes, through willow thickets and blackberry brambles, past clumps of red-orange Indian paintbrush and bright yellow succulents, always with the sea within sight or sound. You stroll through coastal scrub of creamy-blossomed coyote bush, red-leafed succulents, yellow and white yarrow, and bushy yellow beach lupine. Hikers may be joined on this route by equestrians who have descended from the stables on the deteriorating Thornton Beach Road. Where this old road meets the dunes, about 1.2 miles from Fort Funston, hikers reverse direction and retrace their steps.

After trudging north along the dunes, look for an indistict trail to the bluff top at Fort Funston. This is the seldom-used equestrian trail, which hikers can also use. The next trail, 0.1 mile farther north, is the hikers' route, which involves a steady climb back to the bluff top on the sand ladder. Several landing platforms offer the chance to rest and to survey the round-trip route you just followed. The staircase terminates at the hang-glider staging area. Here behind the protection of wind-sculpted trees by the viewing deck, the parked hang-gliders look like a swarm of butterflies with outspread, brilliantly colored wings.

Equestrians can join hikers on the beach below Fort Funston by descending Thornton Beach Road from the equestrian trailhead.

Bicyclists, who followed city streets from Daly City, can join the hikers and dismounted equestrians at the viewing deck built out over the bluff. Together you can look back over this spectacular coastline and over the dunes that the hikers and equestrians traveled. Watching the stream of ship traffic move in and out of the Golden Gate can test your knowledge of seagoing vessels. Especially on weekends, the brightly colored hang-gliders' silent take-off and flight above the strand can provide hours of vicarious aerial thrills. If the day is clear, you may want to stroll along the Sunset Trail or linger longer on the viewing deck for a picnic and more views of this dramatic coast.

The next leg of the Bay Area Ridge Trail starts here in Fort Funston—the first trip in this guidebook. (See *Fort Funston to Stern*

Grove.) If you had begun your journey along the Bay Area Ridge Trail in Fort Funston and had followed all the trips in this guidebook described clockwise around San Francisco Bay, you would have traveled more than 200 miles along the ridges above the bay. Each trip would have offered outstanding views and different perspectives on some very special features of the Bay Area.

APPENDIX 1
Bay Area Ridge Trail Parks At-A-Glance

The chart below is a "snapshot" of the amenities available in parks along the Bay Area Ridge Trail. Please note that this is general information for the parks and is not necessarily what you will find on the Bay Area Ridge Trail route through that park. See also Appendix 2 for phone numbers and contact information.

Where the chart indicates that the section of the Bay Area Ridge Trail route in a park is wheelchair accessible, see the specific trip description for details.

	Dogs	Water	Toilet	Parking	Phone	Picnic Tables	Visitor Center
SAN FRANCISCO							
Fort Funston	leash	✔	✔	✔	✔	✔	✔
Stern Grove	leash	✔	✔	✔	✔	✔	
Presidio	leash	✔	✔	✔	✔		✔
THE NORTH BAY							
Marin Headlands			✔	✔	✔		✔
Tennessee Valley			✔	✔	✔	✔	
Mount Tamalpais State Park:							
Pantoll		✔	✔	fee	✔		
Rock Spring	leash	✔	✔	✔		✔	
Samuel P. Taylor State Park		✔	✔	✔		✔	
Loma Alta OSP	✔/ leash	✔					
Lucas Valley OSP	✔/ leash			✔			
Indian Tree OSP	✔			✔			
Mt. Burdell OSP	✔			✔			
Helen Putnam Regional Park	✔	✔	✔		✔		
McNear Park	✔/ leash	✔	✔	✔		✔	
Petaluma Adobe State Historic Park		✔	✔	✔		✔	
Jack London State Park		✔	✔	✔	✔	✔	
Spring Lake Park		✔	✔	✔	✔	✔	
Annadel State Park		✔	✔	✔		✔	

Camping	Ranger Station	Horse Amenities	Wheelchair Accessible	Other
			✔	native plant nursery, hang-glider viewing deck
				Summer Sunday Concerts
✔				Headlands Institute, Golden Gate Hostel
✔		✔	✔	
✔	✔			
		hitch rack		
✔		✔	✔	
✔		✔		
		✔		
				baseball, tennis, horseshoe, play structures, Boys and Girls Clubhouse
				historic adobe with guided group tours by arrangement, bike racks
				museum, historic structures
✔				swimming
	✔			hitch rack at Marsh/Burma trails junction

	Dogs	Water	Toilet	Parking	Phone	Picnic Tables	Visitor Center
Sugarloaf Ridge State Park		✔	✔	fee	✔	✔	✔
Skyline Wilderness Park		✔	✔	fee		✔	
Rockville Hills Community Park				✔		✔	
Hiddenbrooke Trail				✔			
Blue Rock Springs Park		✔	✔	fee	✔	✔	
Benicia State Recreation Area		✔	✔	fee		✔	
City of Benicia 9th Street Park		✔	✔	✔	✔		
THE EAST BAY							
City of Martinez				✔			
Martinez Regional Shoreline		✔	✔	✔		✔	
East Staging Area	✔/ leash		✔	✔		✔	
Carquinez Strait Regional Shoreline							
John Muir Nat'l Historic Site		✔	✔	✔			✔
Pinole Valley Park		✔	✔	✔	✔		
Sobrante Ridge Regional Preserve	✔						
Kennedy Grove Regional Recreation Area	leash/ fee	✔	✔	fee	✔	✔	
San Pablo Reservoir Recreation Area		✔	✔	fee	✔	✔	

Camping	Ranger Station	Horse Amenities	Wheelchair Accessible	Other
✔		✔		horse rental, guided rides only
✔		✔		archery range, disc golf, native habitat garden, horse arena, RV
				nature programs
				lake, golf course & driving range, play structures
			✔	fishing, barbecues
				beach, windsurfing, boat launching ramp
			✔	restaurants, city park, history museum, historic buildings
		✔		public pier, boat launching ramp, sand beaches, bocce ball, baseball, soccer, horse arena
				self-guiding tour of Muir House, garden, orchard, Martinez Adobe
				water, parking, horse water at Coach Drive entrance
				no amenities
				playground, volleyball, horseshoe, playing field, senior citizen's center
				boating, fishing

	Dogs	Water	Toilet	Parking	Phone	Picnic Tables	Visitor Center
Tilden Regional Park	✔	✔	✔	✔	✔	✔	✔
Sibley Volcanic Regional Preserve	✔	✔	✔	✔		✔	✔
Redwood Regional Park	✔	✔	✔	✔	✔	✔	
Anthony Chabot Regional Park:							
MacDonald Staging Area	✔		✔	✔			
Bort Meadow	✔	✔	✔	✔		✔	
Chabot Staging Area	✔		✔	✔			
Cull Canyon Regional Recreation Area		✔	✔	✔		✔	
Mission Peak Regional Preserve	✔	✔	✔	✔	✔		
Ed R. Levin County Park	leash	✔	✔	✔	✔	✔	✔

THE SOUTH BAY AND SAN FRANCISCO PENINSULA

	Dogs	Water	Toilet	Parking	Phone	Picnic Tables	Visitor Center
Alum Rock Park		✔	✔	fee	✔	✔	✔
Joseph Grant County Park	ltd./ leash	✔	✔	fee	✔	✔	
Coyote Creek Parkway:							
Coyote Hellyer County Park	leash	✔	✔	✔		✔	
Shady Oaks Park	✔/ leash			✔			
Metcalf Park	✔/ leash	✔	✔	✔			

Camping	Ranger Station	Horse Amenities	Wheelchair Accessible	Other
✔		✔	✔	food concessions, swimming
				self-guiding volcanics tour with pamphlet
✔				youth group camping only
				Equestrian Center, marksmanship Range, Lake Chabot Marina, Anthony Chabot Family Camp
✔				
				fishing, swimming (fee), seasonal, snack bar
		✔		hang-glider facilities, equestrian staging at Stanford Ave. entrance
✔		✔		hang-glider facilities, play structures, fishing, group camping
			✔	barbecues, playground, Youth Science Institute, nature programs
✔				equestrian staging area, fishing
				play structures, fishing, velodrome playing field,
				play structures, basketball
			✔	turf, play structures

THE BAY AREA RIDGE TRAIL

	Dogs	Water	Toilet	Parking	Phone	Picnic Tables	Visitor Center
Burnett Park	✔/ leash	✔	✔	✔		✔	
Santa Teresa County Park	leash	✔	✔	✔		✔	
Mt. Madonna County Park	ltd./ leash	✔	✔	fee	✔	✔	✔
Sanborn County Park		✔	✔	✔	✔	✔	✔
Castle Rock State Park			✔				
Skyline Ridge OSP			✔	✔		✔	
Russian Ridge OSP			✔	✔			
Windy Hill OSP	ltd./ leash		✔	✔		✔	
Wunderlich County Park		✔	✔	✔			
Huddart County Park		✔	✔	✔	✔	✔	
Purisima Creek Redwoods OSP			✔	✔		✔	
GGNRA Sweeney Ridge	leash		✔	✔			

Camping	Ranger Station	Horse Amenities	Wheelchair Accessible	Other
	✔		✔	fishing, trails
✔				amphitheater, Henry Miller home historical site, white deer pen
fee				Welch-hurst Sanborn Hostel
✔				
			✔	phone and water at Saratoga Summit Fire Station, Nature Center with observation deck and displays
				restrooms and picnic tables at Anniversary Trail parking area
		✔		
✔				barbecue pits, nature trail, play structures, play fields, archery range, youth and adult camps
			✔	
				vista point, water, restrooms, at Skyline College

APPENDIX 2
Information Sources and Contacts for Parks on the Bay Area Ridge Trail

MANAGING AGENCIES

National Park Service, Golden Gate National
Recreation Area   415-556-0560
Fort Mason
San Francisco, CA 94123
www.nps.gov

San Francisco Presidio	415-556-4323
North District—Marin Headlands	
and Muir Woods	415-331-1540
Point Reyes	415-464-5100
Olema Valley	415-464 5137
John Muir Historic Site	925-228-8860
South District—Fort Funston,	415-239-2366
Sweeney and Milagra ridges	or 415-556-8642

State of California, The Resources Agency
Department of Parks and Recreation   916-651-6916
Box 942896
Sacramento, CA 94296-0001
www.parks.ca.org

Mount Tamalpais State Park	415-388-2070
Samuel P. Taylor State Park	415-488-9897
Petaluma Adobe State Historic Site	707-762-4871
Annadel State Park	707-539-3911
Sugarloaf Ridge State Park	707-833-5712

Benicia State Recreation Area	707-745-3385
Jack London State Park	707-538-8734

East Bay Regional Park District   510-635-2950
Peralta Oaks Court
P.O. Box 5381
Oakland, CA 94605-0381
www.ebparks.org

East Bay Municipal Utility District   510-254-3778
500 San Pablo Dam Rd.
Orinda, CA 94563
www.ebmud.com

Midpeninsula Regional Open Space District   650-691-1200
330 Distel Circle
Los Altos, CA 94022
www.openspace.org

Marin County Open Space District   415-499-6387
Marin County Civic Center
San Rafael, CA 94903
www.marinopenspace.org

San Francisco Recreation and Park Department   415-831-2700
McLaren Lodge, Golden Gate Park
501 Stanyan St.
San Francisco, CA 9411
www.parks.sfgov.org

Sonoma County Regional Parks Department   707-527-2041
2300 County Center Dr.
Santa Rosa, CA
www.sonoma/county.org/parks

Greater Vallejo Recreation District   707-648-4600
395 Amador St.
Vallejo, CA 94590
www.gvrd.org

Santa Clara County Parks and Recreation
Department   408-358-3741
298 Garden Hill Dr.
Los Gatos, CA 95030
www.parkhere.org

San Mateo County Parks and Recreation Department	415-363-4020

County Government Center
590 Hamilton St.
Redwood City, CA 94063
www.sanmateocountyparks.org

City of Petaluma Parks and Recreation   707-778-4380
320 N. McDowell
Petaluma, CA 94954
www.ci.petaluma.ca.us

City of Fairfield   707-428-7428 x 100
1000 Webster Street
Fairfield, CA 94533
www.ci.fairfield.ca.us

City of Benicia Recreation Department   707-746-4285
www/ci.benicia.ca.us

City of San Jose Parks Department   408-277-4000
4 North 2nd Street, Ste. 600
San Jose CA 95113
www.ci.san-jose.ca.us/prns

TRANSPORTATION AGENCIES THAT SERVE PARKS AND PRESERVES ON THE BAY AREA RIDGE TRAIL ROUTE

For all transit agencies, dial your Area Code and 817-1717
or go to: www.transitinfo.org

BART	415-992-2278
	510-465-2278
San Francisco Municipal Railway—MUNI	415-673-6864
Golden Gate Transit	
From San Francisco and Southern Marin County	415-332-6600
From Central and Northern Marin County	415-453-2100
From Sonoma County	707-544-1323
AC Transit	800-559-4636
Valley Transit Authority	800-894-9908

SamTrans

Sonoma Transit

Benicia Transit

Napa Transit

Santa Rosa CityBus

Contra Costa County

CAMPING OPPORTUNITIES ON AND NEAR
THE BAY AREA RIDGE TRAIL ROUTE

Marin Headlands: Kirby Cove, Battery Alexander: group camping, reservations required, 415-331-1540

Hawk Camp: overnight camping and restrooms

Point Reyes: backpack camp reservations, 415-464-5100; commercial campgrounds and inns in Olema

Samuel P. Taylor State Park: reservations Mistix, 800-444-7275; Devils Gulch Horse Camp: reservations, 415-456-5218

Mt. Burdell OSP: Deer Camp

Tilden Regional Park: youth group camping only by reservation, 510-562-2267 (CAMP)

Redwood Regional Park: youth group camping only by reservation, 510-562-2267 (CAMP)

Anthony Chabot Regional Park: large group camping by reservation, 510-562-2267 (CAMP)

Ed. R. Levin Regional Park: group camping by reservation, 408-358-3751

Sanborn County Park: camping reservations, 408-358-3751

Castle Rock State Park: backpack camping at park headquarters: (800) 444-7275

Monte Bello OSP: backpack camping on Black Mountain by reservation, 415-691-1200

Huddart County Park: group camping, youth, equestrian, and backpack by reservation, 650-363-4021

HOSTELS ON AND NEAR
THE BAY AREA RIDGE TRAIL ROUTE

Marin Headlands: Golden Gate Hostel: open daily from 4:30 p.m. to 9:30 a.m., reservations advisable, 415-331-2777

Point Reyes: Point Reyes Hostel, 415-663-8811

Sanborn County Park: Sanborn Welch-hurst Hostel, open year-round, reservations advisable, 408-358-3751

Hidden Villa Hostel: open September to June, 415-949-8648

PICNICKING

Redwood Regional Park: group picnic reservations 510-636-1684

Anthony Chabot Regional Park: group picnic reservations 510-636-1684

HORSE PARKING/AMENITIES ON OR NEAR
THE BAY AREA RIDGE TRAIL ROUTE

Marin Headlands: Conzelman/McCullough roads junction, Bunker Road trailhead, and Miwok trailhead at east end of Rodeo Lagoon near Headlands Institute.

Tennessee Valley: stables and riding lessons

Mount Tamalpais State Park: hitch rack and parking at junction of Laurel Dell Fire Road and east side of Ridgecrest Blvd.; hitch rack at Rock Spring

Samuel P. Taylor State Park: camping at Devils Gulch; water trough on Shafter Trail

Mt. Burdell OSP: Deer Camp: hitch racks, horse water trough (nonpotable), portable toilet (seasonal)

Annadel State Park: hitch rack at Marsh/Burma trails junction

Skyline Wilderness Park: horse arena

Sobrante Ridge Regional Preserve: horse water and parking at Coach Drive entrance

Anthony Chabot Regional Park: Equestrian Center, 510-569-4428

Mission Peak Regional Park: Equestrian staging facilities at Stanford Avenue entrance

Ed R. Levin County Park: Equestrian staging facilities near Sandy Wool Lake

Joseph Grant County Park: Equestrian staging area

Sweeney Ridge (GGNRA): Equestrians begin from private Park Pacific Stables in Pacifica

ORGANIZATIONS THAT SUPPORT PARKS AND SPONSOR ACTIVITIES, NATURE TRIPS, TRAIL MAINTENANCE DAYS, AND OTHER VOLUNTEER ACTIVITIES

Many public agencies offer docent-led nature walks and occasional trail maintenance days. Consult the agency near you from the above list. In addition, local and statewide nonprofit groups sponsor outdoor trips for environmental education and enjoyment. Consult your telephone directory for the Bay Area office of the following groups:

American Youth Hostels

Audubon Society: Bird walks; many chapters in Bay Area

Bay Area Orienteering Club

Bay Area Ridge Trail Council: Publishes a quarterly Outings Calendar of docent-led trips

Bicycle Groups: Bicycle Trails Council of Marin, California Association of Bicycle Organizations, East Bay Bicycle Coalition, ROMP, Western Wheelers

California Native Plant Society: several chapters in Bay Area

Community Colleges: Some offer group hiking classes

Environmental Museums: California Academy of Sciences, Coyote Point Museum, Oakland Museum

Golden Gate National Park Association

Headlands Institute: environmental education programs and conference facilities

Hiking Clubs

Horsemen's Associations

The Nature Conservancy

Presidio project: office and visitor information center

Santa Cruz Mountains Natural History Association

Santa Cruz Mountains Trail Association

Senior Centers: Offer group walks

Trail Councils and Clubs: East Bay Area Trails Council, Santa Cruz Mountains Trail Association

The Trail Center: A 4-county trail information and trail maintenance clearinghouse, based in Los Altos

Youth Groups: Boy Scouts, Girl Scouts, and Campfire Girls units

Sierra Club: Local chapters around the Bay Area offer hiking, bicycling, backpacking, climbing and kayaking trips

Riders on the Los Alamitos/Calero Creek Trail.

APPENDIX 3
Bay Area Ridge Trail Sampler:
Trips for Many Reasons

"BAG A PEAK" ON THE RIDGE TRAIL ROUTE

Stern Grove to The Presidio
Twin Peaks

Mount Tamalpais State Park
Mt. Tamalpais' East Peak is 4+ miles from Pantoll and
1200 feet higher

Mt. Burdell Open Space Preserve
Mt. Burdell

Sugarloaf Ridge State Park
Bald Mountain

Tilden Regional Park to Redwood Regional Park
Vollmer Peak

Redwood Regional Park to Chabot Park
Redwood Peak and Round Top Mountain

**East Bay Municipal Utility District Lands to Cull Canyon
Regional Recreation Area**
Dinosaur Ridge

Mission Peak Regional Preserve and Ed R. Levin County Park
Mission Peak and Monument Peak

Boccardo Trail Corridor
Unnamed hill on side trip

Alum Rock Park
Eagle Rock

Santa Teresa County Park and Los Alamitos/Calero Creek Park Chain
Coyote Peak

Mt. Madonna County Park
Mt. Madonna

Skyline Ridge Open Space Preserve and Russian Ridge Open Space Preserve
Borel Hill and Mt. Melville

Windy Hill Open Space Preserve
Windy Hill summit

FOR OCEAN VIEWS: ON A CLEAR DAY
WITHOUT FOG OVER THE PACIFIC

Fort Funston to Stern Grove
See the Farallones from the hang-glider viewing deck

Stern Grove to The Presidio
From Twin Peaks and adjoining streets

Marin Headlands

  From Golden Gate Bridge North to Tennessee Valley and

  From Tennessee Valley to Shoreline Highway

Mount Tamalpais State Park
From Shoreline Highway to Pantoll

Mount Tamalpais State Park and Golden Gate National Recreation Area

  From Pantoll to Bolinas-Fairfax Road

Golden Gate National Recreation Area and Samuel P. Taylor State Park

Kennedy Grove to Tilden Regional Park
From Inspiration Point

Tilden Regional Park to Redwood Regional Park
From Sea View Trail

Sanborn-Skyline County Park and Castle Rock State Park
Views of Monterey Bay

Saratoga Gap Open Space Preserve to Skyline Ridge Open Space Preserve
From Long Ridge Open Space Preserve

Skyline Ridge Open Space Preserve and Russian Ridge Open Space Preserve

Windy Hill Open Space Preserve
From Windy Hill summit

Purisima Creek Redwoods Open Space Preserve
From Harkins Ridge Trail

Sweeney Ridge To Milagra Ridge
From Mori Ridge and the Discovery Site

Mussel Rock to Fort Funston
From both ends of the trail

FOR SAN FRANCISCO BAY VIEWS: SPARKLING BLUE OR FOG-SHROUDED, IT'S ALWAYS IMPRESSIVE

Stern Grove to The Presidio
From Twin Peaks

San Francisco Presidio
Especially Golden Gate, Richardson Bay and Alcatraz

Marin Headlands

From Golden Gate Bridge North to Tennessee Valley and

From Tennessee Valley to Shoreline Highway
Richardson Bay and Angel Island

Mount Tamalpais State Park
From Shoreline Highway to Pantoll

Indian Tree Open Space Preserve
From Indian Tree summit

Mt. Burdell Open Space Preserve
From the summit of Mt. Burdell

Jack London State Park
From Sonoma Mountain summit

Sugarloaf Ridge State Park
From Bald Mountain

Skyline Wilderness Park
Napa Marshlands on San Pablo Bay

Hiddenbrooke
Views of the Golden Gate, its bridge and the Napa Marshlands

Vallejo-Benicia Buffer
On upper trail

Benicia Waterfront
On the west trail

Carquinez Regional Shoreline Park to John Muir National Historic Site
San Pablo Bay

Sobrante Ridge Regional Park
Views especially of San Pablo Bay

Kennedy Grove to Tilden Regional Park
From Nimitz Way

Tilden Regional Park to Redwood Regional Park
From Sea View Trail

Mission Peak Regional Preserve and Ed R. Levin County Park

Boccardo Trail Corridor
South Bay and its wetlands

Skyline Ridge Open Space Preserve and Russian Ridge Open Space Preserve

Windy Hill Open Space Preserve
Views Up and down the bay from the summit

Sweeney Ridge To Milagra Ridge
Here Portolá first saw the bay

FOR A CHILD'S RIDGE TRAIL BIRTHDAY PARTY: PICNIC TABLES AND RESTROOMS NEARBY

Fort Funston to Stern Grove
Several picnic areas

Stern Grove to The Presidio
Many parks along the Ridge Trail route with picnic facilities, restrooms at Stern Grove and Golden Gate Park only

Presidio
See the World War II gun emplacements and picnic at Rob Hill; Visitor Center at Main Post Parade Ground

Mount Tamalpais State Park
Rock Spring or Bootjack Picnic Areas

Golden Gate National Recreation Area and Samuel P. Taylor State Park
Walk or ride on Cross Marin Trail and picnic in the park

Helen Putnam Regional Park, McNear Park to Petaluma Adobe State Historic Park
> Picnic and play areas at west end and picnic at parks along the way and at Petaluma Adobe

Jack London State Park
> Sample a bit of history and picnic afterwards

Annadel State Park
> Picnic at Spring Lake Park and walk or ride the Connector Trail to Annadel State Park

Sugarloaf Ridge State Park
> Round trip on Stern Trail and picnic by Sonoma Creek

Skyline Wilderness Park
> Play areas and picnic sites

Blue Rock Springs Park
> Picnic tables and play area

Benicia Waterfront
> Walk, bike, or roller-blade on level, paved trail and picnic at one of several park sites along the way

Martinez Regional Shoreline
> Picnic and play areas, large playing fields, fishing pier

Sobrante Ridge Regional Park
> At Pinole Valley Park; many picnic tables on the ridge (after an uphill climb)

Kennedy Grove to Tilden Regional Park
> Picnic sites and level trail at both ends

Tilden Regional Park to Redwood Regional Park
> Many sites at several entry points; Steam Trains at Tilden

Redwood Regional Park and Anthony Chabot Regional Park
> At Redwood Bowl beside the Ridge Trail or after a trip to Chabot Science Center; or walk from the Redwood Regional Park's Moon Gate to the Redwood Bowl (less than 1 mile); other sites available at Redwood Gate and at Bort Meadow

East Bay Municipal Utility District Lands to Cull Canyon Regional Recreation Area and Independent School
> Cull Canyon Recreation Area especially suited to birthday parties with swimming available

Independent School to Five Canyons
Picnic and play areas, swimming, playing fields at
Don Castro Regional Park

Mission Peak Regional Preserve and Ed R. Levin County Park
Sandy Wool Lake picnic sites and children's play area

Alum Rock Park
Play area in mid-park and picnic tables throughout park

Coyote Hellyer County Park to Metcalf City Park
Walk or ride bikes along the trail and return to birthday treats
at several parks along the trail

Santa Teresa County Park and Los Alamitos/Calero Creek Park Chain
Work off extra energy before the party on a short Ridge Trail
trip from Santa Teresa Pueblo Group Area

Mt. Madonna County Park
Picnic tables near visitor center and at amphitheatre; white
deer and more picnic tables near Ridge Trail; fishing for
children 5-12 at Sprig Lake

Skyline Ridge Open Space Preserve and Russian Ridge Open Space Preserve
Hike the trail before picnicking at Horseshoe Lake or Alpine
Pond; Nature Center open on weekends at Alpine Pond

Windy Hill Open Space Preserve
Picnic area adjacent to Skyline Boulevard

Mussel Rock to Fort Funston
Neighborhood parks along the trail in Daly City; watch the
hang-gliders and picnic on the viewing deck at Fort Funston

FOR SPRING WILDFLOWERS' BEAUTIFUL BLOSSOMS: ESPECIALLY IN THE GRASSLANDS

Marin Headlands
From Golden Gate Bridge North to Tennessee Valley
Swaths of mule-ears and bush lupines

From Tennessee Valley to Shoreline Highway
Iris in many hues

Mount Tamalpais State Park
Lavender bush lupine

Mt. Burdell Open Space Preserve
Milkmaids herald spring

Annadel State Park
White fritillary

Sugarloaf Ridge State Park
Lewisia

Rockville Hills Community Park
Blue iris, orange sticky monkey flower

Vallejo-Benicia Buffer
Tall blue brodiaia

Carquinez Regional Shoreline Park to John Muir National Historic Site
Poppies and blue-eyed grass

Anthony Chabot Regional Park
Trillium garden

Mission Peak Regional Preserve and Ed R. Levin County Park
Poppies and white phacelia on high grasslands between peaks

Joseph Grant County Park
Some of earliest and largest displays in Bay Area

Santa Teresa County Park and Los Alamitos/Calero Creek Park Chain
Jewel flower, magenta Clarkia on Stile Ranch Trail

Saratoga Gap Open Space Preserve to Skyline Ridge Open Space Preserve
Masses of blue and cream-colored iris

Skyline Ridge Open Space Preserve and Russian Ridge Open Space Preserve
Acres of wildflowers, especially on Russian Ridge; yellow Johnny jump-ups early in spring

Windy Hill Open Space Preserve
Columbine; many flowers late into summer

Wunderlich County Park to Huddart County Park
Especially Clintonia and bleeding heart

Purisima Creek Redwoods Open Space Preserve
Shade-loving plants: columbine and Clintonia

Sweeney Ridge To Milagra Ridge
Native orchids and host plants for Mission Blue butterfly

Mussel Rock to Fort Funston
Seaside flowers, yellow lizard tail

TRIPS WITH AN OVERNIGHT CAMP OR HOSTEL NEARBY

Not more than 2 miles away—See Appendix 4 for map and
Appendix 2 for contact information

Stern Grove to the Presidio
Two San Francisco International Hostels

Marin Headlands
Golden Gate Hostel, Hawk and Haypress Backpack Camps

Mt. Tamalpais
Pantoll and Shansky Backpack Camps

Golden Gate National Recreation Area and Samuel P. Taylor State Park
Car Camping at Samuel P. Taylor State Park and Horse
Camp at Devils Gulch; Point Reyes Hostel (5 miles from
Olema Hill parking)

Mt. Burdell Open Space Preserve
Group camping by reservation

Annadel State Park
At adjoining Spring Lake Park

Sugarloaf Ridge State Park
Campsites near creek; corrals for horses

Kennedy Grove to Tilden Regional Park
Youth group camps by reservation at Wildcat and Tilden parks

Tilden Regional Park to Redwood Regional Park
Youth group camps by reservation only

Redwood Regional Park and Anthony Chabot Regional Park
Youth group camps by reservation only at Redwood and
Family camping at Anthony Chabot

Anthony Chabot Regional Park
Year-round family camping

Mission Peak Regional Preserve and Ed R. Levin County Park
Group camping at Ed R. Levin County Park

Joseph Grant County Park
Family and youth group campsites

Mt. Madonna County Park
Family campgrounds

Sanborn County Park and Castle Rock State Park
Hostel and walk-in camps in Sanborn Park and backpack camp at Castle Rock State Park.

Wunderlich County Park to Huddart County Park
Group camping at Huddart County Park by reservation only

San Francisco Presidio
Group camping at Rob Hill by reservation

TO HISTORIC SITES: RANCHES, HOMES, FORTS, AND INNS

Fort Funston to Stern Grove
Military site and Trocadero Inn

San Francisco Presidio
Historic Spanish military site and American military base

Marin Headlands
Military site, historic lighthouse at Point Bonita

McNear Park to Petaluma Adobe State Historic Park
Victorian homes and General Vallejo's ranch house

Jack London State Historic Park
Ranch buildings and cottage of literary figure

Annadel State Park
Former Rancho Los Guilicos

Vallejo-Benicia Buffer and Benicia Waterfront
Former General Vallejo rancho; former state capital

Carquinez Regional Shoreline Park to John Muir National Historic Site
John Muir's home

Mission Peak Regional Preserve and Ed R. Levin County Park
Former Mission San José lands

Alum Rock Park
California's first and oldest park; remnants of former steam railroad

Joseph Grant County Park
Historic home and ranch of former Stanford University trustee on former Mexican land grant

Santa Teresa County Park and Los Alamitos/Calero Creek Park Chain
Joaquin Bernal's former Rancho Santa Teresa

Mt. Madonna County Park
Summer home of former land and cattle baron Henry Miller

Skyline Ridge Open Space Preserve and Russian Ridge Open Space Preserve
Former "summer capital" of California Governor James Rolph; historic logging road from west side forests to bay

Windy Hill Open Space Preserve
Former Rancho El Corte de Madera

Sweeney Ridge to Milagra Ridge
First sighting of San Francisco Bay by Portolá's scouts; World War II military sites

ALMOST LEVEL TRAILS—AND MOSTLY PAVED

Fort Funston to Stern Grove

Helen Putnam Regional and McNear parks to Petaluma Adobe State Historic Park

Benicia-Vallejo Waterfront

Martinez Regional Shoreline to Carquinez Strait Regional Shoreline
Martinez City Streets and Shoreline Park

Kennedy Grove to Tilden Regional Park
Nimitz Way segment from Wildcat Canyon Regional Park gate to Inspiration Point

Alum Rock Park
Creek Trail

Joseph Grant County Park
Trails around Grant Lake and near park office

Coyote Creek Parkway North
  From Coyote Hellyer County Park to Metcalf City Park

Coyote Creek Parkway South
  From Metcalf City Park to Burnett Ranger Station

Santa Teresa County Park and Los Alamitos/Calero Creek Trail
Segment on Los Alamitos/Calero Creek Trail

Mt. Madonna County Park
Trail to Miller homesite

Sanborn County Park
Peterson Grove and Trail

Skyline Ridge Open Space Preserve
Trail around Alpine Pond

SHORT TRIPS: LESS THAN 5 MILES ROUND TRIP OR ONE WAY WITH SHUTTLE

Fort Funston to Stern Grove

San Francisco Presidio

Marin Headlands
  From Golden Gate Bridge North to Tennessee Valley

Marin Headlands
  From Tennessee Valley to Shoreline Highway

Loma Alta Open Space Preserve to Lucas Valley Open Space Preserve

Vallejo-Benicia Buffer

Benicia-Vallejo Waterfront

Martinez Regional Shoreline to Carquinez Strait Regional Shoreline

Carquinez Strait Regional Shoreline to John Muir Historic Site

Kennedy Grove to Tilden Regional Park

Mt. Madonna County Park

Sanborn County Park and Castle Rock Park

Windy Hill Open Space Preserve

TRIPS OF 5 TO 10 MILES ONE WAY WITH SHUTTLE

Stern Grove to The Presidio

Mount Tamalpais State Park
  From Shoreline Highway to Pantoll

Indian Tree Open Space Preserve to O'Hair Park

Helen Putnam Regional and McNear Parks to Petaluma Adobe

Annadel State Park

Tilden Regional Park to Redwood Regional Park

Redwood Regional Park to Anthony Chabot Regional Park

Anthony Chabot Regional Park

East Bay Municipal Utility District Lands to Independent School

Independent School to Five Canyons

Mission Peak Regional Preserve and Ed R. Levin County Park

Coyote Creek Parkway North

  From Coyote Hellyer County Park to Metcalf City Park

Coyote Creek Parkway South

  From Metcalf City Park to Anderson/Burnett Ranger Station

Santa Teresa County Park and Los Alamitos/Calero Creek Trail

Saratoga Gap Open Space Preserve to Skyline Ridge Open Space Preserve

Wunderlich County Park to Huddart County Park

Purisima Creek Redwoods Open Space Preserve

Sweeney Ridge to Milagra Ridge

OR ROUND TRIP ON THE RIDGE TRAIL

Loma Alta Open Space Preserve to Lucas Valley Open Space Preserve

Mt. Burdell Open Space Preserve

Sugarloaf Ridge State Park

Skyline Wilderness Park

Rockville Hills Community Park

Boccardo Trail Corridor and Alum Rock Park

Skyline Ridge and Russian Ridge Open Space Preserve

Windy Hill Open Space Preserve

LONG TRIPS: MORE THAN 10 MILES ONE WAY WITH SHUTTLE, OR ROUND TRIP ON SAME TRAIL

Stern Grove to Presidio round trip.

Mount Tamalpais State Park

  From Shoreline Highway to Pantoll round trip

Mount Tamalpais State Park

  From Pantoll to Bolinas-Fairfax Road round trip

GGNRA and S.P. Taylor State Park

  From Bolinas-Fairfax Road to State Park Entrance one way

Tilden Regional Park to Redwood Regional Park round trip

Coyote Creek Parkway

From Coyote Hellyer County Park to Anderson/Burnett Ranger Station one way

All the one-way trips in the 5-10-mile category would be more than 10 miles round trip

LINGER BY A LAKE ON A RIDGE TRAIL TRIP

Fort Funston to Stern Grove
Lakes Merced and Pine Lake

Mt. Burdell Open Space Preserve
Seasonal

Jack London State Park

Annadel State Park
At Spring Lake Park

Skyline Wilderness Park
At trail's end

Rockville Hills Community Park

Vallejo-Benicia Buffer

Kennedy Grove To Tilden Regional Park

Anthony Chabot Regional Park
Short distance off the trail

East Bay Municipal Utility District Lands to Independent School
Cull Canyon Regional Recreation Area
Swimming in season, too

Mission Peak Regional Preserve and Ed R. Levin County Park

Coyote Creek Parkway North

Saratoga Gap to Skyline Ridge Open Space Preserve

Skyline Ridge Open Space Preserve and Russian Ridge Open Space Preserve

TRIPS WITH BUS CONNECTIONS: TAKE THE BUS TO A RIDGE TRAIL ENTRANCE, HIKE AS FAR AS YOU LIKE AND RETURN TO THE BUS STOP

(check with bus company to verify schedule and stops)

Stern Grove to The Presidio
SF Muni at each end

Marin Headlands
Golden Gate Transit at north end of Golden Gate Bridge

Mount Tamalpais State Park
Golden Gate Transit to Pantoll

GGNRA to Samuel P. Taylor State Park
Golden Gate Transit to State Park on Cross Marin Trail

Indian Tree Open Space Preserve
Golden Gate Transit to Novato at San Marin/
Novato Boulevard

Mt. Burdell Open Space Preserve
Golden Gate Transit as in Indian Tree and at San Marin/
San Andreas intersection in Novato

McNear Park to Petaluma Adobe State Historic Park
Golden Gate Transit and Petaluma Transit

Annadel State Park
Santa Rosa city bus and Sonoma Transit

Vallejo-Benicia Buffer
Vallejo Transit

Benicia-Vallejo Waterfront
Benicia Transit

Martinez Regional Shoreline
Contra Costa County Connection from BART

**Carquinez Regional Shoreline Park to John Muir Historic Site—
To historic site**
Contra Costa County Connection and BART

Kennedy Grove to Tilden Regional Park
AC Transit

Tilden Regional Park to Redwood Regional Park
AC Transit

Redwood Regional Park to Chabot
AC Transit to Chabot Space and Science Center

Anthony Chabot Regional Park to Independent School
AC Transit from Castro Valley BART to Cull Canyon Regional
Recreation Area

Independent School to Five Canyons
AC Transit to Don Castro Regional Recreation Area

Mission Peak Regional Preserve and Ed R. Levin County Park
AC Transit to Ohlone College and Mission/Stanford Ave. intersection: Climb the peak from Ohlone College and return or continue on Hidden Valley Trail to Mission Boulevard/Stanford Ave.

Alum Rock Park
Valley Transit Authority

Coyote Creek Parkway
Valley Transit Authority to Yerba Buena Ave. (Northeast of Coyote Hellyer Park)

Santa Teresa County Park and Los Alamitos/Calero Creek Park Chain
Valley Transit Authority Connections near both ends of trail

Sweeney Ridge to Milagra Ridge
SamTrans to Skyline College and Sneath Lane; to Lundy Lane near Mori Ridge trailhead

Mussel Rock to Fort Funston
By BART and SamTrans to Palmetto/Westline from Colma BART and Muni to John Muir Drive/Skyline Blvd. several locations in Daly City

"FAULT-Y " TRIPS AND SERPENTINE STROLLS

ALONG THE SAN ANDREAS FAULT

Trips from Sanborn County Park north through Huddart County Park
lie close to the west side of the fault on the Pacific Plate

Sweeney Ridge to Milagra Ridge on Pacific Plate

At Mussel Rock
the fault drops into the Pacific Ocean, and then re-appears in Marin County

Marin County
trips from the Golden Gate Bridge north to Samuel P. Taylor State Park lie on the east side of the fault on the North American Plate

ALONG THE HAYWARD FAULT

East Bay trips through ridgetop parks
parallel the Hayward Fault, which lies to the west

ALONG THE CALAVERAS FAULT

Alum Rock Park and Boccardo Trail Corridor

MORE FAULTS

Sugarloaf Ridge State Park
St. John's Mountain Fault

Annadel State Park
west lies Rodgers Creek Fault

Rockville Hills Community Park
fault through Green Valley

Hiddenbrooke Trail
St. John's Mine Fault

SERPENTINE STROLLS

San Francisco Presidio
large area of serpentine outcrops on Ecology Trail side trip

Santa Teresa County Park
two areas of serpentine outcrops

Sugarloaf Ridge State Park
serpentine on trip to Bald Mountain

Loma Alta Open Space Preserve
serpentine outcrops along Ridge Trail route

Sweeney Ridge
a weathered serpentine column marks the Portolá
Discovery Site

THREE OR MORE CONTIGUOUS
RIDGE TRAIL SEGMENTS   Total Miles

Fort Funston to Stern Grove
Stern Grove to The Presidio
The Presidio   12.7 miles

Marin Headlands
 From Golden Gate Bridge to Tennessee Valley
 From Tennessee Valley to Shoreline Highway
Mount Tamalpais State Park
Mount Tamalpais State Park and GGNRA
GGNRA and Samuel P. Taylor State Park   33 miles

Kennedy Grove to Tilden Regional Park
Tilden Regional Park to Redwood Regional Park
Redwood Regional Park and Anthony Chabot
  Regional Park
Anthony Chabot Regional Park
East Bay Municipal Utility District Lands to
  Independent School
Independent School through Don Castro Regional
  Recreation Area to Five Canyons   41.9 miles

Sanborn County Park and Castle Rock State Park
  to Saratoga Gap
Saratoga Gap Open Space Preserve to Skyline Ridge
  Open Space Preserve
Skyline Ridge Open Space Preserve and Russian
  Ridge Open Space Preserve   17.5 miles

By combining one or two Bay Area Ridge Trail segments with
adjoining park trails, hikers, equestrians, and bicyclists can make
many fine loop trips and return to trailhead bus stops or car
parking.

APPENDIX 4

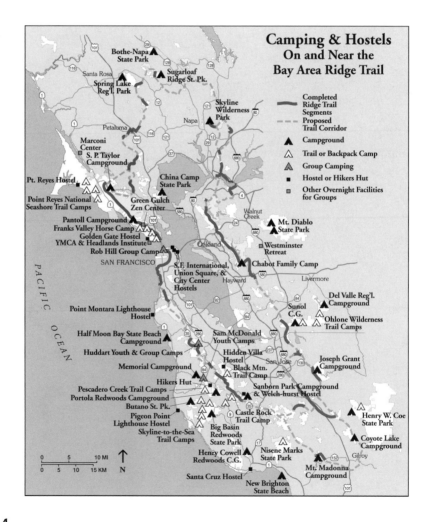

**Camping & Hostels
On and Near the
Bay Area Ridge Trail**

Completed Ridge Trail Segments

Proposed Trail Corridor

▲ Campground

△ Trail or Backpack Camp

△ Group Camping

■ Hostel or Hikers Hut

□ Other Overnight Facilities for Groups

Bothe-Napa State Park
Sugarloaf Ridge St. Pk.
Santa Rosa
Spring Lake Reg'l. Park
Skyline Wilderness Park
Napa
Petaluma
Marconi Center
S. P. Taylor Campground
China Camp State Park
Pt. Reyes Hostel
Point Reyes National Seashore Trail Camps
Green Gulch Zen Center
Walnut Creek
Mt. Diablo State Park
Pantoll Campground
Franks Valley Horse Camp
Golden Gate Hostel
YMCA & Headlands Institute
Rob Hill Group Camp
SAN FRANCISCO
Oakland
Westminster Retreat
S.F. International, Union Square, & City Center Hostels
Hayward
Chabot Family Camp
Livermore
Point Montara Lighthouse Hostel
Del Valle Reg'l. Campground
Sunol C.G.
Ohlone Wilderness Trail Camps
Half Moon Bay State Beach Campground
Sam McDonald Youth Camps
Huddart Youth & Group Camps
Hidden Villa Hostel
San Jose
Joseph Grant Campground
Memorial Campground
Black Mtn. Trail Camp
Hikers Hut
Sanborn Park Campground & Welch-hurst Hostel
Pescadero Creek Trail Camps
Portola Redwoods Campground
Butano St. Pk.
Castle Rock Trail Camp
Henry W. Coe State Park
Pigeon Point Lighthouse Hostel
Skyline-to-the-Sea Trail Camps
Big Basin Redwoods State Park
Coyote Lake Campground
Gilroy
Henry Cowell Redwoods C.G.
Nisene Marks State Park
Mt. Madonna Campground
Santa Cruz Hostel
New Brighton State Beach

PACIFIC OCEAN

0   5   10 MI
0   5   10   15 KM
N

APPENDIX 5
Selected Readings

HISTORY

Arbuckle, Clyde, and Rambo, Ralph. *Santa Clara County Ranchos.* San Jose: Harlan-Young Press, 1968.

Avina, Rose H. *Spanish and Mexican Land Grants in California.* Berkeley: Thesis, University of California, Reprinted, R. R. Research Associates. Saratoga and San Francisco: Robert Reed, Publisher, 1973.

Bogart, Sewall. *Lauriston: an Architectural Biography of Herbert Edward Law.* Portola Valley: Alpine House Publications, 1976.

Brewer, William H. *Up and Down California in 1860-1864.* Berkeley: University of California Press, 1974.

Bruegmann, Robert. *Benicia, Portrait of an Early California Town.* San Francisco, New York: 101 Productions, 1980.

Costanso, Miguel. *The Discovery of San Francisco Bay: the Portola Expedition of 1760-1770: the Diary of Miguel Costanso,* in English and Spanish. Edited by Peter Browning. Lafayette, CA: Great West Books, 1992.

Cowan, Robert G. *Ranchos of California, A List of Spanish Concessions, 1775-1822 and Mexican Grants 1822-1846.* Fresno: Academy Library Guild, 1956.

Gilliam, Harold. *The San Francisco Experience.* Garden City: Doubleday, 1972.

Gudde, Erwin G. *California Place Names.* 4th ed. Berkeley, University of California Press, 1998.

Hart, James D. *A Companion to California*. 2nd ed. Berkeley: University of California Press, 1987.

Hoover, Mildred B. and Rensch, Hero E.; Revised by Douglas Kyle. *Historic Spots in California*. Stanford, CA Stanford University Press, 5th Edition, 1994.

Krumbein, William. *A Teacher's Guide for Annadel State Park*. Glen Ellen: Valley of the Moon Natural History Association, 1990.

Lara, Adair H. *History of Petaluma, a California River Town*. Petaluma: Self-published, 1982.

Loomis, Patricia. *Milpitas, The Century of "Little Cornfields" 1852-1952*. Cupertino: California History Center, Local History Studies, 1986.

Mason, Jack. *Earthquake Bay, A History of Tomales Bay*. Inverness: North Shore Books, 1976.

_____, and Park, Helen Van Cleave. *Early Marin*. Jack Mason Publications: Marin County, 1971.

McCarthy, Francis F. *The History of Mission San Jose, California, 1797-1835*. Fresno: Academy Library Guild, 1958.

Margolin, Malcolm. *The Ohlone Way, Indian Life in the San Francisco-Monterey Bay Area*. Berkeley: Heyday Books, 1978.

Marinacci, Barbara and Rudy Marinacci. *California's Spanish Place-Names*. 2nd ed. Houston: Gulf Publishing Company, 1997.

Payne, Stephen M. *Santa Clara County, Harvest of Change*. Northridge: Windsor Publications, 1987.

Sanchez, Nellie Van de Grift. *Spanish and Indian Place Names of California*. San Francisco: A. M. Robertson, 2nd ed., 1922.

Sepeda, Dolores De Moro. *Hills West of El Toro*. Ann Arbor, MI: Braun-Brumfield Inc., 1978.

Richards, Rand. *Historic San Francisco: a concise history and guide*. San Francisco: Heritage House Publishers, 1991.

Stanger, Frank. *South From San Francisco. San Mateo County, California, Its History and Heritage*. San Mateo County Historical Association, 1967.

Stein, Mimi. *A Vision Achieved, Fifty Years of East Bay Regional Park District.* Oakland: East Bay Regional Park District, 1984.

Woodbridge, Sally B., and Woodbridge, John. *Architecture—San Francisco: The Guide.* San Francisco, New York: American Institute of Architects, San Francisco Chapter: 101 Publications, 1982.

NATURAL HISTORY

Bakker, Elna S. *An Island Called California.* Berkeley: University of California Press, 1971.

Birding at the Bottom of the Bay. Santa Clara Valley Audubon Society, Palo Alto, 2nd ed., 1990.

Burt, William H. and Richard P. Grossenheider. *A Field Guide to the Mammals, North America, North of Mexico,* 3rd ed. Boston: Houghton Mifflin Company, 1980.

California Natural History Guides. Berkeley: University of California Press:

—Berry, William D. and Berry, Elizabeth. *Mammals of the San Francisco Bay Region,* 1959.

—Ferris, Roxana S. *Native Shrubs of the San Francisco Bay Region,* 1968.

—Gilliam, Harold. *Weather of San Francisco Bay Region,* 1966.

—Metcalf, Woodbridge. *Native Trees of the San Francisco Bay Region,* 1959.

—Schoenibert, Allan A. *A Natural History of California,* 1992.

—Sharsmith, Helen D. *Spring Wildflowers of the San Francisco Bay Region,* 1965.

—Stebbins, Robert D. *Reptiles and Amphibians of the San Francisco Bay Region,* 1960.

Conradson, Diane R. *Exploring Our Baylands.* 3rd ed. Fremont: San Francisco Bay Wildlife Society, 1996.

Crittenden, Mabel, and Dorothy Teller. *Wildflowers of the West.* Blaine: Hancock House Publishers, 1992.

Evens, Jules G. *The Natural History of the Point Reyes Peninsula.* Point Reyes: Point Reyes National Seashore Association, 1988.

Murie, Olaf J. *A Field Guide to Animal Tracks.* Boston: Houghton Mifflin, 3rd ed., 1990.

Pavlik, Bruce M. and Pamela Muick, Sharon Johnson and Marjorie Popper. *Oaks of California.* 3rd ed. Los Olivos: Cachuma Press, Inc. and California Oak Foundation, 1991.

Peterson, Roger Tory. *A Field Guide to Western Birds.* Boston: Houghton Mifflin Co, 1990.

National Geographic Society. *Field Guide to the Birds of North America,* 3rd ed. Washington: National Geographic Society, 1999.

Sharsmith, Helen K. *Flora of the Mt. Hamilton Range of California. American Midland Naturalist,* Vol. 34, no.2, September 1945. Special reprint: Berkeley: California Native Plant Society, 1982.

Thomas, John Hunter. *Flora of the Santa Cruz Mountains of California.* Stanford, CA: Stanford University Press, 1961.

TRAIL GUIDES

Bakalinsky, Adah. *Stairway Walks in San Francisco.* 3rd ed. Berkeley: Wilderness Press, 1995.

Backpacking California, Edited by Paul Backhurst, Berkeley: Wilderness Press, 2001.

California Coastal Conservancy. *San Francisco Bay Shoreline Guide.* Berkeley: Universtiy of California Press, 1995

Heid, Matt. *101 Hikes in Northern California.* Berkeley: Wilderness Press, 2000.

Magolin, Malcolm. *East Bay Out.* Berkeley: Heyday Books, 1988.

Rusmore, Jean, Betsy Crowder and Frances Spangle. *Peninsula Trails,* 3rd ed. Berkeley: Wilderness Press, 1997.

Rusmore, Jean, Betsy Crowder and Frances Spangle. *South Bay Trails,* 3rd ed. Berkeley; Wlderness Press, 2001.

Suttle, Gary. *California County Summits.* Berkeley: Wilderness Press, 1994.

Weintraub, David. *East Bay Trails.* Berkeley: Wilderness Press, 1998.

Weintraub, David. *North Bay Trails.* Berkeley: Wilderness Press, 1999.

PERIODICALS

 Bay Nature
Coast and Ocean

APPENDIX 6
Bay Area Ridge Trail Council
Dedication Dates

May 13, 1989
Wunderlich County Park to Huddart County Park
San Mateo County

May 13, 1989
Purisima Creek Redwoods Open Space Preserve
San Mateo County

September 21, 1989
Marin Headlands, Golden Gate Bridge to Morning Sun Trail
Marin County

September 21, 1989
Mount Tamalpais State Park and GGNRA, includes:
Shoreline Highway to Pantoll
Pantoll to Bolinas-Fairfax Road
Bolinas-Fairfax Road to Samuel P. Taylor State Park
Marin County

September 30, 1989
Fort Funston to Stern Grove
San Francisco County

October 7, 1989
Skyline Wilderness Park
Napa County

October 14, 1989
Milagra Ridge and Sweeney Ridge
San Mateo County

October 14, 1989
Sanborn County Park to Saratoga Gap
Santa Clara County

October 21, 1989
Benicia-Vallejo Waterfront
Solano County

June 23, 1990
Wildcat Canyon Regional Park to Cull Canyon Regional Recreation
Area, includes:
Tilden Regional Park to Redwood Regional Park
Redwood Regional Park to Anthony Chabot Regional Park
Anthony Chabot Regional Park
EBMUD Lands to Cull Canyon Regional Recreation Area
Contra Costa and Alameda counties

October 13, 1990
Coyote Creek Parkway (North)
Santa Clara County

October 13, 1990
Mt. Burdell Open Space Preserve
Marin County

October 20, 1990
Sugarloaf Ridge State Park
Sonoma County

September 14, 1991
Santa Teresa County Park and Los Alamitos Creek Trail
Santa Clara County

October 12, 1991
Carquinez Strait Regional Shoreline to John Muir National
Historic Site
Contra Costa County

June 6, 1992
Saratoga Gap, Long Ridge, Skyline Ridge, and Russian Ridge Open
Space Preserves
San Mateo County

June 6, 1992
Windy Hill Open Space Preserve
San Mateo County

September 19, 1992
Mussel Rock to Fort Funston
San Mateo County

October 3, 1992
Kennedy Grove Regional Recreation Area to Inspiration Point
Contra Costa County

October 3, 1992
Samuel P. Taylor State Park (Connector Trail)
Marin County

October 31, 1992
Cull Canyon Regional Recreation Area to Independent School
Alameda County

November 7, 1992
Stern Grove to the Presidio
San Francisco County

April 24, 1993
Rockville Hills Community Park
Solano County

April 24, 1993
Mission Peak Regional Preserve to Ed R. Levin County Park
Santa Clara County

May 22, 1993
Vallejo-Benicia Buffer
Solano County

October 17, 1993
Marin Headlands, Morning Sun Trail to Shoreline Highway
Marin County

October 12, 1994
Skyline Community College (Segment of Sweeney Ridge to
Milagra Ridge)
San Mateo County

April 30, 1995
Coyote Creek Parkway (South)
Santa Clara County

May 6, 1995
Annadel State Park and Connector Trails from Howarth City Park
and Spring Lake Regional Park
Sonoma County

May 21, 1995
Pinole Valley Park (Connector Trail) and Sobrante Ridge
Regional Preserve
Contra Costa County

October 12, 1996
"The Notch" from Mori/Sweeney Ridge Trail Junction to
Skyline College
San Mateo County

November 9, 1996
Jack London State Historic Park
Sonoma County

October 25, 1997
Joseph D. Grant County Park
Santa Clara County

October 17, 1998
Independent School to Five Canyons
Alameda County

November 7, 1998
Martinez City Streets to Carquinez Regional Shoreline
Contra Costa County

October 10, 1998
Indian Tree Open Space Preserve to O'Hair Park
Marin County

October 16, 1999
Mt. Madonna County Park
Santa Clara County

October 28, 2000
Alum Rock Park
Santa Clara County

May 5, 2001
Hiddenbrooke Trail
Solano County

October 28, 2001
Loma Alta Open Space Preserve to Lucas Valley Open Space
Preserve
Marin County

May 11, 2002
Boccardo Trail Corridor
Santa Clara County

SCHEDULED DEDICATIONS

June 15, 2002
River to Ridge
Napa County

August 25, 2002
Sonoma Mountain Trail, Jack London State Park
Sonoma County

September 28, 2002
Lynch Canyon Open Space Preserve
Solano County

October 19, 2002
Brookside Trail
Marin County

October 28, 2002
O'Hair Park to Mt. Burdell Open Space Preserve
Marin County

HEADS UP!

Hiking, biking, and horseback riding are activities that pose risks that you need to be aware of and respect. An element of the beauty, freedom, and excitement of any outdoor adventure is the presence of risks that you will probably not have to face at home. It is your responsibility to ensure your safety whenever you set out on a trail or go for an adventure in the outdoors.

The fact that a trail is described in this book is not a representation that it will be safe for *you*. Trails vary greatly in difficulty and in the degree of conditioning and agility one needs to enjoy them safely. Routes may change and, certainly, trail conditions may deteriorate in the time since this book was published. In the San Francisco Bay Area, this is particularly true. A trail that is safe on a dry day or relatively easy for a highly conditioned, agile, properly equipped adventurer may be completely unsafe for someone else or unsafe under adverse weather conditions.

Minimize your risks by becoming knowledgeable about where you are going and what variables you might encounter. Be prepared and alert; even in the relatively urban parklands of the Bay Area, there have been sightings of mountain lions and the presence of poisonous plants, not to mention the occasional road crossing or possible encounter with an unfriendly or threatening individual.

We don't have the space in this book to provide you with a general treatise on outdoor safety. There are many good books and public courses on safety and first-aid; avail yourself of the resources in your local library or community.

Most importantly: stay alert and cognizant of your natural limitations. Anticipate any adverse conditions that might exist where you are going. If you choose to hike, bike, or horseback ride on your own, tell someone where you are going and check in with them when you return. Find out what is happening with the weather. If conditions change, or if you're not prepared to deal with unexpected problems, choose a different and safer route, get a partner to share the adventure with you, or wait until you are better prepared. It's better to waste a drive than be the subject of a rescue.

We don't want to scare you off the trails. Millions of people enjoy safe outdoor adventures every day. When you hike, you assume those risks. They can be met safely, but only if you exercise your judgment and common sense. Heads up and have fun!

INDEX

GREENBELT ALLIANCE
Protecting Open Space and Promoting Livable Communities

Greenbelt Alliance is the Bay Area's leading land conservation and urban planning non-profit. Founded in 1958, we are dedicated to protecting the region's Greenbelt of open space and making our communities better places to live

Over the years, Greenbelt Alliance has helped save over half a million acres of Greenbelt lands and has helped generate over $550 million to acquire new parklands and other open space. Greenbelt Alliance is unique among conservation groups, because we not only work to protect the land, we also work to improve the long-term livability of our cities.

GET INVOLVED!

There are endless opportunities to help protect the Greenbelt and the Bay Area's quality of life: **Become a member (a bargain at only $35).**

Go on one of our **Greenbelt Outings—free hikes, bike rides and farm tours. (Call 415-255-3233 for more information.)**

Join our Greenbelt Action Network of volunteers.
Join our E-mail Activist Network.

For more information about how you can get involved, visit us on the web **www.greenbelt.org**, call us at **415-398-3730** or (in the Bay Area) **800-543-GREEN**.

Greenbelt alliance

PROTECTING OPEN SPACE AND PROMOTING LIVABLE COMMUNITIES

THE BAY AREA RIDGE TRAIL COUNCIL

Now that you've had a chance to experience the Bay Area Ridge Trail, join us!

Since 1988, the Bay Area Ridge Trail Council has planned, promoted, built, acquired, and maintained the Ridge Trail. We are a nonprofit membership-based organization working with volunteers and agencies to complete this over-400-mile trail.

Your support is vital. Become part of our County Committees or trail crew, join the organization, or make a donation and help us complete this spectacular trail.

For more information, visit the Bay Area Ridge Trail Council's website at **www.ridgetrail.org** or **call** us at **415-561-2595.**